D0931218

THE ROAD TO WAR

Contemporary France
General Editor: Jolyon Howorth, University of Bath

Volume 1
Humanity's Soldier: France and International Security, 1919–2001
David Chuter

Volume 2
The Road to War: France and Vietnam, 1944–1947
Martin Shipway

THE ROAD TO WAR
France and Vietnam, 1944–1947

Martin Shipway

Berghahn Books
Providence • Oxford

Published in 1996 by

Berghahn Books
Editorial offices:
165 Taber Avenue, Providence, RI 02906, USA
Bush House, Merewood Avenue, Oxford, OX3 8EF, UK

Library of Congress Cataloging-in-Publication Data
Shipway, Martin.
   The road to war : France and Vietnam, 1944–1947 / by Martin
Shipway.
      p.   cm. -- (Contemporary France)
   Includes bibliographical references and index.
   ISBN 1-57181-894-4 (alk. paper)
      1. Indochina--History--1945– 2. France--Colonies. I. Title.
II. Series.
DS550.S54 1996
959.7'03--dc20   96-24310
                                                         CIP

British Library Cataloguing in Publication Data
A CIP catalogue record for this book is available from
the British Library.

Printed in the United States on acid-free paper

For my mother and father

CONTENTS

ACKNOWLEDGEMENTS

S ince I began the research which has found its way into this
book, I have accumulated many debts, and been at the receiving end of much kindness and hospitality. I hope that over time I
may be able to repay at least a fair proportion of these debts; my
benefactors may be assured that I am a grateful debtor.

My most particular thanks go to my two successive doctoral
supervisors, John Darwin and Vincent Wright, both of Nuffield
College. Their advice, interest, and support kept me going throughout the somewhat prolonged gestation of my doctoral thesis, and
I am grateful for their continuing encouragement. My work has
benefited enormously from their wisdom and expertise, though I
have no doubt I could have learnt far more from their example. I
am also grateful to my examiners, Professor Douglas Johnson and,
especially, David Goldey, for their sympathetic treatment of the
work which lies behind the present volume. I have greatly appreciated the interest shown in my work, in the shape of invitations to
give papers, by Robert Holland, Institute of Commonwealth Studies, London; Ralph Smith, School of Oriental and African Studies,
London; Marc Michel, Institut d'Histoire Comparée de Civilisations, Aix-en-Provence; and Tony Chafer, Amanda Sackur, et al.,
University of Portsmouth. I have received much help from the
staff of libraries and archives in Oxford, Paris, London, and Bath;
but I am especially grateful to the staff of the Centre des Archives
d'Outre-Mer in Aix-en-Provence, who have contributed to a number of highly productive and enjoyable research trips.

Many friends have helped and supported me with this project.
I must particularly mention Stein Tønnesson, a far more serious
scholar of Vietnam than I could aspire to be, to whom I owe my
initial interest in Indochina. He most generously shared with me
some of his finds from the nether reaches of the archives; my debt

here was compounded by the fact that I was subsequently unable to gain access to those same archives (see Bibliography). For memories of a now-distant summer in Aix I have to thank Stein and many others, not least the irrepressibly hospitable Olivier Vergniot. Amongst my friends in Oxford, it was perhaps Simon Auerbach who was most supportive to me in this project, not least by demonstrating in person how to finish a doctorate. My love of France, and interest in all things French, I owe in the first instance to my oldest French friend, Jean Le Noac'h.

The present work was largely produced while I was a Lecturer in the School of Modern Languages and International Studies, University of Bath. From my erstwhile colleague and present friend Claire Duchen (now translated to Sussex) I gratefully acquired many of the tools of my trade, and to Bill Brooks I owe many things, not least a probably quite healthy taste for the ironies of University life. I would also like to acknowledge the support and encouragement of Professor Jolyon Howorth in backing my research, and to thank him as Series Editor for his guidance. Of course, neither he nor anyone but myself bears any responsibility for the deficiencies of what follows.

Finally, the person whose love, patience, and enthusiasm have made this work possible, and even enjoyable, is Mary Anne Ansell. To her, Victoria, and Jenna, for their moral support, good humour, and friendly disparagement, I offer my special thanks.

Birkbeck College   Martin Shipway
University of London   1996

NOTE ON TEXT

For the sake of the English reader, all French sources have been translated by the author. However, it was felt that the spirit of the French sources was often of sufficient interest to warrant inclusion of the original, which is therefore reproduced in the Notes. No attempt is made to reproduce diacritics in Vietnamese names. French and Vietnamese abbreviations are used throughout, rather than an artificial and often misleading translation. In what follows a 'straight' translation of abbreviated names is provided; the reader is referred to the term's first appearance in the text for further clarification.

Abbreviations

AEF	Afrique Equatoriale Française (French Equatorial Africa)
AOF	Afrique Occidentale Française (French West Africa)
CEFEO	Corps Expéditionnaire Français en Extrême-Orient (French Far East Expeditionary Corps)
CFLN	Comité Français de la Libération Nationale (French Committee of National Liberation)
CNF	Comité National Français (French National Committee)
CNR	Conseil National de la Résistance (National Council of the Resistance)
Cominindo	Comité Interministériel de l'Indochine (Interministerial Committee on Indochina)
DAE	Direction des Affaires Economiques (Economic Affairs Division)
DAP	Direction des Affaires Politiques (Political Affairs Division)
DGER	Direction Générale des Etudes et Recherches (General Directorate for Studies and Research)
DIC	Division de l'Infanterie Coloniale (Division of Colonial Infantry)
DOM	Département d'Outre-Mer (Overseas Department)

Dong Minh Hoi	Viet Nam Cach Menh Dong Minh Hoi (League of Revolutionary Vietnamese Parties)
EMGDN	Etat-Major Général de la Défense Nationale (General Staff for National Defence)
ENFOM	Ecole Nationale de la France d'Outre-Mer (National Academy for Overseas France)
FFI	Forces Françaises de l'Intérieur (French Forces of the Inferior)
FIDES	Fonds d'Investissement pour le Développement Economique et Social (Investment Fund for Social and Economic Development)
FOM	Ministère de la France d'Outre-Mer (Ministry for Overseas France)
FTP	Francs-tireurs et Partisans Français (French Irregulars and Partisans)
GEC	Groupe d'Etudes Communistes (Group of Communist Studies)
GPRF	Gouvernement Provisoire de la République Française (Provisional Government of the French Republic)
Haussaire	Haut-Commissaire (High Commissioner)
MDRM	Mouvement Démocratique pour la Rénovation Malgache (Democratic Movement of Malagasy Renewal)
MRP	Mouvement Républicain Populaire (People's Republican Movement)
OSS	Office of Strategic Services
PCF	Parti Communiste Français (French Communist Party)
PCI	Parti Communiste Indochinois (Indochinese Communist Party)
PRL	Parti Républicain de la Liberté (Republican Freedom Party)
SFIO	Section Française de l'Internationale Ouvrière (French Section of the Workers' International)
UDSR	Union Démocratique et Sociale de la Résistance (Social and Democratic Union of the Resistance)
Viet Minh	Viet Nam Doc Lap Dong Minh Hoi (League for the Independence of Vietnam)
VNQDD	Viet Nam Quoc Dan Dang (Vietnamese National Party)

NB. For abbreviations used in citations of archival sources, see Bibliography.

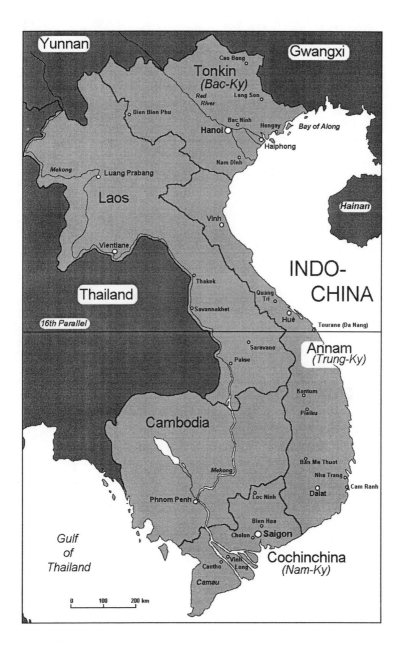

Indochina, 1945

INTRODUCTION

France's experience of decolonisation has generally been studied from published sources in terms of the 'wars, plots and scandals' dominating French post-war history up to Algerian independence in 1962. However, with the gradual opening of the archives, it is becoming possible to investigate the process from the inside, from the perspective of the policy-making elites. Based on archival sources in France (diplomatic and colonial archives, published official papers and memoirs, private papers), this is a study of the role and intentions of policy makers in the French higher administration, and especially in the Ministry of Colonies,[1] during the crucial period of Provisional Government in Paris (1944–1947). The focus is on the crucial case of Indochina, where the French 'return' following the defeat of Japan led within little more than a year to full-scale war between the French colonial regime and Ho Chi Minh's Democratic Republic of Vietnam. This marked the start of seventeen years of colonial war for France, the climax of which caused the downfall of the Fourth Republic in 1958. In Indochina it opened the first round of a thirty-year war of liberation from foreign domination and civil war.

Indochina was the richest and most populous of France's colonial possessions; it was also by force of historical circumstance the most pressing issue facing colonial policy makers at the close of the Second World War. For both these reasons, it was seen by officials in Paris as a test-case, and in many ways even as a model, for determining not only the constitutional, political and administrative shape of the French colonial empire, renamed the French Union (*Union Française*), but also the nature of France's relations with the emerging forces of colonial nationalism. For Indochina

---

1. Renamed the Ministry for Overseas France (*Ministère de la France d'Outre-Mer*) when Marius Moutet became Minister in January 1946.

exemplified most clearly in this period the dilemma facing the colonial administration. On the one hand, a new generation of liberal colonial officials identified the French Union as the means of French restoration to the first rank of Great Powers following the humiliations of the Second World War. This concern was particularly keenly felt given the fact that many of these officials were early supporters of General de Gaulle (*gaullistes de la première heure*) in those colonies of French Equatorial Africa and elsewhere which 'rallied' to de Gaulle in 1940. But on the other hand, France's hold over her colonies was at its weakest, while at the same time the aspirations of the colonial peoples were being given increasingly clear and forceful expression by nationalist movements drawing confidence from the same tide of events which had eroded French power. Thus the new policy presented first at the Brazzaville Conference in January–February 1944, and hence known informally as the Brazzaville policy (*politique de Brazzaville*), was in essence an attempt to balance the terms of an equation of imperial interests or, put another way, to solve a conundrum: how to meet nationalist demands while preserving, and indeed reinforcing, imperial unity. The basis for this new policy was the idea of a Federation, or Union, binding the metropole and colonies.

Given the apparent wealth of good intentions invested in this new policy, how did the French colonial administration become engaged so precipitately in one of its most disastrous policy-making failures? The argument of historical hindsight, that imperial federalism was a clumsy attempt to square a circle and to reconcile the conflicting and inherently incompatible ends of imperialism and national self-determination, appears to be only partially adequate. This study sets out to explore more fully the reasons for the rapidity with which France's liberal policy collapsed, and for the apparent readiness with which French officials acquiesced in that collapse. These reasons are sought in an analysis of the political and administrative mechanisms and the ideological underpinnings of policy making in a period of political turbulence and uncertainty following the Liberation of France.

Starting from a critical examination of the Brazzaville policy as defined by its principal proponent, Henri Laurentie, Director of Political Affairs at the Ministry of Colonies, the study shows how the new policy evolved in response to official perceptions of a 'colonial crisis', manifested not only in Indochina, but also in the crises in Eastern Algeria and in Syria which erupted, as if on cue, at the moment of Victory in Europe. Liberal French officials showed unprecedented concern for this 'colonial' side of the equation and, in particular, an enlightened understanding of the need to make concessions to local nationalists. Even so, even a genuinely liberal imperial policy needed to be couched in terms appealing to metropolitan French values. This had the unintended consequence of reinforcing the longstanding myths surrounding the French colonial mission. Indeed, arising out of Gaullism's 'heroic period', Brazzaville suggested new elaborations of the colonial myth, which were open to interpretation by a variety of actors bringing to bear conflicting ideological concerns and political interests. Over time, the liberal vision of colonial policy makers was contaminated, distorted, and ultimately defeated by French actors pursuing aims which, while distinct from those originally defined by Laurentie and his colleagues, could nonetheless be presented in terms of the Brazzaville policy.

This process of contamination or distortion affected colonial policy making in two principle ways in the specific case of Indochina. First, domestic political factors impinged on the colonial policy-making process. It is suggested that the new policy was drawn up on the basis of an implied model of domestic politics. Working at first within the political vacuum of de Gaulle's improvisatory 'Resistance State' at Algiers,[2] policy makers assumed that politics after the Liberation would operate consistently according to a given set of political parameters; this would allow the administration to focus on external factors, taking for granted domestic factors such as the salience of colonial policy on the domestic political agenda, its acceptability within a given ideological framework, or the continuing solidarity of the institutions on which policy depended. In fact, in common with much of the planning that came out of the Resistance, this initial model was faulty, or at best over-optimistic, and failed to take into account the domestic political crisis which prevailed throughout the period of Provisional Government.[3] As a result, there were continual shifts in the domestic parameters governing the policy-making process. Indeed, the hostile or uncomprehending response to the new policy at Brazzaville and during the internal debate which followed suggested already the potential mismatch between the Brazzaville policy and metropolitan, especially Republican, perceptions of empire.

2. 'Etat Résistant', J.-B. Duroselle, *Politique étrangère de la France, L'âbime, 1939–1945*, Paris, 1982, 473.

3. On the planning of the Resistance, see A. Shennan, *Rethinking France, Plans for Renewal, 1940–1946*, Oxford, 1989.

In this way, policy was adapted to reflect, in particular, the shifting importance or significance of ideologies or ideological trends having a bearing on colonial policy, such as Gaullism, Republicanism, anti-Communism or old-fashioned imperialism. Such a process might at times be conceived as a way of 'selling' the policy, while at others it simply mirrored the extremely rapid evolution of French politics at this period. As the ideological cast of mind of the policy makers altered, so, too, the aims of policy shifted, often quite subtly, so that by late 1946 the colonial administration had apparently lost sight of its original objectives as set down in 1944–45.

The second form of unintended mutation which the Brazzaville policy underwent was the result of more direct and wilful interference. This was the deformation of policy proposals wrought by actors working within the hierarchy of the colonial administration, but who chose to misinterpret, overlook or simply to disobey orders issuing from Paris. The administrative ethos of the French colonial service had long condoned or encouraged independent initiative. Nonetheless, the cumulative effect of acute political instability in Paris, administrative ambiguities concerning the chain of command, and the sheer scale of the problem faced by the colonial administration in Indochina, fostered hitherto unthinkable acts of insubordination by administrators and soldiers working far from Paris. Differences of political, functional or geographical perspective are also highlighted: even allowing for the intrusion of personal agendas and interests, an event or policy was open to quite different interpretation, according to whether it was viewed from Paris, Saigon or, say, de Gaulle's country retreat at Colombey-les-Deux-Eglises; from a ministerial private office or from the corridors of the Rue Oudinot (the quarters of the Ministry of Colonies, opposite the Invalides in Paris); from the High Commissioner's Palace in Saigon or French headquarters in Hanoi. As will be shown, these differences of perspective and interpretation would lead, in the case of Indochina, to the emergence of rivalry between two distinct centres of decision making, in Paris and Saigon. Indeed, the outbreak of war in Indochina marked the temporary resolution of this rivalry in favour of Saigon.

This account of policy making concurs with the findings of other recent research in attributing to the Saigon administration a large part of the blame for the turn of events which led to war. But it goes further, for it argues that the two forms of policy mutation go together. This was for two reasons. First, administrative insubordination was arguably more brazen and effective as a result of domestic political uncertainties. Secondly, Saigon's independent course of action itself fed back into the system, so that *ex post facto* rationalisations were often found for events which had come about directly as a result of breaks in the chain of command. This in turn may help to explain one surprising aspect of the breakdown of policy in Indochina, which is the extent to which it was downplayed or, more usually, simply accepted within the political and administrative establishment, albeit with responses ranging from regret and resignation, at one end of the scale, to relief and enthusiasm at the other. Indeed, by the time of the start of the war, even a beleaguered coalition government was more than equal to the task of explaining away, to a bored and increasingly disillusioned electorate with little interest in colonial affairs, an event eight thousand miles away which could variously be interpreted as an unpleasant but necessary task for the Republican 'civilising mission' (*la mission civilisatrice*), the defence of the Motherland (*la mère-patrie*), the defeat of colonial rebels, or simply as a Red Scare in the early rounds of France's domestic Cold War. In this way the early guardians of the Constitution of the Fourth Republic were to be seen storing up trouble which would ultimately lead to the crumbling of that Constitution.

The period covered by the study is brief, but few would dispute that the tumultuous life-cycle of the Provisional Government (*Gouvernement Provisoire de la République Française*, GPRF) was extremely important in the evolution of the French state, or that the period was remarkably self-contained. It will be observed that colonial policy making described the same downward trajectory as the greater whole of which it formed an increasingly significant part. At the Liberation of Paris, in August 1944, officials at the Ministry of Colonies could be forgiven for thinking, however naïvely or erroneously, that most things were possible. By the time of the outbreak of war in Indochina, the die was cast: France had a Constitution, albeit imperfect and only grudgingly accepted by the voters in the November 1946 referendum; in May 1947, the course of France's domestic Cold War was to be decided by the expulsion of Communist ministers from the Ramadier government; and a semblance of inevitability attaches also to the fate of France's colonial mission, which was dealt a further heavy blow in March 1947 by the insurrection in Madagascar.

The study builds on work accomplished recently by historians of French decolonisation and of Indochina, much of it based on a detailed understanding of the available archival sources. The extent of scholarly attention which at long last is being paid to France's decolonisation process is reflected, for example, in the series of colloquia organised by French research institutes.[4] In respect of Indochina, the work of two historians in particular has proved invaluable. First, Philippe Devillers, whose first history of the war in Indochina was published even before the war ended, in 1952, has published an extensive collection of documents, with commentary, which covers the same period as the present study. Devillers's work combines unique mastery of the sources with an unparalleled understanding of the history of French involvement in Indochina. As he himself comments: 'The archives have confirmed our worst suspicions'.[5] Secondly, Stein Tønnesson's intricate unravelling of the functioning and dysfunctioning of the colonial administration in Indochina on the eve of the war has served both as a mine of information and as a model of scholarship.[6] Apart from reference to published collections of documents, and some careful recourse to the memoirs of some of the actors involved, the study uses the findings of the author's own archival research in Paris (Henri Laurentie's papers at the *Archives Nationales*, files relating to Indochina in the *Archives Diplomatiques*) and Aix-en-Provence (various collections at the *Centre des Archives d'Outre-Mer*).[7]

The present work parts company from its predecessors in both perspective and purpose. Where Devillers and Tønnesson are both primarily concerned to elaborate an understanding of the

4. See especially Institut d'Histoire du Temps Présent (IHTP), *Les chemins de la décolonisation de l'empire français, 1936–1956*, Paris, 1986; Institut Charles-de-Gaulle and IHTP, *Brazzaville, Janvier–Février 1944, aux sources de la décolonisation*, Paris, 1988; G. Pedroncini and P. Duplay, eds, *Leclerc et l'Indochine, 1945–1947, quand se noua le destin d'un empire*, Paris, 1992; and, more recently, Institut d'Histoire Comparée des Civilisations and Institut d'Histoire du Temps Présent, *Décolonisations européennes*, Aix-en-Provence, 1995, and C.-R. Ageron and M. Michel, eds, *L'ère des décolonisations*, Paris, 1995 (Papers of the 1993 Colloquium 'Décolonisations Comparées').

5. 'Les archives ont confirmé ce que l'on supposait de pire', P. Devillers, *Paris-Saigon-Hanoi, Les archives de la guerre 1944–1947*, Paris, 1988, 11; see also his *Histoire du Viêt-Nam de 1940 à 1952*, Paris, 1952.

6. S. Tønnesson, *1946: Déclenchement de la guerre d'Indochine*, Paris, 1987; see also his 'The Outbreak of the War in Indochina, 1946', unpubl. thesis, PRIO, Oslo, 1983.

7. See especially Amiral G. Thierry d'Argenlieu, *Chronique d'Indochine, 1945–1947*, Paris, 1985, comprising the diary and private papers of one of the story's principal actors and myth makers; J. Sainteny, *Histoire d'une paix manquée*, rev. ed., Paris, 1967; M.J. Shipway, 'The Brazzaville Conference, 1944: Colonial and Imperial Planning in a Wartime Setting', M. Phil. thesis, University of Oxford, 1986, and 'France's "crise coloniale" and the breakdown of policy making in Indochina, 1944–1947', D. Phil. thesis, University of Oxford, 1992.

course of events in Indochina, the focus of this study is set firmly on Paris. This reflects a belief that in matters of colonial policy, decisions, wrong decisions, reluctant decisions and even non-decisions were all made in the metropole (or if not made there, then covered, accepted or repudiated there), however many hands were forced, arms twisted or even legs pulled in the process. In this case, as will be seen, the Political Affairs Division (*Direction des Affaires Politiques*) offers a curiously privileged, and yet by the same token detached, perspective on events, some way down the hierarchy between the Government at its pinnacle and the colonial officers at its base. As Laurentie's brief career in the higher administration also illustrates, however, detachment has its frustrations – and its dangers, particularly when the summit of the pyramid is whipped by storms, and its base threatened by subsidence.

Secondly, although Indochina is taken as a case for detailed study, its purpose is more general, that is, to broaden our understanding of the process of decolonisation, and of French decolonisation in particular. The adoption of the metropolitan perspective calls for two *caveats*. First, understanding the point of view of the metropole requires a readiness to accept the premises of the period, but this need not imply any kind of revisionism. As Alfred Grosser warns us, 'Analysing the origin of colonial conflicts after 1944 means understanding first of all that, at the time, France's civilising mission was not simply a formula in which people hypocritically pretended to believe; these days, on the contrary, colonisation is viewed through a distorting prism which makes it seem as if it was nothing but brutality and exploitation'.[8] Secondly, the ending of colonial empires was clearly an event of global significance, and no doubt with global causes, but whose effects in this instance are to be studied within a largely domestic French, Western European, context. Decolonisation was one of two phenomena, along with the Cold War, to have dominated the politics of some West European states such as Britain and France, while largely determining the post-war framework of international relations. As Grosser also reminds us, France's experience of these two phenomena was uniquely concentrated: 'From 1947, the Fourth Republic lived through the drama of being the only European

---

8. 'Analyser la naissance des conflits coloniaux après 1944, c'est d'abord comprendre que la mission civilisatrice de la France n'était pas à l'époque une simple formule à laquelle on jouait hypocritiquement à croire, alors qu'aujourd'hui le prisme déformant fait trop souvent admettre que la colonisation aurait été exclusivement brutalité et exploitation.' A. Grosser, *Affaires Extérieures*, Paris, 1984, 12.

country to experience simultaneously on a domestic front both of the great conflicts which tore the post-war world apart: the antagonism between East and West, and decolonisation'.[9] Understanding decolonisation, as far as possible from the inside, is thus a vital key to understanding France's and Western Europe's post-war history. The study is divided into two parts. **Part One** is concerned with the origins and formulation of the Brazzaville policy, and with the problematic relationship of domestic politics and colonial policy making at this period. *Chapter One* reassesses the Brazzaville Conference, suggesting that a multivalent Brazzaville myth was from the outset inseparable from the intended reality of the Brazzaville policy. *Chapter Two* examines Henri Laurentie's proposals for the Brazzaville policy, and evaluates metropolitan opposition to these proposals. *Chapter Three* examines the ways in which liberal proposals for policy evolved in response to an analysis of impending colonial crisis. *Chapter Four* describes the political, ideological and administrative context for colonial policy making, and examines the policy makers' implied model of domestic politics as relating to colonial policy.

Part Two examines French policy making in Indochina from the preparations for a French 'return' at the end of the Second World War, until the outbreak of war with the Democratic Republic of Vietnam in December 1946. *Chapter Five* considers the period up to the eve of the 'return' in September 1945, as officials sought to make policy aimed at the 'moving target' created by the Japanese takeover in Indochina, the shockingly swift ending of the War in Asia, and the August 1945 Revolution in Hanoi. *Chapter Six* examines the disagreements and ambiguities underlying the negotiating process which led to the Accords of 6th March 1946. *Chapter Seven* charts the development of rivalry between Paris and Saigon following the signing of the Accords. *Chapter Eight* covers the unavailing efforts of the government and administration in Paris to regain the initiative during the Fontainebleau Conference, over the Summer 1946. *Chapters Nine and Ten* trace the disintegration of policy against the gathering gloom of worsening Franco-Vietnamese relations, and despondency and chaos in France, leading to the start of France's futile and bloody war with the Vietnamese.

---

9. 'La IVe République a connu dès 1947 le drame d'être le seul pays européen à vivre simultanément comme conflits internes les deux grands déchirements du monde d'après-guerre: l'antagonisme Est/Ouest et la décolonisation.' Ibid., 9–10.

PART I

THE EXTERNAL AND DOMESTIC PARAMETERS OF COLONIAL POLICY MAKING

1

THE BRAZZAVILLE CONFERENCE AND ITS ORIGINS, 1940–1944

Policy Formulation and Myth Making on the Congo

Historians of French decolonisation have now largely dispensed with the Gaullian myth surrounding the Brazzaville Conference and the benign, supposedly decolonising vision of the 'Man of Brazzaville', de Gaulle himself. Moreover, the conference's insufficiencies as an exercise in liberal agenda-setting have now largely been accepted.[1] The real French African Conference which met at Brazzaville for nine days in January-February 1944, sponsored by de Gaulle's French Committee of National Liberation (*Comité Français de Libération Nationale*, or CFLN) at Algiers, left a highly misleading legacy. An understanding of the origins of the conference, as well as of its highly ambiguous outcome, is therefore unavoidable in any discussion of the policy to which it gave rise.

This chapter thus explores the wartime origins of the post-war 'Brazzaville policy', but it is also concerned with the myth which grew up alongside this policy, and was for the most part indissociable from it. Drawing an analogy with the reformist planning of the metropolitan Resistance, the chapter identifies three reasons for the ambiguity which very rapidly attached to the Gaullists' new imperial thinking. First, although the Brazzaville Conference

1. Institut Charles-de-Gaulle and Institut d'Histoire du Temps Présent (IHTP), *Brazzaville, aux sources de la décolonisation*, Paris, 1988, is the most recent and comprehensive survey, though the title, and the large cover photograph of de Gaulle, would tend to contribute to the myth. See also M.J. Shipway, 'The Brazzaville Conference, 1944: Colonial and Imperial Planning in a Wartime Setting', M.Phil thesis, University of Oxford, 1986.

was the forum for a debate on this new imperial thinking, which was intended as the basis for a policy to be implemented across the French Union following the Liberation, this forum was restricted, largely for practical reasons, to officials of the colonial administration in French Black Africa. Its competence to deliberate on matters of overall policy was thus necessarily limited. Secondly, and despite the caution and muddle which largely characterised the Conference recommendations, Brazzaville was important because it became bound up with the emerging myth of de Gaulle, the emancipator of France and her Empire. Hence, thirdly, the very success of Brazzaville as a propaganda event, even while it was being written off by officials as a partial failure, was to create an immediate source of confusion regarding the thrust and purpose of post-war French colonial policy. For, like many myths, the Brazzaville myth was open to varying interpretations, and thus served as a catch-all term of reference readily appropriated by different actors pursuing often wildly conflicting goals. The origins of the myth, however, lay in the uniquely humiliating French experience of 1940, and in the impact on France's vast imperial territories of metropolitan defeat, occupation, and political schism; the chapter therefore starts with an examination of the record of the wartime French Empire.

The French Empire at War, 1940–1943

French imperial territory was mostly far removed from the various theatres of war either in Europe or in Asia. The impact of the Second World War was nonetheless keenly felt across the Empire, both because French colonies and dependencies experienced the ripple effects of international developments and of the Gaullist war effort, and more directly because they served as the stage, or at least the backdrop, for many of the dramas played out between Frenchmen as a result of the defeat of 1940. These dramas involved, not least, the switch of allegiance to de Gaulle effected at some point between 1940 and 1944, whether voluntarily, by military force, or by the force of events, by every French colonial administration excepting that of Indochina. Thus, the impetus for colonial and imperial reform from 1944 onwards came not only from a reflex of 'gratitude' for the part played by the Empire in effecting a French 'renaissance', but also as a response to the seismic shocks which had seriously shaken and weakened an already over-extended and ramshackle imperial structure.

For the duration of the Phoney War, the conflict was seen as one restricted almost exclusively to Europe, in which the colonies, as in the First World War, would have only a supporting role. With the fall of France, however, two very different conceptions of the Empire's role came into play. According to the first of these, reflected in the armistice, the Empire was to act as a makeweight for France's weakness in the grand design of Hitler's New Europe. Thus, notwithstanding the harshness of the armistices, designed as they were to remove France as an actor on the continent, they made only minor incursions into the French Empire. Neither the navy, shortly to be decimated by the Royal Navy at Mers-el-Kebir, nor the colonial armed forces, were surrendered or demobilised, though they were neutralised. By contrast, de Gaulle's analogy with past French strategy was a more radical one. As the newly appointed Under-Secretary of State for War in the Reynaud government, he sought, ultimately in vain, to persuade the Premier to continue the struggle from colonial exile. The proposed strategy was thus one of a grandiose 'African Marne', a vast rallying of French forces as on the Marne in 1914, before an eventual counter-attack. It is an open question how effective such a strategy would have been. Certainly from the perspective of 1943–44, with France totally occupied, de Gaulle's vision seemed justified. But no contingency plans existed for such a strategy. To have abandoned France to total occupation, and to the rigours of an ill-conceived guerilla war, would have been to put at risk any semblance of legitimacy.[2] Although he was privileged as a rebel to pursue a course from which the government felt compelled to swerve, de Gaulle's foresight was nonetheless remarkable. The basis for his rebellion was his refusal to believe that the conflict was limited to Europe. As he declared from the first, in the 'Appel' of 18 June 1940:

> For France is not alone. She is not alone! She is not alone! She has a vast Empire behind her. She can form a bloc with the British Empire which commands the seas and remains at war. She may,

---

2. It was also feared that, once the Wehrmacht reached the Pyrenees, it would be allowed transit through Francoist Spain and pursue its campaign, if necessary as far as the Suez Canal. J.-B. Duroselle, *Politique étrangère de la France, L'abîme, 1939–1945*, Paris, 1982, 161–63.

like England, make use of the limitless resources of the United States. This war is not bound by the Battle of France. It is a World War.[3]

This conception of the war was in turn reflected by his attitude to the colonies. Both Pétain and de Gaulle believed in the indissoluble link binding France and her Empire. But de Gaulle concluded from this, not that the Empire should acquiesce in France's defeat, but that it should go on fighting while substantial portions of French territory remained undefeated.

De Gaulle's crusade, however, at least for the first three years, is best understood as an inspired tactical and propaganda campaign, in which the aim was to win French loyalty and French territory, and so to establish his legitimacy as the authentic representative of the French nation. The first phase of this campaign, a concerted effort to rally military commanders and colonial administrators to the new cause, must be counted a failure: none of the imperial 'proconsuls' in North Africa or other key territories, some of whom had at first expressed their support for a continuation of the war, was prepared to reject Pétain's authority. Two Governors-General expressing support for de Gaulle, Catroux in Indochina and de Coppet in Madagascar, were removed from office and immediately 'rallied' to de Gaulle.[4] Indochina, now deprived of British support, drifted inexorably into Japanese suzerainty. After the British bombing of the French Mediterranean fleet at Mers-el-Kebir and the failure of the Anglo-Gaullist expedition to capture Dakar, Operation 'Menace', the loyalty of most of the Empire was not in doubt; French North Africa and French West Africa (*Afrique Occidentale Française*, or AOF) quickly emerged as the bastions of Vichy's colonial empire. In the Americas the issue was decided by the Havana Convention of July 1940, by which the American Republics pledged to oppose any transfer of sovereignty in the Western hemisphere. Although this was intended as an instrument to block German incursions, it effectively opposed the Free French also.[5]

---

3. 'Car la France n'est pas seule! Elle n'est pas seule! Elle n'est pas seule! Elle a un vaste Empire derrière elle. Elle peut faire bloc avec l'Empire britannique qui tient la mer et continue la lutte. Elle peut, comme l'Angleterre, utiliser sans limites l'immense industrie des Etats-Unis. Cette guerre n'est pas limitée par la bataille de France. Cette guerre est une guerre mondiale.' C. de Gaulle, *Discours et messages*, 3 vols, Paris, 1970, vol. 1, *Pendant la guerre, juin 1940–mai 1946*, 4.
4. Duroselle, *L'abîme*, 220–40.
5. Ibid., 258.

By the end of 1940, apart from some smaller territories which declared for de Gaulle under British supervision, the Indian settlements, New Caledonia, and Oceania, only the securing of French Equatorial Africa (*Afrique Equatoriale Française*, or AEF) represented a veritable triumph for 'Free France'. Advised by Captain de Hauteclocque (better known by his posthumous post-war title and Resistance *nom de guerre*, Marshal Leclerc), the Governor of the strategically vital territory of Tchad, Félix Eboué, rallied to de Gaulle in August 1940. Following his example, Brazzaville, federal capital of AEF, fell to the Gaullists in a bloodless coup, followed by the rest of AEF and Cameroun, though Gabon was taken only after bitter Franco-French fighting.[6] Eboué was rewarded with the Governor-Generalship of 'Free French Africa'. Brazzaville, although it was to become associated with Gaullist reform after the 1944 conference, was until then chiefly important as the effective capital of Free France, a territorial base to which de Gaulle could retire when relations with Churchill became too difficult in London. As he reflected on his arrival in the makeshift capital, 'I feel how much this land is French'.[7] Further territorial gains were made by the Gaullists on the back of British or Anglo-American initiatives. Thus the Anglo-Gaullist invasion of Syria in 1941 allowed de Gaulle's men to assume the Mandate administration, and de Gaulle negotiated a similar transfer of administrative powers following the British invasion of Madagascar in 1942. Most importantly, the Anglo-American invasion of North Africa in late 1942 not only precipitated the German occupation of the so-called 'Free Zone' of hitherto unoccupied France, but also set in train the complex sequence of events by which de Gaulle was established as head of the CFLN at Algiers in July 1943, thus uniting the remainder of the Empire, barring Indochina, under his authority. It should be noted, however, that even at this crucial stage, the rival claims of the American-backed General Giraud had not yet been fully resolved, and that some territories, notably AOF, preferred Giraud to the 'aggressor' de Gaulle.

Reformism was pushed into the background while the struggle for imperial unity lasted. The degree to which de Gaulle was influenced by the reformist ideas of Eboué, or vice versa, can only be

---

6. See D. Shipley, *White, Black Africa and de Gaulle: From the French Empire to Independence*, Philadelphia and London, 1979, 59–79.

7. '… je sens combien cette terre est française': 26 Oct. 1940, *Discours et messages*, vol. 1, 38.

matter for speculation. At most, de Gaulle showed an awareness that Africa would not emerge from the war as she went in, for example in a speech to the Royal African Society in October 1941:

> A Greek philospher once said that war is a begetter of children. It is certainly true that its hard light throws into relief many previously unrecognised necessities, and that its inexorable thirst for action forces changes which have been denied or delayed in peacetime. Africa is also at war, and we should have no doubt that this tremendous adventure will have a profound influence on its development.[8]

But even here, his sentiments, geared to his audience, were designed merely to stress the importance of a unified Allied African war effort. Indeed, until de Gaulle's arrival in Algiers, and even thereafter, the reality of Gaullist imperialism in Syria, Morocco, Tunisia, and even in Algeria appeared to be a very different story, one of repression and indifference to all pressures for reform.[9]

However, two external factors impelling the Gaullists towards colonial reform need to be addressed before the preparations for Brazzaville are considered: the comparison with Vichy's colonial policy and international pressure for reform, in particular that of American anti-colonialism. Vichy's attitude to Empire was a renewed form of the old doctrine of 'repli impérial', or retreat into Empire. As one typical publication had it, in 1942:

> On her own in Europe, France is merely a devalued piece on the chessboard of the old continent. Because her Empire again gives her the chance to apply her power and exert her long-term influence outside her territory, she has regained value at an international level which can be ignored by none. Through the Empire, France has a chance to count amongst the great nations.[10]

8. 'Le philosophe grec disait que la guerre enfante. Certes, il est bien vrai que sa dure lumière met souvent en plein relief des nécessités jusqu'alors mal reconnues et que sa dévorante activité impose des réalisations que les époques pacifiques rejettent ou retardent. Or l'Afrique est dans la guerre et nous ne pouvons douter que cette gigantesque épreuve doive influer profondément sur son évolution.' 23 Oct. 1941, *Discours et messages*, vol. 1, 128.

9. See C.-A. Julien, *L'Afrique du Nord en marche*, 3rd edn, Paris, 1972; S.H. Longrigg, *Syria and Lebanon under French Mandate*, Oxford, 1958; Shipway, 'The Brazzaville Conference', 45–52.

10. 'La France seule en Europe n'est qu'une pièce démonétisée sur l'échiquier du vieux continent. Grace à son Empire qui restaure en elle des notions de force extériorisée et de permanente influence elle est sur le plan mondial une pièce qui a encore une valeur propre que nul ne peut négliger. Par l'Empire, elle conserve une chance de compter parmi les grandes nations.' *L'Empire notre meilleure chance*, Lyon, 1942, quoted by C.-R. Ageron, *France coloniale ou parti colonial?*, Paris, 1978, 270–71.

Clearly this was largely a propaganda stance, though a significant one. Publications on an imperial theme and local imperial committees (*Comités d'Empire*) were commonplace on both sides of the Armistice line. Between October 1940 and October 1942, 38 percent of news items on the Gaumont-Pathé newsreels were on imperial topics.[11] In practical terms the policy of *repli impérial* was double-edged. Defence of the Empire was a priority from the start, when the regime stuck out in resisting German and Italian demands with regard to the Empire. As noted above, the regime was also largely successful in checking Gaullist infiltration. At the same time, the Empire was seen less as a chesspiece than as a bargaining counter in French attempts to collaborate. Ironically, it was as a result of Vichy allowing the Luftwaffe to fly from Syrian airfields against the British in Iraq, in the Paris Protocols of 28 May 1941, that de Gaulle came to acquire control of Syria and Lebanon following the Allied invasion.[12] A year later, it was as a result of fears that the Japanese would be invited into Madagascar that the British invasion was planned.[13]

Stability and continuity, as primary aims of Vichy colonial policy, were largely achieved. Nationalist activity in the three North African territories was in any case at a low ebb, with militants of the more extreme parties, such as Messali Hadj's Algerian People's Party (*Parti du peuple algérien*) or the Tunisian *Neo-Destour*, safely behind barbed wire, while more moderate nationalists were content to bide their time. The authorities' attention was more particularly directed to the North African Jewish populations. Algeria, for example, saw the repeal of the Crémieux decree, which since 1870 had granted the substantial pre-colonial Sephardic Jewish community full status alongside the settlers.[14] In AOF, the transition to a Vichy regime made little difference and the new Governor-General, Pierre Boisson, who moved to Dakar when the Gaullists overthrew him from his previous post at Brazzaville, was a moderate in his colonial policy. Nonetheless, the colonial freedoms hard-won in the inter-war years were gradually eroded: the *indigénat*, or native penal code, was made harsher, local assemblies were suppressed, and the few black

---

11. Ageron, *France coloniale*, 271.
12. R.O. Paxton, *Vichy France: Old Guard and New Order, 1940–1944*, London, 1972, 117.
13. The Japanese had no designs on the island, though the French were prepared to condone them if they had. Duroselle, *L'abîme*, 353.
14. Julien, *L'Afrique du Nord en marche*, 267–77.

'dissidents' (Gaullists and others) were more harshly treated than their white counterparts.[15]

Only in Indochina was continuity of policy not assured. From 1941, the colony's status was anomalous both in Southeast Asia and within the French Empire. The Japanese garrison was never numerous enough to constitute an occupying force (until the March 1945 coup). Moreover, isolated by the British blockade, the colony was integrated into the Japanese economy, to the advantage of both. At the same time, the new Governor-General, Admiral Decoux, propagated an Indochina 'mystique' to counter the propaganda surrounding Japan's proposed 'Greater East Asia Co-Prosperity Sphere'. To this end he promoted Annamese (i.e., Vietnamese) language and culture, established an ambitious programme of public works, and reorganised administration so as to emphasise the identity of each of Indochina's constituent parts, including for the first time 'Viet-Nam' so called. The new Federal Council contained by 1943 a majority of officially sponsored native representatives.[16] However, Decoux's was perhaps the most authoritarian of the Vichy colonial governments, in which all forms of elected representation were suppressed, while nationalists, communists, and Gaullists were vigorously persecuted. Nonetheless, the embryonic federal system set a precedent for subsequent Gaullist reforms.[17]

The received image of a retrograde and authoritarian regime under Vichy belies the progressive nature of some aspects of its colonial policy. In particular, in the field of imperial economics, Vichy carried forward the debate on economic liberalisation and industrialisation, and displayed a willingness to reform lacking even under the Popular Front. The perception that a measure of imperial industrialisation could have increased French power in 1940 gave a new impetus to moves for economic reform. Some suggested measures made more political than economic sense, such as the revived plan, discussed since 1876, to build a railway from the Mediterranean to the Niger.[18] The ten-year plan unveiled in 1942, on the other hand, allocated a substantial budget for development which involved for the first time the use of public funds for colonial industrialisation. As Jacques Marseille has argued, Vichy's

15. J. Richard-Molard, *L'Afrique Occidentale Française*, Paris, 1949, 165–66.
16. P. Devillers, *L'Histoire du Viêt-Nam de 1940 à 1952*, Paris, 1952, 81–88.
17. See below, Ch. 5.
18. Ageron, *France coloniale*, 270.

resolve in this matter pre-emptively outmatched the economic recommendations of the Brazzaville Conference two years later.[19]
If outdoing Vichy's record was largely an unproblematical aim
of Gaullist colonial policy, facing down the vaguely defined but
potentially disastrous threat posed by American anti-colonialism
was a more serious challenge. This was in part because of barely
concealed American distaste at France's defeat and subsequent
political difficulties: after Pearl Harbor, US relations with Vichy,
although they were maintained for some time on a diplomatic
footing, were never cordial, and became increasingly ambiguous.
Roosevelt's relations with de Gaulle were famously difficult, and
the months preceding the establishment of the CFLN at Algiers
were marred by the US President's unwillingness to relinquish
the upright but politically inept General Giraud as contender for
the French political succession. But alongside British rule in India,
French colonialism at times constituted the principal target for
American anti-colonial opprobrium. Thus Roosevelt thought the
record of French colonialism 'hopeless'. Of his son he asked:

> How do [the colonies] belong to France? Why does Morocco, inhab-
> ited by Moroccans, belong to France? Or take Indo-China. The
> Japanese control that colony now. Why was it a cinch for the Japan-
> ese to conquer that land? The native Indo-Chinese have been so
> flagrantly downtrodden that they thought to themselves: anything
> must be better than to live under French colonial rule![20]

This distaste translated into an increasingly high-handed approach to the future of French Empire. At first, the President and
the State Department proffered formal recognition of 'the sovereign jurisdiction of the people of France over the territory of
France and over French territory'. By January 1943, at Casablanca,
President Roosevelt was claiming that his special adviser in North
Africa, Robert Murphy, had 'exceeded his authority' when he
assured French leaders that their Empire would be restored. To de
Gaulle, whose reaction it is not difficult to infer, he explained that
since 1940 the French had not been in a position to assert their
sovereignty, so that France was 'in the position of a little child
unable to look out and fend for itself, and that in such a case a
court would appoint a trustee to do the necessary'.[21] In particular,

19. J. Marseille, *Empire colonial et capitalisme français*, Paris, 1984, 337–42.

20. E. Roosevelt, *As He Saw It*, New York, 1946, 115.

21. C. Thorne, *Allies of a Kind: The United States, Britain and the War against Japan,
1941–1945*, New York, 1979, 217; *Foreign Relations of the United States (FRUS)*, Washington and Casablanca, 514, 695–96.

international trusteeship for Indochina became a regular theme of Roosevelt's, and it was Chiang Kaishek, rather than the French, whom the President envisaged as trustee. Moreover, as plans for an international 'police force' developed, it was again French territories which came under consideration. In particular, Dakar and New Caledonia, where the Americans already had bases, were thought to pose a threat to international security if left in 'unsure hands'. Meanwhile, Roosevelt and Murphy offered encouragement to the various aspirations of Algerian and Moroccan nationalists and to the Sultan of Morocco, though the exact tenor of this encouragement remained ambiguous.[22]

French policy makers had also to compete with British and Dutch efforts to allay American anti-colonial misgivings. The Dutch showed perhaps the greatest alacrity in seeking to influence American public opinion. Following plans made as early as June 1942, Queen Wilhelmina proclaimed a Commonwealth in December in which 'the Netherlands, Indonesia, Surinam, and Curaçao will participate, with complete self-reliance and freedom of conduct regarding ... internal affairs, but with the readiness to render mutual assistance'.[23] The Declaration served its purpose. Henceforth the Dutch were cited as an example to the British and French in colonial matters, although as Roosevelt admitted to one British diplomat, he found it unlikely that the Dutch, 'poor dears', could have the East Indies back as they imagined.[24] British responses to the American challenge ranged from Churchill's staunch assertion that he had 'not become the King's First Minister in order to preside over the liquidation of the British Empire', to a more nuanced approach. Like the Dutch, the British were concerned to give a more favourable impression of the Empire, now more generally called the Commonwealth, to take on public opinion on its own terms. Welfare was stressed as an essential part of colonialism, and negotiations for the 1945 Colonial Welfare and Development Act, which began in 1943, may in part be seen as an attempt to appease US opinion, in part as a response to those segments of British opinion, foremost amongst whom were the Labour Party, whose hand had been strengthened by American attention. At the same time, concessions were being prepared to counter American

22. *FRUS*, Cairo and Tehran, 485, 509; Julien, *L'Afrique du Nord en marche*, 283–86.

23. Wm Roger Louis, *Imperialism at Bay: The United States and the Decolonization of the British Empire, 1941–1945*, Oxford and New York, 1977, 29.

24. Thorne, *Allies of a Kind*, 218.

plans for international trusteeship, notably in the elaborate plans for 'regional commissions' announced in the House of Commons by the Colonial Secretary, Colonel Stanley, in July 1943.[25]

Bastille Day, 14 July 1943, saw the rallying of Martinique to the Gaullist cause, the final French territory barring Indochina to do so. With the Empire united behind it, the CFLN now had before it the task of repairing the political damage, direct and indirect, wreaked by three years of imperial disunity and disorientation, and of meeting the international challenge to continuing imperial cohesion. It was this complex task which was addressed by the organisers of the Brazzaville Conference, whose efforts are now considered.

Brazzaville: Origins and Inspiration

The Brazzaville myth derived potency from its association with the heroic deeds of wartime Gaullism. Thus, at one level, the Brazzaville Conference was the culmination of more than three years of intermittent debate and discussions amongst a small group of colonial administrators; but at another level, it was the *pronunciamiento* of men who had initially had in common only the fact that they had declared for de Gaulle, during the establishment of 'Free French Africa' in August 1940 or subsequently. The new colonial and imperial thinking which emerged from their discussions may be compared with the planning undertaken by many Resistance groups in occupied metropolitan France, in a spirit both of despair at the circumstances of French defeat, and, more importantly, of idealism for the new France which would emerge from the ashes. Like the planning of the Resistance, that of the Gaullist colonial administration was a by-product of more pressing and active concerns: neither de Gaulle nor Governor-General Félix Eboué allowed their subordinates to forget that their first priorities were the day-to-day running of their colonies and the often punishing demands of the Gaullist war effort.[26]

The perspective of the colonial administration over these years was largely colonial, often specifically African and sometimes absurdly parochial: where other than in the depths of the Sahel

---

25. Louis, *Imperialism at Bay*, 200, 257–58 and passim.

26. E. M'Bokolo, 'French Colonial Policy in Equatorial Africa in the 1940s and 1950s', in P. Gifford and W.R. Louis, eds, *The Transfer of Power, Decolonization 1940–1960*, New Haven, 1982, 177; B. Weinstein, Eboué, New York, 1972, 257–58; on the 'snobisme activiste' which favoured militarily active members of the Resistance, see A. Shennan, *Rethinking France, Plans for Renewal 1940–1946*, Oxford, 1989, 35.

could a senior administrator write in his annual report, under the heading 'important political events', that there was nothing to report for 1944?[27] Yet despite the limitations placed upon it, the new imperial thinking was wide-ranging and ambitious and shared many intellectual characteristics with that of the metropolitan Resistance. In particular, the broad themes of the imperial debate may be likened to the three 'routes' to constitutional renovation identified by Andrew Shennan in the Resistance debate: the route of elite replacement, the institutional route, and the route of moral regeneration.[28] It is under these headings that the new imperial thinking may best be understood.

The question of **elite replacement** was more practical than theoretical in colonial Africa, at least at the level of the higher administration, and by the time of Brazzaville purges had already been undertaken, albeit in a makeshift and unsatisfactory way. Moreover, unlike the metropolitan Resistance, the administration of 'dissident' AEF was already engaged in duties comparable to those of peacetime, and could legislate and act upon at least some of its new ideas.[29] The criterion for the selection of senior personnel was simple: the governors, governors-general and senior administrators of French Africa and Madagascar who constituted the deliberative body at the Brazzaville Conference had been chosen, with very few exceptions, on the basis of their loyalty to de Gaulle. This was notably Eboué's case, whose new political allegiance was, moreover, the logical extension of his deeper convictions: as a Socialist party activist (and a freemason), as a notably liberal Governor of Guadeloupe under the 1936 Popular Front government, and as the highest ranking black in the French colonial administration (born in French Guiana of slave ancestry), Eboué had every reason to oppose Vichy and to identify with the still embryonic Gaullist movement.[30] A similar combination of Gaullism, patriotism, and colonial liberalism may be discerned in Henri Laurentie, Eboué's right-hand man both at the Governor's Palace in Tchad and subsequently at Brazzaville. Not yet forty when he 'rallied' to de Gaulle,

27. Rapport politique, Niger, 1944: AOM, 2G-44–22 (14Mi1853). As he continued: 'The population has calmly pursued the war effort of the last five years.' As noted above, the AOF administration rallied to de Gaulle, and then reluctantly, only in 1943. (For details of all French archival sources, see Bibliography).

28. *Rethinking France*, 38–42.

29. M'Bokolo, however, stresses the discrepancy between the planning and the concrete achievements of the AEF administration, in 'French Colonial Policy', 175, 187.

30. Biographical details from *Fichier des anciens élèves de l'Ecole Nationale de la France d'Outre-Mer*, AOM, 39APOM3; Weinstein, *Eboué*, passim.

Laurentie had served before the war in Cameroun, Guinée and, unusually for a member of the Colonial Corps, for four years in the Mandate administration of Syria. At the outbreak of war he was a District Officer (*commandant de cercle*) in Northern Tchad, before Governor Eboué chose him as his Secretary-General. When Eboué was made Governor-General, Laurentie moved with him.[31] Laurentie emerges as an intellectual and an idealist from the portrait offered of him by Brian Weinstein, regarding the early period of his association with Eboué in pre-Gaullist Tchad:

> A sharp-featured man with a shock of hair over his right forehead, his religion, cutting wit and a disarming modesty were as well-known as his emotional patriotism. Mr and Mrs Laurentie's house had the largest library in Tchad, and many said the young administrator wrote poetry.... Eboué and he were practically the only Frenchmen to address [African dignitaries and civil servants] with the respectful *vous* form in French.[32]

When René Pleven was appointed Commissioner for the Colonies in the CFLN in July 1943, Laurentie was appointed his Director of Political Affairs, and was in this capacity Secretary-General of the Brazzaville Conference.

As the Conference was to reveal, however, Gaullism was no guarantee of professional dynamism, much less of reformism or liberalism. Indeed some senior figures at Brazzaville, including the Governors-General of AOF and Madagascar, Pierre Cournarie and Pierre de Saint-Mart, might never have achieved Governor, let alone Governor-General, had it not been for their loyalty to de Gaulle. The corps of Governors at Brazzaville revealed a preponderance of what Laurentie was later to criticise bitterly as:

> the bureaucratic spirit ... honest, hard-working and ultimately impermeable to any kind of general thinking.... This obstinate refusal to change or make any kind of revolution, this insistence on maintaining colonial paternalism indefinitely is the most deplorable state of mind there is these days.[33]

Moreover, even on the question of Gaullist loyalism some compromise had been necessary: the roll-call at Brazzaville included two Governors who had served in the Vichy administration of

---

31. *Fichier*, AOM, 39APOM3. Henri-Marie-Joseph-Augustin-François Laurentie, born 28 Aug. 1901, at St.-Symphorien (Indre-et-Loire).

32. Weinstein, *Eboué*, 310–11.

33. '... l'esprit 'administrateur' ... honnête, travailleur et à la longue, imperméable à toute espèce d'idées générales.... Cette espèce d'obstination à ne pas

AOF; below the rank of Governor the administration went largely unpurged for reasons of administrative efficiency and continuity.[34] The theme of **moral regeneration** featured prominently in the new imperial thinking, and largely characterised Félix Eboué's contribution to the debate. In late 1941, Eboué convened a small conference at Brazzaville to discuss a new approach to colonial policy. Written up by Laurentie in a circular dated 8 November 1941, subsequently published by the Gaullists in London under the ambitious title 'The New Native Policy' ('La nouvelle politique indigène'), the 1941 conference inspired much of its grander successor's agenda.[35] There was little that was actually new in the so-called Eboué 'thesis', which drew on Eboué's long experience as administrator, ethnologist, and linguist, going back to a first posting in Oubangui-Chari in 1913. Eboué was particularly inspired by the ideas of Marshal Lyautey, the architect of the French regime in Morocco, who was quoted in the circular:

> Therefore we should not disturb a single tradition or change a single custom. *In every society there is a ruling class, born to rule, without whom nothing may be accomplished.* This class should be brought round to our interests.[36]

Moral renewal of the colonial regime, then, was to stem from respect for African civilisation, recognition of traditional structures, and a more equitable relationship between Africans and Europeans, between the administration and its subjects. The circular placed new stress on issues such as family and social customs, the role of an educated African elite, whom Eboué termed 'évolués' (literally 'evolved'), and the status of mixed race, so-called 'métis'.

---

vouloir changer, à ne vouloir faire aucune révolution, à perpétuer indéfiniment le paternalisme colónial est la plus déplorable disposition d'esprit que l'on puisse trouver aujourd'hui': Laurentie to Bayardelle, 4 Aug. 1944, AN, 72AJ538. On Saint-Mart, see *Fichier*, AOM, 39APOM4; on Cournarie, see D. Bouche, 'La réception des principes de Brazzaville par l'administration en A.-O.F.', in Inst Charles-de-Gaulle and IHTP, *Brazzaville*, 207–8.

34. A third Vichyste Governor, Croccichia of Guinée, failed to attend, unable to stomach the occasion. On the purge of the colonial administration, see W.B. Cohen, *Rulers of Empire: The French Colonial Service in Africa*, Stanford, 1971, 169–70: only about twenty officials in AOF lost their jobs at the Gaullist takeover in 1943.

35. Weinstein, Eboué, 270–74; the circular appears in J. de la Roche and J. Gottmann, *La fédération française*, Montréal, 1945, 586–627.

36. 'Donc ne froisser aucune tradition, ne changer aucune habitude. *Il y a dans toute société une classe dirigeante, née pour diriger, sans laquelle on ne fait rien.* La mettre dans nos intérêts.' De la Roche and Gottmann, *La fédération française*, 587. Emphasis in text.

The context for this renewal was unashamedly colonial: Eboué aimed to place the existing colonial regime on a new, more permanent footing. Self-determination and nationalism were both alien to the concerns of the Eboué thesis. However, it made a significant advance in condemning the old 'Jacobin' doctrine of Assimilation, and in rejecting the policy of direct administration derived from it:

> To attempt to make or remake a society in our own image, or at least according to our own mental habits, is to court certain failure. The native has a certain code of behaviour, laws, a nation, which are not the same as our own. We will bring him good fortune neither by applying the principles of the French Revolution, which is our revolution, nor by judging him according to the Napoleonic Code, which is our code of laws, nor by replacing his chiefs with our administrators, who will think for him, but not with him.[37]

It was in this stance that the Eboué thesis was to have a bearing on the later, more general Brazzaville policy.

More directly relevant to the wider concerns of the Empire as a whole was the **institutional** route to imperial reform, which was Laurentie's particular concern. Almost from the start, Laurentie looked beyond the confines of the colonial system for a durable solution to the problems of Empire. As he later recalled: 'From the moment we started discussing it, which was in 1942, I became more and more convinced that only a liberal policy could save the empire, which would have to be transformed, and that meant completely transformed'.[38] This liberal policy evolved around the concept of a French Federation embracing the metropole and colonies. Given that this was the essential guiding principle of the French Union underpinning later policy, it will be discussed in

---

37. 'Faire ou refaire une société, sinon à notre image, du moins selon nos habitudes mentales, c'est aller à l'échec certain. L'indigène a un comportement, des lois, une patrie qui ne sont pas les nôtres. Nous ne ferons pas son bonheur, ni selon les principes de la Révolution Française, qui est notre Révolution, ni en lui appliquant le code Napoléon, qui est notre code, ni en substituant nos fonctionnaires à ses chefs, car nos fonctionnaires penseront pour lui, et non en lui.' Ibid., 585; see M'Bokolo, 'French Colonial Policy', 178–90.

38. '… à partir du moment où on en a parlé, c'est-à-dire à partir de 1942, … s'est formée de plus en plus nettement dans mon esprit, qu'il n'y avait qu'une politique libérale qui pouvait sauver l'Empire. En le transformant, d'ailleurs en le transformant complètement'; in an interview with G. Pilleul, 'Témoignage du gouverneur-général Henri Laurentie', in Institut Charles-de-Gaulle, *Le général de Gaulle et l'Indochine*, Paris, 1982, 239–40.

that context.[39] Nonetheless, the premises of Laurentie's thesis were central to the debate at Brazzaville, and thus must be mentioned here.

The idea of an imperial Federation was intended to resolve the conflicting aims and objectives of Empire, the most important of which was the maintenance of French sovereignty. This was made clear by Laurentie, in the agenda for the Brazzaville Conference, whose starting point was 'that France's political power should be exercised precisely and rigorously across the whole of the Empire'. But this aim had to be seen as only part of a far more complex equation. Indeed, the passage presented the extent of the dilemma facing imperial reformers:

> It is also desirable that the colonies should enjoy considerable administrative and economic freedoms. Equally, the colonial peoples should be able to express these freedoms for themselves, and their freedom should be developed and extended gradually in such a way that they are involved in the running of their own countries.
>
> It is not desirable that the colonies should arbitrarily be involved in the affairs of metropolitan France. Even less should political and business interest groups in Paris be in a position to exert influence in the colonies' internal affairs.[40]

The first problem, then, was how to maintain French sovereignty while recognising and encouraging the colonies' gradual attainment of political responsibility or maturity (loosely termed 'la personnalité politique'). This latter concept implied at the very least the development of a national identity distinct from that of France, but encompassed also the extension of political, administrative, and economic freedoms, hitherto inconceivable even in the French protectorate regimes of North Africa and Indochina. The second

39. See below, Ch. 2.
40. 'On veut que le pouvoir politique de la France s'exerce avec précision et rigueur sur toutes les terres de l'Empire.

'On veut aussi que les colonies jouissent d'une grande liberté administrative et économique. On veut également que les peuples coloniaux éprouvent par eux-mêmes cette liberté et que leur liberté soit peu à peu formée et élevée afin qu'ils se trouvent associés àla gestion de la chose publique dans leur pays.

'On ne veut pas que par une extension arbitraire, les colonies s'entremettent dans les affaires de la France métropolitaine. On veut encore moins que les milieux politiques et d'affaires de Paris soient en mesure de faire pression sur les affaires intérieures des colonies.' Programme général de la Conférence, 20, AOM, AP/2288. The three sentences starting 'On veut ...' appear, out of context, in the Conference's recommendations, in the official record: *La Conférence Africaine Française*, Paris, 1945, 32.

problem, following on from this, consisted in reconciling the Empire's patent diversity with the desire to 'rationalise' imperial structure. This was partly a question of sheer geographical dislocation, but was also a consequence of the enormous variety of France's colonies and protectorates in terms of size, constitutional status, and degree of political evolution. Any plan for the Empire as a whole would have to allow not only for the African territories' almost total lack of modern political development (except, that is, in Senegal), but also for the nominal sovereignty vested in the Bey of Tunis and the Sultan of Morocco; the 'assimilated' status of the Old Colonies in the Caribbean and elsewhere; the diverse constitutional forms present in a single colony, Indochina; the predominance of European settler communities in New Caledonia and in Algeria; and, not least, the constitutional fiction which portrayed the latter colony as an extension of the metropole. The Empire's administrative complexity was also of relevance here, since imperial policy had to be coordinated between three ministries: Colonies, Foreign Affairs (responsible for the North African protectorates and the Levant Mandates), and Interior (which oversaw the Algerian civil administration). Finally, the role of the metropole had to be defined: the Brazzaville agenda, quoted above, evoked not only the well-established pattern of direct administration from Paris (modified according to the lobbying pressure of commercial and financial interests), but also the traditional spectre of an 'assimilated' empire swamping parliamentary politics.

Whatever judgement may be made concerning the workability, or otherwise, of Laurentie's federal idea, its attractions to the originators of the new imperial thinking, on paper at least, are obvious: federation would, at a stroke, permit the evolution of individual territories towards self-government and self-determination; would allow a 'multiple track' approach, whereby each territory could evolve at its own pace; and would unite France with her empire without prejudicing the interests of either. The notion of 'empirical' federalism, as it was called in the Brazzaville agenda, had obvious flaws, not least a considerable oversimplification of the problem. Moreover, the federal plan existed in only skeletal form by the time of Brazzaville, including the institutional structure and constitutional status of an eventual federation. But as a theoretical model conceived in the political vacuum of wartime colonial Africa, it was remarkably comprehensive in its approach. Like Eboué's native policy, the Laurentie thesis also put down an intellectual marker in its refutation of assimilationist doctrine. Building on the assimilation achieved in the 'Old Colonies', federalism dispensed with the assimilationist ideal of Greater France ('la plus grande France'), as well as spurious (but still current) demographic notions of 'the France of a hundred million people', which could henceforth more readily be dismissed as purely rhetorical constructs liable only to confuse the issues.[41]

One further aspect of the new imperial thinking needs to be mentioned. This was the perception of its international context. An essential purpose of the Brazzaville Conference was as a Gaullist affirmation of France's will and fitness to continue its mission as a strong and liberal colonial power. In this the colonial administration aimed to match or surpass the British and Dutch declarations concerning the future of their empires, and to be seen to do so, in order to meet the anti-colonial challenge of the United States. As a consequence of this competitive, rather threatening international environment, Brazzaville was staged partly as a propaganda event. As one advocate of the new imperial thinking argued in the Consultative Assembly in Algiers:

> Do I need to draw attention to the terms of the Atlantic Charter? While all around are rethinking the colonial world, France cannot afford to remain silent or absent. It is only just that, following the deeds and declarations of the Americans, the South Africans, and the Australians, France should also make itself heard, and act.[42]

The temptation to over-statement for propaganda purposes was considerable. Thus, in the same debate, Eboué was somewhat tactlessly offered as living proof of France's lack of racial prejudice.[43] But just as Churchill's refusal to 'preside over the liquidation of the British Empire' came at a moment of rising British confidence in the wake of El Alamein and news from Stalingrad, so it was perhaps inevitable in the circumstances that Brazzaville was the occasion for a good measure of triumphalism. In a partial triumph

41. H. Brunschwig, 'De l'assimilation à la décolonisation', in IHTP, *Les chemins de la décolonisation de l'empire français, 1936–1956*, Paris, 1986, 49–53.

42. 'Ferai-je enfin état de certains termes de la Charte de l'Atlantique? Dans cette grande reconsidération générale du monde colonial la France ne peut demeurer muette, ni absente. Il n'est que juste qu'après les paroles ou les actes d'Amérique, d'Afrique du Sud, d'Australie, la France à son tour se fasse entendre et agisse.' P.-O. Lapie, in the Colonial Debate which preceded the Conference: *Journal Officiel, Assemblée Consultative Provisoire* (JOACP), 13 Jan. 1944, 13. Lapie made no mention of British reformism.

43. Ibid., 14.

of form over content, then, it was almost immaterial what was said at Brazzaville, as long as it was spoken defiantly.

Brazzaville: Execution and Postmortem

By late January 1944, the stage was set for an essentially upbeat, but otherwise rather confusing, piece of theatre on the banks of the Congo. With correspondents of the international and Resistance press in attendance, alongside consular and other representatives of concerned powers (notably Britain, the United States and Belgium), de Gaulle made the Conference the focal point on a triumphal tour of all the colonial capitals of French Africa. In Brazzaville, he unveiled a hideous monument to the eponymous French explorer Savorgnan de Brazza, named a football stadium after Eboué, and opened the Conference. De Gaulle's 'Brazzaville speech' was characteristically sybilline with its promises of vaguely defined reforms, balanced against the more immediate concerns of the impending Liberation of France:

It falls to France, and to France alone, when the time is ripe, to make those structural reforms which she alone will decide in her sovereignty. But meanwhile we must live, and living from day to day means facing the future.[44]

Even here, it will be noted, the priority of maintaining sovereignty was reaffirmed. After the opening day, de Gaulle departed to complete his tour en route for Algiers, and took no further part in the deliberations.[45] Together with his African *realpolitik* of more than a decade later, however, it was apparently enough to ensure veneration of the Gaullist Cross of Lorraine in the region for a long time to come.

The main proceedings of the Conference, conducted behind closed doors, were considerably less satisfactory. The original intention had been to hold a general imperial conference, but for ostensibly practical reasons its remit was limited to the affairs of the Black African colonies (hence its official designation, the French African Conference). Moreover, participation was restricted exclusively to

---

44. '... il appartient à la nation française, et il n'appartient qu'à elle, de procéder, le moment venu, aux réformes de structure qu'elle décidera dans sa souveraineté. Mais en attendant, il faut vivre, et vivre chaque jour, c'est entamer l'avenir.' 30 Jan. 1944, Discours et messages, vol. 1, vol. 1, 394.
45. White, *De Gaulle and Black Africa*, 129.

colonial officials. Apart from the Governors and their subordinates, the Conference was attended, in a non-deliberative capacity, by representatives of the Consultative Assembly, colonial dignitaries such as the Bishop of Brazzaville, Monsignor Biéchy, and by two carefully chosen 'assimilated' Africans. Indochina was considered off-limits for obvious reasons, though it was the subject of a Declaration by the CFLN issued on 8 December 1943, and a message of solidarity was piously offered to 'captive Indochina' at the opening session.[46] Indochina was thus mentioned only in passing. North Africa, conversely, was considered too sensitive a subject for the semi-public forum of the Conference. Defying the advice of René Massigli, CFLN Commissioner for Foreign Affairs, that the Conference was likely to have resonance north of the Sahara, the Moroccan and Tunisian Administrations sent only observers to the Conference, as did the Algerian Government-General. The reason given in Rabat and Tunis, not for the last time in attempts to extend the imperial debate to North Africa, was that their participation would overstep the limitations imposed by protectorate status. In his report to Massigli, Vallat, the senior observer from Rabat, boasted of his moderating influence on the discussions. As he remarked, with old-fashioned, reactionary zeal:

> Inspired by Commissioner Pleven and Secretary-General Laurentie, the Conference delegates were borne along by the generous impulse to put their democratic ideals into practice and to indulge a spirit of sacrifice which seemed to us not always to take into account the more down-to-earth concerns of the French Empire.[47]

Where the Conference addressed themes of relevance in North Africa, in particular those relating to Islam or the use of Arabic in schools, passages were struck from the record, and were left out of the roneotyped transcripts later distributed.[48]

Notwithstanding Vallat's report, Pleven and Laurentie were almost the only ones to be borne along by a generous impulse of any kind at the Conference. As Laurentie put it in his June 1945 briefing on Indochina, it was not the case 'that the recommendations of the

---

46. *Conférence Africaine Française*, 15; see below, Ch. 5.
47. 'Sous l'impulsion du Commissaire M. Pleven et du Secrétaire-Général Laurentie, la Conférence fut dès le début emportée par un généreux élan vers la réalisation d'idéaux démocratiques et animée d'un esprit de sacrifice qui nous parut parfois ne pas assez tenir compte du point de vue plus terre à terre de l'impérium français.' Compte rendu, 'RABAT le 23 février 1944', MAE, Guerre/Alger/683.
48. Shipway, 'The Brazzaville Conference', 56–57, 98.

Brazzaville Conference contained any truly striking innovations'.[49] This was not meant to deny the usefulness of the debates, or of the innovations introduced, here and there, into the Conference recommendations. Much of the Conference turned, naturally enough considering the professional concerns of the conference delegates, on technical and practical questions of day-to-day colonialism, health, education, public works, and so on, and thus had little political resonance anyway. This was the case, even, for the recommendation that the exclusive medium for French education should be French, which reflected Republican orthodoxy going back to the 1875 Constitution, confirmed existing practice, and recognised the failure of British experiments with native languages; the question of Arabic, moreover, was sidestepped.[50] Some of the recommendations represented substantial humanitarian advances. This was notably the case of the recommendation that forced labour and the *indigénat*, the penal code applied by administrators to Africans, should be phased out. Even here, despite the fact that forced labour had been condemned by the International Labour Organisation (ILO) as long ago as 1930, the delegates were guided by extreme caution, allowing five years for the complete abolition of forced labour, and introducing a compulsory labour service ('service obligatoire du travail') in its place.[51]

On economic questions, though here at least the rhetoric was more enthusiastic, the same pattern of liberalism tempered by caution may be discerned. Indeed, as noted above, the supposed novelty of Brazzaville's economic recommendations had already been surpassed by Vichy's colonial planning. Economic issues did not bulk large in the Laurentie thesis. And, as Pleven stressed in his opening speech to the Conference, Brazzaville was intended to mark a shift away from the almost exclusive preoccupation with economics which had characterised earlier Conferences in the 1920s and 1930s. As he argued:

49. 'On ne peut pas dire que dans l'ensemble des recommendations faites par la Conférence de Brazzaville il y ait eu des innovations véritablement éclatantes.' Cours d'Information sur l'Indochine, n.d. (May 1945), AOM, AP/214bis.

50. D.E. Gardinier, 'Les recommendations de la Conférence de Brazzaville sur les problèmes d'éducation', in Inst Charles-de-Gaulle and IHTP, *Brazzaville*, 170–80.

51. H. Almeïda-Topor, 'La question du travail forcé', in Inst Charles-de-Gaulle and IHTP, *Brazzaville*, 115–20. The Conference thus clumsily evoked echoes of Vichy's loathed *Service du Travail Obligatoire*, by which ordinary Frenchmen were despatched to work in Nazi Germany.

The primacy accorded economics reflected the preoccupations of a period dominated by an unprecedented international crisis; this crisis itself stemmed largely from a financial view of the world according to which money, from being an instrument to serve man, became an end in itself.[52]

The main theme of the economic debate at Brazzaville was the end of the so-called Colonial Pact ('pacte colonial'), thus defined and ritually condemned in the agenda:

On the pretext of fairly distributing the world's raw materials, we are still happy to transpose onto the international level the old doctrine, whose origins lie in protectionism if not in the slave trade: Africa, according to this doctrine, will provide raw materials to the industrialised continents which will, in their turn, provide Africa with finished goods.[53]

As Marseille argues, the Colonial Pact was already defunct as a result of inter-war changes in the colonial customs regime; short of reversing this development, which was likely if anything to be reinforced by the foreseeable liberalisation of the post-war international economic system, there was little the Conference could do to innovate on this question. Where innovation was really called for, in colonial industrialisation, delegates merely offered heavily qualified encouragement. This was somewhat surprising, given the Gaullist perception, mentioned in the agenda, that had heavy industry, particularly defence industries, existed in the colonies, the disaster of 1940 might have been prevented. Ironically, and underlining perhaps Laurentie's blind spot for economics, the repudiation of the Colonial Pact was identified by him as one of only two 'new ideas' to come out of Brazzaville (the other being the federal idea).[54]

52. 'Cette sorte de primauté accordée à l'économique était le reflet des préoccupations d'une période dominée par une crise mondiale sans précédent, causée largement par des conceptions financières qui faisaient de la monnaie non plus l'instrument destiné à servir l'homme mais une fin en soi.' *Conférence Africaine Française*, 19.
53. 'Sous prétexte de répartition des matières dans le monde, on se contente volontiers, aujourd'hui encore, de transposer sur le plan international les vieilles doctrines protectionnistes, pour ne pas dire esclavagistes: l'Afrique, dit-on et écrit-on, fournira les matières premières aux continents industriels qui rendront à l'Afrique leurs articles fabriqués.' Loc.cit.
54. J. Marseille, 'La Conférence de Brazzaville et l'économie impériale: «des innovations éclatantes» ou des recommandations «prudentes»?', in Inst Charles-de-Gaulle and IHTP, *Brazzaville*, 107–15. On colonial industrialisation, see Marseille, *Empire colonial*, 332–49. Cours d'Information sur l'Indochine, loc.cit.

Laurentie and his colleagues had staked most on the two innovations outlined above: Eboué's native policy, and the idea of a French Federation. Both were received with a mixture of indifference, incomprehension, and outright hostility. In the session on native policy, Pleven sought to present Eboué's ideas as a new orthodoxy.[55] The Governors, however, refused to take the hint, pulling their punches only out of respect for the ailing Eboué, who was unable to take a very active part in the Conference proceedings as a result of advancing deafness.[56] Some aspects of the new native policy were passed as recommendations, such as the idea of a Statute for 'evolved dignitaries' (*notables évolués*) granting privileges to a small educated elite who would be called on to mediate between Africans and Europeans. This had already been put into limited practice in AEF. But Eboué's doctrine as a whole, which urged respect for African culture, was rejected by the Conference. As Governor Raphaël Saller argued with implacable logic:

> Evidently, the purpose of our civilisation is to bring civilisation to others. So we civilise, that is to say, we are not content to provide merely a surplus of material well-being, but we also impose moral rules and intellectual development. And by what methods and according to whose example should we do this, if not by our own methods and according to the example of our own civilisation, in the name of which alone we may speak? For what authority would we have to speak in the name of the civilisation whose people we are trying to improve?

Further, Saller argued that educated Africans wanted assimilation; anything else would lead to suspicion that they were being offered merely second-class status.[57] In the recommendations, the central ideas of the new native policy, itself 'colonial' in its implications, were either watered down or contradicted. The resulting text was

55. Transcript, 3 Feb. 1944: AOM, AP/2288.
56. He died only four months later, on 17 May 1944: Weinstein, *Eboué*, 310–12.
57. 'Il est évident que le but de notre civilisation est de civiliser. Donc nous civilisons, c'est-à-dire que nous ne nous contentons pas d'apporter un surcroît de bien-être matériel, mais aussi une règle morale et un développement intellectuel. Et par quelles méthodes, en proposant quel exemple, sinon les méthodes que nous pratiquons nous mêmes et l'exemple de notre propre civilisation. Nous ne pouvons parler qu'au nom de celle-ci, autrement quelle autorité aurions-nous pour parler au nom de la civilisation des peuples que nous voulons élever?' Transcript, 3 Feb. 1944, AOM, AP/2288. See P. Isoart, 'Les aspects politiques, constitutionnels et administratifs des Recommandations', in Inst Charles-de-Gaulle and IHTP, *Brazzaville*, 90–96.

thus indistinguishable from the bland doctrinal utterances of the past. The conference organisers' dismay was expressed by Léon Pignon, Laurentie's deputy at the conference and subsequently a key figure in Saigon, who complained that the administration had now opted for the solution which had underpinned French colonial policy since the Revolution: assimilation. As he argued, this was all the more surprising, since the assimilationist stance had been taken, not by parliamentarians unversed in colonial matters, but by 'experienced colonials, in touch with customs and with sociology'. As he commented, if Eboué's doctrine had been passed at all, this was in deference to Eboué, or because the 'dire consequences' of assimilation were so obvious that it could not be swallowed whole.[58]

The Governors did not feel similarly bound by tact and common sense when it came to the Laurentie thesis, except, perhaps, when they recommended that the whole question be studied by a more competent official Expert Commission. By an apparent tactical error, and in contrast to the Conference's work in other subject areas, it had been decided not to appoint a separate committee to deliberate on the federal idea at the conference itself. However, a plenary debate was held on the representation of the colonies in a new French constitution, the minutes of which were reproduced in the official record of the Conference.[59] This debate served only to blur the distinctions which Laurentie was seeking to make. One report presented to the Conference, for example, advocating assimilation, was claimed nonetheless by its author to be a blueprint for imperial federation in so far as it was practicable. Administrator Delmas's conclusions were in almost direct contradiction with Laurentie's, not least his assertion that the present system was generally sound, and needed only to be reformed by administrative and political decentralisation. His vision of the Empire was a rationalisation and extension of past Jacobin models calculated to appeal to a wider Republican audience:

> The Empire should consist of continental France and Overseas France, not associated but united, France One and Indivisible governed by a Fourth Republic, the respectful and grateful inheritor of the three Republics from which it is descended.[60]

58. 'NOTE sur l'attitude de la Conférence de Brazzaville à l'égard de la circulaire du 8 novembre 1941', ref.LP/SC, n.d.: AOM, AP/2288/5.
   59. *Conférence Africaine Française*, 33, 72–82. The Expert Commission was to meet in Algiers, May-Jul. 1944: see below, Ch. 2.
   60. 'L'Empire, ce doit être la France continentale et la France d'outre-mer, non pas associés, mais unies, la France une et indivisible organisée sous la forme d'une IVe

Delmas concluded that the Empire had no need for a separate Constitution; further, that the colonies should be represented in the forthcoming Constituent Assembly. This last idea, translated into one of the more effective Conference recommendations, was also the source of one of the French Union's most enduring ambiguities. For, whilst this 'liberal' measure paved the way for the early careers of a generation of African political leaders (including the first Presidents of independent Ivory Coast and Senegal, Félix Houphouët-Boigny and Léopold Sédar Senghor), it was never more than a token gesture given the parsimonious allocation of colonial seats in the French Parliament, and was the source of much Parisian meddling in colonial affairs and vice versa. So much had been predicted already by Laurentie in the Conference agenda.[61]

The most damaging blow to the Laurentie thesis was struck in the statement heading the Conference's political recommendations, the source of which remains obscure, though authorship has been claimed by Governor Saller, whose stamp it bears:

> The ends of the civilising mission accomplished in the colonies exclude any idea of autonomy, all possibility of evolution outside the French bloc; also excluded is the eventual establishment of self-government in the colonies, even in a distant future.[62]

Apart from its political ineptitude, the Declaration was marked by an apparently wilful confusion of terms, which arose from the Conference debates. Autonomy was central to the federal idea, though it was clear in the agenda that it was a long-term goal even in the more developed dependencies, let alone in the African colonies. At the Conference, however, debate revolved around administrative decentralisation, a subject popular amongst colonial administrators still constrained by a pattern of rule from Paris dating back to the Second Empire of Napoleon III. As Laurentie

---

République, héritière respectueuse et reconnaissante des trois Républiques dont elle sera issue.' Ibid., 77.

61. This is further discussed in M.J. Shipway, 'Madagascar on the eve of insurrection, 1944–1947: the impasse of a liberal colonial policy', *Journal of Imperial and Commonwealth History*, 24, 1 (Jan. 1996), 72–100.

62. 'Les fins de l'oeuvre de civilisation accomplie dans les colonies écartent toute idée d'autonomie, toute possibilité d'évolution hors du bloc français; la constitution éventuelle, même lointaine de self governments [sic] dans les colonies est à écarter.' Ibid., 32; C.-R. Ageron, 'Les préparatifs de la Conférence de Brazzaville et ses enseignements', in Inst Charles-de-Gaulle and IHTP, *Brazzaville*, 39–40.

pointed out, however, more was at stake: the devolution of power to local officials was potentially fatal to the development of local political autonomy. As he argued:

> The problem is the following: does the Conference accept, or not, that the colonies should accept a political identity in the face of metropolitan power? Administrative decentralisation is only a temporary stage which will necessarily be transcended.[63]

The implied answer of the Governors was in the negative. The subject of 'le self government', a term so alien to French thinking it was always cited in English, also led to controversy at the Conference. The agenda had advised caution in developing self-government, in keeping with the proposed evolutionary nature of a federal system. The problem foreseen lay in the relations between a colony's indigenous population and and its European settlers, for although New Caledonia and Algeria were the only French settler colonies ('colonies de peuplement') as such, even tiny settler communities often wielded power disproportionate to their size:

> The term 'self-government' has been applied all too often. It should not be dismissed out of hand, but we have to confront reality, and those who speak of self-government always forget to ask: self-government by whom? and over whom?[64]

When Laurentie raised the subject in the debate on administrative reform, however, Saller headed him off on the grounds that, according to his committee, the question was not admissible. Autonomy and self-government were both admissible within the bounds of the Laurentie thesis; essential also, however, were 'indestructible ties to France and the indelible mark of France', as Laurentie stressed in a draft recommendation on decentralisation (which was rejected).[65] Thus, the Declaration, which deliberately blurred the boundary between these three distinct concepts, was

---

63. '... le problème est le suivant: la conférence accepte ou n'accepte pas que les colonies prennent une personnalité politique en face du pouvoir métropolitain? La décentralisation [administrative] n'est qu'une étape dont il est à prévoir qu'elle sera nécessairement dépassée.' Transcript, 4 Feb. 1944, loc.cit.

64. 'Le mot de self government n'a été que trop souvent prononcé. Nous ne l'écarterons pas àpriori, mais nous désirons d'abord nous placer en face de la réalité. Or, lorsqu'on parle de self government, on oublie toujours de demander: le self government de qui? et sur qui?' *Programme général*, loc.cit.

65. 'une attache indestructible avec la France et une marque française indélébile', Transcript, 4 Feb. 1944, loc.cit.

voted over Laurentie's and Pleven's heads, in the most decisive setback for the new imperial thinking to come out of the Brazzaville Conference.

———— ✠ ————

As the ideologues of the metropolitan Resistance were also to discover, wartime idealism and the planning for the post-war world inspired by that idealism were limited both in perspective and in later applicability. Most of the grand plans conceived in occupied France bore little relation to the schemes devised in the turbulent atmosphere of the Liberation, far less to their implementation in the post-lapsarian world of the Fourth Republic after 1946. As Andrew Shennan argues, this does not make that planning the less valid as a topic for historical study.[66] Thanks to the greater freedom and openness enjoyed by the Gaullist colonial administration, the new imperial thinking was far better coordinated than much of the work of their metropolitan counterparts. For obvious reasons, the internal Resistance was unable to stage an event even remotely comparable to the Brazzaville Conference. Nonetheless, two substantial hurdles lay across the path which led from wartime good intentions to post-war policy making.

First, a common perspective and a common purpose were no guarantee of a homegeneity of views. The controversies and a certain rarefied quality to the debate at Brazzaville may in part be attributed to the fact that the Conference took place in a political vacuum. Although they acted with the authority of de Gaulle, the organisers of the Conference felt bound to present their brainchild to an open forum at which all views were equally valid: the Corps of Governors had been invited in their capacity as colonial experts, after all. What emerged was a clash between the new ideas and a fairly general allegiance on the part of the Governors to old doctrines and practices which the originators of the new imperial thinking had largely discarded. Most disappointing of all was the Governors' continued adherence to the doctrine of Assimilation, a Republican shibboleth which had always been more useful as a rhetorical device in the National Assembly than as a defining principle of colonial policy. Moreover, there was a leisureliness to the debate at Brazzaville which was just as likely to baffle subsequent observers as it was to annoy Laurentie and his colleagues. What, for example, was one

66. *Rethinking France*, 288–89.

to make of Administrator Delmas's magisterial definition of French imperialism?:

It may be observed that all the Latin peoples colonise as we do according to the principle of assimilation. We are inclined to the idea of Empire in the Roman sense and not in the Anglo-Saxon sense, which is the social and juridical reflection of a spiritually distinct civilisation. This, however, does not mean that we should apply Roman solutions: the Roman problem was Mediterranean, whereas ours is global.[67]

At best such statements were likely to persuade commentators that the overall aim of the emerging Brazzaville policy was to defend the status quo ante behind a smokescreen of well-meaning rhetorical nonsense.

Secondly, following on from this, the colonial administration found itself hoist with the petard of the Conference's success as a propaganda event. Having presented the Conference as the epitome of all that was generous and liberal in the French imperial mission, they were stuck with it. The propaganda value of the Conference should not be underrated. Not least, it helped persuade the Americans and the British (who needed less persuading) that the French still meant business as a colonial power. As Ralph Bunche reported for the US State Department: 'There was no recognition [at Brazzaville] that France owed any accountability to the international community in the conduct of her international affairs nor that the international community had any valid interest in such affairs'.[68] Duff Cooper, British Consul-General at Algiers, was more sceptical, and expressed amused bafflement when René Pleven explained to him his 'imperialist policy of the spirit' ('politique impérialiste de l'esprit').[69] Later in liberated Paris, however, the publicity accorded the Conference caused more harm than good; the Brazzaville epithet became a liberal talisman or watchword of political correctness. One senior official, in

---

67. 'Il est à observer que tous les peuples Latins font, comme nous, de la colonisation à base d'assimilation. Nous sommes portés vers l'Empire au sens romain et non vers l'Empire au sens anglo-saxon, manifestation sociale et juridique d'une civilisation spirituelle différente. Ce qui ne veut pas dire que nous ne devons appliquer que les solutions romaines: le problème romain était méditerranéen, le nôtre est mondial.' Transcript, 6 Feb. 1944 *Conférence Africaine Française*, 75.

68. 'The French African Conference at Brazzaville', 6 Apr. 1944, quoted by Louis, *Imperialism at Bay*, 45–46.

69. Quoted in French, in Duff Cooper to Eden, 26 Feb. 1944, PRO, FO371/42216; see Inst Charles-de-Gaulle and IHTP, *Brazzaville*, 321–22.

a pamphlet first published in 1945, commented that the Brazza-ville recommendations 'remain the Tablets of the Law, revealed truth, the taboos which may be alluded to but never questioned'.[70] This left officials with a problem: how to present Brazzaville as a success while disowning its more reactionary findings; and how to ensure that the Brazzaville policy was not taken less seriously than the myth of the same name.

The debate continued, in the meetings of the Expert Commission proposed at Brazzaville, and in the discussions which led to the Declaration on Indochina in March 1945.[71] De Gaulle was also helpful, lending his support to the federal idea, while claiming that this *was* the Brazzaville policy. In July 1944, for example, at a press conference in Washington, he provided an admirably suc-cinct definition of the federal idea and its applicability to Indo-china. Reminding his audience of 'a conference that we held at Brazzaville last winter', he went on:

> I believe that every territory over which flies the French flag must be represented within a federal system which includes the Metro-pole and where the interests of each party may be heard.
>
> The French Empire ... comprises a number of territories, which are developed to very differing degrees; some territories have reached an advanced state of development, others are still at a very low level. The aim of French policy is and will remain to raise all these territories to as high a level as possible, so that every one is able to look after its own interests and to be represented within a federal system. This is the policy that France will pursue, in partic-ular for Indochina.[72]

---

70. '... demeurent les Tables de la Loi, la vérité révélée, les principes 'tabous' aux-quels on se réfère, mais qu'on ne discute pas.' L. Mérat, *Fictions ... et réalités colo-niales*, Paris, 1946, preface by Marius Moutet, 25.

71. See Chs 2 and 5.

72. 'Je crois que chaque territoire sur lequel flotte le drapeau français doit être représenté à l'intérieur d'un système de forme fédérale dans lequel la Métropole sera une partie et où les intérêts de chacun pourront se faire entendre.

'L'Empire français ... comprend plusieurs territoires dont l'évolution est très var-iée; certains territoires sont parvenus à un degré élevé d'évolution, d'autres sont encore très bas. La politique de la France est, et sera, d'élever tous ces territoires le plus haut possible pour que chacun ait la possibilité d'administrer ses intérêts et d'être représenté à l'intérieur d'un système d'ordre fédéral. Telle est la politique de la France et en particulier pour l'Indochine ...' 10 Jul. 1944, *Discours et messages*, vol. 1, 418–19. At a later press conference, de Gaulle stated that French policy had been fixed after Brazzaville, thus dismissing the conference's importance, perhaps unconsciously: 25 Oct. 1944, ibid., 464–6.

The real work of policy making, however, still remained to be undertaken by the time of the Liberation of Paris in August 1944, when the Commissariat for the Colonies moved from cramped quarters in Algiers to the Ministry of Colonies in the Rue Oudinot. It is the Brazzaville policy in its full-blown form that is considered in the following chapter.

2

THE REPUBLIC STRIKES BACK, 1944–1945

Brazzaville Policy and the Metropolitan Critique

The long-term effects of the myths and ambiguities surrounding the Brazzaville Conference were, by their very nature, incalculable. In the shorter term, however, the Conference's partial failure was a disappointing but not insuperable obstacle to the promotion of a new imperial policy. This chapter therefore considers the colonial administration's efforts to 'sell' the new policy to an expert audience, but shows how these efforts were met here too with hostility, suggesting already that metropolitan acceptance of the new policy would be at best problematic. Henri Laurentie soon returned to his brainchild, and the convening of an Expert Commission to discuss the political and constitutional basis for future imperial policy, as recommended at Brazzaville, provided him with the chance to expound the Federal idea in a more focused and detailed way than had been possible at the Conference. Chaired by Laurentie, the Expert Commission met in Algiers over the spring and early summer of 1944.[1] The debate continued in the meetings of a Working Party *(Bureau d'Etudes)* called in March 1945 to prepare the agenda of the Commission chaired in Paris by Gaston Monnerville, whose most urgent task it was to decide the

---

1. René Pleven, eschewing a snappier title, called it the 'Commission charged with the study of the measures needed to grant the Colonies their rightful place in the new French Constitution' ('… chargée de l'étude des mesures propres à assurer aux Colonies leur juste place dans la nouvelle constitution française'. The papers (cited as 'Commission') are in AOM, AP/214 and MAE, Alger/683. This Commission has been generally neglected, but is discussed by M.J. Shipway, 'The Brazzaville Conference, 1944: Colonial and Imperial Planning in a Wartime Setting', M.Phil thesis, University of Oxford, 1986, 100–114; and by A. Shennan, *Rethinking France, Plans for Renewal 1940–1946*, Oxford, 1989, 148–51.

basis for colonial representation within the forthcoming Constituent Assembly.[2] And on 24 March 1945, the new policy had its first and most extensive public airing, in the GPRF's Declaration on Indochina, which made first official use of the term 'Union Française' (French Union), and which set out the Provisional Government's position on colonial self-government within the new imperial structure. Laurentie played the major role throughout this debate, as Director of Political Affairs first in the Commissariat for the Colonies at Algiers, and subsequently in the Ministry of Colonies in liberated Paris.

The chapter's focus is on Laurentie's ambitious plans for a federation, or Union, of France's colonial territories and protectorates, as developed in the period following Brazzaville. It is not intended to judge the cohesiveness or logic of Laurentie's proposals, but they will be matched against the terms of an implicit imperial equation balancing metropolitan interests against colonial demands and aspirations. Perhaps inevitably, Laurentie's thinking was dominated by the 'colonial' perspective, and the primary aim of liberals in the colonial administration was to bring about a transformation of empire in order to meet the perceived colonial and international pressure for reform. Increasingly, however, the metropolitan half of the equation would have to be taken into account, and it was here that considerable doubt arose concerning the extent to which the new approach to the problems of Empire could be shared by French political opinion. Of chief interest here, therefore, is the nature of the critique made by those expert commentators called upon to debate the policy proposals. The chapter identifies the major problem arising from the metropolitan side of the imperial equation, which lay in the fact that France would be called upon to make sacrifices of her power and sovereignty in order to construct the new imperial structure. After the evasiveness of the delegates at Brazzaville, the chapter shows how objections to the new imperial thinking were now increasingly raised on the largely unanswerable grounds of constitutional unworkability and political unfeasibility. Whereas at Brazzaville the rather amateurish doctrinal opposition to the Federal idea had been merely exasperating, now Laurentie and his colleagues found their proposals subjected to the more rigorous scrutiny of legal and constitutional experts, of ministerial representatives with

---

2. Bureau d'Etudes Constitutionnelles (hereafter cited as 'Bureau d'Etudes'), AOM, AP/214bis.

competing interests, and of seasoned parliamentarians bringing to bear the full force of Republican ideals and traditions. The intentions of these men were irreproachable – for instance, perhaps the fiercest opponent of federalism in this debate was the worthy Socialist future minister Jules Moch – and the interests which they represented were *prima facie* valid and legitimate. Nonetheless, as will be argued, the fact that their perspective differed so radically from that of the colonial administration was highly problematical for the advocates of the Brazzaville policy. For, if federation provoked scepticism even at a theoretical level from experts without an obvious partisan interest, it was unclear what would make the Federal idea acceptable in an open political forum, and thus workable as actual policy. Before turning to this debate, the chapter considers the terms of the Brazzaville policy in the form elaborated by Laurentie over the course of the debate. It concludes with an examination of the March 1945 Declaration on Indochina, the administration's first attempt to reconcile the theory and practice of colonial policy making.

The Federal Idea and the Imperial Equation

The Federal idea was an attempt to provide a comprehensive and intellectually satisfying set of answers to the predicted problems of post-war colonial empire. In its most general terms, federation was intended to strike a balance between the two halves of the imperial equation while avoiding the extremes. In other words, it was to allow the broadest possible measure of constitutional, political, and economic reform of France's colonial dependencies while ensuring, and indeed strengthening, their ties with the metropole. However, although Laurentie's proposals addressed both sides of this equation, his overriding preoccupation was with the 'colonial' side of the equation. Even at this early stage, therefore, the principal champion of the Brazzaville policy was laying the policy open to metropolitan attack.

Laurentie's emphasis on colonial needs and ambitions, as opposed to metropolitan interests, was perhaps clearest and, by the same token, least problematical in the new policy's emphasis on an evolutionary hierarchy of colonial territories. Thus, in stark contrast with the doctrine of Assimilation, federation was built upon an understanding of the diversity of Empire, and on the need to provide for the political evolution of each individual territory even within a 'finished' federal structure. Laurentie thus proposed three broad categories of French dependencies. The first category consisted of assimilated 'external provinces' (*provinces extérieures*), or, as they came to be known after the passing of the Law of 7 May 1946, the Overseas Departments (*départements d'Outre-Mer*). In part, this was a category designed to incorporate previous historical practice: the 'Old Colonies' of Senegal, the Antilles, and Réunion had been represented in the pre-war Chamber of Deputies (along with Cochinchina, French India, and Algeria), and would retain this privilege. But the possibility of other territories wishing to acquire assimilated status was not excluded.

The second category, and perhaps the principal innovation of the Federal idea, consisted of countries which were considered to have attained some degree of political maturity (*personnalité politique*). The implications of this prized attribute remained unspecific, but, notwithstanding the restrictive terms of the Brazzaville recommendations, the concept potentially embraced autonomy and self-government, if not independence. In the Expert Commission, for example, René Cassin, constitutional lawyer and perhaps the best-known Frenchman to have rallied to de Gaulle in the early days of 1940, described the first aim of federation as being to raise each colonial territory to self-goverment.[3] These more highly developed countries, known ultimately as Associated States (*Etats Associés*), included in the first instance Indochina, Madagascar, and New Caledonia. Morocco and Tunisia were at first categorised separately as international protectorates at the insistence of the Commission's observers from the Commissariat for Foreign Affairs. As René Cassin argued, however, one of the advantages of federation was its appeal to countries which might attain total independence outside a federal system. Subsequently, protectorates were included theoretically as Associated States.[4]

The third category of territories comprised the remaining dependencies: the African Federations of AOF and AEF, Cameroun (a League of Nations 'B'-Class Mandate which was intended to merge with AEF to form a new Federation of French Central Africa), the French Somali Coast, French Oceania and the French

---

3. '... l'élevation vers le Self Government', Commission, 2nd session, 9 May 1944.
4. Commission, Report and 7th session, 20 Jun. 1944. The Associated States were initially referred to as *pays fédéraux* or *pays unis*.

Indian Settlements.[5] These countries, to be known no longer as colonies but as Federal Territories or United Territories, were deemed not yet to have reached the required degree of political and economic evolution, and would therefore remain under the colonial administration's provisional trusteeship (*tutelle provisoire*) until they were deemed to have attained political maturity. As Laurentie explained to the Working Party:

> All French territories are destined to attain their political majority. Some have already achieved this: Morocco, Tunisia, Indochina, New Caledonia. Others have some way to go, and they will remain under the control of the French executive, which will also retain some measure of legislative control. But this executive control will be provisional: the United Territories will evolve as is appropriate in each case, either towards the assimilated status of Overseas Departments, or towards the status of Associated States.[6]

This divergent development was vital, and it was considered by no means to be a foregone conclusion as to which path would be adopted by any given territory. In May 1945, for example, Laurentie suggested that, while Tunisia, where he had made a highly successful presentation of the Federal idea to local dignitaries, would be likely to 'come down on the side of association', Senegal might well opt for assimilation.[7] The mechanism by which such a choice might be expressed and implemented was open to question. Neither was any mention made of a timetable for this evolution towards assimilation or self-government. As was common for such planning, however, the implied timespan was one of decades, even generations. Clearly the success of the Federal idea would depend on the changes in the status of these countries

---

5. Ibid. The Indian Settlements were included in a separate category in the Commission report; so too was the Anglo-French condominium of the New Hebrides.

6. 'Tous les Pays Français ont la vocation à la majorité politique. Certains y sont parvenus: le Maroc, la Tunisie, l'Indochine, la Nouvelle-Calédonie. D'autres n'y sont pas parvenus: ils resteront en tutelle sous l'Exécutif, qui restera pour eux, dans une certaine mesure, le législateur. Mais la tutelle de l'Exécutif sera temporaire: les Territoires unis, suivant leurs affinités, évolueront, soit vers l'assimilation, pour devenir des départements d'outre-mer, soit vers l'association pour devenir des Pays-Unis.' Bureau d'Etudes, 3rd session, 20 Mar. 1945.

7. Cours d'information sur l'Indochine, n.d. (May 1945), AOM, AP/214bis; Note, 'Voyage de M. Laurentie à Tunis', n.d. (early 1944), AN, 72AJ535. United Territories were thought unlikely to opt for Overseas Department status, but cf. the Gabonese leadership who, according to the last Governor of Gabon, Louis Sanmarco, were refused Department status by de Gaulle: L. Sanmarco, *Le colonial colonisé*, Paris, 1983, 210–11.

being seen as substantial rather than mere tinkering with their subordinate status.

The categorisation of French dependencies was generally accepted by the Expert Commission, notwithstanding some rough edges to Laurentie's tidy scheme. Thus, Madagascar was viewed sometimes as an Associated State, sometimes as a United Territory, an ambiguity reflecting a real confusion in the minds of the colonial administration, never entirely sure whether to view Malagasy nationalists as the mediators of an authentic national culture or merely as troublemakers.[8] Even greater ambivalence surrounded the place of Algeria in the proposed structure. Political and constitutional dogma dictated that Algeria was assimilated, its populated coastal regions being divided into Departments on the metropolitan model. And yet it was difficult to make a clear distinction between Algerian national aspirations and those of its Moroccan and Tunisian neighbours, except by stating, as did one Commission member, that its populations were not sufficiently advanced to aspire to political maturity. On the other hand, as the Algerian Governor-General's observer, Jacques Berque, saw it, Algeria had suffered too long from metropolitan control and from what he called the 'universalising tendency of France's genius'. The problem of Algeria's European settlers was also raised here, though only in passing, when Cassin warned against the potential abuses of political autonomy by the ruling French minority.[9] On the whole, however, as one commentary put it, the list of categories was logical, 'in that it corresponds to reality'.[10]

More controversial in terms of the general debate was Laurentie's exegesis of an institutional structure for the new Union, which was similarly designed with a view to the 'colonial' side of the equation, but concerning which the metropolitan implications were more immediate and obvious. Thus, the institutions proposed by Laurentie and his department (the *Direction des Affaires Politiques*, or DAP) in the Working Party sessions were designed in the first instance to meet the needs of the imperial hierarchy already drawn up. The initial proposal was for four levels of Assembly: the metropolitan parliament, comprising six hundred

8. See M.J. Shipway, 'Madagascar on the eve of insurrection, 1944–1947: the impasse of a liberal colonial policy', *Journal of Imperial and Commonwealth History*, 24, 1 (Jan. 1996), 72–100.

9. Commission, 3rd session, 16 May 1944; 9th session.

10. Comité de l'Afrique du Nord, 'NOTE relative à l'intégration des Protectorats Tunisien et Marocain dans l'Union Française', 4 Mar. 1946, AOM, AP/214.

members; a 300-strong Representative Overseas Assembly (*Assemblée représentative des pays d'outre-mer*) which would assist the Head of State in the drafting of legislation for Overseas France; a Federal Assembly comprising the combined metropolitan and overseas Assemblies; and a National Assembly with the same membership, meeting only to revise the Constitution. The second of these assemblies, the Representative Assembly, was to be composed of one-third metropolitan delegates, one-third overseas French citizens, and one-third non-citizens.[11] In the final session some significant modifications were proposed to this model, to meet Laurentie's anxieties that the system as outlined would create a gulf between the metropole and the overseas territories. For instance, in the Federal Assembly, Indochina's twenty-five million inhabitants would be represented by forty members, and thus swamped by the metropolitan representation of eight hundred. Morocco and Tunisia would be similarly under-represented. Moreover, in the Representative Assembly the Associated States (here called *pays unis*) would often be concerned with drafting legislation for the United Territories. As Laurentie commented, the problem was to find a solution which did not resemble a trap, particularly with regard to the all-important Associated States. Laurentie proposed giving the Associated States elected representatives in the Federal Assembly only, and the Overseas Departments representation in the metropolitan parliament only. The Representative Assembly would thus be composed only of elected delegates of the United Territories and their metropolitan counterparts, reflecting again the provisional status of this category of territories. This Assembly, although smaller, would be allowed significant influence and marks of prestige (a palace, formal channels of consultation with the Head of State and the Minister of Colonies), such as had been denied its toothless pre-war forerunner, the Higher Council of the Colonies (*Conseil Supérieur des Colonies*).

The French Union's most important institution would thus be the Federal Assembly. The Associated States' autonomous status would be significantly enhanced by their representation in this Assembly alone. The bulk of their affairs would be decided by their own organs of self-government, to be laid down in separate statutes for each country. (The Declaration on Indochina of 24 March 1945 was sometimes taken as a model for such a statute). The Federal Assembly, although massively unwieldy with its nine

---

11. Bureau d'Etudes, 2nd session, 16 Mar. 1945.

hundred members, would be effective because its main work would be done by Committees in permanent session, with the Assembly meeting in plenary session only once annually. The powers of this Assembly were to be chosen according to two criteria, the first of which was relevance to the problems of Empire, e.g., communications, or customs. The second was that issues should be of public concern, in an Assembly which might otherwise be doomed by public indifference and apathy. Defence was one such issue: the Associated States' relatively modest representation would thus reflect their contribution to France's defence effort. But most important of all in this respect would be the referral of economic issues to the Assembly, such as economic relations between the countries of the Union.[12]

Both in their plans for the articulation of an eventual federation, and in the schemes devised for its institutional arrangements, Laurentie's and his colleagues' instincts were much more those of colonial administrators than of Constitution-writers. Indeed, as will be seen subsequently, these instincts were equally finely tuned both with regard to the nationalist question, and in respect of the need for administrative reform. It was this 'colonial' bias which the Expert Commission was in part called upon to correct; its aim was to draw up a workable version of the Federal idea which could be studied by the Constituent Assembly, and not merely regarded as 'a brilliant idea lacking in substance', as Laurentie put it in the Commission's report.[13]

Moreover, Laurentie occasionally intimated a kind of political agenda, particularly with regard to his perception of the need to bring the Empire to the centre of French political concerns in the run-up to the drafting of a new Constitution. As he speculated before the Expert Commission:

> If we could extend liberalism to the point of integrating the colonies into the government of France, we would have a more complete conception of France itself.[14]

Implicit in this ideal was an apparent assumption that the Fourth Republic, when it emerged from the debates of the Constituent Assembly, would conform to Gaullist wishes, particularly

---

12. Bureau d'Etudes, 3rd session, 20 Mar. 1945.
13. Loc.cit.
14. '… si nous avions à pousser le libéralisme jusqu'à pouvoir intégrer les colonies dans le gouvernement même de la France, nous avons vraiment conçu de la France une idée plus complète.' Commission, 8th session, 27 Jun. 1944.

concerning the establishment of a strong executive. Laurentie took for granted, for example, that the French Union would be subject to a constitution 'in which Ministers would be responible only to the President of the Council [i.e., the Prime Minister] and not to Parliament', and in which conflicts between the constituent territories of the Union would thus be more readily resolved. As Professor Lampué warned, it was unlikely that a Constituent Assembly would share Laurentie's point of view. Everything depended on trends of political and public opinion, which nobody could predict in present circumstances.[15] By March 1945, when this discussion took place, the validity of these reservations had already been strongly suggested by the course of a debate on the Federal idea, in which the metropolitan perspective was at last given its due.

The Metropolitan Critique

By concentrating in the first instance on the base of the hierarchy, rather than on its head, Laurentie had effectively turned upside down the traditional approach to empire. Nonetheless, the other half of the imperial equation remained inescapable, and the nub of the debate in both Algiers and Paris turned not on the theoretical freedoms to be held by the constituent parts of the new Union, but on the powers which would continue to be exercised by metropolitan France. How far, for example, could the Federal idea be equated with authentic federalism? Conversely, how, if at all, could it be squared with the Republican ideal of the One and Indivisible Republic? What were the theoretical powers to be exercised by the Federation, and what would remain within the exclusive domain of metropolitan France? To debate these questions, the panel assembled by René Pleven included constitutional and political experts alongside representatives of the colonial administration and the observers from the North African administrations. The debate served to inject a welcome dose of realism into the federalists' 'brilliant idea', and pointed up some of the contradictions inherent in the blueprints drawn up by Laurentie and his colleagues. Indeed, some of the most pertinent positive criticism came from a consistent supporter of the Federal idea, René Cassin. But the more worrying aspect of the discussions in Algiers was the running skirmish, which showed every sign of

15. Bureau d'Etudes, 3rd session.

developing if the need arose into a full pitched battle, between the supporters of the Federal idea and the representatives, most notably at Algiers in the person of Jules Moch, of a doctrine more formidable than facile assimilationism: old-fashioned and full-blooded Republicanism. Their encounters did not offer great hopes for the realisation of the Federal idea in anything other than truncated or illusory form.

In part, Laurentie and his colleagues pre-empted expert criticism of the Federal idea by insisting on its innovatory quality, and on the need for fresh attitudes and a fresh vocabulary. At times, this exercise smacked merely of modishness, for example in the suppression of the terms 'colonial' or 'imperial', and in the self-conscious correction of anyone referring to 'France', instead of to 'metropolitan France'. France's colonies remained colonies even if renamed 'territories' and governed by a High Commissioner, rather than a Governor-General. Nonetheless, a genuine attempt was made to strike free of precedent and example. Where unwanted precedents were evoked, the terms were changed, most notably that of Federation to designate the new structure. The initial choice of the term seems to have been made merely for terminological convenience: if one enthusiast of the idea was to be believed, 'Federation' was chosen above 'Union', 'Confederation', 'Community' ('communauté' was also the usual translation of 'commonwealth'), and, of course, 'Empire', because it was both French-sounding and new.[16] Not for the last time, the federalists had misjudged their audience. French it might be, but Federation evoked the wrong historical resonances in the face of French Jacobinism, by referring back to the *Girondin* movement of the post-1789 Revolutionary period. Moreover, federation had too precise a legal meaning, and the notion of France as merely *primus inter pares* was clearly unacceptable. The term was discreetly dropped, first by de Gaulle who, in his October 1944 press conference, reiterated his support for the Federal idea while discounting its given name, preferring the vaguer notion of 'a French system where everyone would have a role to play'.[17] By the following spring, Laurentie was promoting the neutral term 'Union': 'The term

16. P.-O. Lapie (SFIO), *Journal Officiel, Assemblée Consultative Provisoire* (JOACP), 1944, no. 6, 14.

17. '… un système français où chacun jouera son rôle.' C. de Gaulle, Discours et messages, 3 vols., vol. 1, *Pendant la guerre, juin 1940–janvier 1946*, Paris, 1970, 25 Oct. 1944, 464–65.

'French Union' has the advantage of possessing no precise juridical meaning. By adopting this term, we avoid reference to a political system which does not correspond to reality'.[18] The term was finally made official in the Declaration on Indochina, made public by Pleven's replacement as Minister of Colonies, Paul Giacobbi, on 24 March 1945.

In the same spirit of innovation, other models and precedents were considered and largely rejected, including the lessons that could be drawn from the British and Dutch cases. These included Queen Wilhelmina of the Netherlands' December 1942 Declaration of a Commonwealth of Dutch colonial possessions: as was pointed out, the Dutch Empire was extremely homogeneous, and its imperial problems were concentrated for the most part in a single territory, the Dutch East Indies.[19] The British model was more congenial, because of its size and apparent cohesion, but here the problem was the opposite: not only was the British Empire more heterogeneous even than the French, but its backbone consisted of white settler colonies which could be compared only with France's most problematic colonial possession, Algeria (and even then the comparison was remote). Moreover, relying on bonds of 'kith and kin', and on economic ties, the British had no need to consider the more rigorous restraints of federation. Apart from specific comparisons, therefore, for example with British emphasis at this period on schemes for Colonial Welfare and Development, appeals to the British model were largely the product of wishful thinking. One of the legal experts sitting on the Working Party summed up this attitude when he argued that the new Union should be seen as having 'moral unity' rather than a 'rigid juridical framework and the character of a political entity'.[20] Professor Solus's explicit model for this was the British Commonwealth. But as was pointed out, such a French 'Pax' (along the lines of the *pax Romana*) existed already as a temporary measure intended to last

---

18. 'Le titre d'Union Française présente l'avantage de n'avoir aucun sens juridique précis. En l'adoptant, on évite à évoquer un système politique qui ne correspondrait pas à la réalité des faits.' Bureau d'Etudes, 3rd session. Confusion was also avoided with the Federations of AOF, AEF and, following the March 1945 Declaration, Indochina.

19. Commission, 1st session, 1 May 1944; W.R. Louis, *Imperialism at Bay*, Oxford and New York, 1977, 29.

20. '... bien plutôt sous l'aspect d'une unité morale ... que sous celui d'un organisme ayant un cadre juridique rigide et prenant l'aspect d'une entité politique.' Bureau d'Etudes, 1st session.

until French political legitimacy and stability were fully restored. This was deemed to be no longer sufficient in a period of Constitution making.

If anything, the preferred model was that of the USSR, interpreted according to the letter, rather than the Stalinist spirit of the 1936 Constitution. The appeal of the Soviet model must be ascribed in part to extraneous political factors, such as the importance of the French Communist Party (PCF), and the high regard in which France's least abrasive ally was held, particularly after de Gaulle's signing of the December 1944 Franco-Soviet Treaty. Reservations were expressed, for example during the preparations for Brazzaville, concerning the realities of the Soviet system; as one of Laurentie's colleagues commented, too little was known about the means by which the Soviet Republics were achieving their reportedly astonishing development, including the rumoured large-scale population transfers; or about the extent to which this progress was merely on paper.[21] Nonetheless, the comparison illuminates the idea behind federation: regional autonomy under the firm leadership of a central federal member, assisted by an enlightened 'nationality' policy, and reinforced by a plan for decentralised industrialisation. Given the final choice of 'Union' to designate the new empire, the model must be taken seriously.

Ultimately, however, whatever it was called or compared with, the new structure would chiefly be judged according to how – and whether – it worked, and this issue constituted the core of the debate initiated at Algiers, and also provided the thrust of the metropolitan critique of the Federal idea. For here it was a question, not so much of what the Federation had to offer France, but of what France would be obliged to sacrifice to the Federation. The unavoidable implications of the notion of federalism for France were spelt out by René Cassin. As he explained: 'Federalism occurs when a given number of autonomous entities abandon certain attributes of sovereignty for the benefit of the collectivity'.[22]

21. 'Notes sur le programme général de la conférence de Brazzaville', de Curton, 20 Oct. 1943, AOM, AP/2288/4. This paper was perhaps a source of one of the obscurer Brazzaville recommendations, calling for a delegation to study the Soviet Union's *kolkhoz* system of collective farming: *La Conférence Africaine Française*, Paris, 1945, 52. For a contemporaneous appreciation of Soviet 'national' policy bordering on the utopian, see Alfred Cobban, *The Nation State and National Self-Determination*, London, 1st ed., 1946.

22. '... ce qui caractérise le fédéralisme, c'est l'abandon par un certain nombre d'entités autonomes au profit de la collectivité de certaines attributions de souveraineté.' Commission, 2nd session, 9 May 1944.

However, in the French case this could not apply, since it was clearly metropolitan France which held all the attributes of sovereignty. Thus, in order for a federation to be established, France would inevitably be called upon to give up certain powers. The question which Cassin put before the Expert Commission was therefore as follows:

> What do we consider to be fundamental? What are the fundamental attributes of which France cannot divest herself?... Since France has all the powers, what do we consider to be indispensable, what cannot be given away?[23]

Much of the Commission's work addressed these questions, and it is here that serious flaws in the Federal idea became apparent. For, as the Commission members examined Foreign Affairs, Defence, Communications, Economics, and Education in turn, as well as the powers of an eventual Federal Assembly, it became clear that it was going to be difficult to devolve much responsibility to the Federation at all.

Foreign Affairs was a case in point. There was agreement that the Foreign Minister should be responsible to France first, and to the Federation second. Regional interests might be represented, for example in the Far East, by French envoys assisted by Indochinese representatives. But as Moch insisted, to general agreement, 'all essential questions in foreign affairs, which is to say nine-tenths of our foreign affairs, are France's exclusive responsibility'.[24] Defence proved more controversial. Again, on one central point, disagreement was slight: military command would be centralised in Paris. Devolution of military responsiblity was unthinkable, especially given the desire to strengthen France through the Empire. As Cassin remarked: 'Given that the American and British are inclined to throw their weight around, France should gather her strength to do the same'.[25] On the other hand, Cassin put his support behind the idea of decentralisation in the question of munitions, and the spreading of military resources around the Empire: this was common sense

---

23. 'Qu'est-ce que nous considérons comme fondamental? Quelles sont les attributions fondamentales dont la France ne peut pas se dépouiller?... Puisque c'est elle qui avait tous les pouvoirs, qu'est-ce que nous considérons comme irréductible, qu'on ne peut pas lui enlever?' Ibid.

24. '... toutes questions essentielles des Affaires Etrangères, c'est-à-dire, les 9/10 des Affaires Etrangères sont du ressort français'. Ibid.

25. '... avec la tendance des Américains et des Anglais de devenir des 'big' la France devra ramasser toutes ses forces pour être 'big' elle aussi.' Commission, 3rd session, 16 May 1944.

both in the light of the experience of 1940 and with a view to the prospect of a truly global international system after the war.

Two further controversies on this subject went to the heart of the issue of federalism by raising the question of the proposed institutional structure of the new Union: what would be the role of the Federal Assembly, in military recruitment or in the voting of the military budget? Properly conceived, the idea of federation would require the devolution of military recruitment: in Metropolitan France, it was Parliament, and not the Military High Command, which voted recruitment measures, and in a Federation, it should fall to each Federal entity to do the same. However, in the event of a local national elite assuming real political power in one of the North African territories, say, it was unlikely that it would still act as a human reservoir ('réservoir d'hommes'), as the French army would require. Clearly discounted was the French myth of colonial loyalty, supposedly proven on the field of battle in both 1914–18 and 1940, although the political advantages of the idea were self-evident: Cassin referred in this respect to 'that rather overdone delusion that blacks and North Africans were somehow a kingpin for France'.[26] The second point of contention concerned the military budget. Could a Federal Assembly decide on the military budget for the Federation as a whole, as a federal system would require, or only, as Moch insisted, on that part of the budget which the colonies themselves had contributed? Moch was prepared to back a purely consultative Assembly, but if the Assembly was to deliberate on matters concerning French (i.e., Metropolitan French) interests, he was opposed to it. Indeed, he saw himself uncompromsingly as 'an opponent of the Federal idea when French interests are at stake'.[27] Moch, and with him probably a majority of the French, was not prepared to make the imaginative leap which the federalists advocated, which would enable him to equate French interests with the interests of her Empire as a whole.

As the debate also underlined, there were areas where the idea of federalism implied a greater degree of centralism than had previously obtained. Thus, in a long discussion at Algiers on the subject of airborne communications links (a subject which preoccupied the planners of the period), it proved difficult to conceive of any

26. '... ce mirage un peu exagéré d'après lequel les nègres ou les musulmans de l'Afrique auront été les chevilles ouvrières de la France'. Ibid.
27. Ibid.

system other than one in which Paris formed a central 'hub' for journeys even across Africa.[28] Of more central importance was the question of economic planning. Starting from the principle, derived from the Brazzaville recommendations, that any planning would emanate from Paris, debate centred on the extent to which metropolitan powers would decide on economic strategy, and how far this could be devolved to the Federation. Colonial industrialisation had been cautiously encouraged at Brazzaville; and yet federalism would provide a democratic forum for increased tension between metropolitan and colonial interests in the Federal Assembly. Economic conflicts were already a feature of the pre-war empire, and significantly, the example used, that of competition between rice and maize imports from Indochina and home produce, concerned the proverbial primary goods of colonial production; how much more contentious might be a dispute over industrial goods?[29] As Laurentie predicted, even with a Socialist government in power, there would inevitably be conflict between those anxious to encourage metropolitan investment in colonial industrialisation and those representing entrenched interests in France who saw the prospect as a threat to the economic life of the metropole.[30]

Centralism of a different kind was suggested by the debate on Education, an area where the Governors at Brazzaville had adopted an apparently retrograde, but largely practical, recommendation, that French should be the language of colonial education. But the question assumed an almost spiritual dimension as conceived by the federalists, for not only opponents of the idea argued for revisiting the 'mystique of Greater France', as Moch called it.[31] Education was described by Cassin as 'a powerful means of attaining spiritual unity and dynamism', the purpose of which was partly a new version of the French civilising mission, but chiefly as the unifying factor overriding the institutional questions of Federation. Models and comparisons came into their own here: Pleven lamented the fact that the French Empire lacked the symbolic

---

28. Commission, 4th session, 23 May 1944. Cf. projects extant at this period for the transfer of the Government-General of AOF, for reasons including ease of air travel, away from Dakar to the Sahelian hinterland, e.g., to Bobo-Dioulasso (in present day Burkina Faso): NOTE pour le Directeur du Cabinet, 30 Nov. 1945, AOM, AP/974.

29. Commission, 5th session, 30 May 1944.

30. Commission, 5th session, Report.

31. '... la mystique nouvelle de la plus grande France'. Commission, 9th session.

focus of loyalty which the Crown supplied within the British Commonwealth and on which depended the strength of economic, military, and racial ties binding the Dominions.[32] The Soviet model was also invoked in this context. As Laurentie noted, Soviet unity and cohesion were provided by the Party; although abhorrent to a nation of individualists, a parallel role was envisaged for the colonial education system. In the face of this mysticism, Moch's position, that he was not opposed to a unified education system across the Empire but resisted the introduction of colonial educational norms in France, seems positively curmudgeonly.[33]

Jules Moch's contribution to the debate was significant not only for the blunt, down-to-earth quality of his arguments, but also for his self-appointed role as a representative of the political classes to whose scrutiny the Federal idea would have to be submitted. His critique of the Federal idea was consistent throughout the meetings of the Algiers Commission, but was summarised in his response to Laurentie's draft report. First, he criticised the idea of federating polities which, in direct contradiction to the idea of federalism, were profoundly unequal. When Laurentie conceded that the Federal idea was 'ahead of its time', he replied that it was usual to federate already existing states, and that it was impossible to 'federate a developed state – metropolitan France – with a political vacuum – which is what most of our overseas territories amount to'.[34] Second, he underlined the inconsistencies in Laurentie's hierarchical system, especially concerning the problem of Algeria. Third, he argued that it would be difficult to draw up a homogeneous body within an eventual Federal Assembly, given the diversity of the Union. As he pointed out, with the sole exception of the present Consultative Assembly, the product of very particular historical circumstances, French constitutional tradition determined that any Assembly be composed of 'men chosen by the same means, and mandated by the expression of at least a portion of popular sovereignty'.[35] This essential Republican principle

32. Commission, 1st session. Perhaps this is what Pleven meant when he suggested to an amused Duff Cooper that France was pursuing 'une politique impérialiste de l'esprit', quoted above, Ch. 1.

33. Commission, 5th session.

34. 'En effet, on fédère des Etats préalablement existants. On ne fédère pas un Etat évolué – la métropole – avec le néant politique – la plupart de nos territoires d'outre-mer.' Commission, 9th session.

35. '… une réunion d'hommes semblablement désignés et mandataires d'une fraction ou de la totalité de la souveraineté populaire.' Ibid.

would be infringed if representatives were officially appointed, rather than elected by universal suffrage. Or, as he put it more bluntly: 'How can the colonies be run by those directly concerned? At present I am against giving the same rights to African chiefs and to representatives of France'.[36] Further, he objected to the ambiguities that would arise concerning the status of federal ministers. It was a central proposition of the federalists that many ministers, although probably metropolitan appointees, would hold federal portfolios and be answerable to the Federal Assembly. How, then, could disputes be resolved when the Federal Assembly lost confidence in a minister enjoying metropolitan support?[37]

Although his procedural objections were valid and challenging, it was Moch's fidelity to Republican principles that was so forbidding to the federalists. These principles were expressed partly, to be sure, in terms of Assimilation. Even here Moch went far beyond the bland assimilationism rehearsed at Brazzaville. As an alternative to federation, Moch thus advocated a system based on 'Assimilation with broad autonomy for the few developed territories, and for the others, a system of local representation.'[38] The most important element of this proposal was its insistence on the need for a gradual approach, which Laurentie had hitherto neglected, but which was to an extent reflected in his report. But Moch's objections to the Federal idea arose from political instincts that went far deeper than mere caution: 'I am a spiritual descendant of the men who have led four Revolutions in 150 years in order to restore full sovereignty to the people. My view is that that sovereignty is inalienable'.[39] By underlining the extent to which the Federal idea conflicted with the tenets of Republican doctrine, Moch's stance in the Commission already prefigured the reception which awaited the idea in the forum of the Constituent Assembly.

The fate of the Federal idea overall had largely been mapped out by the end of the Algiers Commission: attractive as it might

36. 'Comment peut-on faire administrer les colonies par des gens directement intéressés? Je suis pour l'instant hostile à donner les mêmes droits aux chefs nègres et aux représentants français.' Commission, 3rd session.

37. Commission, 9th session.

38. '… la notion d'Assimilation avec une très large autonomie locale des quelques territoires évolués, et pour les autres, un régime de représentation locale.' Commission, 1st session.

39. 'Je me sens spirituellement l'un des dépositaires des hommes, qui, depuis plus de 150 ans ont fait quatre Révolutions pour restituer au peuple sa pleine souveraineté. Elle demeure, selon moi, inaliénable.' Commission, 9th session.

have been from the imperial perspective, it was difficult to suppose the Federal idea faring any better in Paris. Little progress was made in the meetings of the Working Party, at which Laurentie elaborated the institutional arrangements for the new Union with the not entirely benign or willing cooperation of legal experts and of representatives of the colonial 'establishment' in Paris nominated by two powerful lobby groups, the Committee of the French Empire (*Comité de l'Empire Français*) and the Academy of Colonial Sciences (*Académie des Sciences Coloniales*). As Andrew Shennan has argued, given the evident unworkability of the 'increasingly baroque' structures devised by the DAP, what chance was there of an eventual Constituent Assembly finding a more elegant structure? Not without some justification did Professor Solus complain of the suggested system's *inelegantia juris*.[40]

Laurentie and his colleagues could nonetheless take heart from the fact that, notwithstanding the objections raised to the principle of an imperial federation, they had at least set a new agenda. Henceforth, no debate on the Empire could take place without reference to Laurentie's 'thesis' and to the Brazzaville Recommendations (where relevant), and without considering *both* terms of the imperial equation. Reflecting a shift in the international climate, the new imperial thinking had given new prominence to the needs and aspirations of the colonial peoples, although not yet to the demands of colonial nationalism. And even the most diehard Republicans would have to admit the need to square some measure of colonial self-determination with the doctrine of the One and Indivisible Republic. Moreover, sooner or later, and irrespective of the findings of the Constituent Assembly, France still needed a concrete colonial policy, and one based preferably on something more solid than the complacent temporisations of pre-war policy. The course of events in 1944 brought with it a decisive shift in the political climate. The Liberation and the transfer from Algiers to Paris of de Gaulle's committee, newly elevated to the status of GPRF, acted as a rush of oxygen into the vacuum. Buoyed by the authority of de Gaulle, and given a new sense of purpose by their (re-)establishment in the rue Oudinot, the staff of the Ministry of Colonies prepared the new policy for Empire. The first major statement of the new policy came in the Declaration on Indochina of 24th March 1945, to which we now turn.

40. Shennan, *Rethinking France*, 158; Bureau d'Etudes, 3rd session.

The Declaration on Indochina

Indochina was an obvious topic for a specific policy statement. In the first place, it lay outside the purview of the Brazzaville Conference. Secondly, as France's richest and most populous colonial possession, and as the French dependency with arguably the most highly developed sense of its own variegated national identity, it was a clear candidate for elevation to Associated Statehood. There was little discussion in the Expert Commission of the individual 'statutes' proposed by Laurentie for the constituent parts of the new Union. This was partly for lack of concrete information or specific expertise: as Laurentie informed the Commission, detailed studies had been requested from the various Governments and Governments-General in order to provide recommendations for the statute of each individual territory.[41] In the case of Indochina, this lack of expertise was particularly to be regretted, given the likelihood that the United States would judge French plans by what was said about Indochina.[42] Thirdly, Indochina circa 1944–45 was an agreeable model for policy making, in that the Ministry of Colonies could work largely unimpeded by the constitutional and diplomatic niceties which beset policy making in North Africa. In administrative terms also, Indochina policy was relatively free of inter-ministerial rivalries and jealousies, although the Declaration itself was held up for several months because of disagreements between the Ministries of Colonies and Foreign Affairs.[43] For all these reasons, Indochina became the focus for liberal hopes concerning the Empire. The Declaration was the most comprehensive statement of government thinking at this period regarding the eventual status of the all-important Associated States within a new French Union. By the time it was made, however, its content had already been outpaced by events, and in particular by the complete Japanese takeover in Indochina, which suggested a new, more urgent rationale for colonial reform.

Although, as will be seen in subsequent chapters, the Declaration served a quite separate purpose in a specifically Indochinese context, in general terms its wording manifested the balance which policy makers hoped to strike between the two halves of the imperial equation. Thus, after a short preamble, the Declaration defined

41. The author has found no trace of these in the archives.
42. Commission, 2nd session.
43. See below, Ch. 5.

the relationship envisaged between Indochina and the new imperial structure as a whole:

> The Indochinese Federation will join with France and the other parts of the French community to form a 'French Union', whose external interests will be represented by France. Indochina will enjoy its proper freedom within this Union.[44]

The Declaration was vague and unspecific at key moments, not least as to what constituted 'proper freedom', which was all that served to define Indochina's constitutional relationship with France. Moreover, many crucial decisions were left to the French Government and an eventual French Constituent Assembly. From the local perspective much remained to be discussed also: was the Declaration meant to represent the maximum or the minimum that France was prepared to offer; was it the statement of a bargaining position, or a declaration of actual policy?

Notwithstanding this studied vagueness, the balance between metropolitan and colonial interests was maintained throughout. Thus, considerable freedoms were to be accorded the Indochinese Union. The five 'lands' (*pays*) of Indochina, a highly problematic concept in themselves, were to be headed by a federal government composed of ministers drawn from both the Indochinese and the French communities in Indochina; an Upper House (*Conseil d'Etat*), 'in which will sit the Federation's most eminent personalities', would be responsible for drawing up federal legislation; an Assembly, 'elected according to the most appropriate electoral system for each of the Federal lands, and in which French interests will be represented', would vote on taxes and the budget, and deliberate on proposed legislation and on treaties. The Declaration made considerable advance upon the Brazzaville recommendations in according both Indochinese citizenship and a new status of French Union citizenship guaranteeing free access to posts within the Federation and within the French Union, as well as in the armed forces. It promised freedom of the press, of belief and of association; a primary education system that was to be 'compulsory and effective', and the development of secondary and further education. The study of local languages and culture would be closely

---

44. 'La Fédération indochinoise formera avec la France et avec les autres parties de la communauté une 'Union française', dont les intérêts à l'extérieur seront représentés par la France. L'Indochine jouira, au sein de cette Union, d'une liberté propre.' JOACP, no. 31, 25 Mar. 1945, 547. Reproduced in J. Dalloz, *La guerre d'Indochine*, Paris, 1987, 287–89.

tied to French culture; and an independent labour inspectorate would provide for the 'social education and emancipation of Indochinese workers'. Finally, the Federation would enjoy economic autonomy; industrialisation was to be encouraged, in order that 'Indochina confront its demographic situation'.

On the other side of the equation, the prime attributes of sovereignty were to be maintained firmly in France's grasp, or rather in the grasp of a Governor-General who would lead the Government, and to whom both ministers and the Upper House would be answerable. It was difficult to suppose that he would be other than a metropolitan appointee. Indochina was to be represented internationally by France, and Indochinese armed forces would be constituted 'under metropolitan supervision and within the general system of defence of the French Union'. Moreover, the terms of Indochinese participation within the Union, as well as the definition of French Union citizenship, were left to a French Constituent Assembly to decide.[45] Finally, although the 'appropriate institutions of liberated Indochina' were to be consulted, their identity was unclear, and 'consultation' did not allow a veto.

The Declaration was the most complete single public statement of the ideas which fed the imperial debate in Brazzaville, Algiers, and Paris. In the present context, it is chiefly important as the opening gambit of France's ambitious attempt to regain control of its Far Eastern imperial stronghold. With hindsight, the Declaration's importance may be appreciated in one further symbolic respect, which is that it followed hard on the heels of the violent end of Admiral Decoux's Vichyite administration, which survived the fall of Vichy itself only to be overthrown by the Japanese in a swift coup executed on 9 March 1945. The Ministry of Colonies was naturally obliged to present the Declaration as a matter of policy uninfluenced by short-term considerations; as mentioned, the Declaration had indeed been planned and discussed over many months prior to March 1945. In a circular to the Governors and Governors-General, Laurentie thus took pains to depict the Declaration as a 'decisive turning point in French colonial policy':

> The essential idea we must stress is that the French Union, creation of which flows from this Declaration, is not an ad hoc measure but

---

45. The notion of French Union citizenship marked a shift away from the previous policy of granting French citizenship to an elite, which represented the *summum bonum* of pre-war assimilation policies.

a system in the fullest sense which will determine the future of every French possession.[46]

Even in March 1945, this sounded very much like whistling in the wind. For, in making what was meant to be a generous and liberal offer of approximate self-government, the Declaration still fell far short of what nationalists in Hanoi and Phnom Penh were seen to be taking for themselves. Within three days of the Japanese takeover, with the encouragement of their Greater Asian suzerains, the Emperor Bao Dai and the young Cambodian Prince Sihanouk had declared independence for the nationalist governments already being established in their respective capitals. Two months later, the crises in Eastern Algeria and in Syria were to call further into question the remaining certainties of French imperial rule.

Like the Brazzaville Conference, the debate conducted by the Expert Commission and the Declaration on Indochina were equally unsatisfactory in one crucial respect: neither was in close touch with reality. Thus, the experts' critique of the Federal idea was no doubt justified to the extent that Laurentie and his collaborators had overlooked the need for policy to conform, or be seen to conform, to French political and ideological norms. Indeed, it was in part this need to adopt policy to a shifting set of domestic parameters of policy which was to have such a decisive effect on subsequent Indochina policy. And yet, it was easily possible to argue too far the other way. Thus, at no stage during the Algiers Commission, any more than at Brazzaville, was any real fear expressed that the Empire was in any sense vulnerable, except perhaps to American interference.

The Japanese takeover in Indochina clearly put paid to such complacency. While it was no doubt alarming for liberals within the colonial administration to have the initiative taken so decisively away from them, just as they were preparing to implement their new policy, the ensuing crises were in a sense helpful to Laurentie and his colleagues, in that they ostensibly demonstrated the forces involved in the imperial equation, which hitherto had

<hr />

46. 'L'idée sur laquelle il convient essentiellement d'insister c'est que l'Union française dont la création découle de cette déclaration constitue non pas une mesure d'occasion mais un véritable système qui déterminera le destin de toutes les possessions françaises.' Tel., Colonies to Dakar, Douala, Brazzaville, Tananarive, no. 154/AP, ref HL/og, 24 Mar. 1945, AOM, Tels/888.

seemed a largely theoretical exercise in policy prescription. Laurentie's message, therefore, over the spring and summer of 1945, was that the brewing crisis across the empire was the consequence of a colonial policy centred too exclusively on the metropolitan perspective. It remained to be seen whether the deep-seated hostility to the Federal idea revealed in the post-Brazzaville debate could be countered through deft deployment of the panic button.

3

'WE ARE IN THE MIDST OF COLONIAL CRISIS'

The Response to International and Colonial Change

> *'There is only one argument for doing something; the rest are arguments for doing nothing.'*[1]

By the spring of 1945, as liberated Paris prepared itself for the relief and triumph of Victory in Europe, the Brazzaville Conference, the Expert Commission, and the Working Party of the Monnerville Commission had all declined to endorse in anything other than the most qualified terms Laurentie's proposals for the reorganisation of Empire along federal lines. Returned to Paris as Director of Political Affairs in the Ministry of Colonies, Laurentie was apt to rail against both the undynamic atmosphere which reigned in the 'dark corridors of the Rue Oudinot' and against the lack of imagination of the average 'administrative mind'.[2] Every centimetre the French equivalent of Cornford's 'young man in a hurry', however, Laurentie had so far failed to provide a satisfactory answer to a simple but pertinent question: why should the GPRF commit itself to a quite radical idea for imperial reform which not only ran counter to past policy, but which also directly denied the validity of the doctrine underpinning that policy? This chapter thus examines the shift effected by Laurentie in the rationale for the Brazzaville policy, in response to perceived critical changes in France's international and colonial situation. It shows the unprecedented extent to which Laurentie took into account

---

1. F.M. Cornford, *Microcosmographia Academica*, Cambridge, 1908.
2. Laurentie to Pignon, 22 Sep. 1944, AN, 72AJ539; Laurentie to Bayardelle, 4 Aug. 1944, 72AJ538.

factors such as, notably, the rise of nationalism. And yet, it will be argued that Laurentie's proposals amounted to an uncomfortable compromise, retaining 'colonialist' features, while still begging the question of domestic acceptability. Laurentie's case was that, while the normalisation of France's relations with her allies had removed the perceived external threat to Empire, one outcome of World War had been to foster a potentially more serious imperial danger, from the emerging and newly confident forces of colonial nationalism. He contended, moreover, that the effect of often harsh colonial policy initiatives undertaken by the Gaullists, far from eliciting the much-vaunted 'loyalty of the colonial populations', had in fact served to prepare the ground for the propagation of nationalist aims and ideas. This impasse was dramatically symbolised for Laurentie by the eruption of the Algerian and Syrian crises in May 1945. Laurentie's analysis, for all its perspicacity, not only increased the responsibilities of an administration which had already shown little commitment to reformism; but also it emphasised just how far the most energetic and committed proponent of the federal idea was out of step with French public and political opinion on the imperial question.

The Changing International and Imperial Stakes

Laurentie's re-evaluation of the basis for the Brazzaville policy was in response to three developments in France's international and imperial standing which came to a head in the first half of 1945. First, by the end of the war in Europe, relations between the three Western Powers had largely been normalised, and this normalisation was reflected in no area more clearly than in France's imperial affairs. Secondly, however, the receding of the tide of war revealed the extent to which the former strength of the colonial powers had been sapped by the events of the war, and the effects this had had in encouraging colonial nationalism. Thirdly, following on from this, the colonial administration was now apparently beginning to pay the price of harsh Gaullist colonial policy, in terms of colonial unrest and a growing nationalist challenge to French policy and even to French rule.

By the time of Roosevelt's death in April 1945 at the latest, the American threat to the integrity of the colonial empires, which had anyway been more rhetorical than actual, had largely faded. As argued above, the Brazzaville Conference had played its part in helping to persuade international opinion of France's continuing colonial ambitions. Indeed, as early as July 1944, emerging from a meeting with Roosevelt in Washington, de Gaulle could assert that 'it is not the intention of President Roosevelt, the American Government, or the American people to annex a single French territory'.[3] The US President's unprecedented fourth election victory in 1944 removed another, electoral, reason for the vehemence of his anti-colonial sentiments. But it was perhaps largely for reasons of *realpolitik* that the US Government started to soften the force of its anti-colonial rhetoric: as the end of the war loomed, America needed strong and stable allies more than it needed ideological purity. It has been argued that, even on the question of Indochina, the ailing President had gone some way by the time of his death towards abandoning the campaign for the internationalisation of the colony.[4] Anti-colonialism was still very much an issue between the United States and the colonial powers, but this was now more a matter of posture than of substance. Moreover, more confident following the much delayed granting of international recognition to the GPRF, in October 1944, the French felt increasingly able to take a back seat in the public debate, allowing their more accommodating British counterparts to bear the brunt of American concerns. This was the case, for example, at the January 1945 Conference at Hot Springs, Virginia, called to discuss the Japanese problem and more general colonial and economic issues, at which the colonial powers displayed a newfound will to regain the high ground of international morality. Their position was one of pragmatic gradualism, according to which it came naturally to give expression to the colonies' supposed interests:

> The countries of the Empire support the view that more harm than good can be expected from decision making which, moreover, would throw those countries into a world in which there is as yet no effective system of security. There is thus a question of time which has to be appreciated.[5]

3. '... le Président Roosevelt, le Gouvernement américain, le peuple américain n'ont aucune intention d'annexer aucun territoire français.' C. de Gaulle, *Discours et messages*, 3 vols, vol. 1, *Pendant la guerre, juin 1940–juillet 1946*, Conférence de presse, 10 Jul. 1944, 442.

4. S. Tønnesson, 'The Longest Wars: Indochina 1945–75', *Journal of Peace Research*, vol. 22, no. 1, 1985, 4.

5. 'La thèse soutenue par les pays de l'Empire appuie sur le fait qu'il y aurait plus de mal que de bien à attendre d'une décision hâtive risquant en outre de jeter ces pays dans un monde où la sécurité générale n'était pas encore effective. Il y a donc une question de temps qu'il faut apprécier.' Tel. Washington to Paris, A/S

Moreover, as the French and British pointed out, backed on this issue alone by a vociferous Indian delegation, American doctrines of anti-colonialism were in large measure hypocritical, as was reflected in the Conference's Southern venue.

French anglophobia notwithstanding, Hot Springs revealed the extent of the substantial grounds for solidarity between the colonial powers. Gaullist mistrust of 'the Anglo-Saxons' continued to play a part: as Jean de la Roche, head of the French mission, explained, French diffidence at Hot Springs was partly because official French policy was 'trailing behind British doctrines, which means it is even more remote from American inclinations', partly out of concern that the British and Americans might achieve reconciliation on the backs of the French.[6] But the period saw marked efforts to achieve cooperation between the colonial powers in Africa and elsewhere. Laurentie's time was thus in part taken up with missions of liaison to Brussels and to London, where an Anglo-French conference was in preparation, to take place at Achimota in Ghana.[7] Returning from one such mission to the Belgian capital, Laurentie argued vigorously to de Gaulle that colonial collaboration should be a key factor in ensuring Western cooperation:

> The other colonial powers have clearly understood the way we are playing, and they approve. Colonial solidarity is becoming a reality, and it has the advantage of matching the balance of Western Europe.[8]

Although this observation was largely a matter of common sense, this apparently self-evident solidarity was to be profoundly shaken a few months later over the Syrian crisis, which most French political opinion would choose to see as reflecting Anglo-French, rather than Franco-Syrian, tensions. Although in itself inconclusive on matters of policy, the Hot Springs Conference pointed the way forward to the San Francisco Conference which met in April 1945. To be sure, not only the United States, but also the Soviet Union enjoyed considerable propaganda victories at San Francisco with

---

Travaux de la Conférence de Hot Springs (5–19 janvier), 25 Jan. 1945, MAE, Y 1944–49 (Conférences internationales), vol. 123.

6. '… en retrait des doctrines britanniques …', c'est-à-dire plus loin qu'elles encore des tendances américaines.' Ibid.

7. The Conference was cancelled at the last moment by the British Colonial Office.

8. 'Les autres puissances coloniales ont vu clair dans notre jeu et l'ont approuvé. Une solidarité coloniale est en train de se former, qui à l'avantage de correspondre à l'équilibre de l'Occident européen.' NOTE PERSONNELLE pour M. le Général de Gaulle, 28 Dec. 1944, AN, 72AJ535.

the dissemination of the vocabulary of Trusteeship, on the American side, and with calls for colonial independence by the Soviet and pro-Soviet delegations.[9] However, colonial affairs played only a small part in the proceedings at San Francisco. Moreover, the main colonial issue to be resolved there worked in France's favour: the issue of International Trusteeship, which had clouded in particular the future of French sovereignty over Indochina, was quietly dropped.[10] This outcome was in part the result of the Japanese takeover in Indochina in March, which in itself made the future for France even more uncertain. In the eyes of the French government it was nonetheless significant that the matter was no longer one for international concern.

These developments, however welcome, had only partially let the French off the hook. It was too easy, in May 1945, to believe that France's five-year odyssey was over now that the Empire had been restored after playing its part in ensuring French victory. As Laurentie was well aware, the reality was very different. In contrast with earlier, largely European, wars, no part of the French, or any other, empire, had remained untouched, directly or indirectly, by the effects of the 1939–45 conflict. The cosy system of 'European collective security for colonial empire', as Ronald Robinson calls it, was no more.[11] In the French case, all parts of the Empire had experienced at least one change of sovereignty, and many had seen foreign invasion or occupation (including US bases at Dakar and Noumea). Since 1940, France had suffered a drastic decline in power, in both absolute and relative terms, in common with the other colonial powers: even Britain, the bastion of European imperial power, had experienced in 1941–42 'some particularly dark and difficult days'; the Netherlands had been militarily defeated

9. Cours d'Information sur l'Indochine, Conférence par Monsieur le Gouverneur LAURENTIE, n.d., AOM, AP/214bis: hereafter cited as 'Cours d'Information'. J. Marseille gives the date of this briefing as 22nd May, 'La Conférence de Brazzaville et l'économie impériale: «des innovations éclatantes» ou des recommandations «prudentes»?', in Institut Charles-de-Gaulle and IHTP, *Brazzaville, aux sources de la décolonisation*, Paris, 1988, 107.

10. W.R. Louis, *Imperialism at Bay, 1941–1945: the United States and the Decolonization of the British Empire*, Oxford and New York, 1977, 46; Tel. Fouques-Duparc to Bidault, San Francisco, 28 Jun. 1945, a 'bilan provisoire et sommaire des résultats obtenus du point de vue français', MAE, Y 1944–1949, vol. 125: the Trusteeship issue ranks seventh and last.

11. 'Imperial Theory and the Question of Imperialism after Empire', in R. Holland and G. Rizvi, eds, *Perspectives on Imperialism and Decolonization*, London, 1984, 84.

also, and while Belgium had maintained its colonial status in Africa, this was only 'because of its geographic situation and had nothing to do with its own efforts'.[12] If victory had been achieved in most theatres of war by May 1945, therefore, and largely assured even in the Far East (though it was still unclear at what cost that victory would be obtained), the continued survival of the colonial empires was far from certain.

In contrast with the crumbling position overseas of the European powers, Laurentie outlined what amounted to a coalition of opposing factors. First was the emergence of two avowedly anticolonialist superpowers, the United States and the Soviet Union. Even after San Francisco, it was clear that a combination of American power and anti-colonialism would continue to have an imponderable effect on colonial morale. The influence of the Soviet Union was as yet more diffuse and intangible outside Europe. But, as Laurentie argued, 'an image of Russia has been accepted fairly generally and it is all the more appealing because it remains an enigma'.[13] Two other general factors argued, in Laurentie's thesis, against the idea of a restored colonial status quo: the full participation of two Asian nationalist powers, China and Japan, in the international system; and the resurgence of nationalism in the Middle East. In the case of the first factor, Laurentie argued that the United States' acceptance of China as an ally and an ostensible equal was as decisive as the effects of the Japanese war effort since 1941. As he pointed out:

> Japan conducted the war as a matter of race, as if it were a question of championing the Orientals. It failed in its efforts. Japan has as good as lost the war, but this ideal of an Oriental champion has not been lost, and has obviously been taken up by China.[14]

China would be weak for some time (though, one might add, not weak enough to prevent it from playing a considerable spoiling role in Indochina 1945–46), but the important fact was that a government led by Asian nationalists would henceforth be seen as an

12. '... du fait de sa position géographique et nullement du fait de sa vigueur propre.' Cours d'Information.
13. '... une image de la Russie se répand un peu partout et qui est d'autant plus attrayante qu'elle reste énigmatique'. Ibid.
14. 'Le Japon ... dirigeait son action belliqueuse comme une affaire de races, comme une espèce de championnat de la race jaune. Il a échoué dans cette entreprise. On peut dire aujourd'hui que la guerre japonaise est perdue; mais ce qui n'est pas perdu, c'est l'idée du championnat de la race jaune; ce championnat est repris évidemment par la Chine.' Ibid.

equal of the Western powers. The final beneficiary from the rout of the European powers was the cause of nationalism in 'that running sore which is the Middle East'. The countries of the Middle East had played little direct part in the war, though the region had been strategically vital. But the disequilibrium left by the war could only favour 'the virulent authority of political Islam' whose influence had previously been neutralised by the now vanished 'solid position of the colonial powers'.[15]

One further factor weighed heavily in Laurentie's thinking. This was the effect on colonial morale of various aspects of colonial policy since the Gaullist takeover. Official rhetoric notwithstanding, the Empire had chiefly been important to de Gaulle as a source of men and supplies, as a territorial base from which to conduct his campaign, and as a source of legitimacy. As Laurentie has suggested: 'He wanted first to make use of it, and then to put it back together and hand it back intact in peacetime to the legitimate French authorities'.[16] Brazzaville-style liberalism, or the limited but undoubtedly liberal reforms promised by de Gaulle in his speech at Constantine (Algeria) on 7 March 1944, were thus of a low order of priority compared with the need to gear the empire to the needs of the war effort, and to govern until a legitimate government was reconstituted in Paris.

The strains of the war were already telling by the time of Brazzaville, even in those territories which only came under Gaullist authority with the formation of the CFLN in 1943. The war effort took two principal forms in the two African federations and in Madagascar. The first consisted of military recruitment. Already in 1939–40, eighty thousand men from the African colonies served abroad, many in the Battle of France. The feats of Black African troops under Gaullist command are part of Gaullist legend. However, the bulk of colonial manpower was provided by AOF, which only rallied to de Gaulle after the resolution of the Giraudist debacle in 1943, and where recruitment was already underway in 1942. The concluding campaigns of the war involved a total of 23,000 European settlers, 2,500 Senegalese and 102,500 Africans from the rest of AOF. The chief limiting factor on such recruitment was the rule that recruitment maintain a fixed proportion of about 20

---

15. Ibid.
16. 'Il voulait d'abord s'en servir … ensuite le reconstituer et assurer sa remise le jour de la paix aux autorités légitimes de la France.' 'Témoignage du gouverneur-général [sic] Laurentie', in Institut Charles-de-Gaulle, *Le général de Gaulle et l'Indochine*, Paris, 1982, 232.

percent Europeans. Tens of thousands more Africans were recruited for service on public works and in the plantations. More immediately serious for the administration was the economic war effort, for which the CFLN's demands, maintained by the GPRF in Paris, were clearly in excess of AOF's real productive capacity. In a grotesque parody of the received idea of colonial exploitation, the administration sought to maximise production by African and European planters, smallholders, and the large numbers of Africans still recruited by force. Even so, as Joseph-Roger Benoist has shown, for most major categories of exports from AOF, targets were not achieved or even approached.[17]

It is not the task of this survey to assess the importance of specific instances of unrest, such as the riot of repatriated troops held at a transit camp at Thiaroye, near Dakar, in December 1944, which underline the tensions experienced at the time.[18] The gravity of the issues arising out of the economic war effort may more readily be discerned in Ivory Coast, where the liberal Governor Latrille joined forces with the newly formed African Farming Union (*Syndicat Agricole Africain*), led by the young Félix Houphouët-Boigny, to defend the interests of African cocoa planters against the politically dominant and economically privileged settler community.[19] More usually, the effects of the war effort were experienced by local administrations as a general but increasingly acute malaise. In Madagascar, which rallied to de Gaulle following the British invasion of 1942, General Legentilhomme, Gaullist High Commissioner for the Indian Ocean, conducted the war effort with such ferocity that Pleven was obliged to make a special trip in December 1943, on his way to Brazzaville, in order to announce important political concessions.[20] Even in France's most peaceable and least troublesome territory, French Equatorial Africa (AEF), which had also been under Gaullist control the

---

17. D. Bouche, 'Problèmes de sécurité en AOF à l'heure de la réorganisation de l'armée française', in Institut Charles-de-Gaulle, *De Gaulle et la Nation face aux problèmes de la défense*, Paris, 1983, 242; J.R. Benoist, *L'Afrique Occidentale Française*, Dakar, 1980, 16–17. Although known as *Tirailleurs sénégalais*, these troops were in fact recruited across AOF.

18. Bouche, 'Problèmes de sécurité', 242–44.

19. R. Schachter-Morgenthau, *Political Parties in French-Speaking West Africa*, Oxford, 1964, 176–88; P.H. Siriex, *Félix Houphouet-Boigny*, Dakar, 1975.

20. It was at this period that the two secret organisations were formed, the Parti National Socialiste Malgache (PA.NA.MA.) and JINA, which are now generally held responsible for the Insurrection of March 1947: J. Tronchon, *L'insurrection malgache de 1947*, Paris and Fianarantsoa, 1974/1986, 22–23.

longest, the privations and pressures of the war effort were taking their toll: already by 1943, AEF's annual deficit had risen from 15 million francs in 1940 to as much as 40 million.[21]

Notwithstanding the tensions caused by the war effort, Gaullists faced their greatest colonial challenge from the volatile forces of Arab and Maghrebine nationalism in North Africa and the Levant. If by VE-Day they had not come off worst, this was mainly at the cost of liberal promises broken, and of old reputations confirmed. One of the first actions of the CFLN had been to depose the Bey of Tunis, the Tunisian sovereign supposedly protected by the 1881 Treaty of Le Bardo. Accused of collaboration with the Axis, his real crime was to have formed a nationalist government in December 1942 while Tunisia was still ruled from Vichy.[22] In Morocco, a new Istiqlal ('Independence') Party was formed in December 1943 with the moral support of the Sultan, whose nationalist sympathies were encouraged by Roosevelt, but the arrest of Istiqlal leaders in January 1944 led to violence in several cities, in ironic counterpoint to the Brazzaville Conference. The Sultan was obliged by Massigli, Foreign Affairs Commissioner, to declare before his vizirs that 'the word "independence" must disappear from our hearts and from our lips'.[23]

It was in Algeria and Syria that the Provisional Government found itself implicated in the most spectacular crises, which erupted at the moment of victory in Europe. In Algeria, the moderate nationalist Ferhat Abbas issued a 'Manifesto of the Algerian People' (*Manifeste du Peuple Algérien*) in February 1943, which called for substantial autonomy, and which met with a limitedly favourable response. However, de Gaulle's proposed reforms of March 1944 were extremely guarded. By May 1945, political tensions were compounded by food shortages as a result of the war effort. On VE-Day, these erupted into violence against the European population in Sétif in Eastern Algeria, which in turn provoked reprisals by the settlers and by the combined French army, navy, and airforce. The violence claimed 102 European lives; nine hundred Algerian deaths were recorded, but the figure was believed to be nearer six thousand. French intelligence believed

---

21. J. Suret-Canale, *Afrique noire occidentale et centrale, L'ère coloniale (1900–1945)*, Paris, 1964, 587–95.
22. C.-A. Julien, *L'Afrique du Nord en Marche*, Paris, 3rd edition, 1972, 98–99, 176.
23. '... le mot indépendance doit disparaître de nos coeurs et de nos bouches'. Ibid., 344–48.

that unrest was spontaneous, but had prematurely triggered a full-scale insurrection.[24] The crisis in Syria had been simmering since the Gaullists took over the Mandate administration in 1941, following the Anglo-Gaullist overthrow of General Dentz's Vichy adminstration. Independence was promised in late 1941, but on the understanding that it would be granted at war's end, on a number of conditions guaranteeing French interests. Free elections were finally held in November 1943 and returned nationalist governments in Beirut and Damascus. When the Lebanese government declared an end to the Mandate, its members were arrested. The French came out of the November 1943 crisis badly, which accelerated the transfer of powers to the new governments, and by May 1945 this process was largely complete. In the spring, the French sponsored Syrian and Lebanese admission to the United Nations, and the two states were represented at the San Francisco Conference. However, the French still had control of the so-called Special Troops (*troupes spéciales*) in Syria, a body of twenty-five thousand gendarmes recruited largely from the minorities, and made matters worse by sending troop reinforcements, ostensibly to counter British troop numbers, but effectively to put pressure on the Syrians. The crisis escalated, and by the end of May, French forces were bombing Damascus, Aleppo, Homs, and other Syrian cities. Finally, under pressure from London and after appeals from President Quwatli of Syria, the Commander of British Forces in the Levant, General Paget, issued orders restricting French troops to barracks under pain of being fired upon by their British allies.[25]

Neither the Levant states nor Algeria could be understood as straightforward examples of French imperial rule. From the perspective of the Ministry of Colonies, both crises could be seen as the result of policies distinct from, and contrasting with, any emanating from the Rue Oudinot. Moreover, more than for any part of France's colonial domain per se, there was significant ideological

24. Report by Carvell (Consul-General, Algiers), PRO, FO371/49275. For recent accounts of these events see J.C. Jauffret, 'The Origins of the Algerian War: The Reaction of France and its Army to the Emergencies of 8 May 1945 and 1 November 1954', trans. C Watkins and M. Sparling, in R. Holland, ed., *Emergencies and Disorder in the European Empires after 1945*, London, 1994, 17–29; A. Clayton, *The Wars of French Decolonization*, London, 1994, 28–33.

25. De Gaulle refers modestly to the deployment of 'two cannons and an aircraft' in *Mémoires de guerre*, 3 vols, vol. 3, Le salut, 227. See W.R. Louis, *The British Empire in the Middle East*, 1945–51, Oxford, 1984, 147–72; Clayton, *The Wars*, 33–38.

and emotional investment in both cases, derived from the myth of Algeria as an extension of metropolitan territory on the one hand; and, on the other, from the history of French involvement in the Levant going back to the sixteenth century (or even to the crusades). Neither was it a difficult matter to find scapegoats for both crises. In the Syrian case, this role was amply filled by the British: the Consultative Assembly debate in mid-June called on witnesses for the prosecution as diverse as Major-General Spears, the hated former British Resident, T.E. Lawrence, Kitchener (*in re* Fashoda) and Richard Lionheart.[26] Indeed, both Duff Cooper, at this time British Ambassador in Paris, and the historian Roger Louis suggest that French suspicions were not unfounded.[27] In the Algerian debate in July, there was little to distinguish the vehemence of opinions expressed from Left and Right, except that Communists blamed the Sétif risings on the settlers, described by one speaker as 'a miserable bunch of idlers, traitors, and fascists'; while defenders of French Algeria saw the risings as either the work of gullible natives, 'simple men through and through who only understand brute force', or as 'a terrible revolt prepared and organised methodically against French sovereignty'.[28]

From the perspective of the Rue Oudinot, however, Laurentie had little doubt as to the cause of the two crises. To be sure, the Ministry despatched the official, anti-British, version of the Syrian crisis to the colonies, even while governors were ordered to monitor their territories for possible knock-on political effects, for example amongst the Levantine trading communities of the West African colonies. In the event, the only signs of discontent came from Togolese political activists, mindful of their country's status under a League of Nations mandate, and with an eye to Ewe propaganda distributed from the Gold Coast.[29] But in a memorandum to Giacobbi in June, Laurentie interpreted the eruption of crisis thus:

> We are in the midst of colonial crisis. Feelings of disillusionment, disaffection, defiance, and hatred are so general as to be dangerous.

26. *Journal Officiel, Assemblée Consultative Provisoire* (JOACP), no. 44, 15 Jun. 1945, 1113–30; no. 45, 19 Jun. 1945, 1134–50.

27. A. Duff Cooper, *Old Men Forget*, London, 1953, 354; Louis, *The British Empire*, loc.cit.

28. '… une poignée de misérables oisifs, traîtres et fascistes'; 'êtres simplistes par excellence, ne connaissant que la force'; 'une terrible révolte préparée, organisée avec méthode contre la souveraineté française'. JOACP, nos 56–57, 11 Jul. 1945, 1344–67, 1371–84; no. 59, 18 Jul. 1945, 1397–1418.

29. Tels. collected in AOM, AP/214bis.

Our counterweight is a feeble one: the apathy of the colonial masses can never offset the nationalism which is being born or proclaimed across the empire.[30]

Laurentie blamed the crises squarely on the accumulated effect of the factors described in this chapter: French weakness, both in absolute terms and relative to the strengths of other international actors, and the challenge of nationalism, which was both buoyed by these developments and encouraged by the repressive policies of the Gaullist administration. As he argued, this crisis could not have been worse timed:

Nationalism is finding expression at the exact moment when our only hope of keeping the Empire is to undertake a massive operation to capture hearts and minds. Providing we make substantial sacrifices here and there, we can hope to reaffirm through renewal the bonds which unite France to her overseas territories. For want of real power we must deploy different weapons.[31]

It is to the implications of this stance for policy making that we now turn.

Laurentie's Appeal to 'Hearts and Minds'

Laurentie's case, which he had been strengthening since the partial failure of the Brazzaville Conference, was given perhaps its fullest and most persuasive exposition in his briefing to fellow administrators and cadets at the National College for Overseas France (Ecole Nationale de la France d'Outre-Mer, or ENFOM) in

---

30. 'Nous sommes en pleine crise coloniale. Les sentiments de déception, de désaffection, de défiance et de haine se décèlent sur tant de points que cela forme un dangereux ensemble. Le contrepoids est léger: l'apathie des masses ne saurait balancer le nationalisme qui, un peu partout, naît ou s'affirme.' NOTE, 20–21 Jun. 1945, AN, 72AJ535.

31. 'Ce nationalisme s'exprime au moment précis où nous n'avions pas d'autre moyen de conserver l'Empire que d'entreprendre et réussir une grande opération du coeur et de la raison; moyennant plusieurs renoncements de notre part, nous pouvions consacrer en les renouvelant les liens qui unissent les territoires d'outre-mer à la France. Faute de puissance réelle, nous faisions jouer d'autres armes.' Ibid. This key document is discussed at length in M.J. Shipway, '"Nous sommes en pleine crise coloniale …"' : French decolonisation, state violence, and the limits of liberal reformism', in J. Windebank and R. Günther, eds, *Violence and Conflict in the Politics and Society of Contemporary France*, Lewiston/Queenston/Lampeter, 1995, 117–34.

May 1945. Although this was intended as the first of a series of briefings on Indochina policy, no other from the series survives, if it was ever completed. This may be read as the most complete extant version of Laurentie's thesis in its revised form.[32] Laurentie's rationale for radical reform was based on three arguments: that reform was dictated by pragmatism rather than generosity, in order to maintain imperial unity in the face of crisis; that policy should be consistent aross the empire; and that it should be founded on the proposition that an accommodation with nationalism was both necessary and possible.

First, then, Laurentie made the fairly general but nonetheless potentially startling observation that the choice of a genuinely liberal imperial policy should be dictated, not by the usual professions of French generosity, but purely by pragmatism and, more specifically, by the recognition of French weakness. As Laurentie argued, the Gaullist campaign since 1940, culminating in the triumphal return to Paris, had served to counteract the effects of defeat and capitulation, but 'our slow resurrection' could only ever be incomplete:

> Although today we have achieved Victory in Europe, it is obvious that France did not at all fully participate in that victory, and that she is not one of the principal victors in this war. This realisation will have an effect on the minds of our colonial populations.[33]

Clearly, for Laurentie, policy should be based on this weakness. Indeed, this notion had already found expression in his December 1944 memorandum to de Gaulle, which generously glossed the thinking which had led to Brazzaville:

> We understood at Algiers. Deprived of the means to exercise our power – army, air force, navy – we decided to replace them with the ideas and sentiments needed to revive and confirm France's rights to a colonial empire. It was in this spirit that the Brazzaville Conference was conceived and organised.[34]

---

32. See also the Circular distributed to Governors and Governors-General in September 1945, AOM, AP/2167.

33. 'Si aujourd'hui la victoire est obtenue en Europe, il est visible que la France n'y a participé que d'une façon tout à fait partielle, qu'elle n'est pas parmi les grands vainqueurs de cette guerre et cette constatation aussi influera sur l'esprit des populations coloniales.' Cours d'Information.

34. 'On l'avait compris à Alger. Dépouillés de nos moyens de puissance, armée, aviation et marine, nous avions décidé de les remplacer par des idées et des sentiments propres àrajeunir et confirmer les titres coloniaux de la France. Ainsi fut conçue et

Pragmatism suggested also that the use of force merely reinforced the impression of French vulnerability (a perception which might fruitfully have been applied to other areas of Gaullist policy, such as de Gaulle's ill-conceived bid to annex the Valle d'Aosta). Thus, commenting on the coincidence of the Syrian and Algerian crises, Laurentie warned that the French risked gaining the reputation for recidivism:

> The arguments which we thus allow the nationalists to use against us, including the appearance of weakness which clings to us with the repeated use of force, are such that we now run the risk of being dragged into a chain of events which we can no longer control. One more 'incident', if we are unlucky, would be enough to set off the final avalanche.[35]

This was an argument which was to be of particular moment in Indochina, although, as will be seen, Laurentie's arguments were not applied to the show of force, which was still considered to be essential for the effective wielding of French authority.

Laurentie's other arguments had even more momentous implications for policy making. With his second argument, that France faced a general 'colonial crisis', Laurentie was in part contending that a general imperial policy should take the place of the piecemeal and improvisatory policies of the past. It was an essential part of Laurentie's role as a 'Young Turk' within the colonial administration to contest the supposedly expert opinion of 'old hands' whose experience was an effective means of blocking innovation. As he argued, in ironic vein, in the pages of a journal representing colonial interests, French colonial policy had for too long been the exclusive domain of 'those in the know':

> These so-called experts will first tell you that there is not one single colonial question but as many colonial questions as there are colonised countries. This is a convenient argument which serves to undermine anyone who has not spent fifteen or twenty years in a country but who nonetheless has the effrontery to take an interest

---

réunie la Conférence de Brazzaville.' NOTE PERSONNELLE pour M. le Général de Gaulle, 28 Dec. 1944, AN, 72AJ535.

35. 'Les arguments fournis au nationalisme, y compris cette allure de la faiblesse, que nous donne l'emploi répété de la force, sont tels que nous pouvons craindre d'être désormais entraînés dans une suite de faits dont nous ne serons plus les maîtres. Un autre 'incident', avec un peu de malchance, suffirait à déterminer l'avalanche.' NOTE, 20–21 Jun. 1945, loc.cit.

in it. It should be understood, therefore, that in order to discuss Indochina, one must first have done the rounds at the right sort of Hanoi tea party, or glimpsed Lyautey's profile in order to have anything to say about North Africa, or, in the case of Madagascar, one must have slept on the paper mattresses which protect the island's silence.[36]

But his arguments went deeper than this. Brazzaville policy was an attempt to find a general solution to what was perceived to be a general problem. As he further argued:

France's colonial policy can only be general, because what confronts France is also a general problem: we are looking at colonial revolution.[37]

Similarly, those attending Laurentie's briefing on Indochina could be forgiven for expecting to hear a summary of plans for the resumption of French rule in Indochina following the Japanese takeover. Instead, Laurentie delivered a lecture on the general principles of France's colonial policy across the French Union; for, as he explained, 'there is no colonial issue which is not of relevance to the Far East'.[38] Crucially, also, colonial discontent across the Empire was seen as part of the same general movement. In his response to the May crises, for example, Laurentie extended his scope to embrace the situation in the less troubled territories under his own Ministry's administration: in West Africa, which was 'rapidly wakening to [political] consciousness and showing undeniable signs of unrest'; in Madagascar, still slumbering but whose awakening was to be feared; even in the Antilles, where there were dreams of a Caribbean Federation; neither should the

36. 'Ces *experts* vous diront d'abord qu'il n'y a pas *une* question coloniale mais autant de questions coloniales que de contrées colonisées. Argument commode, et qui permet de révoquer en doute ceux qui n'auraient pas commencé par passer quelque quinze ou vingt ans dans un pays et prendraient la liberté de s'y intéresser. Il devrait être entendu que, pour discuter de l'Indochine, il faudrait avoir fait ses classes dans les thés mondains de Hanoï, ou de l'Afrique du Nord, avoir aperçu la silhouette de Lyautey, ou de Madagascar, avoir dormi sur les matelas de papier qui protègent le silence de la Grande Ile.' 'Précisions sur la politique coloniale', *Marchés coloniaux*, Jan. 1946; typewritten ms. in AN, 72AJ535.

37. '... la politique coloniale de la France ne peut être que générale, parce que l'événement qu'elle confronte est également général; il s'agit de la révolution coloniale.' Ibid. The term 'révolution coloniale' was applied also in a Note, DAP, 1er et 3ème Bureaux, n.d. (Jul. 1945), AOM, AP/214bis/V.

38. '... il n'y a pas, à vrai dire, de question coloniale qui soit propre à l'Extrême-Orient.' Cours d'Information.

upheavals in the French Indian settlements or New Caledonia be overlooked.[39]

Thirdly, Laurentie was in no doubt as to the effect of this, and the other factors outlined above, on France's colonial populations: 'the fairly ubiquitous growth of nationalism, or rather its more explicit and confident expression'. This nationalism either took a precise, mature form, as in the Levant, or was for the moment only latent 'and hidden beneath a kind of racism'. Thus, nationalism was a force with which the French would have to come to terms, and nationalists were no longer a local nuisance who could be ignored or suppressed. But, by extension, it was crucial to work on the assumption that some accommodation was possible:

> It is a fact that nationalism exists. But I believe we should consider it axiomatic that this nationalism need neither harm nor exclude us, and that at bottom, it is presented to us by its negative rather than its positive side.[40]

The key to any accommodation with nationalist forces, therefore, was the recognition of nationalism's underlying motivation. For Laurentie, nationalism was chiefly an expression of opposition to 'the spirit of colonisation, or, if you prefer, of colonialism'. By this was understood in general terms the infringement of individual liberties, most notably by the imposition of the *indigénat* (the code of punishments exacted directly on colonial subjects by the administration); and the refusal of equality, both through the statutes of colonial rule, which still distinguished between 'citizens' and 'subjects', and through the French assumption of superiority, which led to the exclusion of adequately trained colonial subjects from all but a handful of responsible positions.[41]

Laurentie thus advocated the employment in positions of responsiblity of a whole class of intellectuals (*évolués*). This was clearly a key element of the March 1945 Declaration on Indochina: as Laurentie pointed out, a properly recruited administration within the proposed Indochinese Federation would constitute not only the essential 'armour' holding the new polity together, but also a guarantee of French good faith in its relations with the

39. Note, 20–21 Jun. 1945, loc.cit.

40. '… c'est un fait que le nationalisme existe. Néanmoins, ce nationalisme, et je crois que nous devons considérer cela comme un axiome, ce nationalisme n'est pas nécessairement virulent ni exclusif, et au fond, se présente plutôt d'une façon négative que d'une façon positive.' Cours d'Information.

41. '… l'esprit même de la colonisation ou si l'on veut du colonialisme'. Ibid.

emerging Associated States.[42] At the same time, he warned of the possible danger that these intellectuals would act as a screen between the French and the masses. As he argued, even in Africa there was a place for mass political parties over which the French could hope to preserve some influence. This influence was intended, not so much to create an opposition between the masses and the 'ruling class', but to ensure that this class did not obstruct social policies of little direct interest to them. Speaking perhaps from his personal experience in the Near East, Laurentie was critical of the 'nationalist aristocracy' which he saw operating not only in Syria, where 'three hundred families' had created a screen between the French administration and ordinary people, but also in Indochina and in Madagascar. Whereas in Indochina, French loss of contact following the Japanese takeover would mean that the French would be obliged to deal with already existing political parties, in Africa and Madagascar the French were still working on a relative *tabula rasa*: the task of the local administrations would therefore be one of surveillance and guidance as colonial society rapidly evolved modern forms of political organisation.[43]

While permitting and encouraging the development of locally recruited political and administrative institutions, therefore, France's aim should be to preserve the power of arbitration (*arbitrage*), in order to prevent oppression by one race or political class. Laurentie thus favoured the development of internal federal systems: here again, the Declaration on Indochina was an obvious model, providing for a federation of five *pays* or 'lands': Cambodia, Laos and the three regions (*ky*) into which Vietnam had traditionally been divided by the French administration. In his Indochina briefing, Laurentie cited also the example of Madagascar, where internal federation was seen as the solution to France's perceived main policy-making problem on the island: how to prevent the predominance of the Merina (or *hova* as they were misleadingly called by the French) over the other races or clans on the island.[44] One final aspect of Laurentie's rationale for the Brazzaville policy needs to be mentioned, namely the question of economic development. As has already been suggested, this was

42. Ibid.

43. Ibid.

44. Ibid. The Merina had dominated the island before the French invasion of 1896. 'Hova' (pronounced, and sometimes written, 'houve') has various meanings, including 'noble' and 'commoner', according to region: Tronchon, *L'insurrection malgache*, 13.

relatively and perhaps surprisingly low on Laurentie's order of priorities. Nonetheless, as he argued in his Indochina briefing, equality could only be established between the various member countries of an eventual French Union on the basis of the 'appropriate economic means'. On this question, however, Laurentie went no further than to point out that, given both the parlous state of France's own economic situation and the likely liberalisation of the international economic order, the basis for economic development would have to come from some form of international collaboration. On the question of the limits to which economic autonomy would be assured, Laurentie contented himself with concluding rather blithely that, in the all important case of Indochina at least, 'autonomy has already been promised, and is therefore a foregone conclusion'.[45] Laurentie's cursory examination of this crucial topic reflects perhaps both his perception that politics would precede economics, and also his awareness of the extent to which economic development lay outside the powers of the colonial administration.

Like many prophets of imperial *perestroika*, Henri Laurentie and his fellow liberals risked falling between the two stools of reformism and conservatism. On one hand, there was much in his analysis to impress the historian of decolonisation, not least his perception that French weakness and loss of prestige would, unless a break was made with the heavy-handed policies of the past, place the empire in real danger of dissolution. As he encapsulated the dilemma facing French policy makers:

> It is a matter of knowing whether we will manage to resolve the contradiction between the colonial peoples' desire for independence on the one hand, and on the other France's weakness, which makes it difficult to sustain the authority needed to pursue a liberal but progressive policy.[46]

Even here, however, from the perspective of 1945, an obvious danger of such dramatic policy presentation was that Laurentie would be seen to overstate the case. This was a trap of which he was

---

45. '..l'autonomie est d'ores et déjà promise et par conséquent acquise'. Ibid.

46. '... il s'agit de savoir si nous arriverons à résoudre la contradiction: aspiration des populations vers l'indépendance d'une part et d'autre part faiblesse de la France qui lui permet difficilement de mener avec une autorité continue une politique libérale mais [sic] progressive.' Cours d'Information.

constantly aware: as he wrote in February 1945 to his friend and colleague Aimé Bayardelle, Governor General at Brazzaville, he took uneasily to the role of Cassandra.[47] Like Cassandra, Laurentie ran the very real risk of being uncomfortably right but never heeded. Indeed, quite apart from bureaucracy's elective affinity with the established order, powerful reasons dictated the apparent conservatism of both the Corps of Governors at Brazzaville and the colonial experts assembled in Algiers and Paris. In particular, the wartime Gaullist campaign had been fought with the double-edged sword of reform and legitimacy. While in his speeches de Gaulle often dwelt on promises of 'national renewal' (*rénovation nationale*), his more obvious and immediate concern was to restore legitimacy and continuity. If it was both impossible and undesirable, therefore, to return to the status quo ante, reforms had to be seen to be granted by de Gaulle from a position of strength. Brazzaville, and thus also the Brazzaville policy in whatever form, was *prima facie* more about imperial restoration than it was about colonial reform, however pressing the reasons for the latter.

On the other hand, Laurentie's analysis still betrayed the reflexes of colonial rule. First, his notion of arbitration was difficult to distinguish from classic colonial policies of 'divide and rule'. So much is clear already from Laurentie's chosen examples: in the case of Indochina, the division of Vietnam into three *ky* on the spurious grounds of culture, race, and tradition could more clearly be interpreted as a way to maintain the French colonial bastion of Cochinchina, the Southern *ky* (as will be seen in later chapters); while in Madagascar, the distinction between the *Hova* and the supposedly downtrodden 'coastal peoples' was a largely factitious one which, according to Jacques Tronchon, 'corresponds more to an ideological split than to any ethnographic or geographic reality'.[48] Secondly, Laurentie's definition of nationalism, however liberal in its admission of the need to meet the material and political aspirations of the peoples under France's tutelage, fell far short of recognising the validity of perhaps the most fundamental and powerful stated aim of nationalism, namely the right of self-determination. Thus, although the Brazzaville policy went far further than previous policy to provide a framework for political, and to a lesser extent economic, development, the ideological assumptions of

47. Laurentie to Bayardelle, 9 Feb. 1945, AN, 72AJ535.
48. '... correspond plus à un clivage idéologique qu'à une réalité ethnographique ou géographique'. Tronchon, *L'insurrection malgache*, 13.

that framework were still resolutely French, and implicitly colonial. By extension, it would fall to the French colonial administration to decide whether or not a given nationalist party or movement was 'acceptable' in the limited terms of French policy, or whether it could be condemned out of hand as 'extremist', 'inauthentic', or as yet another example of Laurentie's troublesome and obstructive 'nationalist aristocracy'.

Finally, returning to the metropolitan perspective, Lantie's account of the crisis facing the French Empire at war's end begged two questions. First, how would these decisions be formulated or mediated within the hierarchy of the colonial administration? The second concerned perhaps the most serious limitation of Laurentie's rationale for the Brazzaville policy. This was its ready assumption of an almost exclusively 'colonial' perspective, which thus apparently ignored or took for granted a more properly metropolitan view of imperial affairs. Laurentie had provided a controversial, if plausible, account of the current state of Empire and of the need for reform; but had so far failed to couch his arguments in terms readily assimilable within a domestic political or ideological framework. So how far could colonial policy be squared with domestic concerns at a time when these were more preoccupying even than usual? It is this question which the next chapter addresses.

4

THE DOMESTIC PARAMETERS OF COLONIAL POLICY MAKING AFTER THE LIBERATION, 1944–1946

So far the proposals which emerged from Brazzaville have been considered chiefly in terms of parameters having a direct bearing on policy. These parameters of policy might be taken to include such factors as: the coherence and comprehensiveness of policy; its relevance to clearly identifiable and legitimate aims such as, in this case, the maintenance of Empire or, more specifically, the restoration of French control or influence in Indochina; the theoretical capacity of policy to respond and to adapt to changing external factors, such as shifts in the international system, or the rise of nationalism; an awareness of the limits of policy as reflected, for example, in the rejection of assimilationism and of the use of force. These parameters concerned colonial policy makers most urgently and, measured against them, the framework of the Brazzaville policy was largely complete by the summer of 1945, awaiting only the moment for implementation in the Far East.

In itself, the Brazzaville policy's emphasis on the external parameters of policy was unsurprising.[1] After all, it was drawn up by colonial administrators, and bore from the start the *imprimatur* of a figure whose ideological outlook was dominated from the outset by external concerns. Moreover, in the circumstances of wartime Gaullism, any reference to metropolitan politics was purely hypothetical. Nonetheless, as has been suggested in earlier chapters, it was insufficient for the Brazzaville policy to be rational and comprehensive in its own terms, as if conceived in a domestic political

1. N.B. Alfred Grosser's definition of 'la politique extérieure', embracing colonial affairs, in *Affaires extérieures*, Paris, 1984, 8–9.

vacuum. Thus, when drawing up the new colonial policy, officials implied or assumed a model of domestic politics. This chapter considers the parameters governing this model, and seeks to determine the extent to which domestic politics after the Liberation conformed to it. In particular, the chapter examines the effects on these domestic parameters of the prolonged domestic crisis which accompanied the Constitution-writing process, especially following de Gaulle's resignation as President of the GPRF in January 1946. The ideal in domestic terms would presumably have been a period of relative stability during which policy makers could concentrate on meeting rapidly changing external pressures and constraints. Even as France confronted an unprecedented challenge to her position as a colonial power, however, the colonial administration also had to come to terms with conditions of considerable volatility and confusion in Paris. As the chapter argues, although at first conditions in Paris conformed adequately, if imperfectly, to the domestic parameters of policy as set out below, the first cracks soon appeared in the policy makers' preferred model. This construct was to prove no match for the intensifying seismic tremors of domestic political crisis.

Three domestic parameters of policy may be identified, the first of which is that of **political salience**. To what extent did colonial policy warrant or receive government and/or parliamentary priority? In Algiers, the Brazzaville 'spirit' had almost sufficed to ensure a high degree of political interest in colonial policy; but after the return to Paris, in the face of the tremendous economic and political problems which awaited the GPRF, it was an open question as to how far and why colonial policy mattered to the government and to French party-political and public opinion. However, it is also suggested that a high degree of salience for colonial affairs did not always have an entirely constructive effect on policy.

This first parameter also depends closely on the second, that of ideological acceptability. Ideology, here understood in its general sense as '... the integrated assertions, theories and aims that constitute a socio-political program',[2] plays so fundamental a role in policy making that it is often taken as a given. Given the volatility of politics at the Liberation, however, as will be shown, this was

2. Webster's *Third International Dictionary*, quoted by H.M. Johnson, 'Ideology and the Social System', *International Encyclopedia of the Social Sciences*, ed. D.L. Sills, vol.VII, New York, 1979, 76.

very far from being the case. The importance of ideology for policy making may be conceived in three stages. First, ideology provides a context in which policy may be understood and presented as important or necessary. Thus, in the case of the Brazzaville policy, it would be impossible to imagine Laurentie describing the aims of policy or its international context 'objectively', ie. without making assumptions determined by a particular ideological framework (in this case, broadly speaking, Gaullist). Second, ideology informs the terms of that policy or, rather, policy is formulated according to given ideological norms: hence the significance of Laurentie's attempt to define the Brazzaville policy in terms acceptable to Republican doctrine. Third, ideology legitimates policy, enabling policy makers to explain their aims in terms recognizable and acceptable to their audience. The theme of 'gratitude' for the sacrifices of Empire serves as a straightforward example of this phenomenon: a liberal imperial policy was thus portrayed as repayment of a debt (rather than giving something away for nothing). As will be argued, the Brazzaville policy reflected in part the convergence of two powerful ideologies, Gaullism and Republicanism. The chapter examines what happened as these two ideologies diverged in their imperial aims, and how far policy was affected by other ideological influences, such as an emergent strain of anti-Communism, or the resurgence of old-fashioned imperialism.

The third parameter is that of **institutional solidarity**. The highly ambitious reforms envisaged in the Brazzaville policy depended on two institutional factors: a clear chain of command, and administrators' unquestioning acceptance of the authority of Paris. But how strong were the institutions on which the new policy depended, and how loyal were the agents of that policy? The prospects for the new tenants of the Rue Oudinot were mixed in this respect. On the one hand, de Gaulle's authority, and that of his most loyal supporters, had been imposed on the colonial hierarchy from an early stage in the Gaullist campaign. On the other hand, this authority was reinforced by only a limited rationalisation of the colonial hierarchy in the specific case of Indochina. Moreover, the colonial administration had a long tradition of autonomy from Paris. The great colonial proconsuls of the past, such as Marshal Lyautey, had prided themselves on their capacity to act independently of Paris and even in defiance of Paris's orders. But as late as 1940, as Bernard Lanne points out, a Governor-General could still count on his personal authority in order to act without reference to the Ministry of Colonies.[3] It was perhaps in this respect that the Brazzaville policy was to be put most acutely under strain by the pressures of French politics, particularly following de Gaulle's resignation. The chapter considers in turn the political and ideological parameters of policy, and the institutional structures underpinning policy. It then examines the effects of domestic political crisis after January 1946.

The Political and Ideological Model Holds, 1944–1945

The priority accorded colonial policy in Algiers and Brazzaville was clearly never going to survive the return to Paris at the Liberation. The relative salience of colonial affairs thus dropped dramatically in the face of the problems which now faced the Provisional Goverment amidst the political, economic, and moral devastation of metropolitan France. Indeed, this shift in priorities was symbolically marked within a few weeks of the GPRF's return to Paris, when René Pleven, the able and dynamic Minister of Colonies, was moved to the much more important portfolio of Economy and Finance.[4] Nonetheless, this partial return to the traditional low salience of colonial affairs in French domestic politics was offset by a continuing high degree of ideological support for the new policy, which in turn was reflected in an admittedly rather ambiguous consensus on the part of the emerging and re-emerging political parties. At the same time, de Gaulle's continued leadership as President of the GPRF ensured the loyalty of the colonial administration and the smooth functioning of its institutions. Thus the reality of political life seemed to be working, albeit imperfectly, in favour of the Brazzaville policy.

Colonial officials and those politicians with an interest in colonial affairs could claim some limited success in their efforts to foster interest in imperial affairs. After all, the new policy had received the endorsement of de Gaulle, and the Brazzaville 'spirit' ensured that at least lip-service was paid to the importance of empire. Gaston Monnerville, Chair of the Consultative Assembly's

---

3. B. Lanne, 'Le Tchad pendant la guerre', in IHTP, *Les chemins de la décolonisation de l'empire français*, Paris, 1986, 440.
4. His predecessor, Aimé Lepercq (no party), had been killed in a car crash.

Overseas France Commission, was merely reflecting the mood of the times when he declared:

> Ladies and Gentlemen, let us never forget: without the Empire, France would be merely a liberated country. Thanks to her Empire, France counts amongst the victors.[5]

To meet supposed French interest in the Empire, an Information Division (*Direction de l'Information*) was created at the Rue Oudinot and in March 1945, Paul Giacobbi, Pleven's successor as Minister, sponsored a small Colonial Exhibition, remembering no doubt the Great Colonial Exhibition of 1931, which had awakened Parisians to the exoticism of Empire, if not to its political importance.[6] Starting in July, Laurentie gave a series of talks on the radio, commenting weekly on a theme of colonial interest. The message could reasonably be supposed to be striking home: in an poll conducted in May 1945, only 10 percent of respondents disagreed with the proposition that France was once again a Great Power; as the pollsters commented, 'If France was still great, it was because of the Empire and its resources'.[7]

However, it was doubtful whether this new awareness of empire could be translated into backing for the new policy. Imperial reformism was too readily overshadowed by other issues; politics was largely dominated by the purges of Vichy supporters and collaborationists, by de Gaulle's jockeying for position with the Communists and other Resistance groups, by the problem of food and fuel shortages, and by the question of economic reconstruction. Notwithstanding the rhetoric of imperial 'gratitude' and pride, commentators readily gained the impression that the domestic preoccupations of the Liberation had, if anything, hastened the return to time-honoured French traditions of indifference to the affairs of Empire. Thus, George Orwell, passing through Paris in March 1945, noted that the Japanese overthrow of the French administration in Indochina had 'set many people talking about

5. 'Mesdames, messieurs, ne l'oublions jamais: sans l'Empire, la France ne serait aujourd'hui qu'un pays libéré. Grâce à son Empire la France est un pays vainqueur. (Applaudissements.)' *Journal Officiel, Assemblée Consultative Provisoire* (JOACP), no. 39, 15 May 1945, 1049.

6. See R. Girardet, *L'idée coloniale en France de 1871 à 1962*, Paris, 1972, 25.

7. 'Si la France était grande, c'était par l'Empire et ses ressources'; C.-R. Ageron, 'L'opinion publique et l'Union Française', in IHTP, *Les chemins*, 34. The texts of Laurentie's radio talks are in 'Chronique', AN, 72AJ535.

the half-forgotten problem of the French colonies'. As he argued, the French were 'not Empire-minded':

> the average Frenchman is only intermittently interested in imperial policy.... This has been especially true since the Liberation. Except when something violent happens, the French overseas territories hardly find their way into the French press.[8]

Orwell's arguments were borne out by a lacklustre colonial debate in the Consultative Assembly, the first since the Liberation, also in March, in which, as Monnerville commented, the empty benches were a disappointing reminder of earlier days. In ironic counterpoint to Orwell's observations, one delegate's explanation of the lack of imperial press coverage was simple: 'It's the paper shortage!'[9]

This period of relatively low salience for colonial affairs coincided with Laurentie's development of the liberal doctrine underpinning the Brazzaville policy: there was perhaps something to be said for policy making out of the glare of public attention. Moreover, colonial liberals could draw comfort from the extent to which the new policy conformed to the terms of two prevailing and, in this field at least, overlapping ideologies: Gaullism and Republicanism. As will be seen, whilst neither ideology offered unambiguous or unqualified support for the Brazzaville policy, the ideological case was still relatively clear in favour of the new policy as of 1945.

Gaullism was the most obviously instrumental ideology at each of the three stages described in the introduction to this chapter. It provided first and foremost a context for colonial policy making: the Brazzaville policy was not only the reflection of the imperial perspective which necessarily dominated wartime Gaullism, but it also formed an essential part of the Gaullist programme for rebuilding French greatness (*grandeur*). Thus, too, the theme of French imperial gratitude might largely be glossed as *Gaullist* gratitude for proving de Gaulle right in his 'Appel' of 18 June 1940.[10] Moreover, as Jean Lacouture reminds us, the Empire formed part of the triptych of attributes which de Gaulle claimed to have kept in trust and restored to France at the moment of the

8. 'De Gaulle Intends to Keep Indo-China. But French Apathetic on Empire', *Observer*, 18 Mar. 1945.

9. 'C'est la crise du papier!'. JOACP, no. 27, 20 Mar. 1945, 556–74; and no. 28, 21 Mar. 1945, 579–92.

10. E.g., Laurentie's lecture at the Palais de Chaillot in January 1945, on the no doubt stirring theme of 'L'Empire au secours de la métropole': text in AN, 72AJ535.

Liberation: 'independence, the Empire, the Sword'.[11] Second, Gaullist aims informed and infused the Brazzaville policy. Thus, as has been shown, Laurentie's institutional model for the French Union assumed that Gaullist constitutional ideals of a strong executive would be reflected in an eventual Constitution.[12] Third, de Gaulle's imprimatur as the Man of Brazzaville was a powerful instrument for legitimizing the new concern for liberal imperial reform. The Brazzaville epithet was not always applied responsibly or greeted with universal approval, but it did carry weight in Paris after the Liberation. Gaullists tended to stress the General's pronouncements best suiting their purposes: for Laurentie this was de Gaulle's helpfully explicit support for a federal imperial system, or at least for 'a French system where everyone would have a role to play'.[13]

More generally, Gaullism suggested a new pragmatic methodology for imperial policy, according to which reform was geared to a calculation of French interests (chiefly understood in terms of greatness). As has been suggested, it was from this basic imperial equation that the new Federal idea was derived. By the same token, however, the pragmatism of de Gaulle's own apparent attitude to Empire belied any idea of a deep commitment to imperial affairs on his part, much less of the powers of a prophet of decolonisation, as implied in his *War Memoirs*.[14] It followed that the terms of the imperial equation could be altered to match changes, or perceived changes, in French interests. These interests, however, could often be interpreted quite narrowly: as the Syrian furore demonstrated, contradicting Laurentie's subtleties, de Gaulle could easily be distracted by more traditionally 'imperialist' concerns, in this case good old-fashioned Anglo-French rivalry. As will be seen in Part Two, the reversion of Gaullism to a simple imperialist attitude of 'what we have we hold' had a decisive influence on Indochina policy. Is it possible to distinguish between

11. 'L'indépendance, l'Empire, l'épée'. J. Lacouture, *De Gaulle*, 3 vols, vol. 2, *Le politique, 1944–1959*, Paris, 1985, 154; C. de Gaulle, *Mémoires de Guerre*, 3 vols, vol. 3, *Le salut*, Paris, 1970, 1, 91.

12. See above, Ch. 2.

13. '… un système français où chacun jouera son rôle.' C. de Gaulle, *Discours et messages*, 3 vols., vol. 1, *Pendant la guerre, juin 1940–janvier 1946*, Paris, 1970, 25 Oct. 1944, 464–65. See Chs 1 and 2.

14. E.g., *Mémoires de guerre*, vol. 3, 213. J. Touchard is sceptical not of de Gaulle's sincerity but of its timing: as he points out, this third volume of the *Mémoires* appeared in the shops shortly after de Gaulle's offer of Algerian self-determination on 16 September 1959, in *Le gaullisme, 1940–1969*, Paris, 1972, 82.

Gaullism and what might be called De Gaullism, an ideological attitude determined primarily or exclusively by loyalty to the General? The distinction which may be made is a subtle one. On the one hand, as will be seen in Part Two, Gaullists such as Laurentie displayed a clear capacity to diverge from the General's policy, though during his tenure as President of the GPRF they did so at their peril. On the other hand, Gaullism was still a radically new ideology which depended in large part on the contiuous, if not necessarily consistent, input of its founding 'charismatic ideologist'.[15] Certainly the concept of Gaullism without de Gaulle at the helm was as yet unthinkable, and would remain so for a quarter-century.

Republicanism was more established and less volatile than Gaullism, but no less problematic in its application to colonial policy. The difficulty lay in deciding which tenets of Republican doctrine to apply to colonial policy, and which to downplay. Indeed, this was a problem which had exercised both Republicans and colonialists since the early days of the Third Republic.[16] Republicanism, understood as the extension of the 1789 Declaration of the Rights of Man and of the Citizen and of the principles of 'Liberty, Equality, Fraternity' to the peoples of Overseas France, was a lofty ideal to which the delegates at Brazzaville and leftist politicians could readily lay claim. This was in large part what was understood by the Brazzaville 'spirit', an entity which was as often alluded to as it was imprecisely defined. More significantly, this aspect of Republicanism found concrete expression both in the humanitarian reforms recommended at Brazzaville and in the text of the March 1945 Declaration on Indochina. Moreover, in the left-wing atmosphere of Parisian politics in this period, the experience of the Popular Front offered a useful if cautionary precedent for the application of Republican principles to colonial policy. The Brazzaville policy could thus be depicted, without too much imagination, as a second chance to carry out the colonial reforms which had been promised but never realised in 1936–37. The Syrian crisis acted in this sense as a warning shot across French bows, as the Consultative Assembly was reminded by Madame Viénot, widow of the Popular Front minister Pierre Viénot (SFIO) who had negotiated the ill-fated treaties of 1936 with the Syrian and Lebanese nationalists.[17] This impression of continuity with pre-war aims was

15. H.M. Johnson, 'Ideology', 78.
16. Girardet, *L'idée coloniale*, passim.
17. JOACP, no. 29, 21 Mar. 1945, 1120.

reinforced by the continued political role of the architects of the Popular Front's colonial policy, Léon Blum and Marius Moutet, the latter of whom returned to the Rue Oudinot as Minister of Overseas France in January 1946.[18]

Two substantial stumbling-blocks hindered any attempt to harness Republican ideals too tightly to the Brazzaville policy. These were the doctrine of the One and Indivisible Republic, and the intellectual nemesis of Laurentie's thesis, Assimilationism. The obstacle which both doctrines represented for the proponents of the Brazzaville policy has already been illustrated in the persistence of assimilationist ideas at Brazzaville, and in the arguments of Jules Moch in the internal debate on federalism.[19] However, the real danger was not that Republicans would reject the new policy, but that they would dilute or compromise it. This danger was already apparent in the inclusion of African representation in the Constituent Assembly, following one of the more durable recommendations of the Brazzaville Conference. This was a measure which was acceptable within a federalist framework only if it did not set a precedent for an eventual Constitution (which it did). As will be seen below, the application of Republican doctrines to colonial policy would become a matter of urgency once the Constituent Assembly sat down in early 1946 to the process of drawing up a set of French Union articles for the new Constitution.

The combination of low political salience (except in the aftermath of the Syrian and Algerian crises) and ideological convergence in favour of imperial reformism was apparently enough to ensure a consensus on the part of the political parties, which shared de Gaulle's preoccupation with domestic politics, and which were anyway in the process of reorganisation or formation. Here again, a return to the pre-war status quo could be detected: colonial affairs had rarely been a party issue and, as Orwell noted, the left-wing parties possessed little of the anti-imperialist tradition of the Labour Party (even if this last was 'no doubt partly hypocritical').[20] As Andrew Shennan has shown, the parties were slow to formulate a response to the momentum achieved at Brazzaville, and colonial policy remained the province of a handful of

18. See Ch.-A. Julien, 'Léon Blum et les pays d'outre-mer', in P. Renouvin and R. Rémond, eds, *Léon Blum, Chef de Gouvernement*, Paris, 1967, 377–90; W.B. Cohen, 'The Colonial Policy of the Popular Front', *French Historical Studies*, VII, 3, 1972, 368–93.

19. See above, Chs 1 and 2.

20. Orwell, 'De Gaulle Intends'.

'experts', in many instances the same men who had already participated in the imperial debate in Algiers: this was notably the case for Pierre-Olivier Lapie (SFIO), Paul-Emile Viard (MRP, Dean of the Algiers Law School), and André Mercier (PCF), who had sat on the Algiers Expert Commission.[21] Moreover, in many instances, these colonial specialists were in close contact with the Ministry of Colonies: Lapie corresponded with Laurentie, as did another MRP colonial spokesman, Jean-Jacques Juglas, a future Minister of Overseas France (briefly, in the Mendès-France government, 1955).[22] Overseas *députés* elected to the Constituent Assembly in October 1945 further added to the ranks of colonial specialists (and future Ministers), including Léopold Senghor (SFIO, Sénégal, Non-Citizens' College), whose literary talents as an academic historian were to be called upon in the Constitutional Commission, and Dr Louis Aujoulat (MRP, Cameroun, Citizens' College), a medical doctor employed at the Catholic Mission in Yaoundé and thus one of the first to symbolise the link between the brand new People's Republican Movement (*Mouvement Républicain Populaire*, or MRP), and the missions.[23]

What passed for a consensus might perhaps better be described as a doctrinal fudge, blurring the distinction between federalism and assimilation which was to form the somewhat artificial basis for the disagreements of the following year. In one form or another, this ambiguity may be detected in the position of all three major parties at the Liberation: MRP, Socialists, and Communists. In a sense, Laurentie had least to fear from the Christian Democratic MRP, which was formed partly as the ex-Resistance party of Gaullist loyalism, and which professed a liberal, Republican Catholicism resembling Laurentie's own. Ronald Irving has clarified, to an extent, the apparent contradiction in MRP colonial policy, which saw the party support progressive colonial reformism, at the same time as its followers within the administration were responsible for some of its most retrograde actions (notably Governor-General Pierre de Chevigné, the 'pacifier' of Madagascar

---

21. A. Shennan, *Rethinking France*, Cambridge, 1989, 44. Viard and Mercier also sat on the 1944 *Commission des Réformes Musulmanes*: see G. Pervillé, 'La commission des réformes musulmanes de 1944 et l'élaboration d'une nouvelle politique algérienne de la France', in IHTP, *Les chemins*, 357–65.

22. AN, 72AJ535.

23. G. Wright, *The Reshaping of French Democracy*, London, 1950, 18; Bulletins de vote, AOM, AP/935. Aujoulat's liberal colonial credo is established in *La vie et l'avenir de l'Union Française*, Paris, 1948.

after the 1947 Insurrection).[24] Nonetheless, early doctrinal discussions marked a clear distinction between the assimilationist position of Viard, which he expounded to the first Constitutional Commission, and the more advanced theses of Aujoulat, reflected in the MRP's first Congress Resolution on the subject.[25] As Irving shows, these two positions merged in Georges Bidault's concept of 'progressive federalism', although in Bidault's case this amalgam concealed a far more conservative basic instinct.[26]

The two major Marxist parties adopted the traditional fence-sitting position of parliamentary parties of the Left on this issue, which might be resumed in Augustinian terms as 'independence, but not yet'. This position was eloquently expressed by Léon Blum in his speech to the National Assembly accepting the fait accompli of hostilities in Indochina, on 23rd December 1946:

> According to our republican doctrine, colonial possession only reaches its final goal and is justified the day it ceases, that is, the day when a colonised people has been given the capacity to live emancipated and to govern itself. The coloniser's reward is then to have earned the colonised people's gratitude and affection, to have brought about interpenetration and solidarity in thought, culture and interests, thus allowing coloniser and colonised to unite freely.[27]

More concretely, however, the same divergence may be traced in SFIO doctrine as in that of the MRP between the enthusiastic federalism of Lapie and the more traditional position of Marius Moutet who, in a meeting of colonial specialists at the Rue Oudinot, only two weeks before he became Minister, confessed that he believed in 'France's gift for assimilation'.[28] Moutet's opposition to federalism may be overstated, however, since his main objection,

24. *Christian Democracy in France*, London, 1973, 199–230.
25. Wright, *Reshaping of French Democracy*, 148–49; André Colin, Sec.-Gen. MRP to Soustelle, no. 325/CAB, 28 Dec. 1945, enclosing the 'Motion Coloniale adoptée par le 2e Congrès National du MRP', AOM, AP/214bis.
26. *Christian Democracy*, 202–03.
27. 'Dans notre doctrine républicaine, la possession coloniale n'atteint son but final et ne trouve sa justification que le jour où elle cesse, c'est-à-dire le jour où le peuple colonisé a été rendu pleinement capable de vivre émancipé et de se gouverner lui-même. La récompense du peuple colonisateur est alors d'avoir suscité dans le peuple colonisé des sentiments de gratitude et d'affection, d'avoir créé la pénétration et la solidarité de pensée, de culture, d'intérêts, qui permettent à l'un et l'autre de s'unir librement.' *Journal Officiel, Assemblée Nationale, Débats* (JOAN), 24 Dec. 1946, 320.
28. '… si j'avais quelque chose à dire, je croirais à la vertu assimilatrice de la France'. 'Séance de la Commission du jeudi 10 janvier 1946', AOM, AP/215. The

in line with one of Jules Moch's arguments largely conceded by Laurentie in Algiers, was that federalism should only be allowed to develop gradually:

> I do not believe that we will create federalism just like that. It comes about and may arise out of history or politics, but it is not simply created. You can only federate what already exists.... In politics you have to work with reality. Things come into being but it is very difficult to create them.

Moreover, Laurentie could be reassured on one crucial point: concerning Indochina, Moutet believed that the French would be obliged to 'adopt a policy aimed at liberty, like that adopted by the Americans in the Philippines'.[29]

Ironically, however, it was perhaps the PCF's colonial doctrine which was closest to that of liberals at the Rue Oudinot. The ambiguity of its position was thus of a different order. It was now a decade since the Communists had abandoned their Leninist anticolonialism in favour of the Popular Front strategy. (The period of the Nazi-Soviet pact, 1939–41, was largely overlooked.) Participants in both the CFLN at Algiers and in the GPRF, Communists revived the concessionary position on the colonies adopted at the time of the Popular Front of 1936–37, that 'the right to divorce does not mean the obligation to divorce'.[30] The reasoning behind the PCF's position, as explained by Henri Lozeray, the Party's chief colonial specialist, in an article in a party journal, could readily be squared with two essential justifications for the Brazzaville policy, namely anti-capitalist suspicion of 'trusts', also a Gaullist tenet, and nationalist suspicion of 'the Anglo-Saxons':

> 1. Because it is the aim of the French nation, in its fight against the trusts which betray us at the same time as they plunder the colonies, to install a true democracy; this aim cannot fail to bring democracy to the colonial populations;

---

meeting was called by Jacques Soustelle, Minister of Colonies from November 1945 until de Gaulle's resignation. On Lapie, see M.J. Shipway, 'The Brazzaville Conference, 1944: Colonial and Imperial Planning in a Wartime Setting', M. Phil. thesis, University of Oxford, 1986, 66–67.

29. 'Je ne crois pas qu'on fera le Fédéralisme. Il se crée, il naît historiquement et politiquement, mais on ne le fait pas. On ne fédère que ce qui existe.... Il faut travailler politiquement dans le réel. Les choses deviennent, mais il est bien difficile de les créer.... [Nous serons] 'obligés ... de prendre une politique qui l'orientera vers la liberté, comme les Américains ont donné aux Philippines'. Ibid.

30. '... le droit de divorcer ne signifie pas l'obligation de divorcer': see Cohen, 'Colonial Policy'.

2. Because the lands occupied by these populations are threatened by covetous external forces, at a time when they are not in a position to ensure for themselves a truly independent existence.[31]

Moreover, the shift detected by Grégoire Madjarian, from the out-and-out assimilationism of the war years to recognition of the importance and legitimacy of colonial nationalism (shown elsewhere in Lozeray's article), served to bring the PCF line even closer to Laurentie's. Even in the face of growing Cold War tensions, and increasing official anti-Communism, this line remained remarkably consistent, while Party ministers and *députés* alike maintained a low profile on the colonial issue. For example, notwithstanding the Party's enthusiastic welcome for Ho Chi Minh and the Viet Minh delegation to the Fontainebleau conference in summer 1946, for example, its official representative, Lozeray, maintained a tactful, if watchful, silence during the whole of the conference proceedings.[32]

The political and ideological basis for policy could thus be said to be shaping up quite acceptably for the champions of the new liberalism on the eve of France's first substantial post-war imperial venture: the 'return' to Indochina. Given a state of benign public indifference, a high degree of ideological support and a wide measure of party acquiescence, only one element remained to be assessed: to what extent was the administration either willing or able to carry out the tasks allotted to it?

Institutional Solidarity and the Administrative Hierarchy

The parameter of institutional solidarity, identified in the introduction to this chapter, was in a sense more closely determined by

31. '1° Parce que la nation française en lutte contre les trusts qui la trahissent en même temps qu'ils pillent les colonies, veut instaurer une démocratie véritable, qui ne pourra qu'apporter la démocratie à ces populations coloniales;

'2° Parce que les terres habitées par ces populations sont l'objet de convoitises redoutables pour elles, alors qu'elles ne sont pas en état de garantir une existence vraiment indépendante.' H. Lozeray, 'La question coloniale', Cahiers du communisme, no. 6, Apr. 1945, 71–76, partially reprinted in J. Moneta, *La politique du Parti communiste français dans la question coloniale, 1920–1963*, Paris, 1971, 150–52.

32. G. Madjarian, *La question coloniale et la politique du Parti communiste français, 1944–1947*, Paris, 1977, 240–41; A. Ruscio, *Les communistes français et la guerre d'Indochine, 1944–1954*, Paris, 1985, 116–18. On Fontainebleau, see below, Ch. 8.

pre-war practice, and therefore more predictable. Thus, whilst the makers of the new imperial policy had clear ideas as to the faults of the pre-war system, and ambitious plans for reforming it, and whilst the question of official loyalty was of particular relevance in the aftermath of Vichy, the policy makers' task was more a question of fitting their model to the pre-existing administrative structure than vice versa. Indeed, it was only in the case of Indochina that any substantial institutional change was effected by the GPRF. If qualified satisfaction was warranted, therefore, both on the question of loyalty and in terms of institutional structure, it was an open question, here too, as to how far these factors would withstand the rigours of domestic political crisis.

Official loyalties were much called into question in the early days following the Liberation, but were never really an issue. Initially, perhaps, the Brazzaville policy was important as a propaganda tool in the Gaullists' struggle for acceptance and legitimacy. But the veterans of Brazzaville in the colonial administration shared the predicament of the GPRF as a whole: how to ensure both loyalty to the new ideals and administrative continuity. Almost inevitably the former of these two goals took lesser priority, and though the Ministry of Colonies had its own Purge Committee (*Commission d'Epuration*), the function of this committee was more to intimidate than it was to punish those with lingering sympathies for Vichy. In all but a very few cases the old personnel were retained, though there were some notable, and perhaps arbitrary, victims.[33] As Laurentie argued, in a letter to Pignon, the problem was one of official morale as well as of political loyalties: 'You cannot imagine what it is like for an administration to have lived under this crushing regime for four long years and to have had nothing useful to do for two years'.[34] The Brazzaville policy served therefore as a means of ensuring loyalty and cooperation, though it is doubtful whether this tactic could achieve more than the substitution of one form of conformism for another.

---

33. H. Deschamps, *Roi de la brousse*, Paris, 1975, 88: Deschamps (Gvr, Côte Française des Somalis, 1940; Gvr, Côte d'Ivoire, 1941–43) resigned in 1945 when Giacobbi questioned his 1940 decision not to resist the Italian invasion of Djibouti. See also P. Novick, *The Resistance versus Vichy: The Purge of Collaborators in Liberated France*, London, 1968, 86–93.

34. 'Vous ne pouvez imaginer ce que c'est pour un service administratif d'avoir vécu sous ce régime écrasant pendant quatre années et de n'avoir rien eu à faire d'utile depuis deux ans.' Laurentie to Pignon, 25 Sep. 1944, AN, 72AJ539.

Considerable resentment was evinced by senior officials who had stayed at their posts during the Vichy period. They now saw their authority usurped by Gaullists who were either new to the service or who, like Laurentie, had been relatively junior at the outbreak of war. Amongst those who had endured the Occupation in this way was Louis Mérat, the director of Moutet's private office in 1935/36 (*directeur du cabinet*, a post he regained when the veteran SFIO minister returned to the Rue Oudinot in 1946), and whose public denunciation of the hypocritical Brazzaville 'spirit', and of tardy or opportunist Gaullist supporters ('rallieurs de la dernière heure'), has already been quoted.[35] For their part, the newcomers amply reciprocated the old guard's mistrust. Like that of many Gaullists, Laurentie's vehemence was in part highly personal: his return to Paris enabled him to make contact with his four children, but not with his wife, who, denounced as a 'dissident', was still in captivity 'in a camp somewhere in Mecklenburg, where she is certainly enduring considerable suffering'. It was galling to suspect that her informer was most probably still working in the Ministry.[36]

As Part Two will demonstrate, the implementation of the Brazzaville policy would depend in large part on the functioning of the administrative hierarchy, and on questions concerning the chain of command and the exercise of authority, both within the Ministry and between the ministry and the colonial administration in the field. First, then, how great was Laurentie's authority as Director of Political Affairs to impose the Brazzaville policy? On the one hand, he had been catapulted, as a relative junior in both age and rank, into potentially the most influential post within the colonial hierarchy. Noted already by Eboué for 'his strong personality and brutal frankness', Laurentie's modus operandi at the Rue Oudinot was nothing if not abrasive.[37] But he was temperamentally well-suited to his highly proactive view of his office, and relished the thought that the odds were stacked against him. As he wrote to de Gaulle, 'We have a magnificent colonial policy, but there are only

35. See above, Ch. 1.

36. Laurentie to Pignon, 25 Sep. 1944, loc.cit; a 'Note pour Monsieur le Ministre', HL/og, 6 Apr. 1945, identifies the likely culprit, still working in the *Direction du Personnel*, AN, 72AJ535. Mme Laurentie returned to Paris the following summer.

37. '… sa forte personnalité et sa brutale franchise', AOM, 39 APOM 2–3. Laurentie's successor, Robert Delavignette, was four years his senior, and was promoted Governor-General on his appointment in March 1947.

a dozen of "us" in France and the colonies'.[38] On the other hand, Laurentie had to confront longstanding ambiguities within the administrative chain of command. Whilst Laurentie appeared to be 'number two' within the Ministry, he was in reality second among equals within the colonial administration as a whole.[39] The Director of Political Affairs was obliged to compete for the Minister's ear not only with other senior personnel within the ministry, but also with the 'proconsuls', i.e., the Governors and Governors-General. Whilst the Political Affairs Division (*Direction des Affaires Politiques*, or DAP) was arguably the most influential within the Ministry, and was certainly conceived as such, the Directors were all of equal status, and the Divisions existed in parallel series at one remove from the Minister. Laurentie thus competed with Georges Péter, Director of Economic Affairs, and with Raphaël Saller, Planning Director, a post created in February 1945 to administer the Investment Fund for Social and Economic Development (*Fonds d'Investissement pour le Développement Economique et Social*, or FIDES) set up the following year. The ethos of the different Divisions was well caught in an anonymous memorandum sent to Governor-General Cournarie, which contrasted the DAP's 'socio-political liberalism which no-one in the colonies asked for' with the 'capitalist tendencies' of the Economic Affairs Division (DAE) and the 'socialist tendencies' of the Planning Division.[40] This competition was particularly marked between the DAP and Péter's DAE, whose primary preoccupation (particularly while the war continued) was with meeting economic targets irrespective of longer-term political goals.

The greatest prospective headache for policy makers, however, had its source not in the Ministry of Colonies but in the palaces of the Governors-General. The four Governments-General at Dakar, Brazzaville, Tananarive, and Hanoi had been established around the turn of the century in order to impose policy emanating from Paris more effectively on recalcitrant colonial governments; the High-Commissioner for the Cameroun in Douala was added to their number in 1920. However, the proconsuls' independence from Paris was an essential part of the French Colonial Service's

38. 'Nous avons une grande politique coloniale, nous, c'est-à-dire, en France et aux colonies, une douzaine de personnes.' NOTE PERSONNELLE pour M. le Général de Gaulle, 28 Dec. 1944, AN, 72AJ535.

39. W. Wainwright in Institut Charles-de-Gaulle, *Le général de Gaulle et l'Indochine*, Paris, 1982, 9. See Appendix I, The Administrative Structure of Empire, 1945.

40. 'Situation en AOF à fin juillet 1945', 22 Jul. 1945, AOM, Cab/14.

unofficial tradition, enshrined over decades. Despite successive ministers' efforts, notably Moutet's in 1936-38, the proconsuls' power was still intact in 1944–45; this power favoured stability and continuity, not reform. As Laurentie complained to de Gaulle:

> Our Governors and Governors-General are conscientious administrators almost to a man, very sensitive to the problems of a sub-district, but with no understanding of general political questions.[41]

Proconsular power, combined with the bureaucrat's elective affinity with the established order, was amply in evidence over the summer of 1945, as Laurentie lost the battle to implement the Monnerville Commission's liberal proposals for the electoral system in Black Africa. Although plans were drawn up for rationalising the colonial hierarchy in favour of Paris, these largely came to nothing.[42]

The arbiter in these internal contests was the Minister. Laurentie lost his principal backer when Pleven moved to the Ministry of Economy and Finance (where he continued to champion the Brazzaville policy).[43] His successor, Paul Giacobbi, was a less bankable proposition. A Radical senator from Corsica, Giacobbi had voted against the granting of full powers to Pétain in July 1940; he was thus one of only a few experienced parliamentarians in the Consultative Assembly in Algiers. Notwithstanding his membership of the 1944 Commission for Muslim Reforms, his passport to the Rue Oudinot consisted of his 'powerful antennae in Corsican circles, which still have such an influence amongst colonial personnel.'[44] Giacobbi's was not a forceful personality, and he lacked both the enthusiasm and the imagination of his predecessor. Within a few weeks of his arrival, Laurentie complained to de Gaulle that the service seemed to have 'sunk back into the rut so beloved by the

41. '... nos gouverneurs et même nos gouverneurs-généraux sont, sauf exception, de bons agents consciencieux ..., fort attentifs aux soucis d'une subdivision, fort incompréhensifs des problèmes politiques généraux.' NOTE PERSONNELLE pour M. le Général de Gaulle, loc.cit; J.-R. Benoist, *La balkanisation de l'Afrique Occidentale Française*, Dakar, 1979, 45–47.

42. D. Bouche, 'L'administration de l'Afrique occidentale française et les libertés démocratiques (1944–1946)', in IHTP, *Les chemins*, 467–79; R. Saller, Note, 'Les réformes nécessaires', 12 Jun. 1945, AOM, AP/214.

43. In August 1945 Laurentie appealed twice to Pleven over Giacobbi's head: see AN, 72AJ535. Laurentie was later to act as Pleven's Technical Adviser (*conseiller technique*) during the latter's second, brief, premiership in 1951.

44. '... des antennes puissantes dans le milieu corse toujours influent au sein du personnel colonial'. Pervillé, 'La commission des réformes musulmanes'. See also C. de Gaulle, *Mémoires de Guerre*, vol. 2, *L'unité, 1942–1944*, Paris, 1970, P.-H. Siriex, *Félix Houphouët-Boigny, L'homme de la paix*, Paris and Dakar/Abidjan, 1975, 5.

majority, but unbearable to the others'.[45] However, Giacobbi's lack of dynamism arguably enhanced the influence of his Director of Political Affairs, who retained a higher profile than his Minister, often drafting notes and telegrammes sent out over his superior's signature. Giacobbi was, for example, merely the mouthpiece for the March 1945 Declaration on Indochina.[46] Moreover, Laurentie enjoyed sufficient favour with de Gaulle to be spared when he overstepped the mark, as he did spectacularly over Indochina policy in September 1945.[47] Inevitably, after the brief interregnum of Jacques Soustelle, from November 1945 until de Gaulle's resignation, Laurentie's influence was to lessen under the leadership of Marius Moutet, a man with far clearer ideas of reform than Giacobbi and with a far greater status within government. This state of affairs was nonetheless welcomed by Laurentie, who noted an improvement in the atmosphere at the Ministry and commented to a colleague that 'for the first time in a long time we have the impression of keeping abreast of events'.[48]

One further aspect of the overall structure of France's colonial administration needs to be considered, concerning the fact that France's colonies and protectorates were the responsibility of three fiercely independent ministries. Thus, Laurentie's reaction to the Algerian and Levant crises in May 1945 was one not only of alarm but also of frustration that his own services could only look on as the local administrations apparently prepared for 'the avalanche'. As he lamented:

> This urgent and dangerous situation is handled by an incoherent and inept administrative system. Unity of action, which is so obviously necessary, is ruled out because of the simultaneous responsibility of two separate ministries.[49]

45. 'Après un mois de son règne, on a l'impression d'avoir retourné à l'ornière, chère au plus grand nombre, insupportable au reste.' NOTE PERSONNELLE, 28 Dec. 1944, loc.cit.

46. See above, Ch. 2. Cf. Shennan, *Rethinking France*, 151–53: all three documents cited by Shennan were Laurentie's work. Giacobbi's *directeur du cabinet*, Max Defond, is all but invisible in the archives.

47. See below, Ch. 5.

48. '… pour la première fois depuis longtemps, on a le sentiment que l'on marche de pair avec les événements'. Laurentie to Bayardelle, 3 Apr. 1946, AOM, 72AJ538.

49. '… à cette actualité pressante et périlleuse on ne consacre pourtant qu'un système gouvernemental incohérent et incapable. L'unité d'action, manifestement indispensable, est contredite par la compétence simultanée de deux départements ministériels.' Ibid.

Moreover, neither of these was directly concerned with colonial affairs: Algeria was governed by a single Division within the Ministry of the Interior, while the Africa-Levant Division similarly held sway at the Quai d'Orsay. An interministerial North Africa Committee existed to coordinate policy: as Laurentie commented, 'Is it not rather a matter of directing policy?' As he summed up the situation in North Africa:

> North Africa's 'colonial' problem, which is both intrinsically serious and highly contagious, thus eludes the Government's 'colonial' efforts, even as the problem grows more acute by the day.[50]

Indeed, the debate concerning the structure of the French Union itself provided an example of the working of the so-called 'sealed bulkheads' ('cloisons étanches') which separated off North African policy from other areas of colonial concern. Thus the protectorates were at first included in a separate category within the proposed imperial hierarchy in order not to contravene their internationally guaranteed status; and one of the reasons for the limiting of the agenda of the Monnerville Commission was because of the refusal by the Africa-Levant Division at the Quai d'Orsay to discuss the inclusion of the protectorates within the French Union in the absence of an 'extensive preliminary study'.[51]

It was perhaps in its very complexity that reform of the administrative hierarchy of the Empire was most urgent and least likely. Laurentie for one envisaged a radically reformed administrative system which would combine the virtues of regional specialisation and central metropolitan control. Thus there would be a Ministry for Indochina, one for North Africa and at least one other to cover Black Africa, Madagascar and other colonies. Nor would it be excessive to put so many separate administrations to work, given the Empire's state of flux, which meant that precedents and traditions were increasingly irrelevant. At the same time, the need for political unity and governmental efficiency remained imperative; Laurentie proposed the creation of a colonial 'super-Minister' who alone would sit in the Council of Ministers and would be

50. 'Ne s'agirait-il plutôt d'ordonner?... Le problème 'colonial' de l'Afrique du Nord, avec tout ce qu'il comporte de mal intrinsèque et de contagion, échappe à l'action 'coloniale' du Gouvernement, cependant qu'il devient chaque jour plus aigu.' Ibid.

51. '... une étude préalable et approfondie'. Commission d'études de la représentation des territoires d'outre-mer à l'Assemblée Constituante, 1ère séance, 11 Apr. 1946, AOM, AP/215. See above, Ch. 2.

constitutionally responsible for colonial policy overall. Such calls for a shake-up of the administrative system constituted a recurring theme in the DAP's campaign for imperial reform.[52]

In the event, however, structural reform was introduced in only one relatively minor way, which nonetheless had far-reaching consequences. This account of administrative structures has so far given little attention to Indochina. Indeed, Indochina policy was something of an exception in the eyes of officials since it was largely a theoretical issue until a full year had passed after the Liberation. Partly for this reason, however, it was an exception also in that the Indochinese administrative structure alone underwent significant change at this period. Much of this change was related to the March 1945 Declaration, and will be examined in the following chapter. One change, however, reflects chiefly on the overall question of institutional solidarity as considered here. This was the creation in February 1945 of an Interministerial Committee for Indochina (*Comité Interministériel de l'Indochine*, or Comindo). Indochina had traditionally been a fiefdom of the Ministry of Colonies. Nonetheless, it was clear that neither the Action Committee (*Comité d'Action*) established in 1944 nor the ad hoc negotiations which led to the March 1945 Declaration on Indochina provided an adequate framework for the interministerial approach needed for a successful 'return' to France's richest and most complex colony.[53] The Committee thus placed Indochina policy firmly under the control of de Gaulle, its Chairman ex officio. Also on the Committee sat the Ministers of Colonies (Vice-Chairman), Economy and Finance, War (a post also held by de Gaulle), and Foreign Affairs, and the head of intelligence (*Directeur-Général des Etudes et Recherches*). The Ministers were supported and often represented by senior officials: in the case of Colonies, this meant Laurentie, who played a key role on the Committee and who had an important ally in the Secretary-General of the Committee, François de Langlade, another Gaullist loyalist. Crucially, communications were to pass through the Secretariat-General. However, the corollary of better coordination and the concentration of power in de Gaulle's hands was that the influence of the Rue Oudinot was neutralised if necessary. Although broadly speaking

52. Eg. Laurentie's 'Schéma d'un programme général concernant l'organisation politique, administrative et économique d'outre-mer', 25 Jun. 1946, AN, 72AJ535.
53. See below, Ch. 5.

positive, therefore, the move had the possibly intentional effect of restricting the scope of potentially over-ambitious liberals in the Ministry of Colonies.

If policy makers at the Rue Oudinot could draw some satisfaction from the state of affairs in Paris in the year following the Liberation, this was because two basic requirements were met for successful policy making. First, a high degree of ideological support for the Brazzaville policy suggested that political leaders would not oppose the new policy. Ironically, political and public indifference to colonial affairs served to reinforce an official sense of security in this regard. But, as Orwell suggested, and as the Syrian and Algerian crises demonstrated, this complacency was shaken as soon as 'something violent' happened. Secondly, de Gaulle's authority provided considerable reassurance, but here, too, there were clouds on the horizon: the appointment of Admiral Georges Thierry d'Argenlieu, the ultimate Gaullist loyalist, as High Commissioner for Indochina in August 1945, suggested already that de Gaulle set store more by loyalty than by liberalism, at a time when Laurentie was pushing hard to impose a liberal policy in Indochina. As Laurentie commented: 'It is enough to make you wonder whether we have not completely gone off our heads, and whether, unlike Mr. Churchill, some of us would not like to be seen as the gravediggers of Empire'.[54] These were family squabbles, however, and de Gaulle's continued presence as Head of the GPRF at least ensured that the chain of command, somewhat tautened in the case of Indochina, would continue to be respected. What would happen when the domestic parameters of policy were no longer satisfied? As the onset of political crisis in 1946 was to reveal, this was a far from theoretical eventuality.

Crisis Breaks, 1946

Two major developments may be identified in French politics in 1946: the resignation of de Gaulle in January, and the drafting, rejection, and revision of a new Constitution. Both had a profound impact on colonial policy making. On the one hand, de Gaulle's unexpected departure removed at a stroke one of the principal

---

54. 'C'est véritablement à se demander si nous n'avons pas complètement perdu la tête et si, à l'inverse de Monsieur CHURCHILL, certains ne veulent pas être les fossoyeurs de l'Empire.' Laurentie to Bayardelle, 1 Sep. 1945, AN, 72AJ538.

ideological and institutional pillars of the Brazzaville policy. On the other hand, the process of Constitution making not only hastened the end of the ideological synthesis in favour of the Brazzaville policy, unstable though it may have been, but also turned colonial policy, very much to its detriment, into a matter of domestic political controversy. The specific impact of these changes on policy making will be studied in Part Two, in respect of Indochina. The rest of this chapter considers the changes wrought to the policy makers' model of domestic politics, both directly and indirectly, by the political crisis in Paris.

As has been argued, de Gaulle's importance for the Brazzaville policy was ultimately more as a focus of authority, loyalty, and legitimacy than as a colonial liberal. His departure from office on 20 January 1946 thus left a void at the centre of French politics at a moment of crucial importance, not least for Indochina policy. Over the following year in particular, his absence would be felt acutely in two ways. First, the command structure which he had adapted to his needs by the creation of Cominindo was now controlled by the unstable Tripartite coalition of MRP, SFIO, and PCF which succeeded de Gaulle. As will be seen, this was to be a matter of great importance, given the ministerial crises ensuing from the troubled gestation of the new Constitution. At crucial moments both for domestic politics and Indochina policy, in June and November-December 1946, France was without a properly constituted government, leaving Cominindo staffed by caretakers. Second, his resignation prompted a subtle but decisive shift in the ideological outlook of his supporters, in which the 'Man of the Eighteenth of June' ('l'homme du 18 juin') acquired an almost Arthurian aura as the guardian of legitimacy whose inevitable return would herald the hoped-for New France. Thus Philippe Devillers recalls High Commissioner d'Argenlieu's assertion in August 1946 that de Gaulle would soon be back, and that his own role was merely to 'keep things going while waiting for his return'.[55] D'Argenlieu's journal makes explicit his views on the post-de Gaulle Republic:

> With President de Gaulle's resignation, all authority disappears from the reborn State. For myself and so many others, this retreat from power signifies not merely a government crisis but a metamorphosis of the regime.[56]

55. '... [je] maintiens les choses en attendant qu'il revienne'. Institut Charles-de-Gaulle, *De Gaulle et l'Indochine*, 201.

56. 'Avec ce retrait du président de Gaulle, c'est l'autorité même de l'Etat renaissant qui s'en va. Pour moi et ... tant d'autres – ce retrait ne marque pas une crise

What future insubordination and betrayals were not possible according to this analysis? Moreover, de Gaulle continued to exert a strong, not entirely beneficial influence on policy. Thus, in his speech at Bayeux on 16 June 1946, with which he marked his partial return to the political fray, he advocated a form of Federation in which imperial unity clearly preceded liberal reform.[57] By August 1946, his advice on Indochina to his erstwhile protégé was limited to a lapidary and distinctly obstructive injunction: 'Laurentie, don't give Cochinchina to Ho Chi Minh!'[58]

The primary effect of the Constitution making process on perceptions of the Brazzaville policy was to bring to an end the consensus which had been achieved in favour of the new policy. The internal contradictions of this consensus may be deduced from the Union articles of the first Constitutional draft, drawn up at the request of the Constitutional Commission by the members of the Commission for Overseas France, who were considered to be better equipped for the task.[59] Many commentators have demonstrated the incoherence of this text, which failed to distinguish between the One and Indivisible Republic and the promise of a 'free, consented Union' ('une Union libre et consentie'), and which promised freedoms indiscriminately to individuals, on the principle of assimilationism, and to 'the peoples of Overseas France', as suggested by the federal principle.[60] Although generally applauded at the time, and initially accepted as the basis for the Union articles in the second draft following the May 1946 referendum, this first attempt dismayed Laurentie so much that he was on the point of offering his resignation. As he explained to Moutet, he stayed only to await the results of the referendum, 'with a last glimmer of hope, which was in fact realised'.[61]

In the eyes of the administration, things went from bad to worse in the debates surrounding the second draft. It was clear by the

ministérielle mais une métamorphose du régime.' G. Thierry d'Argenlieu, *Chronique d'Indochine, 1945–1947*, Paris, 1985, 27.

57. *Discours et messages*, vol. 2, *Dans l'attente, février 1946–avril 1958*, Paris, 1970, 5–11.

58. 'Laurentie, ne donnez pas la Cochinchine à Hô Chi Minh!'. 'Témoignage du gouverneur-général [*sic*] Henri Laurentie', in Institut Charles-de-Gaulle, *Le général de Gaulle et l'Indochine*, 231, 238.

59. Wright, *Reshaping French Democracy*, 145.

60. A. Grosser, *La IVe République et sa politique extérieure*, Paris, 1961, 247–49.

61. '… avec un reste d'espoir qui fut exaucé'. Note personnelle pour Monsieur le Ministre, 'Situation politique des colonies au début de juin 1946', 4 Jun. 1946, AOM, AP/214bis.

time of de Gaulle's Bayeux speech at the latest that Gaullist and Republican views of colonial policy had diverged: while Gaullist attitudes merged imperceptibly into imperialism, along with those of MRP conservatives such as Bidault, Republicans bickered in the Assembly over an exclusivist definition of 'Frenchness' which was the less palatable corollary of assimilationism. By a paradox, the equation of Assimilationism with colonial liberalism was made even as colonial Nationalist *députés* were being called upon to justify their presence in a French Assembly.[62] Federalism, meanwhile, by the indirect agency of de Gaulle, and Bidault's direct intervention, was adopted as the conservative option for the French Union, as MRP *députés* and others insisted on imposing the federal system from above, rather than allowing it to evolve over time. Even after the Rue Oudinot's intervention, the Union articles in the second constitutional draft were more coherent than in the first, but disappointing, in that they provided only the husk of an institutional structure for the French Union devoid of political substance. As Alfred Grosser argues, these articles were the fruits of a well-nigh impossible attempt to reconcile liberalism and centralism. Since Assimilation was the only doctrinally acceptable way to do this, and since the logical outcome of Assimilation, as spelled out by Edouard Herriot in the Assembly, was that 'France would become the colony of her former colones', a compromise had to be reached. As Grosser concludes wrily: 'It so happens that it is more tempting and easier to betray a moral principle than to go back on an administrative and political tradition'.[63]

Officials' declining confidence in the face of political crisis may be discerned more specifically in two shifts in the domestic parameters of policy, the effects of which will be discussed in Part Two, but which need to be mentioned here. The first of these concerned the policy's ideological acceptability, as policy makers came under the influence of a new ideological factor: anti-Communism. This was less a coherent ideology than a staining agent, gradually colouring policy as France edged closer to its own domestic Cold War. Initially, the Rue Oudinot had taken its lead from de Gaulle, who viewed the actions of the PCF with wary pragmatism: thus, in November 1945, de Gaulle admitted Communists into the GPRF,

---

62. Grosser, *La politique extérieure*, 250–51.
63. 'Il se trouve qu'il est plus tentant et plus facile de tricher avec un principe moral qu'avec une tradition politique et administrative', ibid., 250. Herriot's warning, that 'la France devient alors une colonie de ses anciennes colonies', is in JOANC, 27 Aug. 1946, 3334.

as they had participated also in the CFLN, but denied them ministerial control of the 'three levers which control foreign policy: Diplomacy, which expresses that policy, the Army, which supports it, and the Police, which guarantees it'.[64] Initially, there was little reason for the colonial administration to adopt anything other than a positive attitude, given the Communists' constructive role as described above. Rumours of infiltration by Communists or fellow-travellers into the administration were by and large dismissed, and Communist Study Groups (*Groupes d'Etudes Communistes*, or GEC) in major West African cities went largely unnoticed by the compilers of colonial political reports.[65] Crucially, the same realism informed the attitude of policy makers to those nationalists encountered in the colonies who happened to be Communists. This was the case with the Mahajana party in the French Indian Settlements, which was allied with both Congress and the All India Communist Party. As will be seen, it was most particularly the case with the GPRF's dealings with Ho Chi Minh's party, the *Viet Nam Doc Lap Dong Minh Hoi* (Viet Minh).

This effortful tolerance of Communist involvement in domestic and colonial affairs went against the grain, however, and in the event, it took only de Gaulle's precipitate departure from office, and the start of the Constituent Assembly's work, to tip the balance. There is no evidence to suggest that the PCF changed its tactics between the autumn of 1945 and the following spring. Nonetheless, its role in the Constitutional Commission was highly influential, not least regarding the drafting of the French Union articles. This was apparently enough to convince Laurentie and others like him of Communist disloyalty. As he wrote in his June 1946 memorandum to Moutet:

> In March 1946, when it was becoming obvious that world peace was not around the corner, the Communist Party started to interfere in the affairs of the still embryonic French Union, and at once completely distorted any understanding of the problem.[66]

64. '… les trois leviers qui commandent la politique étrangère, savoir: la Diplomatie qui l'exprime, l'Armée qui la soutient, la Police qui la couvre', de Gaulle, *Discours et messages*, vol. 1, 17 Nov. 1945, 650.

65. One supposed fellow traveller was André Latrille, Governor of Côte d'Ivoire, who reported with glee the whispers that his Palace in Abidjan was 'a nest of Stalinists' ('un repaire de Staliniens'): Rapport du Directeur des APAS, Dakar, no. 395 APS, Jun. 1945, AOM, 2G-45-115. On the GEC, see D.B. Marshall, *The French Colonial Myth and Constitution-Making in the Fourth Republic*, New Haven, 1973, 50–51.

66. 'Au mois de mars 1946, alors qu'il est visible que la paix du monde ne se fera pas, le parti communiste fait irruption dans l'Union Française qui s'échafaude à

This new attitude of open hostility on the part of the administration thus marked the almost predictable end of an uneasy honeymoon period. Without de Gaulle to keep the threat at bay, officials were now prepared to see conspiracy in every Communist initiative: reflecting on the party's support for the Malagasy *députés* in the Constituent Assembly, for example, Laurentie remarked that, having hesitated between ascribing this move to 'incompetence' or to 'treason', he had now decided on the latter. Conspiracy to what end? In the same note, Laurentie revealed a rather alarming streak of paranoia, concerning the strategies of the Great Powers in a hypothetical 'looming war'. Even without recourse to such apocalyptic predictions, however, officials were increasingly intolerant of Communist political success. This had an inevitable knock-on effect on attitudes towards colonial nationalists, especially the Viet Minh. The theme of Ho Chi Minh's adherence to Communist doctrines and tactics will thus recur with increasing insistence in the following chapters. Less than three months after the outbreak of war in Indochina, two months before the expulsion of PCF ministers from the Ramadier government, President Truman enunciated his own Cold War doctrine, on 12 March 1947, in a speech which lent international credibility to the trend in French political attitudes.

The second shift which may be observed, and which will be traced in the following chapters, was a wave of official disenchantment, not only with the emerging 'rule of the parties' ('régime des partis'), as de Gaulle slightingly referred to it, but also with the machinery of government and decision making. Colonial affairs were high on the political agenda in Parisian politics for much of 1946, but the situation was highly volatile. The French Union articles dominated, and indeed threatened to take over, the second Constituent Assembly's deliberations, but the price of political salience in this case was a highly acrimonious, and unproductive, contest between two clearly defined camps. On the one hand, colonist sympathies were given a focus by the second gathering of the new colonial lobby, the grandiosely styled Estates-General of French Colonisation (*Etats-Généraux de la Colonisation Française*), held in Paris in July 1945. While on the other hand, the increasingly vociferous colonial *députés* formed an Intergroup in the second Constituent Assembly dominated by Ferhat

peine et fausse d'emblée toutes les données du problème.' Note personnelle, 4 Jun. 1946, loc.cit.

Abbas's liberal Algerian nationalist movement (the *Amis de la Manifeste)* and the three elected Malagasy representatives of the newly formed Democratic Movement for Malagasy Renovation (*Mouvement Démocratique de la Rénovation Malgache*, or MDRM). An additional source of tension, from June to September, lay in Ho Chi Minh's presence in Paris, at the head of the Viet Minh delegation to the Fontainebleau Conference, which was as irksome for the Right as it was a source of encouragement to PCF and nationalist *députés* alike.[67]

Within two months of the inconclusive ending of the Fontainebleau negotiations, however, the salience of the colonial question had come full circle. As Laurentie commented bitterly on the eve of the November 1946 legislative elections:

> Colonial policy may have provided a pretext for slanging matches between the parties, but it is hardly enough to whet their appetites, and no-one in France is going to vote one way or the other because of Indochina or even Algeria. In other words, our cries of alarm do not penetrate beyond the antechambers of power.[68]

Laurentie and his colleagues were thus in a double bind: either colonial policy was viewed through the filter of domestic political concerns, and distorted, or it was ignored. Worse was to follow: the elections left France without a government for a full five weeks, during which time, as will be seen, the fate of liberal Indochina policy was largely sealed.[69] In these circumstances, the temptation for officials at all levels to take matters into their own hands was strong indeed and, as the following chapters will reveal, the liberal but headstrong Laurentie eventually proved to be no Saint Antony in this respect.

If at first it was hoped that prevailing political conditions in Paris might continue to fall within the political, ideological, and institutional parameters assumed by colonial policy makers, this hope

67. Wright, *Reshaping French Democracy*, 204–05; J. Tronchon, *L'insurrection malgache de 1947*, Paris and Fianarantsoa, 1974/86, 335–37: Malagasy *députés* presented Ho with a copy of their plans for the French Union.

68. '... la politique coloniale peut être devenue prétexte à injures entre les partis, mais c'est àpeine un hors d'oeuvre et personne ne votera en France en considération de l'Indochine, pas même de l'Algérie. Autant dire que nos cris de détresse se perdent dans le désert des antichambres.' Laurentie to Pignon, 9 Nov. 1946, AN, 72AJ539.

69. See below, Ch. 9.

was swept away by the political crisis of 1946. Thus, in terms of political salience, the affairs of the French Union moved briefly to the forefront of domestic political concerns, but this was at the expense of the momentum which had previously favoured the Brazzaville policy. The ideological acceptability achieved through a broad-based consensus lending credence to the new policy was no more. And the required institutional solidarity was increasingly jeopardised once the Brazzaville policy was out of the hands of de Gaulle, the vital source of ideological inspiration and institutional credibility.

What were the effects on policy of this constant shift in the domestic factors underpinning it? In a sense it was a distraction when it came to Indochina policy which, after the signing of the Accords of 6 March 1946, was arguably a matter for direct negotiation between the Republic of Vietnam and the GPRF. But it was partly the fact of this distraction which was so potentially damaging to colonial policy making: as Andrew Shennan comments, 'the colonial problem was all along viewed as a domestic problem which could be solved by domestic decisions'.[70] On the other hand, this view ran counter to the perception of liberals at the Rue Oudinot, who stressed the external perspective on the future of the French Union. Thus, pulled in both directions, policy makers in Paris did their best to ensure that policy did not explode in their faces. We now turn to their efforts over two years in Indochina, culminating in the biggest failure of all—the outbreak of war.

70. *Rethinking France*, 168.

PART II

POLICY MAKING IN INDOCHINA AND ITS BREAKDOWN, 1945–1947

5

CALCULATING THE STAKES

The Brazzaville Policy and the 'Return' to Indochina,
December 1943–September 1945

Throughout the course of the debates and developments discussed in the preceding chapters, the question of Indochina remained in suspense. Alone amongst the territories of Overseas France at the time of the Brazzaville Conference, Indochina stayed outside Gaullist control. Both in Algiers and subsequently in liberated Paris, policy makers found themselves posing a series of as yet only hypothetical questions; their perplexity was barely concealed by the bravado of two political Declarations on Indochina, in December 1943 and March 1945. How should the principles of the Brazzaville policy be put into practice in France's richest, most populous, and most complex colonial dependency? What role would be left for France in the Far East once the upheavals of the War in the Pacific were over, and how could this role be squared with local and international pressures for imperial reform? Should France be prepared to parley with the forces of Indochinese, and especially Vietnamese, nationalism? And who *were* these forces? What account should be taken of Admiral Decoux's Vichy administration, and especially of its reform programme? Uncertainties relating to these questions were heightened by the Japanese take-over of 9 March 1945, which interrupted the continuity of French rule in Indochina, and which seemed for a while to signal an end to France's presence in the Far East altogether. Nowhere was Laurentie's analysis of 'colonial crisis' of greater moment, as nationalists declared independence in all the Indochinese capitals. Just how far should the GPRF go in making concessions as France prepared to attempt her 'return' to the Far East? What sort of balance could the French now hope to achieve between the apparently incompatible aims of a restoration of French sovereignty on the one hand and the meeting of nationalist demands on the other?

This chapter traces the colonial administration's changing answers to these and related questions over the period from the first Declaration on Indochina until the eve of the Expeditionary Corps' arrival in Saigon in the autumn of 1945. It examines the accelerated evolution of 'liberal' thinking within the Ministry of Colonies over this period, as officials moved from the even-handedness of the early Brazzaville policy to a concessionary position more consistent with the analysis of colonial crisis across the Empire. At the same time, it illustrates the limitations of this liberal approach. This was not only because the new liberalism was hedged around with qualifications and ambiguities, but also, as will be shown, because the further liberal evolution of the Brazzaville policy was already threatened by the more consistent – or more obdurate – approach to Indochina apparently adopted by de Gaulle, and by his readiness to operate a veto at strategic moments.

Already present in this gestation period of the new Indochina policy are many themes which are to be developed in subsequent chapters. First, the chapter demonstrates the potential for dominance of the external perspective in colonial policy making, as suggested in an earlier chapter.[1] By the same token, it shows how officials were forced to respond to rapidly shifting external pressures, and to make policy as if shooting at a moving target. In this way, important principles of policy were often improvised on the spot. Thus, until March 1945, the issue seemed to be the recuperation of Indochina within the fold of French sovereignty and legitimacy represented by the GPRF; or, as Paul Isoart puts it, paying off the Japanese 'mortgage'.[2] After the Japanese takeover, and especially during the international chaos which reigned over the summer of 1945, it was argued by officials that the stakes were much higher, as they sought to determine the price of avoiding total French expulsion. Secondly, however, the chapter illustrates the dangers of policy making in a political void, with little or no reference to the attitudes or interests of domestic decision makers. Some of the reasons for this stance have already been outlined,

1. See above, Ch. 3.
2. '... la levée de "l'hypothèque nippone"': P. Isoart, 'Aux origines d'une guerre: l'Indochine française (1940–1945)', in P. Isoart, ed., *L'Indochine Française, 1940–1945*, Paris, 1984, 1–71. Admiral Decoux's formula quoted, ibid, 4.

such as the not-unwarranted official assumption that the Brazza-ville policy was supported by a broad ideological consensus, even while colonial policy largely failed to distract the Government and public opinion from domestic concerns.[3] The consequences of such autonomous action may be measured, however, in the extent to which it created a widening gulf between colonial liberals and the domestic outlook which dominated in Paris. Thus, the highly liberal Indochina policy conceived over the summer of 1945 seemed for a while to have been merely a phantom pregnancy.

Indochina Policy, 1943–45: '... to keep Indochina for France'[4]

Gaullist Indochina policy in the period up to and including the Declaration of 24 March 1945 was approached from two quite distinct directions. On the one hand, the obvious consequence of Indochina's continued absence from the Gaullist fold was a preoccupation with the question of sovereignty and with the mechanics of an eventual Gaullist takeover of power from the Decoux administration, in the wake of Japanese defeat. On the other hand, the fact that Indochina was not under Gaullist control implied the need for a fresh start when the moment came. This meant that Indochina's future could be discussed in agreeably theoretical terms, without reference to precedent or to the traditional thinking which had impeded progress at Brazzaville. The case of Indochina could thus be understood as a potential model for the application of the Brazzaville policy across the Empire, particularly after the perceived partial failure of the Brazzaville Conference. While the process of policy formulation which led to the March Declaration could be seen to a certain extent as 'going through the motions', it provided the basis for future policy, even if that basis had to be substantially rethought after the Japanese takeover of 9 March 1945.

Like Banquo's ghost, Indochina was an uninvited and silent but, in the minds of many, inescapable presence during the proceedings of the Brazzaville Conference. Both as a forum for debating future imperial reform and as a propaganda exercise, the Conference was, albeit indirectly, almost as much concerned with

3. See above, Ch. 4.
4. '... conserver l'Indochine à la France': Note, Affaires Politiques, Ière Division, ref.LP/SC (Pignon), n.d. (Jul.–Aug. 1944), AOM, NF/134/1214.

'captive Indochina' (as it was piously alluded to in a message of greeting) as it was with French Africa. Thus, Laurentie's federal idea was of obvious relevance to Indochina, which, unlike the African colonies, was an obvious candidate for Associated State status within Laurentie's proposed hierarchy. Moreover, no-one was in any doubt that Indochina would be the first target for American plans for 'international trusteeship', as France's most vulnerable colonial possession, and as the symbolic focus of President Roosevelt's anti-colonialism. As if to underline the colony's importance to France, therefore, the CFLN issued a Declaration on Indochina in the month before Brazzaville, on 8 December 1943. The Declaration may be understood as astute political footwork that gave little away. Thus it offered a stirring and tendentious account of the history of relations between Indochina and the Gaullists in London and Algiers, stressing the loyalty of the 'Indochinese peoples' (their sovereigns were also praised), while making a determined appeal to international opinion with the correct progressive vocabulary, and holding out an olive branch to Nationalist China, which stood to gain most clearly from Roosevelt's schemes. At its heart, however, was a general but nonetheless substantive promise of reform:

> To those peoples who have thus affirmed both their national feeling and their sense of political responsibility, France intends to grant a new political statute within the French community, which will extend and recognize the liberties of the various countries of the Union within the framework of a federation: where the liberal character of the institutions will be enhanced without detriment to Indochinese civilisation and traditions; and where the Indochinese will have access to all posts and functions of State.[5]

The Declaration introduced ideas which would be developed in the March 1945 Declaration: respect for democratic liberties and national identity within an overarching French federal 'communauté' (the equivalent of the British term 'Commonwealth'). Clear also, however, was the dominant theme of the early Brazzaville

---

5. 'A ces peuples qui ont su ainsi affirmer à la fois leur sentiment national et leur sens de la responsabilité politique, la France entend donner, au sein de la communauté française, un statut politique nouveau où, dans le cadre de l'organisation fédérale, les libertés des divers pays de l'Union seront étendues et consacrées: où le caractère libéral des institutions sera, sans perdre la marque de la civilisation et des traditions indochinoises, accentué; où les Indochinois, enfin, auront accès à tous les emplois et fonctions de l'Etat.' Text in: Institut Charles-de-Gaulle, *Le général de Gaulle et l'Indochine, 1940–1945*, Paris, 1982, 253–54.

policy, which lay the stress on France's generosity and liberalism in according these new freedoms. Thus, the underlying message, as at Brazzaville, was an affirmation of the durability and legitimacy of French imperial rule.

Over the following fifteen months, indeed, the substance of French Indochina policy lay in measures designed to assure continued French sovereignty. Lying outside the province of the Brazzaville policy as such, and having been amply treated elsewhere,[6] these measures need nonetheless to be mentioned in the present context as having a bearing on the relative priority accorded Indochina policy. Two broad approaches may be identified alongside Brazzaville-inspired reformism. First, the Gaullist regime worked vigorously to assure French involvement in the Far East and in an eventual military campaign against the Japanese on the Asian mainland. The patent political purpose of this latter goal was eventual Allied recognition of French sovereignty. By the end of 1944, the GPRF's successes to this end included French diplomatic representation in Chungking (from July 1943), a string of listening posts along the Sino-Indochinese border, and a French Military Mission attached to the headquarters of Mountbatten's South-East Asia Command (SEAC) at Kandy. The forward staging post for missions to Indochina was the French Colonial Mission at Calcutta. Less successful were French attempts to circumvent American hostility to the idea of a French return to the Far East, which hindered French action both directly, through the Office of Strategic Services (OSS), and indirectly, since Mountbatten was not prepared to jeopardize relations with the American-commanded China Command for the sake of the French. Ironically, it was the Japanese takeover which reversed the thrust of Roosevelt's attitude to Indochina, a month before his death in April 1945. Even thereafter the OSS played a considerable spoiling role.[7]

Although the perceived long-term threat to French sovereignty in Indochina came from the US or China, the immediate threat came from the Japanese. The second approach adopted by de Gaulle in the Far East thus involved, exceptionally in the whole of his wartime campaign, the establishment of contacts with members of an

---

6. E.g., Isoart, 'Aux origines', 25–35. Cf. also C. Hesse d'Alzon, *La présence militaire française en Indochine (1940–1945)*, Vincennes, 1985.

7. On Roosevelt's change of heart, see S. Tønnesson, 'The Longest Wars: Indochina 1945–75', in *Journal of Peace Research*, vol. 22, no 1, 1985, 11. More generally, see the testimony of the OSS commander in Indochina, A. Patti, in *Why Vietnam? Prelude to America's Albatross*, Berkeley, 1980.

administration loyal to Vichy, in the hopes that resistance might be organised in the event of a Japanese attack. There was no doubt as to the loyalties of Admiral Decoux, the author of a peculiarly fervent Pétain cult, who made no secret of his hostility to 'that sad legion of misguided so-called Gaullists',[8] and who, after the Liberation of Paris in August 1944, was to assume full powers in accordance with a law he had passed the year before, on 18 February 1943, rather than recognising the CFLN's authority. Nonetheless, by early 1944, contacts had been made with his Commander-in-Chief, Mordant (an ambitious man who reportedly coveted Decoux's position), and a Resistance network amongst French Army officers was in place by the time of the Japanese takeover. It remains unclear how effective this resistance ever could have been; the Army was quickly routed by the Japanese after 9 March 1945. By the same token, Decoux's subsequent thesis, that the creation of a pro-Gaullist Resistance provoked the Japanese, seems implausible.[9] By such a thin thread did the maintenance of French sovereignty hang even before it was severed by the Japanese in favour of local nationalists. At the very least, however, the internal resistance in Indochina served the political end of reinforcing in the minds of France's somewhat reluctant Allies the strength of France's case.[10]

Conducted by the CFLN on a diplomatic front and as a curious side-skirmish in de Gaulle's four-year contest with Vichy, the phoney campaign preceding the Japanese takeover had also to be viewed in political terms of what could be offered the Indochinese. It became clear after Brazzaville that a general statement such as the Declaration was insufficient to meet the complexities of the CFLN's task with regard to Indochina. In July 1944, therefore, Léon Pignon was placed at the head of a new Indochina Division (*Direction de l'Indochine*) within the Commissariat for the Colonies (still in Algiers) with a view to formulating a more precise policy. Pignon was the obvious man for this job, as a former Indochina hand and as Laurentie's close associate during the Brazzaville Conference. As he explained:

8. '… cette triste légion d'égarés que l'on nomme gaullistes'. Isoart, 'Aux origines', 19–22.

9. Amiral J. Decoux, *A la barre de l'Indochine*, Paris, 1949, 315.

10. The American official view in 1940–41 was that 'The title of France to Indochina was clouded by the failure of the Vichy government to resist Japanese aggression': quoted by C. Thorne, *Allies of a Kind: Britain, the United States and the War against Japan, 1941–1945*, New York, 1979, 217.

Naturally it would have been easier to work out our plans on the spot, in the first few months after arriving in the Union, protected by a regime of military occupation; we could then have contented ourselves for the moment with fairly sincere but deliberately vague promises, such as those contained in the Declaration of 8 December 1943.[11]

Such an approach was ruled out, however, because the success of French action would depend on the ability of an expeditionary force to establish itself more rapidly and comprehensively than such a reflective, circumspect approach would allow.

The major obstacle in the way of policy making over the summer of 1944 was the lack of intelligence from within Indochina. As Pignon commented, 'We are working for the moment with our knowledge of the Indochinese parties and their tendencies as we knew them in 1939'.[12] It was essential, therefore, for contact to be made with the 'qualified spokesmen for native opinion', to work out the interests of the various parties, as well as their strength and influence, and, in the case of the Communist Party or the Chinese-backed nationalist parties, the degree of foreign influence or contact. Information about pre-war institutions was vital: what was the state of the village council system, the mandarinate, or for that matter, the monarchies in Annam, Cambodia or Laos? This need for intelligence was the origin of several missions into Indochina over the autumn and winter of 1944–45. In particular, de Langlade's mission to Tonkin in October-November 1944 established a reasonably clear intelligence picture of the emerging political groups.[13] Much was as expected: the pre-war parties on the metropolitan model, such as the Socialist and Communist parties, had been officially dissolved, though the Communists had successfully established clandestine cells; the mandarinate was thought to have retained its sympathy for the French cause, while seeming to believe that it would constitute the underlying structure of any regime, except perhaps a Communist one; the

11. 'Sans doute aurait-il été plus facile d'élaborer sur place, dans les premiers mois suivant notre entrée dans l'Union, et à la faveur d'un régime d'occupation militaire, notre programme, en nous contentant pour l'instant de promesses d'un accent sincère, mais volontairement assez imprécises, comme celles contenues dans la déclaration du 8 décembre 1943.' Note, ref LP/SC, n.d. (Jul.–Aug. 1944), loc.cit. On Pignon, see *Fichier des anciens élèves de l'ENFOM*, AOM, 39APOM3.

12. 'Nous vivons en ce moment sur la connaissance des partis indochinois et de leurs tendances, tels qu'ils nous étaient connus en 1939.' Ibid.

13. NOTE, Nov. 1944, AOM, INF/133/1210. Isoart, 'Aux origines', 37–38.

main desire of the peasantry was 'above all to be well supplied with rice, cloth, salt, and other essential goods'. Bao Dai's position was thought to be pro-French, since it was French sovereignty which guaranteed his throne, but irrelevant, 'because he reigns in name only and does not personally govern at all'.[14] Amongst anti-French groups, Communist or Nationalist, the strongest and most influential grouping was already apparent: the *Viet Nam Doc Lap Dong Minh Hoi*, or 'League for the Independence of Vietnam'. As de Langlade commented:

> In principle this group is made up of Annamites and nationalists ... but in reality this is the Communist Party with a nationalist label attached in order to attract and assemble the greatest number of members possible. The party is usually known by the abbreviated title Viet Minh. It is the most important and best organised revolutionary party.

It was even believed that its leader, now known as Ho Chi Minh, was 'none other than Nguyen Ai Quoc'.[15] The Viet Minh wanted the eviction of both French and Japanese; another Communist grouping (soon absorbed into the Viet Minh) was opposed to the Japanese only.

A further element of uncertainty concerned Decoux's reforms, and the extent to which these should be taken up by the Gaullists. As Pignon commented: 'The impression should not be given by our political services that everything positive that the Vichy Government has done for the natives will be taken away by us'.[16] These reforms, indeed, were not insubstantial, including the promotion of the national idea in the different lands of Indochina, and even official use of the proscribed term 'Vietnam'; the creation of a unified 'Indochinese Union'; and, most important in Pignon's

14. '... car il ne règne que de nom et n'exerce aucun gouvernement personnel'. Ibid.

15. 'Il est formé en principe d'Annamites et de nationalistes ... mais en réalité il s'agit du Parti Communiste affublé de l'étiquette nationaliste pour attirer et grouper le plus grand nombre possible d'adhérents. Ce parti est surtout connu sous nom abrégé: VIET MINH. C'est le parti révolutionnaire le plus important, le mieux organisé.' Loc.cit. Nguyen Ai Quoc = 'Nguyen the Patriot'; Ho Chi Minh = 'He who Enlightens'. Ho, the leader of the Indochinese Communist Party during the Yen Bay revolt, was thought to have died in gaol in Hong Kong in the early Thirties: J. Dalloz, *La guerre d'Indochine, 1945–1954*, Paris, 1987, 41–43.

16. 'Il est bien évident que nos services politiques ne devront, en aucune manière laisser croire que tout ce qui a été pris en faveur des indigènes par le Gouvernement de Vichy sera retiré par nous.' Note, loc.cit.

analysis, the opening of federal employment, partly for reasons of manpower shortages, to local cadres.[17]

Notwithstanding the need for intelligence, and despite the liberalism which was seen as the sine qua non of the new French attitude in Indochina, Pignon's proposals stopped far short of direct negotiations with the 'spokesmen for native opinion' whose opinion was to be sought. An eventual constitution for Indochina would be bestowed by France ('octroyée par la France'), even if it was essential for it to be drawn up in a manner likely to be acceptable. This was all the more crucial given the pre-eminent position within the French Union which befell Indochina as a consequence of its high state of 'economic and intellectual development'. It was important, at the same time, not to antagonise the French in Indochina, whose cooperation would be needed, and whose morale it was important to maintain in the face of the continuing Japanese presence. Finally, lest the essential principle underlying this process be overlooked, Pignon added an important rider: 'Of course our intentions with regard to Indochina are most sincerely liberal, but the ultimate aim of our policy is nonetheless and above all to keep Indochina for France'.[18] In the balance between the demands of nationalism and the maintenance of sovereignty, there was never any doubt as to the ultimate priority.

This same blend of unilateral liberalism and defensive pragmatism characterised the Declaration on Indochina presented by Giacobbi on 24 March 1945. This Declaration came out of Laurentie's and Pignon's deliberations at the Ministry of Colonies, but had to be negotiated with representatives of the Ministry of Foreign Affairs: Jean Chauvel, Secretary-General of the Ministry of Foreign Affairs, and Philippe Baudet, head of the Asia-Oceania Division (*Direction d'Asie-Océanie*), also at the Quai d'Orsay. As Pignon subsequently commented: 'Drafting the Declaration of 24 March was a long and difficult process; it was sent back to the drawing board at least seven times, and it is very largely the result of a compromise between fairly divergent tendencies'.[19] Thus, the March Declaration and, in many ways, the credibility of French

17. P. Devillers, *Histoire du Viêt-Nam de 1940 à 1952*, Paris, 1952, 83–88; Isoart, 'Aux origines', 15–18.

18. 'Sans doute avons nous à l'égard de l'Indochine les intentions les plus sincèrement libérales, mais l'objet final de notre action n'en est pas moins, et avant tout, de conserver l'Indochine à la France.' Pignon, loc.cit.

19. 'L'élaboration de la déclaration du 24 mars a été longue et difficultueuse: elle a été remise sur le chantier au moins sept fois et, dans une large mesure, elle constitue

Indochina policy were early victims at this period of inter-ministerial wrangling and of the lack of institutional coordination so often criticised by the colonial administration.

Because of the delays caused by this wrangling, the Declaration, originally intended to mark the anniversary of the Brazzaville Conference, had not yet been issued when, on 9 March 1945, Japanese troops attacked French garrisons across Indochina. This swift and devastating *coup de force* followed an ultimatum to Admiral Decoux, demanding his immediate agreement (within two hours!) to the placing of French troops under joint French-Japanese command under the terms of a 1941 Defence Agreement. French resistance was brave but ineffective, and French forces were rapidly captured or decimated, or fled to Southern China. Within days, the Japanese effected what Isoart has called 'the de facto disappearance of French sovereignty'.[20] At Hué and Phnom Penh, the Emperor of Annam, Bao Dai, and the young King of Cambodia, Norodom Sihanouk, declared independence, encouraged by their Japanese suzerains within the Greater East Asia Co-Prosperity Sphere. The King of Luang Prabang followed a month later. The Nationalist government in Hanoi under Tran Trong Kim's premiership indicated a new independent legitimacy. Ironically, this Japanese masterstroke was overshadowed for French and international opinion by American successes on the Rhine and at Iwo Jima.[21]

The crisis turned on their head the GPRF's prior assumptions with regard to Indochina, and brought out in stark relief the contradictions underlying France's imperial dilemma. Was the GPRF to stick by the as yet rather limited provisions of the Brazzaville policy and to seek to make the best of its promises of reform? This was naturally the official position, as staunchly defended by de Gaulle in his first public response to the Japanese takeover:

> In truth, never has the Indochinese Union been more bitterly opposed to its Northern enemy, nor more staunchly resolved, with France's help, to find within itself the means of its own political, social, economic, cultural and moral development in order to realise its great future. Henceforth the veils are torn down and the

---

un compromis entre des tendances assez divergentes.' Note, 'Examen des critiques énoncées dans la note du 18 mai 1945', 24 Jul. 1945, AOM, CP/185. No trace of the negotiations has so far emerged in the files of the *Direction d'Asie-Océanie*, MAE, AO.

20. '... la disparition de fait de la souveraineté française'. 'Aux origines', 42. On the Japanese takeover, Dalloz, *La guerre d'Indochine*, 61–65.

21. P. Devillers, *Paris-Saigon-Hanoi, Les archives de la guerre, 1944–1947*, Paris, 1988, 53.

French Government will soon announce the ways and means by which this development is to be achieved.[22]

Alternatively, were they to start by admitting the shortcomings of French policy, and to accept that further concessions would be needed? Was the Declaration of 24 March the definitive expression of French policy intentions, or was it merely a starting point for negotiations with the nebulous 'appropriate institutions' evoked with delicious vagueness in the Declaration itself? If so, just how far were the French prepared to go? The magic word 'independence' had been uttered. Could this be included in any definitive French bargaining position, and if so, what meaning would be ascribed to the term? These two sets of questions characterised two parallel but distinct debates within the administration, one turning on the terms of the Declaration, the other on the extent to which France would have to bow to *force majeure* within Indochina. These two debates will be examined in turn.

The Declaration and Its Critics

The more impatient members of the colonial administration could be forgiven for finding rather futile a debate on a policy which had already been outpaced by events. This would, however, be to mistake the purpose of the internal discussions which followed the Declaration of 24 March 1945. A parallel could be drawn with the debate on the idea of imperial Federation which had been conducted in Algiers and Paris in something of a political vacuum, and turned largely on the application of metropolitan principles such as liberalism, universal suffrage, and Republicanism. Indeed, as has been shown, the Declaration served the more general purpose of outlining the French Union as a whole. Moreover, this interpretation is wholly consistent with Léon Pignon's view, quoted above, that an eventual constitution for Indochina should be 'bestowed' rather than negotiated. However, the discussions following the Declaration took almost as their starting point the

22. 'En vérité, jamais l'Union Indochinoise n'a été plus opposée à l'ennemi venu du Nord, ni plus résolue à trouver en elle-même, avec l'aide de la France, les conditions de son propre développement dans tous les domaines: politique, économique, social, culturel, moral, où l'attend son grand avenir. Désormais les voiles sont déchirés et le Gouvernement français va faire connaître incessamment dans quels voies et par quels moyens cela sera réalisé.' C. de Gaulle, *Discours et Messages*, 3 vols. vol. 1, *Pendant la guerre, juin 1940–janvier 1946*, 14 Mar. 1945, 534.

proposition that further concessions would have to be made. Thus, the purpose of the debate was to establish the extent to which French policy was acceptable, and what modifications would be necessary. One of the unintended consequences of the March Declaration was the reaction of representatives of the thirty thousand Vietnamese (*Annamites*) living in France, including the militant General Delegation of the Indochinese in France (*Délégation Générale des Indochinois en France*), and, to a lesser extent, political groups in Southern China. These were monitored by the Indochina Division, which added its own comments in a report dated 18 May 1945. In late July, from his new post as Political Counsellor to General Alessandri, Commander of the French Expeditionary Corps in the Far East (CEFEO), Léon Pignon responded as co-author of the Declaration, and reported on opinion amongst nationalists and 'revolutionaries' in Southern China.[23] The debate is an indicator of the administration's flexibility over this critical period.

The Declaration was much criticised for being, as Isoart puts it, 'much better adapted to the French way of thinking than to the deeper aspirations of the Indochinese themselves'.[24] Thus, even a relatively sympathetic commentator such as Nguyen Quoc Dinh, co-author of perhaps the most cogent critique of the Declaration, recognized the competing interests which France was seeking to reconcile, but doubted whether this would be possible within the new French Union:

> The formation of the French Union, the keystone of tomorrow's French imperial system, seems to have been conceived with the aim of finding a compromise between two apparently contradictory principles: the *freedom* of Indochina, which is apparently to be recognised, and the *unity* of the Empire, which is equally fundamental.[25]

23. NOTE pour M. le Directeur des Aff.Pols, a/s la déclaration du 24 mars 1945 concernant le statut futur de l'Indochine, 18 May 1945, AOM, CP/185; Pignon, Note, 'Examen des critiques ...', loc.cit. On the *Délégation Générale*, Dalloz, *La guerre d'Indochine*, 77.

24. '... beaucoup plus adapté[e] à l'esprit français de l'époque qu'aux aspirations profondes des Indochinois'. 'Aux origines', 46.

25. 'La formation de l'Union Française, pièce maîtresse du système impérial français de demain, paraît conçue dans le but de trouver un compromis entre deux principes apparemment contradictoires: la *liberté* de l'Indochine qu'on semble vouloir reconnaître et l'*unité* de l'Empire qui est également fondamentale.' Nguyen Quoc Dinh and Nguyen Dac Khê, *Le futur statut de l'Indochine. (Commentaire de la Déclaration Gouvernementale du 24 mars 1945)*, Paris, 1945, 36–37. (Emphasis in text). Dinh, a

Moreover, the political presentation of the Declaration was felt to leave much to be desired. Thus, the Indochina Division noted the inappropriateness of a reference to the Brazzaville Conference, given its exclusive preoccupation with Africa and its denial of self-government. As Pignon reflected, it was inconceivable not to mention such an 'event of international importance', and besides, since de Gaulle's October 1944 press conference, 'the formula ruling out self-government must be considered outdated'. Also criticised was the text's ambiguity and lack of precision. For Pignon, what was important was to 'justify in the eyes of our interlocutors the cautious position adopted by the Government'.[26] As he noted, the Government was in fact being scrupulous in providing for consultation with 'the appropriate institutions within liberated Indochina' in the Declaration, in order that the future statute of Indochina be submitted to discussion by the people's representatives.

Perhaps the Declaration's most serious presentational drawback concerned the lack of guarantees for the promises it made. Quite apart from a history of bad faith and broken promises, what was the worth of a Declaration made by a provisional government? Could it not be likened merely to the Declarations made by incoming governments in the Third Republic? As the Indochina Division commented: 'The Indochinese complain that they cannot see, either in their experience of contact with French colonisation, or in the circumstances surrounding the Declaration of 24 March, any good reason why they should believe that any promises made to them will be honoured'.[27] Such criticism was unanswerable, as the Declaration had been made partly in the spirit of improvisation, given the impossibility of concrete action. As Pignon noted, this most sensitive point was confirmed by his contacts in China, although, as he argued, the Government's provisional nature was

---

constitutional lawyer, participated in official committees on colonial affairs. Laurentie commented on this work in a radio broadcast in the series *Chronique*, 24 Jul. 1945, text in AN, 72AJ535.

26. '... la formule excluant la constitution de selfs governments [*sic*] doit être tenue pour dépassée et périmée. ... justifier aux yeux de nos interlocuteurs la position prudente que le gouvernement a adoptée'. Loc.cit. On de Gaulle's statement, see above, Ch. 1.

27. 'Les Indochinois se plaignent de ne trouver, ni dans l'expérience de leur contact avec la colonisation française, ni dans les circonstances qui ont entouré la Déclaration du 24 mars 1945, les raisons d'avoir foi dans l'exécution des promesses qui leur sont faites.' NOTE, 18 May 1945, loc.cit. This was a major theme of the Indochinese campaign in France: see 'Les Indochinois ne croient plus aux promesses', *Combat*, 11 Jul. 1945.

not an issue, nor was Gaulle's authority to speak for France in any doubt. It was the business of revolutionaries to enumerate their grievances, and many of these would seem justified. Consequently, their propaganda would readily carry conviction even with their relatively francophile or moderate compatriots. The best that could be hoped for was that the return to Indochina would allow the French to introduce a number of reforms quickly to provide the necessary psychological shock.[28]

Of the more substantial criticisms of the Declaration, two concerned issues which went to the heart of the French dilemma in Indochina: the powers of the new Governor General; and the vexed question of the distinction between the five constituent parts of Indochina, according to which the territory of Vietnam was to continue to be divided into three separate regions or 'ky'. Given that Franco-Vietnamese negotiations were to revolve around these issues over the following eighteen months, the initial French position on these still hypothetical questions is of considerable interest. This was certainly the case for the first of these issues. One of the Declaration's principal innovations was to grant vast new powers to the new Governor General. In contrast to the functionary of the Third Republic, appointed by the Ministry of Colonies and answerable to Parliament, the new appointee would be a far more politically active figure, appointed by, and representing, the head of the French Union (that is, the President of the Republic), heading the executive and playing the role of arbiter. More powerful within Indochina than either the President or the Prime Minister within France, his role would be comparable to a dictator's, and the temptation to abuse his power would be considerable. Too much would depend on the choice of one of the most powerful figures in the Fourth Republic. Indeed, as the Report suggested, the system would succeed or fail according to whether the chosen Governor General was or was not 'the right man in the right place'.[29] This was also Nguyen Quoc Dinh's most serious criticism. As he noted, the French Union, as apparently envisaged in the Declaration, approximated to a partially federal system dominated by France ('un système fédéral à prépondérance de la France (fédéralisme mitigé)'); as such it afforded less freedom to Indochina than might do a properly federal system, or a more informal system such as the British Commonwealth, seen as leading logically to political

---

28. Note, 'Examen des critiques …', loc.cit.
29. Quoted in English: NOTE, 18 May 1945, loc.cit.

independence. As a result, much came down to the question of the main beneficiary of the reduced autonomy (or 'decentralisation', as he called it) which the system would allow. If it were the 25 million-strong Indochinese people, either alone or in collaboration with the French in Indochina, then proper self-government would develop. Dinh, however, pointed to a third beneficiary, the Governor General 'who will effectively be the head of the Federation and who, moreover, will have no ties with the Indochinese population'.[30]

Pignon took a less drastic view. As he argued, once the system was in place the Governor General would quickly come to regret the power given his subordinates: it would be virtually impossible for him to govern against the Assembly's will or to hire and fire ministers as he might wish. The Declaration pointed clearly in the direction of a true parliamentary system. Add to this the rights of local governments, provided for in the Declaration, i.e., in the five 'countries' of the Union, and it was clear that the 'dictator' label had been misapplied to 'the least enviable and most difficult job in the whole of the French Union'.[31] In the short term, the Governor General's powers would indeed be as wide as the Declaration implied. Much remained to be resolved, including the composition of an eventual Indochinese Constituent Assembly, 'for which it would be difficult but not impossible to recruit members'.[32]

The issue prefiguring most clearly the impending clash between the French and Vietnamese nationalists was the internal division of the Indochinese Federation. Here the Declaration was unequivocal, if somewhat disingenuously phrased: 'The five lands which comprise the Indochinese Federation, and which are distinguished by civilisation, race and traditions, will maintain their individual characters within the Federation'.[33] In other words, not only were Cambodia and Laos to retain a separate identity but also Vietnam, like ancient Gaul in the eyes of an earlier coloniser, was to be divided into three parts. It had always been an essential part of French colonial ideology in the Far East that the French had

30. '… qui sera le chef effectif de la Fédération indochinoise et qui, au surplus, n'aura aucune attache avec la collectivité indochinoise'. *Le futur statut*, 43–46.

31. '… le poste le moins enviable et le plus difficile de toute l'Union Française'. NOTE, loc.cit.

32. '… dont le recrutement sera malaisé mais non pas impossible'. Loc.cit.

33. 'Les cinq pays qui composent la Fédération indochinoise et qui se distinguent entre eux par la civilisation, la race et les traditions, garderont leur caractère propre à l'intérieur de la Fédération.' Loc.cit.

come as protectors, defending the kingdoms of 'Indochina' (a French geographical concept) from the expansionist appetites of the Empire of Annam: Cambodia and Laos had been established as French protectorates, as well as Annam itself, which was divided into three *ky* or regions, of which one, Cochinchina, was made a colony. The ancient name of 'Vietnam' (The South of the Viets), which was revived by twentieth-century nationalists, was to be avoided, although Decoux had used it as part of his own propaganda.[34] The Japanese takeover and the declarations of Vietnamese independence had finally let the national cat out of the bag: Vietnamese refugees in China were now committed to the idea of national unity, whilst the 'urban youth' of Tonkin were reportedly following with enthusiasm the Kim government's efforts to 'bring Vietnam into being'.[35] The Indochina Division's problem, as noted in its report, was that, in seeking to rationalise a formerly confused and arbitrary administrative system, they had laid themselves open to charges of seeking to 'divide and rule'. For demographic, economic, and administrative reasons it was felt that the five-way division was 'necessary for the maintenance of French power and of Cambodian and Laotian freedoms'.[36] However, this administrative necessity had been explained in an insensitive, not to say inaccurate, way. Indeed, Dinh damningly confined to a single footnote his discussion of this clause of the Declaration which, he suggested, was based on an obvious historical error.[37] Pignon defended the French case on grounds of linguistic and ethnic differences between North and South, though he discounted 'the concept of race which is now rejected by all modern ethnologists'. These differences were at least as marked as those existing within France, and yet Annam since the seventeenth century had known neither a truly national dynasty nor 'a

34. Cochinchina, Annam, Tonkin in Vietnamese: *Nam Ky, Trung Ky, Bac Ky* (= South, Central and Northern Regions). The regions have been known as *Bô* (= *ky* without the colonial overtones) since 1945. Imperial rule in Tonkin was delegated to the French *Résident-Supérieur*, while the cities of Hanoi and Haiphong were French concessions. Outside the small kingdom of Luang Prabang, Laos also came under direct French rule. Decoux's aim was to combat 'the eventual allure of "Greater East Asia", Japan's brainchild' ('les éventuelles séductions de "la Grande Asie orientale" chère aux Japonais'): Isoart, 'Aux origines', 15–16.

35. '… réaliser le VIETNAM'. Pignon, 'Examen …', loc.cit.

36. '… nécessaire au maintien de la puissance française et des libertés propres au Cambodge et au Laos'.

37. '… qui procède d'une erreur historique évidente.' *Le futur statut*, 9.

single capital with its capacity to devour and assimilate, in the way that Paris has done in France'.[38]

As will be seen below, Pignon was by no means a conservative, and he largely shared Laurentie's perspective on the colonial problem at this date. His chief criticism of the Indochina Division's report was thus that it conceded too much too easily. The point of his counter-arguments was therefore to keep the case open: by accepting the Vietnamese position, the Indochina Division displayed 'a real inferiority complex', which he felt was unjustified. It was better to be prudent and not to make a commitment either way. Outclassed in its political impact by the pressure of events, the March Declaration should not simply be abandoned, as Pignon concluded with characteristically robust pragmatism: 'The Declaration nonetheless constitutes a political act on both the international and the Indochinese stages which we cannot allow to sink into oblivion, and which could be easily revived by some astute propaganda'.[39] On the other hand, it was increasingly accepted that the Declaration's content was to be regarded as provisional, intended mainly for the phase immediately following the 'Liberation'; if it appeared vague and imprecise, this was to allow the Indochinese themselves to participate in the elaboration of their future institutions.

At least implicitly, then, some concessions were possible. This much was clear already in mid-June from the Rue Oudinot's instructions to the French Colonial Mission in Calcutta, commanded by Administrator Jean de Raymond:

> After all France's aim is to build the French Union on the basis of freedom and absolute equality. In this regard you should thus let it be known that the Government's Declaration represents a starting point to be equated more with the needs of the transitional period following the Liberation [i.e., of Indochina] than with Indochina's ultimate destiny.[40]

38. '… la capitale unique dévorante et assimilatrice que PARIS a constitué pour la FRANCE'. Loc.cit.

39. 'La Déclaration … constitue néanmoins sur le plan international et sur le plan indochinois un acte que nous ne pouvons pas laisser tomber dans l'oubli et qu'une propagande bien faite doit revigorer.' Ibid.

40. '… malgré tout la France tient à construire l'Union Française sous le signe de la liberté et de l'égalité absolue. Vous pouvez à cet égard laisser entendre que la Déclaration du Gouvernement est un point de départ et correspond plutôt aux besoins de la période transitoire qui suivra la libération qu'à la destinée définitive de l'Indochine.' Télégramme, Ministre des Colonies pour de Raymond, 12 Jun. 1945, AN, 72AJ539.

The nub of the debate turned, therefore, on the possible extent of these concessions. For some within the administration, the conviction was growing that they would have to include the utterance of one fateful word: independence.

The Debate Around Vietnamese Independence

Arguing over the March Declaration was a kind of displacement activity for the colonial administration over the summer of 1945, as the GPRF made its military and political preparations for a 'return' to Indochina, the circumstances of which it was virtually powerless to control, and even the timing of which it could do nothing to predict. One thing was certain: following their total loss of initiative as a result of the Japanese takeover, the French position in Indochina had never been weaker. Indeed, this weakness was accentuated by two momentous decisions made over France's head: the decision at Potsdam to divide Indochina between two rival Commands for the purpose of receiving the Japanese surrender; and the American decision to drop the A-bomb on Japanese cities, which precipitated that surrender and initiated the Viet Minh's August Revolution in Vietnam. What was France to do in these circumstances? Independence had been declared across Indochina; could it be included in France's bargaining position, and if so, what meaning could be ascribed to the term? The debate on this issue increasingly pointed to conclusions far overreaching the provisions of the Brazzaville policy. Its participants, however, had reckoned without de Gaulle's intransigent and defiant reflexes.

The starting point for the internal debate was an appreciation of the full implications for France of the Japanese takeover, the definitive statement of which came in an extensive report by Captain Paul Mus. A pre-war academic expert on Indochina, Mus had conducted two intelligence missions into Indochina over the winter of 1944/45, and returned from the Far East only in May. Alluding to Laurentie's diagnosis of a general colonial crisis, he applied it also to Indochina:

> We talk of 'malaise'. But this term is a euphemism, given that the local nationals in this country that we have just lost are claiming independence, or at least not disavowing those who are. We are confronted with a growing crisis characterised by the fact that the

Indochinese elite have recognised it more rapidly and thoroughly than we have.[41]

As Mus argued, over the last few years, Indochina had attained its political majority. This was not so much in quantitive terms, since the levels of education and productivity amongst the population at large were still deficient, but constituted 'a qualitative majority', in that trained cadres existed in sufficient number to 'do at least as good a job as their French counterparts from the metropole'.[42] Even amongst 'the Indochinese masses', and especially amongst the Vietnamese who constituted 19 millions out of the total Indochinese population of 23 millions, Mus acknowledged a degree of social and political education sufficient to ensure that a modern state need not be constructed entirely from scratch. Mus dated this development from before 1940, when 'the traditional administrative framework' had been in place; this framework had now been destroyed by the Japanese takeover. The implications for continued French rule were far-reaching, in that the traditional power roles of coloniser and colonised had now effectively been reversed, with the French in the weaker position. To this diagnosis of the current situation Mus added a perceptive analysis of the roots of Vietnamese nationalism in a culture which had proved its resilience during two millenia of conflict and rivalry with the Chinese to the north. But France was not absolved from blame: Mus reiterated Laurentie's criticisms of the French administrative system, raising doubts as to whether the GPRF could make good the consequences of French 'mistakes, hesitations and a sort of functional ineptitude on the part of our central services, conceived with other ends in mind in a bygone era'.[43] Reiterating a point made by George Orwell, he questioned official commitment to Indochina, commenting bitterly on de Gaulle's speech at the Tet celebrations in February 1945 which dwelt on two themes: 'our

41. '"Malaise", reconnaît-on. Mais ce terme est un euphémisme, quand les nationaux de ces pays que nous venons de perdre nous réclament l'indépendance totale ou ne désavouent pas ceux qui la réclament.... Nous sommes devant une crise de croissance, et ce qui la caractérise, c'est que l'élite indochinoise s'en est aperçue plus vite et plus complètement que nous.' Note sur la Crise Franco-Indochinoise, par le Capitaine Paul Mus, 1 Aug. 1945, AOM, INF/134/1219. On Laurentie's Note, 20/21 juin 1945, see above, Ch. 3.

42. '... faire jeu égal, et parfois mieux, avec leurs émules français de la Métropole'. Ibid.

43. '... de nos fautes, de nos atermoiements, ...d'une sorte d'inaptitude fonctionnelle de nos services centraux, conçus à d'autres fins, à une autre époque'. Ibid.

beloved Indochina' and 'faithful Indochina'. From his speech, there was no way of telling whether de Gaulle knew of the famine which threatened Tonkin and North-Annam, nor whether he had grasped 'the profound evolution of a mentality which can only be called national'.[44]

Mus's analysis, like the Report on the Declaration discussed above, was based in part on an understanding of Vietnamese opinion within France. But his views were confirmed by the contacts which had been made with the political parties grouping within Indochina and on its border with China. French intelligence remained patchy, but by the summer of 1945 provided a reasonably clear idea of the shifting balance of forces, and of the attitude of those forces towards France. This was particularly the case after Giacobbi authorised the French Mission in Calcutta to open discussions ('pourparlers') with the various groups identified by de Langlade, Mus, and others, and particularly with the Viet Minh. The results of these initial contacts were not entirely encouraging, as Pignon reported the following month.[45] Pignon considered the government of Tran Trong Kim and his Dai Viet party to have outlived any suspicion of their collusion with the Japanese. The government was made up of well-known and respected figures ('personnalités marquantes et respectées'), and the national idea which it represented stood a chance of succeeding even if the government itself was brought down. Little contact had been made with other nationalist groups, many of whom now looked to China, and in particular to the Guomindang for inspiration, and who remained 'reserved and hostile'.

Contacts with the Viet Minh had been considerably more fruitful, but the signals coming out from this still mysterious organisation were riven with ambiguities. Nonetheless, the sort of *realpolitik* which was to lead to the Accords of 6 March 1946 was already discernible. In May, Jean Sainteny reported back from Kunming to Calcutta that the Viet Minh differentiated between French troops already in Indochina, whose Vichy sympathies were equated with fascism, and those of an eventual Gaullist

44. '… l'évolution profonde d'un esprit qu'il faut bien dire national'. Mus, NOTE, loc.cit; see also a Note, 'Têt de la Libération', 13 Feb. 1945, AOM, INF/123/1119; G. Orwell, 'De Gaulle Intends to Keep Indo-China. But French Apathetic on Empire', *Observer*, 18 Mar. 1945, see above Ch. 4.

45. Tel., Ministre des Colonies pour de Raymond, 12 Jun. 1945, loc.cit; Tel. no 237/AP, Pignon to Colonies, 11 Jul. 1945, AOM, CP/185.

expeditionary force; the implication was that eventual collaboration on the battlefield leading to the expulsion of the Japanese might lead them to accept more prolonged cooperation within the terms of French proposals.[46] By July, however, Pignon was reporting that the attitude of the Viet Minh had become more intransigent, largely because of their awareness of their own strength. The price demanded by the Viet Minh for collaboration was arms, and they stipulated that their objective was total independence for Indochina.[47] It was also in July that Sainteny's mission at Kunming received a message from the Viet Minh via the American OSS which laid out, in English, a five-point programme: elections by universal suffrage to a new Indochinese parliament; independence within a period of at least five and at most ten years; economic reforms to be conceded by France; the granting of all freedoms defined by the United Nations; and the prohibition of opium.[48] Contacts with the Viet Minh over the following few weeks were sporadic, and severely hampered by the monsoon season. However, as Devillers has discovered, a text was prepared by Sainteny, Pignon, and de Raymond which went a long way towards accepting each of the five points, including, on the second key point, the proposal of a referendum to decide the 'form of independence most likely to satisfy the aspirations of the Indochinese peoples, within the framework of the French Union'. Bad weather prevented further contact with the Viet Minh and the text was never sent.[49] By this time, anyway, in mid-August, events were moving into a new decisive phase.

For two years the GPRF and its predecessor, the CFLN, had been grappling with a situation in which the initiative lay in other hands. Two further events in July-August 1945 were to render the French even more powerless. First, during the meeting of the Big Three at Potsdam, on 23rd July, it was decided to divide Indochina along the 16th Parallel for the purposes of receiving the Japanese surrender. To the north of this line, Indochina was to be occupied by the Chinese, to the south by the British. This marked the resolution of a long-standing dispute between the SEAC and the China Command

46. Sainteny to Calcutta, 19 May 1945, quoted by Devillers, *Paris-Saigon-Hanoi*, 59–60.

47. Tel. no 237/AP, Pignon to Colonies, 11 Jul. 1945, loc.cit.

48. Translation in J. Sainteny, *Histoire d'une paix manquée*, Paris, 1967, 57–58.

49. '… la forme de l'indépendance la plus propre à satisfaire les aspirations des peuples de l'Indochine, dans le cadre de l'Union française'. 16 Jun. 1945, reproduced in Devillers, *Paris-Saigon-Hanoi*, 65–67.

under General Wedemeyer.[50] For the French, it meant effectively that, having improved relations with one potentially hostile power, the United States (notwithstanding the continuing ambiguity of the OSS's policy), they were now confronted with another with more obviously rapacious inclinations. As Pignon noted, not only had a Vietnamese Nationalist delegation been received by Chiang Kaishek himself, but Chinese generals along the frontiers were openly encouraging anti-French feelings amongst the revolutionary groups and seeking to effect a union of the different parties; their territorial designs on Tonkin, which they were now to occupy, were only too clear.[51] At least in the south the position for France was reasonably assured, since it was fair to assume that the British would offer no resistance to the idea of a French return.

Secondly, the American decision to use its new nuclear technology, thus precipitating the Japanese capitulation, caught the French by surprise, but also set in train the events which brought the Viet Minh to power. In a note outlining future policy, dated 31 July 1945, Laurentie reported SEAC's estimate that the war in Asia would last a further two to six months.[52] In fact the nuclear bombardment of Hiroshima and Nagasaki was to bring about a Japanese surrender in just over a fortnight. In Vietnam, news of the bombing of Hiroshima contributed to the upheavals within an already unstable political situation. On 7 August, Tran Trong Kim, in the face of material difficulties and the Viet Minh's provocations, offered his resignation, which was refused by Bao Dai. On 10 August, Ho Chi Minh launched the call for general insurrection. On the 16th, following their capitulation, the Japanese ceded power to the Nationalist government. Bao Dai, having appealed to four of the Big Five for international support for Vietnamese independence, and separately to de Gaulle along the same lines,[53] accepted Kim's resignation on the 22nd, and a Viet Minh cabinet was formed under Ho's Presidency. Bao Dai abdicated on the 25th, accepting the honorary post of Supreme Counsellor (*Conseiller Suprême*) and re-taking his civilian name Vinh Thuy. By 25 August, the Viet Minh's August Revolution had largely succeeded, and the new government's authority was being felt over the whole of Vietnam. On 2

50. *Foreign Relations of the United States*, Berlin, II, 1319–21. Thorne, *Allies of a Kind*, 626–27.

51. Pignon, Tel., 11 Jul. 1945, loc.cit.

52. Note pour Monsieur le Ministre des Colonies (a/s de la reprise de l'administration en Indochine), ref. HL/ocg, 31 Jul. 1945, AN, 72AJ535.

53. His letter to de Gaulle is reproduced in Devillers, *Paris-Saigon-Hanoi*, 70.

September, Ho proclaimed independence and the formation of the Democratic Republic of Vietnam.[54]

A further threat was created by the local American services commanded by General Wedemeyer. Notwithstanding an uneasy truce between the new US President and de Gaulle, who paid a state visit to Washington in mid-August, the Vietnamese propaganda effort was apparently intended for the special benefit of the Americans. Thus, it was an astute move on Ho's part, declaring independence, to appeal to the precedent of the American, rather than the Bolshevik, Revolution. Moreover, the American Office of Strategic Services (OSS) was openly supporting the forces of Vietnamese independence: when the OSS's Captain Patti accompanied Jean Sainteny to Hanoi in the wake of the Viet Minh takeover, he was greeted as a friend; Sainteny, by contrast, was kept a virtual prisoner, although he chose as his prison the 'gilded cage' of the Governor General's palace.[55] None of the French agents parachuted into Indochina escaped death or capture.

The internal debate on Indochina thus took place against the background of extraordinary chaos marking the end of the War in the Pacific. The terms of the debate were set by Laurentie in his Note of 31st July, in which he sought to galvanise the GPRF into making preparations for the fatal moment of France's return (in two to six months): as he commented bitterly, there had been many delays and the Ministry's collective bid to make up lost time 'is reminiscent of the debate about the sex of angels'.[56] By the end of July, the High Commissioner, as the head of the new Indochinese administration was to be called, remained to be nominated. But Laurentie was relatively sanguine with regard to the international situation. As he argued, no plan existed, whether American or Chinese, let alone British or Soviet, which considered French sovereignty to be 'non-existent, subject to revision or permeable' ('nulle, révisible ou perméable'): in principle, nothing stood in France's way. The Vietnamese perspective was very different:

> Our interlocutors are not favourably or even neutrally disposed towards us. They have had a taste of independence, French officials have been evicted and their positions would seem to have gone for good. No party with popular support has sufficient ties with us to

54. Devillers, *Histoire*, 132–43.
55. Sainteny, *Une paix manquée*; on the OSS's pro-Viet Minh stance, see Patti, *Why Vietnam?*
56. '... rappelle le débat sur le sexe des anges'.

counterbalance the nationalists. Thus the voice of the masses, whatever they may feel, will not be heard.[57]

At best the French could hope that the nationalists would provoke opposition on the part of the 'masses', who might then turn to them for protection; should the French appear empty-handed then this slim chance would be forfeit.

What were Laurentie's pre-conditions for a successful re-establishment of French authority? The first was a timely display of force, and, specifically, four divisions on the spot at the crucial moment. There was little disagreement on this point in principle, since preparations were well advanced for the despatch of the Expeditionary Corps which, following the Comonindo meeting of 26th May, was to be commanded by General Leclerc.[58] The strength of the CEFEO was a matter of greater controversy. Four divisions was the accepted ideal, as General Blaizot, Leclerc's predecessor, argued to the Chiefs of Staff, who accepted Blaizot's case but doubted whether 'the economic and demographic situation will allow us such a luxury'. As Laurentie commented, without sufficient military support, however tardily despatched to the Far East, 'we must prepare public opinion for the certainty of losing Indochina'.[59] Military force, however, served a more subtle purpose than mere old-fashioned colonial militarism, as Mus explained:

> We will not get back on our feet simply by putting garrisons back into Hanoi, Saigon, Langson and elsewhere.... In such a politically and psychologically difficult situation, force is not accepted for its own sake. But it nonetheless has a wide impact beside its value for its own sake, on condition that it is given, so to speak, a moral purpose. It has demonstrative effect. One can deduce from it that it is reinforced by and founded in something deeper.[60]

57. '... nous ne rencontrons ni adhésion, ni même neutralité. On a goûté à l'indépendance, les fonctionnaires français ont été évincés et leurs places semblent bonnes. Aucun parti populaire n'est socialement assez attaché à nous pour balancer le pouvoir des nationalistes. Ainsi la masse, quels que soient ses sentiments, ou même ses regrets, n'aura pas la parole.' Loc.cit.

58. Commandant G. Bodinier, ed., *Le retour de la France en Indochine, 1945–1946*, Vincennes, 1987, 5.

59. '... que la situation démographique et économique de la France actuelle nous permet un tel luxe': ibid., 26–27; '... c'est à la perte certaine de l'Indochine qu'il faut préparer l'opinion', Note, 31 Jul. 1945, loc.cit.

60. 'Nous ne rétablirons pas simplement nos affaires en remettant nos garnisons à Hanoi, Saigon, Langson et ailleurs.... Dans ce domaine, politiquement et psychologiquement si difficile, la force n'est pas acceptée pour elle-même. Elle n'en a pas moins, outre sa valeur de fait, un rayonnement étendu, mais sous la condition

This proof of political 'virtue' (Mus had perhaps been reading Machiavelli's *Discourses*) was more essential given the extent to which French authority and prestige had been eroded.

Military force, then, provided the essential underpinning for Indochina policy, but it was no substitute for a clear political plan, and it was here that the line taken by the administration with increasing insistence was to prove most controversial. The essential principle for Laurentie was unequivocal: 'Our aim is to hold out, by whatever means'.[61] However, this was meant in a liberal sense and, as he argued, his proposed policy called for the utmost innovation and flexibility on the part of the incoming French forces and administration:

> We should not shrink from proclaiming Annamite independence, and acting sincerely upon such a proclamation, if that is the best or only means at the critical moment to gain the friendship without which we will be evicted.
>
> That, however, is an extreme solution. The structure set down by the Declaration of 24 March represents the opposite extreme. It is highly unlikely that we will be able to abide by it. Between the two extremes, everything is possible.[62]

The new High Commissioner's task would be to work between these two extremes of policy: colonial restoration on the one hand, the acceptance of Vietnamese independence on the other. The interim period of military occupation would allow the French to re-establish contact with the population, and to effect urgent relief work. The most pressing issue here was the famine in Tonkin, caused by the failure of the northern spring harvest and the breakdown in communications between the North and the fertile South. This too had political significance, however, as 'others' unnamed were all too eager to take charge if the French did not.[63]

---

d'être, si l'on ose dire, moralisée. Elle fait preuve. On déduit d'elle ... qu'il y a derrière elle autre chose qui la fonde.' 'La crise morale franco-indochinoise', loc.cit.

61. 'Notre but consiste à durer, quelle que soit la forme de notre persistance'. Note, 31 Jul. 1945, loc.cit.

62. 'Nous ne devons pas nous reculer devant la proclamation de l'indépendance annamite, proclamation suivie d'effets sincères, si c'est, au moment critique, le meilleur ou le seul moyen de gagner l'amitié faute de laquelle nous serons évincés.

'C'est pourtant là une solution extrême. L'organisation prévue par la Déclaration du 24 Mars en serait une autre, en sens inverse. Il est peu probable que nous pouvons nous y tenir. Entre les deux, tout est imaginable.' Loc.cit.

63. Ibid.

Officials both in Paris and in the Far East were increasingly moving in favour of the former, more radical, of the options presented by Laurentie. In a cable despatched from the Rue Oudinot in early August, authorisation was given for the fatal word 'independence' to be uttered in dealing with the Viet Minh. It is an indication of the degree of confusion reigning in Paris that in a further cable these instructions were recanted by Laurentie, following consultations with his colleagues Mus and de Langlade.[64] The frustration of French agents in the Far East was recorded in a telegramme drafted by Pignon for Alessandri, despatching the texts of recent Vietnamese messages, including Bao Dai's to de Gaulle. As he argued:

> Observations resulting from various contacts with the Nationalist parties, and especially with the Viet Minh, would seem to coincide in suggesting that it is still possible for us to collaborate with them, as long as we can utter the word 'independence' at the right moment. No other word will do.

What was meant by 'independence', however, was not unfavourable to French projects in the Far East. Pignon had already used the term in his draft text replying to the demands of the Viet Minh. This was now taken further, developing an argument which was to be reprised during the negotiation of the March 1946 Accords:

> Moreover, it is certain that the Annamites prefer the letter to the spirit, that they are above all asking us to help them save face, and that any promise by us leading to independence can be hedged around with safeguards ensuring that in the short to medium term we establish Dominion status with fairly strong ties to France.[65]

64. Tels no. 1247/1255 and 1303/1304, n.d. (early August). Both tels were cited in Alessandri's tel., Calcutta to Paris, 20 Aug. 1945, transmitted in a further tel., Colonies to de Gaulle, Washington, 22 Aug. 1945, AOM, INF/133/1207. In a letter to Pignon, 12 Sep. 1945, Laurentie states that the earlier cable, 'which had seemed so appropriate', had been vetoed by de Langlade and Mus, and was therefore to be seen as 'some ideas and commentaries and not at all as instructions emanating from the Government' ('une somme d'idées et de commentaires non pas du tout comme des instructions émanant du Gouvernement.'). AN, 72AJ539.

65. 'Diverses observations concordantes résultant des contacts avec les partis nationalistes, et surtout avec le Viet Minh, prouvent,... qu'une collaboration est encore possible, à condition de savoir prononcer,... le mot «indépendance» à l'instant opportun. Aucun autre mot ne peut le remplacer. ... Il est, d'autre part, certain que les Annamites préfèrent la lettre àl'esprit et qu'ils nous demandent surtout de leur sauver la face, et que nous pouvons sans doute entourer une promesse à terme d'indépendance de garanties qui s'aboutissent àétablir dans un délai plus ou

The telegramme then went on to suggest that a provisional declaration should be made, if necessary by de Gaulle in Washington, in more liberal terms than the 24 March Declaration. Such a declaration would pre-empt American attempts to steal any initiative gained by the French in their discussions with the Viet Minh. The urgency of the situation was stressed in a telegramme from the more cautious de Raymond, who also proposed the granting of Dominion status to Indochina.[66]

Laurentie's position was a difficult one in late August, not least because both his Minister and de Gaulle were away from Paris. Personally favouring the independence option, he nonetheless felt obliged to pour oil on troubled waters, and drafted a commentary, over Pleven's signature, which accompanied Alessandri's telegramme of 20 August on its way to de Gaulle in Washington. As he argued, Wedemeyer was acting on his own initiative, in the absence of 'precise instructions from Washington in our favour'. Thus, Alessandri was looking at American policy from an extremely local perspective.[67] In a report addressed to de Gaulle a week later, Laurentie still stopped short of unconditionally advocating independence. His own information was apparently incomplete, since he believed Kim to be still in power, albeit under Viet Minh control. Nonetheless, in a 'situation as vague as it is confusing', one thing was clear: 'that independence is the underlying theme of all the programmes which will be submitted to us, especially that of the Viet Minh'.[68] Whilst it was therefore not yet necessary to talk of independence and thereby to 'give up on the seductive formula of an Indochinese Union forming part of a French Union',[69] it was essential for French agents to enter into negotiations with the Viet Minh, even before the arrival of the High Commissioner, provided that for their part the Viet Minh desisted from negotiating with French 'allies'.

---

moins long un statut de dominion comportant des liens assez étroits avec la France.' Loc.cit.

66. De Raymond's tel quoted in: Note à l'attention de M. le Ministre des Colonies, Secret, 28 Aug. 1945, AOM, INF/133/1207.

67. Loc.cit. As Pignon retorted, this was the angle that counted, since Wedemeyer was free to do as he liked: Pignon to Laurentie, 30 Aug. 1945, loc.cit.

68. '… que le thème de l'indépendance est à la base de tous les programmes qu'on nous soumettra, et notamment au programme du Viet-Minh.' Note au sujet de la politique intérieure à suivre en Annam et en Indochine, 29 Aug. 1945, AN, 72AJ539.

69. '… renoncer par là même à la séduisante combinaison de l'Union Indochinoise, membre de l'Union Française'. Ibid.

As is clear from his correspondence with Pignon, Laurentie was champing at the bit, regretted the hesitations and reversals of policy over the preceding month, and in particular was critical of the inertia shown by the GPRF As he commented to Pignon, reflecting on his own radical preferences, 'it is more and more difficult to extract a decision from the government, especially when it is required to stick its neck out as in this case'.[70] Laurentie was most outspoken at two press conferences in September, the first for journalists, the second a confidential briefing for newspaper editors. The ostensible aim in both cases was to stress France's delicate situation in Indochina and the important role of the press in guiding public opinion. As he explained at the editors' conference, Indochina could be lost 'as a result of errors or the prevalence of unfavourable currents of opinion'.[71] But in essence, Laurentie was going public on his highly concessionary interpretation of Government policy.

The furore resulting from one official's indiscretion was the more remarkable for the fact that Laurentie played down the drama of the situation in the Far East. For example, he made light of Sainteny's semi-imprisonment within the Governor General's palace in Hanoi, which he had been ordered to leave, and from where he was, after all, free to send cables. Laurentie sought also to allay fears of American policy, 'a curious mixture of idealism and an eye for business', which had so far helped only Chinese aims in Indochina. As he predicted with some accuracy (not to say understatement): 'they're soon going to realise that the Viet Minh is a pro-Communist party; that will annoy them tremendously'. On the other hand, he noted also that France would need American economic backing for reconstruction in Indochina.[72] There was no mistake, however, as to the thrust of Laurentie's proposals, even if he pulled his punches at the first conference. Thus, for public consumption, he argued that the main concern of all

70. '… il est de plus en plus difficile d'obtenir une décision gouvernementale et surtout dans le sens d'une telle hardiesse.' Laurentie to Pignon, 12 Sep. 1945, AN, 72AJ539.

71. '… par suite d'erreurs ou de mauvais courants d'opinion qui pourraient … se faire jour'. Transcripts, 'Conférence de presse', 13 Sep. 1945, 'Conférence de presse (Directeurs de journaux)', 14 Sep. 1945., in AN, 72AJ535. The first was reported in *Monde*, 15 Sep. 1945.

72. '… la politique curieuse [des Américains] … un mélange d'idéalisme et d'esprit d'affaires …aujourd'hui ils vont s'apercevoir qu'en réalité le Viet-Minh est un parti communisant; ça va les embêter énormément'. Conférence de presse (Directeurs de journaux), 14 Sep. 1945, loc.cit.

Indochinese from Bao Dai downwards was that 'France should no longer consider Indochina to be a colony'.[73] So much, whatever it meant, had already been conceded at Brazzaville. At the second conference, however, he presented a frank, if nuanced, case for concessions, based on the understanding that it was in the Viet Minh's interest to collaborate. Thus, Laurentie recognized the talent and scope of Ho's government for propaganda, while pouring scorn (on the basis of very little evidence) on its day-to-day capabilities: 'It does not have the practical administrative wherewithal to govern. It does have control of every means of communication. It alone can be seen and heard, which is very important'. At the same time, he argued that this was the best on offer, and that France should negotiate while it had the chance, before the arrival of the Expeditionary Corps: 'However the Viet Minh may seem to us, there is no denying that the government's only possible policy today is to do business openly, not necessarily with them directly, but at least with the nationalist aspiration which they represent'.[74] On the two key issues, national unity and independence, Laurentie made substantial concessions. First, he spoke of Annam's (here meaning Vietnam's) complete freedom and unity, thus accepting the principle of uniting the three *ky*. But did he advocate independence? While he had nothing against the term in itself, he did not believe that the moment had come for independence. He argued, however, that it was an error to issue blanket prohibitions on 'the use of certain words'. His prognosis was essentially optimistic: whereas in Syria, the nationalists were used to 'playing tough', the Vietnamese were not disinclined to deal fairly with the French, and were not about to 'throw themselves into the arms of their enemy in order to obtain an illusory independence'.[75]

---

73. '... c'est que la France considère que l'Indochine n'est plus une colonie'. Conférence de presse, 13 Sep. 1945, loc.cit.

74. 'Il n'a aucun moyen pratique administratif de gouverner. Il a tous les moyens moraux de s'exprimer. On ne voit que lui, on n'entend que lui et c'est un point important ... quelle que soit l'allure du Viet-Minh,... indiscutablement la seule politique qui s'offre au gouvernement aujourd'hui est, je ne dis pas de traiter expressément avec lui, mais de traiter expressément avec l'aspiration nationale qu'il représente.' Ibid.

75. '... se jeter dans les bras de l'adversaire pour obtenir une fausse indépendance'. Laurentie's comments on the Syrians were fairly pungent: there was, he claimed, 'enough to eat and drink' in Syria ('il y avait à boire et à manger'), and nationalists had '[l']habitude du jeu, du truquage'. Conférence de presse (Directeurs de journaux), 14 Sep. 1945, loc.cit.

Laurentie's comments, even at the more confidential gathering of newspaper editors on 14 September, contained nothing that had not been debated internally, and his ideas were largely accepted within the Ministry of Colonies. In essence, Laurentie proposed to apply in Indochina the principles enunciated by him in respect of the Brazzaville policy. However, in proposing policy in the semi-public forum of a press conference, albeit behind closed doors, Laurentie had transgressed in two ways. First, he had committed a breach of protocol, as he later admitted (while protesting perhaps too much):

> The General was furious. I fully understand: an insignificant ministerial director has absolutely no right to dictate policy to the Head of the Government. That was what I had allowed myself to do.[76]

As has been shown, Laurentie took a highly iconoclastic view of his duties as Director of Political Affairs. His inclination to act independently increased over the summer of 1945 with his frustration at the Government's apparent incomprehension of the situation in Indochina. In August, for example, Laurentie addressed two memoranda to his former boss René Pleven in an attempt to divert the GPRF's attention from the preoccupying issues of continuing domestic crisis and German policy. Indeed, his feelings were shared by other high-ranking officers responsible for Indochina: when Sainteny visited Paris to put the case for negotiating with the Viet Minh in July, he met with the indifference of all but Pleven, Laurentie, de Langlade, Colonel Passy (the *éminence grise* of Gaullist intelligence), and the staff officer Captain (later Admiral) Barjot.[77] This neglect was compounded by de Gaulle's absence from Paris at key moments, and by Giacobbi's inaction. Laurentie was thus acting in character, if rather recklessly. De Gaulle's response, however, was surprisingly lenient: Laurentie was merely summoned by his Minister and informed that de Gaulle had desisted from sacking him 'out of kindness and friendship'.[78]

---

76. 'Il était furieux, le Général.... Je comprends parfaitement: un petit directeur de ministère n'a absolument pas le droit de dicter sa politique au chef du Gouvernement. C'était ce que je m'étais permis de faire.' 'Témoignage du gouverneur-général Henri Laurentie', in Institut Charles-de-Gaulle, *De Gaulle et l'Indochine*, 239.

77. Note personnelle pour M. Pleven, n.d. (early August), and Note à M. Pleven, n.d. (mid-Aug.), AN, 72AJ539; Sainteny, *Une paix manquée*, 49–50.

78. '... par bienveillance et amitié'. 'Témoignage', 239, 242. Meeting Mme Laurentie at a reception for returned internees, de Gaulle advised her to tell her husband to behave himself ('d'être sage').

The second transgression committed by Laurentie and his colleagues within the administration was to have diverged from the policy of the General. How had this breach occurred? De Gaulle's policy statements were at best enigmatic, and they had been infrequent on the subject of Empire. Not since his press conference in October 1944, where he gave his endorsement to the Brazzaville policy, had he spoken on the colonies other than in the grand manner criticised by Mus. His Message to Indochina, on 19 August, was an exercise in the usual rhetoric of colonial 'faithfulness' to the 'Mother Country' ('la mère-Patrie'). As Isoart has shown, of his revisions to this text, only the striking-out of a reference to the 'five countries' of Indochina was of political importance. A few days later, in answer to a journalist's question on Indochina in Washington, he provided a laconic summary of the March Declaration.[79] More worrying still, during the recent Syrian affair, his attention had remained fixed on the perfidy of the British, rather than on possible lessons to be learnt as to the nature of modern nationalism. Indeed, as late as the end of September, on the eve of the British landings in Saigon, de Gaulle warned of a possible British hidden agenda ('arrière-pensées').[80]

Further warning of de Gaulle's likely approach to the Indochina question came with his decision to appoint as High Commissioner the frosty, unbending Admiral d'Argenlieu, a stalwart of de Gaulle's campaign since 1940, but with little administrative experience. A naval officer in the Great War, he was a Carmelite monk between the wars, and was to resume his vows in 1947. In 1942–43, he was de Gaulle's High Commissioner in the Pacific, based at Noumea. Whatever his qualities, d'Argenlieu surely did not closely fit the Indochina Division's job description for the new post, which called for 'flexibility, patience, sincerity, political sense, moral probity, strength of purpose, local knowledge'.[81] General Leclerc's appointment as Supreme Commander of French Forces in the Far East was less controversial, though it argued further for de Gaulle's desire to be assured of the full loyalty and community of view of his lieutenants. At one stage, Laurentie was considered as High Commissioner; and following d'Argenlieu's

79. Isoart, 'Aux origines', pp. 54–55; de Gaulle, *Discours et messages*, vol. 1, 24 Aug. 1945, 642.

80. Tél. personnel du Gén. de Gaulle à d'Argenlieu et à Leclerc, AN, 72AJ539.

81. '... souplesse, patience, sincérité, sens politique, valeur morale, indépendance, fermeté, connaissance des hommes et des choses du pays'. NOTE, 18 May 1945, loc.cit.

appointment, he was lined up to act as his Political Counsellor (*Conseiller politique*). But by mid-September, his copy-book was irremediably blotted.[82] Any doubts as to the direction of de Gaulle's policy in the Far East were dispelled by his eloquently brief instructions to the new High Commissioner, which described his primary mission as being 'to restore French sovereignty over the territory of the Indochinese Union'.[83]

Thus, while officials in the Ministry of Colonies engaged in debate on the shifting parameters of France's policy options in Indochina, and moved a long way towards adapting policy to match changing conditions, de Gaulle's aim remained relatively fixed. If anything, it was reduced to its essential element: the maintenance of sovereignty. Consequently, while a narrow interpretation of the March Declaration was uncontroversially seen at the Rue Oudinot merely as a baseline for French policy, for de Gaulle it defined a precise policy to be followed. As he instructed d'Argenlieu and Leclerc in a telegramme at the end of September, responding to the call by officials in the Far East for a new, more liberal Declaration of policy:

> It is out of the question for the French Government now to issue a further Declaration concerning Indochina. The March Declaration is sufficient. A new Declaration would in the circumstances give every impression of backing down, and that would further complicate the siutation in Indochina and beyond.[84]

---

82. 'Témoignage ...', 239. In his *Chronique*, d'Argenlieu, surprised at his appointment, names another candidate to de Gaulle: '- Pas lui! tranche de Gaulle': *Chronique d'Indochine 1945–1947*, Paris, 1985, 30–31. Might this be Laurentie? On his possible nomination as Political Counsellor, see Tel. HC de France en Indochine à M. le DGER, Tel. pour Raymond et al, marked 'non parti', 24 Aug. 1945, AOM, INF/123/1116. See P. Duplay, 'Le choix des responsables', in G. Pedroncini and P. Duplay. *Leclerc et l'Indochine, 1945–1947*, Paris, 1992, 83–93.

83. '1. Le Haut-Commissaire de France pour l'Indochine exerce les pouvoirs de Gouverneur général de l'Indochine et ceux de commandant en chef des forces terrestres, navales et aériennes basées en Indochine ou désignées pour s'y rendre.

'Il a pour première mission de rétablir la souveraineté française dans les territoires de l'Union indochinoise.' De Gaulle to d'Argenlieu, 16 Aug. 1945, d'Argenlieu, *Chronique*, 29–30.

84. 'Il est exclu que le Gouvernement français fasse actuellement une nouvelle déclaration concernant l'Indochine. Celle de Mars se suffit à elle-même. Le fait d'en édicter une nouvelle dans les circonstances présentes aurait toutes les apparences d'une reculade qui compliquerait davantage la situation en Indochine et à l'extérieur.' Télégramme personnel du Général de Gaulle à MM. l'Amiral d'Argenlieu et le Général Leclerc, 29 Sep. 1945, AN, 72AJ539.

This was wholly in line with Leclerc's thinking that everything depended on what happened on the ground, and provided little comfort for those hoping to see in the short term a liberal, and above all peaceful, solution effected in Indochina.[85]

———— ∞∞∞ ————

Notwithstanding the divergence in approach to Indochina policy which brought the Ministry of Colonies into near collision with the President of the GPRF in September 1945, Laurentie continued to press for a liberal and concessionary policy with regard to Vietnamese nationalism. On 16 October, for example, he drafted a set of political instructions, over Giacobbi's signature, for the new High Commissioner.[86] The elements of policy outlined in the telegramme were a distillation of the new thinking as it had evolved over the preceding months: the need for negotiations in present circumstances, even given the undesirability of the Viet Minh as negotiating partners; the acceptance in principle, and only if absolutely necessary, of some notion of independence, with guaranteed cultural, economic, and military rights for France; the toleration of a united Vietnam on a number of conditions, the most important of which was the continued political and territorial integrity of Cambodia and Laos; the maintenance of the Indochinese Union. As he concluded: 'Prudence is essential, but you must be very obviously sincere'.[87] Meanwhile, the Expeditionary Corps's arrival in Saigon in October, and Leclerc's impressively effective campaign across the paddy-fields of the Mekong delta indicated a far more vigorous approach to the use of military force than that suggested by Laurentie and Mus. Within six months, however, from the marriage of these two approaches issued the Accords of 6 March 1946, signed by Jean Sainteny as Commissioner for the Republic in Tonkin and North Annam, and by Ho Chi Minh. The Accords policy ('politique des accords') which led to this historic agreement is examined in the next chapter.

The reasons for the breach are nonetheless instructive, and its consequences were considerable in institutional terms. For his part, Laurentie was in no doubt as to the cause of his own frustrations.

85. '... toute la question sera une affaire d'exécution', Leclerc to d'Argenlieu, 28 Aug. 1945, AOM, INF/124/1116.
86. Tel. Colonies à Hau[t Commi]ssaire Indochine, 16 Oct. 1945, AN, 72AJ539.
87. 'Il faut être prudent, mais il faut que votre sincérité éclate'. Ibid.

In a highly critical note to Giacobbi, Laurentie revealed that he had contemplated resignation in the face of de Gaulle's, and now d'Argenlieu's, apparent game of 'hide-and-seek': as he explained, he took issue less with stated intentions than with the way these were put into practice.[88] In particular, he criticised the delays which had altered the effects of policy, notably concerning the March Declaration; the backtracking of the Government on some issues (he mentioned the colonial elections to the Constituent Assembly, but doubtless a similar case could have been made for Indochina); the lack of clarity concerning official pronouncements; and the continued employment of personnel opposed to the re-formist trend of current policy. Further, Laurentie was highly crit-ical of the apparent Eurocentrism of current French foreign policy, which, he believed, might still lose France her Empire in the face of 'America's destructive designs', an eventuality which the Soviet Union would do nothing to impede. As he commented, in a phrase not unworthy of the great colonisers of the late nineteenth century: 'The left bank of the Rhine will provide me with no con-solation for losing Africa and Asia'.[89]

There was condiderable justice to Laurentie's case; in particu-lar, as has been shown, policy makers had had to contend with the GPRF's apparent lack of interest over the summer of 1945 until it was almost too late. On the other hand, the administra-tion, too, learned the lesson that it made policy independently of the Government at its peril, especially if it did so with insufficient respect for the political, ideological, and institutional parameters governing domestic political life. In particular, loose talk of grant-ing 'independence', however hedged around with qualifications, was injudicious in the extreme when France was on the point of achieving one of its principal aims as defined by Gaullist ideol-ogy, namely the restoration of sovereignty over the national ter-ritory (which included Indochina). Laurentie paid the price for his preoccupation with the external perspective: his influence was diminished by his spat with de Gaulle, to the extent that, notwithstanding the apparent success of 'his' policy, he and his Ministry played a more obviously back-seat role thereafter. No doubt, this development was in part attributable also to the fact that, after September 1945, the Government could deal directly

88. Directeur des Affaires Politiques à M. le Ministre des Colonies, ref HL/bp, 11 Oct. 1945, AN, 72AJ539.
89. 'La rive gauche du Rhin ne me consolera pas l'Asie et l'Afrique perdues'. Ibid.

with the new High Commission through the channel of Comin-indo, as de Gaulle had all along intended. Indeed, the game of hide-and-seek described by Laurentie was to become more chancy after January 1946, when the resignation of de Gaulle left the infinitely more elusive and inconstant d'Argenlieu as the principal player.

6

THE PRIMACY OF ACTION

From the 'Return' to Saigon, October 1945, to the
Signing of the Accords of 6 March 1946

On 3 October 1945, the first detachments of the French Expeditionary Corps to the Far East (*Corps Expéditionnaire Français
en Extrême-Orient*, or CEFEO), under the command of General
Leclerc, steamed into Saigon aboard the light cruiser *Le Triom-
phant*.[1] By the end of that month, Admiral d'Argenlieu had also
arrived in Saigon to take up residence at the Norodom Palace as
High Commissioner. Already by this time, Indochina was well-
established as the focus for the GPRF's new policy for the French
Union. As suggested in the previous chapter, this policy had become separated out into two distinct, though not necessarily
opposed strands. First, officials within the colonial administration,
reacting – perhaps too precipitately – to the rapid changes in the
international system and within Indochina, had argued increasingly for a liberal and concessionary interpretation of the relatively conservative vision presented in the Declaration of 24
March 1945, and indeed for a fresh Declaration on which to base
policy. This revised policy might even include the recognition of
some kind of independence for the emerging forces of nationalism
in Indochina, and in particular for the revolutionary Hanoi government established by the Viet Minh, following their August
Revolution. The second strand of policy was that represented by
de Gaulle and his lieutenants, including the new High Commissioner, who were still apparently drawn to the idea of a more traditional 'return' to Indochina, in which French generosity backed

1. Commandant G. Bodinier, ed., *Le retour de la France en Indochine, 1945–1946*,
Vincennes, 1987, 33.

by military strength would ensure the maintenance of French sovereignty and prestige in the Far East.

This chapter is concerned with the process by which these two strands of policy were bound back together, a process which led the French into negotiations with the Vietnamese, as well as with the Chinese occupying Tonkin and North-Annam, and which resulted within barely more than five months in the signing of the Accords of 6 March 1946. The chapter examines the ambivalent record of colonial officials at the Rue Oudinot during the first few months following France's 'return' to Indochina. Three reasons may be identified why the influence of the Ministry of Colonies was at a low ebb. First, as suggested in the previous chapter, the liberal thesis championed by many officials was clearly out of tune with the instincts of de Gaulle, as shown by his furious reaction to Laurentie's two press conferences in September. Second, the hierarchy established by de Gaulle, according to which Indochina policy was controlled by him through the direct channel of the Interministerial Committee on Indochina (Comindo), now came into play, and was to continue to function effectively even after he resigned in January 1946. Moreover, the key appointees in the new Indochina regime, d'Argenlieu and Leclerc, had been chosen primarily for their loyalty to de Gaulle, even if, in Leclerc's case, this loyalty did not preclude independence of mind and a strong streak of colonial liberalism.[2] But third, inevitably, the Ministry's stock-in-trade – declarations of policy, official and press briefings, internal analysis and debate, instructions to the new High Commissioner – after October 1945, all took second place to action on the ground.

On the other hand, even while the direct influence of colonial liberals was eclipsed, the return to Indochina was seen as a crucial test of the as yet only theoretical terms of the liberal thesis. Thus, what had before been a largely abstract debate was now translated into concrete policy. And in this early phase of France's new Indochina policy, the liberal thesis would be favoured by the pressure of events, and reinforced by the counsel of hard-nosed pragmatism, which in turn stemmed from a wholly Gaullist calculation of French interests. By the same token, however, the chapter argues that the Accords signed on 6 March 1946 were marked from the outset by profound ambivalence: while officials sought to portray them as a triumph and a model for the working of the

2. See G. Pedroncini & P. Duplay, eds., *Le Maréchal Leclerc et l'Indochine, 1945–1947, quand se noua le destin d'un Empire*, Paris, 1992.

French Union and other colonial empires, they could more accurately be interpreted as merely an uncomfortable compromise designed to oust the Chinese and to reinstall a French military presence in their place. This ambivalence was such as to dissipate rapidly the momentum generated before 6 March. Moreover, de Gaulle's resignation would leave considerable scope thereafter for the teasing-out of ambiguities woven into the negotiating process. Before unravelling this process, this chapter first examines the extent of the disagreements which still opposed 'liberals' and 'conservatives' within the administrative hierarchy responsible for Indochina in the Autumn of 1945, and the means by which both sides came to advocate negotiation.

What Is to Be Done? The Internal Debate Continues

Notwithstanding the apparent gulf which existed in September 1945 between the respective positions of de Gaulle, on the one hand, and Laurentie and his colleagues on the other, the debate was still open concerning future policy in Indochina. While Laurentie's *faux pas* was perhaps more revealing in institutional terms, the intellectual basis for his disagreement with de Gaulle might be seen as a clash of political priorities occasioned chiefly by considerable uncertainty, between the concern of the colonial administrator to preserve or restore good colonial relations and pre-empt crisis, and that of the statesman who made a positive virtue of standing firm, especially when the odds were against him. The major cause of this uncertainty was at least partially overcome with the arrival of the Expeditionary Corps. It was thus both easier and more pressing for differences to be aired, and if possible for a reconciliation to be found between the liberal thesis of officials in Paris and the more traditional, conservative stance of de Gaulle and his new High Commissioner. Indeed, a partial consensus – flawed and misleading but sufficient to the task in hand – was gradually established on four key issues confronting the French over the Autumn of 1945: Indochina's status within the French Union; the internal division of the Indochinese Union, and in particular the question of Vietnamese national unity; the identity of France's negotiating partners and collaborators in an eventual new regime; and the question of means, that is, the case for a what came to be called the Accords policy ('politique des accords') as against a tougher, less conciliatory policy.

The first topic for debate, though in many ways still the most theoretical, was the question of Indochina's, and especially Vietnam's, relations with France and the outside world. The Declaration of 24 March 1945 had established two principles in this respect, one hard-and-fast, and one more or less debatable. First, the Declaration's basic formula, of an Indochinese Union within the French Union, was to be retained. On the other hand, considerable leeway remained for the Indochinese to establish their status within this organisation. The various options advocated ranged on a sliding scale between a return to the status quo ante of 1940, and independence for the constituent parts of the Union, including a united Vietnam. As has been shown, de Gaulle's initial instructions to d'Argenlieu suggested something close to the former option, giving the High Commissioner the primary task of restoring French sovereignty.[3] D'Argenlieu's view of his role emerges from his instructions for his new administration, drawn up at Kandy (where the Expeditionary Corps were in training) in early September. Eschewing the task envisaged for him by liberals in Paris, as the enlightened leader of a self-governing Indochina, d'Argenlieu apparently saw himself as an old-fashioned Governor-General whose aim was to 'restore France's protection of the Indochinese peoples', though d'Argenlieu regretted that the term 'protectorate' would have to be discarded for its unwanted colonialist associations. 'Independence' was also banned from the discussions, because it was not policy to discuss it, but also because the notion of independence 'presupposes the attainment of political maturity and a basis for action, when these are precisely what we have to bring about'.[4]

Notwithstanding d'Argenlieu's and de Gaulle's resistance, however, independence remained on the agenda. Putting behind him the setbacks of September 1945, Laurentie set out afresh the terms of his proposed policy for Indochina, in his drafting of Giacobbi's instructions to d'Argenlieu. For Laurentie, 'the essence of the debate is the question of independence'. What was meant

3. See above, Ch. 5.
4. '... reconstituer une véritable protection de la France à l'égard des populations indochinoises ... [la notion d'indépendance] supposerait que la maturité politique et les moyens d'action qu'il s'agit précisément d'acquérir sont déjà réalisés'. 'Instructions politiques de l'Amiral d'Argenlieu, Haut-Commissaire de France pour l'Indochine', Kandy, 8 Sep. 1945, in G. Thierry d'Argenlieu, *Chronique d'Indochine, 1945–1947*, Paris, 1985, 421–22. P. Devillers describes these as 'both literary and unreal', in *Paris-Saigon-Hanoi, Les archives de la guerre, 1944–1947*, Paris, 1988, 88.

by independence, however, was a nuanced and qualified, not to say highly slippery, concept. As the text continued:

No doubt this is more a matter of appearances than a fundamental demand. Moreover, given Indochina's (and not only Annam's) current circumstances, the Government believes that it is unreasonable to talk of independence, and that it would be dangerous for France if we conceived of an independence without conditions attached.[5]

Indeed, the term independence was to be avoided if possible; and independence of any kind could be granted only over time, and on condition of continuing military, cultural, and economic collaboration. In any event, Indochina was to remain in the French Union, but Indochina's membership of the Union would gradually shift to a voluntary basis ('libre adhésion') in case of independence. Thus, Laurentie envisaged something akin to British Dominion status.

The first part of Laurentie's argument, that the term 'independence' would be acceptable even if devoid of content, was familiar from the policy debate over the summer. It was now extended by Jean Sainteny, in his first report to d'Argenlieu as Commissioner for the Republic (*Commissaire de la République*) in Tonkin and North Annam:

Although admission of the term 'independence' is a precondition to any negotiations, it is also the case that the champions of 'independence' have forgotten to ask what it means, or even to consider its implications. We should not forget that we are dealing with a highly literary culture.[6]

As France's negotiating position strengthened, so the appeal of this linguistic sleight of hand increased. Reporting to de Gaulle in late December, even d'Argenlieu contemplated uttering the fateful word, which he equated simply with the idea of 'being master in

5. '... l'essentiel du débat porte sur l'indépendance ... il s'agit sans doute d'avantage d'une question de façade que d'une exigence de base. Au surplus, le Gouvernement estime déraisonnable, dans l'état actuel de l'Indochine (et pas seulement de l'Annam), de parler d'indépendance immédiate et dangereux pour la France d'imaginer que l'indépendance soit inconditionnelle.' Tel. Colonies to Hau[t Commi]ssaire Indochine, 16 Oct. 1945, AN, 72AJ539.

6. 'Si le mot "indépendance" est la condition préliminaire à toute négociation, il n'en est pas moins vrai que les champions de ce mot ont oublié de demander ce qu'il signifiait, ou tout au moins d'en délimiter la portée. N'oublions pas que nous avons affaire à un peuple de lettrés.' Note du 3 octobre 1945, in Devillers, *Paris-Saigon-Hanoi*, 98.

one's own house', though he still couched it in a variety of qualifying phrases:

> Independence within the Indochinese Federation.... Independence within the French Union.... A large measure of independence within the Federation.... A degree of independence compatible with membership of both the Indochinese Federation and the French Union.... Autonomy within the Indochinese Federation with a large measure of independence for the latter within the French Union.... Would these sorts of formulae be rejected out of hand by the French Government?[7]

However, in a memorandum dated 12 February, on the eve of Sainteny's breakthrough in negotiations with Ho Chi Minh, d'Argenlieu took a more restrictive view, preferring the terms 'self-government' or 'Doc Lap' (the Vietnamese term for both freedom and independence), on the grounds that 'these words have no exact equivalent in French'.[8] Thus, if there was no clear disagreement in the French debate on this issue, officials were fooling no-one other than themselves in supposing that such a solution might be acceptable to the Vietnamese.

The second topic, concerning the internal organisation of Indochina, included most notably the burning issue of the three *ky*. The March 1945 Declaration had provided for an Indochinese Federation comprising five units, i.e., Laos, Cambodia and the three regions, or *ky*, of Vietnam: Cochinchina, Annam, and Tonkin. Inevitably, the question of Laos and Cambodia, relatively docile, under-populated, and largely taken for granted by the French, was of little importance beside that of Vietnam. As discussed above, for Vietnamese nationalists it was a self-evident matter of national self-determination that Vietnam should be united. Laurentie had given some ground on this issue in his policy proposals over the summer of 1945, and in his October instructions he

---

7. 'Indépendance au sein de la Fédération indochinoise.... Indépendance au sein de l'Union française.... Large indépendance au sein de la Fédération.... Indépendance compatible avec le maintien, d'une part, dans la Fédération indochinoise, d'autre part, dans l'Union française.... Autonomie dans la Fédération indochinoise jouissant elle-même de la plus large indépendance au sein de l'Union française.... Est-ce que des expressions de ce genre seraient *a priori* rejetées par le Gouvernement français?' D'Argenlieu to de Gaulle, 28 December 1945, in d'Argenlieu, *Chronique*, 110.

8. '... ces mots ne peuvent trouver d'équivalents exacts en langue française'. Note, 12 Feb. 1946, in d'Argenlieu, *Chronique*, 133–34. *Doc Lap* was promised to Bao Dai by d'Argenlieu's successor as High Commissioner, Emile Bollaert, in late 1947.

regarded as negotiable the notion of 'Annamite unity', but only on certain conditions: first, and this was to be considered absolute, the formal recognition by 'Annam' of a separate status, juridical equality and integrity for Cambodia and Laos; the autonomy of the 'Moi lands', that is, the uplands inhabited by non-Vietnamese ethnic minorities; and possibly some frontier changes in favour of Cambodia, Laos, and the ethnic minorities. The Indochinese Union would be maintained at the very least as 'a common institution which may be conceived as a light form of federal government', one of the main purposes of which would be to guard against 'Annamite expansionist designs'.[9]

D'Argenlieu, for his part, stuck more rigidly to the conception of a five-way organisation of the Indochinese Union. In his Instructions, he argued for French caution and restraint on the issue of Vietnamese national unity, which for him was apparently analogous with the concept of *Grossdeutschland*:

> We should not speak prematurely of fusing Tonkin, Annam and Cochinchina. It is far from certain that this conception of a Greater Annam corresponds to the wishes of Annamite elements within Cochinchina particularly.[10]

In September, d'Argenlieu set understandable conditions for the discussion of the problem of uniting the various 'elements of the Annamite people'. These included liberation from the Japanese, the evacuation of allied troops, and the restoration of public order. The effect of the allied occupation, however, friendly in the South, more hostile in the North, was to create a mentality of 'what we have we hold'. In his letter to de Gaulle in December, d'Argenlieu was at pains to stress that none of his variations on the theme of ersatz-independence (quoted above) implied 'accepting the thesis of a Greater Annam'.[11] By this stage, events seemed to favour the five-way split: Cochinchina and Cambodia were largely 'pacified' as a result of Leclerc's campaign, and the way was clear for a Cambodian *modus vivendi*, signed on 7 January 1946. By February, setting out limits for negotiations with Hanoi, d'Argenlieu was

9. '... un organe commun qu'on peut concevoir comme un gouvernement fédéral léger,... les desseins de l'expansion annamite'. Tel., 16 Oct. 1945, loc.cit.

10. 'Il convient de ne pas parler prématurément de la fusion Tonkin-Annam-Cochinchine. Il est bien loin d'être sûr que cette conception d'un Grand Annam corresponde notamment aux désirs des éléments annamites de Cochinchine.' Instructions, in d'Argenlieu, *Chronique*, 422.

11. '... nulle ... n'implique une adhésion à la thèse du Grand Annam'. D'Argenlieu to de Gaulle, 28 December 1945, loc.cit.

apparently attempting to box the Viet Minh into their stronghold of Tonkin and North Annam:

> France is ready to negotiate officially and immediately with the Annamite government in Hanoi, but this does not mean that she is arbitrarily adopting a position on the principle of a Vietnam bringing together the three ky in a single territorial and political unit. In the name of freedom, France reserves for Cochinchina the right to express its own wishes at an appropriate moment.
>
> Still less does France recognise the right of the Hanoi Government to speak for the whole of Indochina.[12]

Thus, even before the signing of the March Accords, the High Commissioner was steeling himself for the controversies still to come over Cochinchinese separatism.

The second topic thus merged into the third, and in many ways most pressing, question facing the French, concerning the identity of France's interlocutors. There was no question in French minds following the August Revolution as to the pre-eminence of the Viet Minh within Indochina. Communist dominance, however camouflaged, within the Viet Minh organisation had also been recognized and largely accepted, as had Ho Chi Minh's revolutionary past.[13] The importance of the Viet Minh as negotiating partners was argued on pragmatic rather than idealistic grounds. As Laurentie saw it, France might have expected normally to outwit or disrupt a movement such as the Viet Minh, which did not represent true Annamite aspirations, or did so only badly. However, given that 'Annamite nationalism' was an unavoidable phenomenon, and that 'the Viet Minh today find themselves in the spotlight', it was better to face the problem directly, in other words, to negotiate.[14] Like Laurentie, d'Argenlieu disputed the representative nature of the Viet Minh, and called for contacts with other parties, less coherent perhaps, but just as representative, if not more so. It is striking, however, that d'Argenlieu made no reference either to the August

12. 'Si la France est prête à traiter officiellement et dès maintenant avec le Gouvernement annamite d'Hanoi, elle ne prend pas arbitrairement position sur le principe du Vietnam fondant en une unité territoriale et politique les trois ky. Elle réserve, au nom de la liberté, à la Cochinchine le droit de se prononcer, l'heure venue.

'Encore moins reconnaît-elle au Gouvernement d'Hanoi des titres pour parler au nom de l'Indochine entière.' Note, 12 Feb. 1946, loc.cit.

13. See above, Ch. 5.

14. '... le Viet-Minh se trouve aujourd'hui tenir la vedette devant le monde'. Tel, 16 Oct. 1945, loc.cit.

Revolution which had established the Viet Minh as the party of government, or to Ho's declaration of independence, made the week before these instructions were issued, on 2nd September. Not for the last time, d'Argenlieu gave the impression of formulating policy with only scant reference to reality.[15]

Circumstances argued against the Admiral's scruples, however, and the Chinese occupation tended increasingly to bring the French and Viet Minh together as negotiating partners. Indeed, Sainteny saw the two sides as natural allies. As he argued, first, an entente would improve France's international standing, by removing all the 'fine humanitarian excuses for Chinese occupation or American involvement'.[16] But second, he predicted that the Chinese occupiers' 'almost routine excesses' would fuel age-old Vietnamese hatred for their Northern neighbours. Chinese aims in Vietnam were complex and in part self-contradictory. At one level, the Chinese occupation was merely a bargaining chip in a campaign to gain control of the Yunnan railway and force the abandonment of extraterritoriality and transit rights in China which, along with the concessions at Shanghai and Hangkeou (already regained by China) and the annexed territory of Kouang Cheou Wan, formed the legacy of French imperialism in China. As Devillers comments, Chungking was apparently motivated by the desire for revenge.[17] Negotiations between the GPRF and the Chungking government, starting in October 1945, aimed at meeting Chinese interests and relieving Chinese troops with French in line with the Potsdam agreement. However, many Chinese saw the occupation of Vietnam as an opportunity to extend Chinese influence, and to this end promoted pro-Chinese nationalist parties in order to ensure the expulsion of French colonialism. In particular the Yunnanese General Lu Han, commanding the Chinese occupying forces, made no secret of his own ambition, as distinct from the aims of Chiang Kaishek, to turn Vietnam into a Chinese 'trusteeship'. Chinese occupying forces therefore brought with them the leaders of potentially friendly nationalist groupings. These included the old *Viet Nam Quoc Dan Dang* (VNQDD, or Vietnamese National Party), founded in 1927 on the model of the Guomindang, and the Dong Minh Hoi (the *Viet Nam Cach Menh Dong Minh Hoi*, or 'League of

15. Instructions, loc.cit.

16. 'L'entente franco-annamite ferait disparaître aux yeux du monde tous les beaux prétextes humanitaires militant en faveur d'une occupation chinoise ou d'une ingérence américaine.' Rapport, loc.cit., 97.

17. Devillers, *Paris-Saigon-Hanoi*, 99–100.

Revolutionary Vietnamese Parties'), a Chinese-sponsored amalgam of various groups formed in 1942 (and initially embracing both the VNQDD and the Viet Minh, which had since split away).[18] The Viet Minh were doubly threatened by Chinese intrigue, since anti-communism meant as much to the Chinese as anti-colonialism: the Guomindang had no interest in seeing Communists flourish on their Southern flank while Mao remained a threat. Finally, the Chinese were playing for lucrative material gains from their occupation: progress on talks in Chungking turned initially on the agreement of a massive indemnity payable by the French for the 'costs' of the Chinese occupation; and talks were almost suspended in November when, on the High Commissioner's orders, the Bank of Indochina withdrew from circulation the 500-piastre note issued by the Japanese after 9 March 1945, which was the favoured denomination of Chinese racketeers.[19]

Viet Minh manoeuvres made them not only acceptable as negotiating partners, but also more amenable to the idea of negotiation. In October, Ho succeeded in duping the Chinese temporarily by forming an alliance with 'friendly' Dong Hinh Hoi members. As Pignon noted in a report to d'Argenlieu, dated 28 October:

> There are signs of major divisions at the heart of the revolutionary government.... Notwithstanding all the fuss made over announcing it, the union between Viet Minh and Dong Minh Hoi remains for the moment simply a statement of principle. The struggle between the two factions goes on behind the scenes, and there has not so far been any question of a government reshuffle.[20]

The following month, the Communist Party was dissolved, ostensibly because it had achieved its aims, but in fact to appease the Chinese. In view of the Franco-Chinese tension provoked by the 500-piastre note crisis, the Viet Minh met Chinese wishes further by agreeing to form a Government of National Unity with the

18. P. Devillers, *Histoire du Viet-Nam de 1940 à 1952*, Paris, 1952, 56, 59–61, 104, 109.

19. Devillers, *Paris-Saigon-Hanoi*, 100, 109. Chinese pressure led to the measure being rescinded north of the 16th Parallel; there followed lucrative trafficking in the withdrawn notes between North and South: Devillers, *Histoire*, 198.

20. 'Au sein du Gouvernement révolutionnaire, de grandes dissensions se manifestent.... L'union du Viet Minh et du Dong Minh, proclamée à grand fracas, demeure pour l'instant une simple proposition de principe. La lutte continue dans l'ombre entre les deux factions, et aucune modification dans la composition du Gouvernement n'est encore intervenue.' Rapport Comrep Tonkin to Haussaire Saigon, 28 Oct. 1945, in Devillers, *Paris-Saigon-Hanoi*, 105. At this time Pignon was Sainteny's Political Counsellor (*Conseiller Politique*) in Hanoi.

VNQDD and Dong Minh Hoi. But they refused to cancel the elections set for 23 December, and fearing a Chinese-backed coup against them, continued discreet 'talks about talks' with Pignon and Sainteny in Hanoi. Overtures in November were deemed unacceptable, but it was agreed to maintain contact: in a three-point plan dated 12 November, Ho called for immediate independence; safeguards for French 'prestige' and economic and cultural concessions; an immediate ceasefire in Cochinchina and an end to arms supplies during negotiations.[21] Reporting to d'Argenlieu in December, Pignon doubted that dissolution of the Viet Minh was in the French interest: the Viet Minh included the most prominent and disinterested political figures, which made them not only more dangerous, but also more likely to act consistently and to keep their word if it were in their interest. As Pignon noted:

> There is no doubt that the only figure of any stature is Ho Chi Minh. Any solution proposed by Ho in line with general opinion will be accepted by the masses. No other party leader could achieve this.[22]

However, he also believed that the 'Annamite problem' was secondary to the 'Chinese problem', and that the key to the former lay with the solution found to the latter. Thus France's negotiations would be not bilateral, but based on a triangle in which each apex depended on the other two. While this arrangement would oblige Ho to give ground to the French, it also kept the French from playing their hand too rashly for fear of provoking a Sino-Vietnamese *rapprochement*.

With full-scale negotiations almost in sight in December 1945, d'Argenlieu was fingering an alternative trump card. Apart from the various formulae discussed above for skirting the issue of independence, d'Argenlieu alluded to a 'new development' ('un fait nouveau') which might force a solution. As he explained rather coyly, he had in mind '... the entrance of an Annamite figure who, given that Ho is now largely discredited, might take his place while saving his face, and who might also rally around him a dynamic minority of prominent and committed individuals, alongside the usual rabble of malcontents, glory-seekers and

---

21. Devillers, *Paris-Saigon-Hanoi*, 109.
22. 'Indéniablement, le seul vrai caractère est celui de Ho Chi Minh. Une solution proposée par celui-ci et allant dans le sens de l'opinion générale sera certainement admise par la masse. Aucun autre chef de parti n'en est capable.' D'Argenlieu approved of this 'well-crafted report' ('rapport bien charpenté'), in *Chronique*, 101.

weaklings'.[23] The Admiral was thinking of the ex-Emperor Duy Tan, last of the Nguyen dynasty, who had been forced to abdicate in 1916 in favour of the younger branch, whose scion Bao Dai was now 'Supreme Counsellor' (*Conseiller Suprême*) in Hanoi under his civilian name Vinh Thuy. From an 'painful exile' on the island of Réunion, under the name Vinh San, the older ex-Emperor volunteered in early 1945 to serve the French and Annamite cause. Despite a reference from Tananarive, where snide officials believed him 'sincere as Asiatics go' ('sincère à la manière des Asiatiques'), his arrival in Paris was not greeted with enthusiasm at the Ministry of Colonies in June. Laurentie encouraged Vinh San to join the Army in Germany, but, as he stressed to his colleague de Raymond, 'He will not be employed in a political capacity'.[24] De Gaulle had other ideas: receiving Vinh San on 14 December (after he had served a spell in the Army), he offered to reinstate him as Emperor in the Spring. De Gaulle had not mentioned this to d'Argenlieu, who was kept informed by de Langlade, Secretary-General of Cominindo.[25]

The trump card was never played: returning to Réunion to see his family, Vinh San died when his plane crashed in French Equatorial Africa on 28 December 1945. As de Gaulle lamented to an aide, 'France certainly is unlucky!'; the accident apparently contributed to the General's disillusionment shortly before his resignation as President of the GPRF.[26] This abortive episode stands as a singularly unpromising side road leading off the path of the Accords policy, which d'Argenlieu and de Gaulle nonetheless were apparently eager to take. On what intelligence did d'Argenlieu base his perception that Ho was discredited? Who were the 'prominent and committed individuals' who would rally to the side of Vinh San? And what popular support could be found for a figure who, after almost thirty years in the Indian Ocean, would at best have appeared a hapless French puppet? Answers to these

---

23. '... l'entrée en scène d'une personnalité annamite capable, sans lui faire perdre totalement la face, de se substituer au chef du Viet-Minh largement démonétisé et de rallier à elle outre l'armée classique des mécontents, ambitieux et pusillanimes qui fait masse, une minorité dynamique de personnalités marquantes et convaincues.' D'Argenlieu, *Chronique*, 110.

24. 'Il ne sera pas employé à titre politique'. Dossier 'Vinh San', AOM, INF/123/1105; Tel. Colonies to Boulé, Dir. de l'Information Indochinoise, Tananarive, 3 Jul. 1945; Colonies to de Raymond, 12 Jun. 1945: AN, 72AJ539.

25. In d'Argenlieu, *Chronique*, 112–13; Devillers, *Paris-Saigon-Hanoi*, 118.

26. 'La France n'a décidément pas de chance.' Institut Charles-de-Gaulle, *Le général de Gaulle et l'Indochine*, Paris, 1982, 73–75.

questions might refer to d'Argenlieu's propensity for wishful thinking; to the honourable but politically hopeless leaders of the Autonomous Republic of Cochinchina (after June 1946); and to the range of popular responses, from apathetic to hostile, to the later Bao Dai solution, for which this plan was the blueprint. Paul Mus also recorded de Gaulle's reaction to the news of Vinh San's death: looking up from a report delivered by Mus in person, the General declared: 'We are going back to Indochina because we are stronger'.[27] On such uncertain foundations rested the planned edifice of the Accords policy.

Fourth and finally, underpinning the policy debate, the question of means was less a topic for debate than a source of constant tension between the dictates of reason, which increasingly favoured the Accords policy, and the temptation to go in guns blazing, to which the soldierly instincts of de Gaulle, Leclerc et al. were occasionally prey. Laurentie's argument against the use of force had been usefully applied over the summer of 1945 in the case of Indochina. This argument was now developed by Sainteny, who saw the military option as politically suicidal. As he argued, France could go in alone, or with 'an ally', by which he meant the Viet Minh:

> If we choose the first solution then we must be prepared to be strong and to go in with arms at the ready. There can be no doubt as to the outcome of such a reconquest, provided it is well-timed. Within weeks we will have swept aside their vague attempts at resistance, and the people will be under our thumb just as much as in the past. Physically and materially reconquered it may be, but morally speaking we will have lost Indochina forever.[28]

A show of force was a different matter. For de Gaulle this was a matter of asserting sovereignty: as he wrote to Leclerc at the end of September, 'it is vitally urgent that French authority should be exercised on the spot'. As a further note issued on the same date made clear, however, this precaution was in part the result of de Gaulle's continuing Anglophobia after the Syrian affair: de

27. 'Nous rentrons en Indochine parce que nous sommes les plus forts.' Ibid. On Cochinchinese separatism, see next chapter.

28. 'Si la première solution est retenue, il faut qu'elle y revienne forte et les armes à la main. L'issue de cette reconquête, déclenchée à un moment propice, ne peut faire de doute. En quelques semaines, les velléités de résistance des nationalistes annamites seront balayées, et le peuple aussi soumis que dans le passé. L'Indochine sera reconquise physiquement, matériellement, mais définitivement perdue moralement.' Loc.cit., in Devillers, *Paris-Saigon-Hanoi*, 97.

Gaulle had no desire to leave the field clear for the British, whose motivation was dubious at best.[29] Neither was the idea of a timely show of force inimical to liberals such as Laurentie and Mus: Laurentie himself had argued in July that the French position should be established in the first instance with 'four divisions on the spot at the crucial moment'. This thinking was reflected in principle in the telegramme drafted by Laurentie in mid-October, though in the circumstances it was considered best for negotiations to be initiated before, rather than after, the arrival of French troops, in order to profit from what Laurentie described as 'an unstable balance of forces'.[30]

This latter proposal, however, was rapidly overtaken by events. Leclerc's initial impulse on arriving in Indochina seems to have been in favour of a swift military victory. In a letter to de Gaulle in mid-October he argued that it would be a mistake to enter into negotiations with the Viet Minh 'before we have shown our strength'. Clearly Leclerc had more in mind than Laurentie's symbolic display of authority: as d'Argenlieu wrote to de Gaulle, Leclerc was 'absorbed by dreams of reconquest'.[31] Moreover, with the arrival on 28 October of Colonel Massu's armoured batallions, Leclerc was apparently in a position to realise his dreams, as he embarked on a dramatic campaign of 'pacification' intended to wrest control of the towns and the main arterial routes from the revolutionary committees and guerilla forces of the Viet Minh. Even before the arrival of Massu's tanks, Saigon was largely under Franco-British control, and detachments had been sent by air to Phnom Penh and to Pakse (southern Laos) to dislodge the fledgeling nationalist governments established in Cambodia and Laos. On 7 January 1946, a *modus vivendi* was signed with Prince Sihanouk, sovereign of a self-governing Cambodia. Over the course of the three months from the end of October, Cochinchina and much of South-Annam were indeed 'pacified'. The Viet Minh's organisation in the South was fragmented and its retreating forces reduced

29. '... il est essentiel et urgent que l'autorité française soit présente sur place'. Tel. personnel du Général de Gaulle à d'Argenlieu et à Leclerc, 29 Sep. 1945; Note, Très Secret, pour l'Amiral d'Argenlieu et le Général Leclerc, 29 Sep. 1945, AN, 72AJ539.

30. '... un équilibre instable'. Instructions, loc.cit; see above, Ch. 5.

31. '... avant d'avoir montré notre force', Leclerc to de Gaulle, 13 Oct. 1945, quoted by P. Isoart, 'Aux origines d'une guerre: l'Indochine française (1940–1945)', in P. Isoart, ed., *L'Indochine française, 1940–1945*, Paris, 1983, 68; '... tout acquis au rêve d'une reconquête', d'Argenlieu to de Gaulle, 25 Oct. 1945, d'Argenlieu, *Chronique*, 74.

to pursuing a drastic scorched earth policy, which lost them much political support in the countryside. On 28 January, General Gracey, Commander of the British occupying forces, handed over his powers to Leclerc and left Saigon.[32]

By the end of January 1946, therefore, an approximate consensus had been achieved within the colonial administration, largely on the basis of a compromise between the ideals of a Brazzaville-inspired policy and the pragmatic calculations of the moment, on each of the key issues of the policy debate. Momentum was now building in favour of negotiations with the Viet Minh in Hanoi and their Chinese occupiers. Indeed, such was the force of this momentum that it survived even the shock of the first, and most decisive, of the year's changes of government, with the resignation of de Gaulle as President of the GPRF. The changeover occurred swiftly on this occasion, and on 24 January 1946, only three days after de Gaulle's surprise announcement, the Socialist Félix Gouin was invested as President of the GPRF, the first to lead the 'tripartite' coalition of SFIO, MRP and PCF. Of the three ministers principally responsible for Indochina, two, Edmond Michelet at the Ministry of Armies and Georges Bidault at Foreign Affairs (both MRP), retained their posts, while the veteran Socialist Marius Moutet sought to lend a new image to the Ministry of Colonies, which was renamed the Ministry of Overseas France (*Ministère de la France d'Outre-Mer*). Negotiating as if on auto-pilot, however, the administration was storing up trouble for the future. It is to the ambiguities of the negotiating process that we now turn.

The Ambiguous Accords of 6 March 1946

The dismay recorded by d'Argenlieu,[33] and experienced no doubt by other Gaullists at de Gaulle's resignation in January 1946, had little discernible effect on the process which led to the Accords of 6 March 1946. Events were moving too rapidly for that. Indeed, in late January French policy was starting to make substantial progress simultaneously on three fronts: while plans went ahead to extend Leclerc's campaign to the north, breakthrough was imminent both

---

32. Devillers, *Histoire*, 163–69. On Gracey's role in Leclerc's campaign, see P.M. Dunn, *The First Indochina War*, London, 1985; D.J. Duncanson, 'General Gracey and the Viet Minh', *Royal Central Asian Journal*, Vol.LV, 1967, 288–97.
33. Quoted above, Ch. 4.

in negotiations with the Chinese in Chungking, and with Ho in Hanoi. Within six weeks of de Gaulle's departure from office, France was the co-signatory of a set of historic Accords with a Nationalist government which nonetheless awakened conservative anxieties just as surely as they reflected liberal proposals.

First, then, military preparations were underway for troop landings in Tonkin. In mid-January, General Valluy, commander of the 9th Division of Colonial Infantry (9e DIC), was despatched to Paris to discuss these landings and their military and diplomatic implications. On 26 January, at the first meeting of Comonindo following the change of government, Valluy explained the risks of the proposed operation and its urgency, since the optimal timing for landing was as early as late February or early March: Valluy noted the expected unilateral withdrawal of part of the Chinese occupation forces by that time, the onset of the monsoon by May–June, and the pitiable situation and morale of the French in Tonkin.[34] Equally, he stressed the unfeasibility of a purely military campaign ('une action militaire pure') since, as he argued in a note dated 3rd February, this would antagonize both the Chinese and the Vietnamese, provoke a massacre of the French in Hanoi and Haiphong, put at risk French collaboration with the Tonkinese, turn into a long and hard guerilla campaign involving Chinese irregular troops even if the regular army withdrew, and have profound repercussions both internationally and within Indochina. Any military operation, then, 'must necessarily be backed up'.[35]

Second, partly to 'back up' plans for the reoccupation of the North, the French were starting at long last to make progress in their negotiations with the Chinese. Indeed, it was increasingly clear that the Chungking government, as opposed to General Lu Han, supported a French return to the North, which would allow Chinese withdrawal in accordance with the Potsdam agreements, while assuring the maintenance of law and order. The condition was that the Communists should be kept at bay, especially since the pro-Chinese parties had proved unfit opponents for the Viet Minh. On 1 January, a new Provisional Government of National Unity had taken power, including VNQDD and Dong Minh Hoi ministers. But in general elections on 6 January, the Viet Minh won

---

34. Tel. no. CI/00644, 1 Feb. 1946, Comonindo to Haussaire, 'Compte rendu conférence du 26 janvier 1946, a.s. relève des troupes chinoises', MAE, AO/IC/179.

35. '… doit être obligatoirement *couverte*'. Note, Général Valluy, 'Conditions de notre réinstallation au Tonkin', 3 Feb. 1946, MAE, AO/IC/179. Emphasis in text.

an overwhelming landslide victory; the opposition parties were represented in the new National Assembly only because of a pre-arranged seventy-seat quota.[36] Opposition fury, largely taken out on the French in the North, furthered the case for agreement for French, Chinese, and Viet Minh alike. A slim alternative to negotiation with Ho still existed. As Pignon reported after seeing Chinese envoys in Hanoi, the Chinese aimed to 'see Ho Chi Minh and the Viet Minh disappear from the political and administrative scene in Tonkin'; unable to rely on the pro-Chinese parties, they now sought a bargain with the French, who had shown the way forward with the Cambodian *modus vivendi*. This was the deal:

> As of today, 28 January, it would seem that the Chinese Government, via its highest ranking intermediaries, is proposing, as a last resort, to establish a government that would be acceptable both to them and to us; this means it will be non-communist if not actually anti-communist. Such a government will give the Chinese sufficient guarantees of liberalism. They will then lean on this government to negotiate with us and will smooth the process of relieving their troops with ours.[37]

This left only the question as to whether the Chinese could be trusted. To a certain extent the French had no choice in this, and would inevitably be caught in a Chinese-laid trap. At the same time, Pignon considered it unwise to 'hasten the disintegration of the Viet Minh, with whom we should not lose contact'.[38] He spoke even of finding a hypothetical third party to support, acceptable both to the Chinese and to the Viet Minh. D'Argenlieu vetoed the Chinese proposals, though, as Isoart comments, his intention was possibly to force an agreement with the 'pseudo-government' at Hanoi, simply to ensure the return of French troops, thus enabling the French to negotiate from strength as they had done in the South.[39]

---

36. Devillers, *Paris-Saigon-Hanoi*, 120, 127.

37. '... voir Ho Chi Minh et le Viet Minh disparaître de la scène politique et administrative du Tonkin.... A l'heure actuelle, 28 janvier, il semble que le Gouvernement chinois, par ses représentants les plus qualifiés, nous propose, en dernier ressort, la constitution d'un gouvernement acceptable par eux et par nous, c'est-à-dire, sinon anti-communiste, du moins sans communistes. Ce gouvernement devra aux yeux des Chinois présenter des garanties suffisantes de libéralisme. Ils lui imposeraient alors de traiter avec nous et faciliterait la relève de leurs troupes par les nôtres.' Rapport, 28 Jan. 1946, in d'Argenlieu, *Chronique*, 141.

38. '... hâter la désagrégation du Viet-Minh, avec qui nous ne devons pas perdre le contact'. Ibid.

39. 'Aux origines', 69.

The key factor was the progress made on the third front of French policy, in its moves towards agreement with the Hanoi government. Both in public and in private contacts with the French, the Viet Minh was promoting the idea, in the face of Chinese and pro-Chinese machinations, that it was 'from France that Vietnam can expect most help and understanding'. On 2 February, at the height of the Tet festival (the Vietnamese New Year), Ho visited the victims of anti-French violence in hospital. On 8 February, receiving General Salan, he again rejected the Declaration of March 1945 as being 'long out of date', but appealed to French generosity in the accustomed manner, and even pointed the way forward in negotiation:

> The term 'independence' is not important to me, but its content is important. We want to live in freedom. Of course, we would like extensive trading relations, broader cultural links, French technicans and advisers in every sphere, but we want to be masters in our own home.[40]

Salan reported that the 'inscrutable' Ho had been visibly startled at the news that French landings were imminent, though when Salan commented that 'we are very powerful, why not recognise the fact', Ho promised prolonged resistance by the Vietnamese people.[41] Meeting Pignon and Sainteny on 9 February, General Salan urged them to step up their conversations with Ho. He took the same tack with d'Argenlieu on 11 February. The following day, the High Commissioner, about to leave for his first meeting with the new government in Paris, drew up instructions for Sainteny, already cited, setting out his preferred negotiating position.[42] The day after d'Argenlieu left, on 14 February, Leclerc wired Paris, summarising the official mood in Saigon and calling for a rapid political decision. As he argued, his own objectives had been achieved and the time was now ripe for concessions, especially since continued use of force would embroil France in a long war. In particular the word 'independence' should no longer be taboo:

40. '"C'est de la France que le Vietnam peut attendre le plus d'aide et de compréhension".... "Peu m'importe le terme 'indépendance', ce qui m'importe c'est le contenu. Nous voulons vivre libres. Certes, nous voulons des échanges économiques très nombreux, des relations culturelles plus étendues, des cadres, des techniciens français dans tous les domaines, mais nous voulons être maîtres chez nous".' Entretien du Gén. Salan avec Ho Chi Minh, 8 Feb. 1946, in Bodinier, *Le retour*, 203.

41. '... nous sommes très forts, pourquoi ne pas le reconnaître'. Ibid.

42. D'Argenlieu's instructions to Sainteny, in d'Argenlieu, *Chronique*, 146–47, Devillers, *Paris-Saigon-Hanoi*, 131–34.

Giving way on the utterance of this word four months ago was tantamount to admitting our impotence. At present we have reaffirmed French sovereignty and power, restored order in Cochinchina, Cambodia and in parts of Laos and Annam, and we are just about to arrive in force at the gates of Tonkin. Now we can talk to the Annamites and make concessions, as a soverign power and on the terms most favourable to us.[43]

Leclerc's position, advocating negotiation from militarily acquired strength, may thus be seen as the synthesis of the two strands of the French debate.

With expectations running high for further progress, the desired breakthrough was not long in coming. In the event, the first, crucial concessions were made by Ho Chi Minh. Salan returned to Hanoi on 14 February to inform Lu Han of French plans for troop landings at the beginning of March, and to urge Sainteny to proceed with negotiations. Following a meeting with Ho on 16 February, Sainteny flew to Saigon, and that evening Leclerc sent news of the basis for a Franco-Vietnamese agreement, arrived at in what was described as a 'long and decisive conversation'. The political terms of agreement were largely in France's favour:

1. French Government recognises in principle Vietnam's self-government, but this recognition is subject to the following conditions: Vietnam will remain within the French Union, will accept French advisers and technicians, will guarantee the maintenance and indeed the development of France's economic privileges, will adopt the same position in cultural matters, and will invite the French army to relieve Chinese troops in Tonkin at the earliest opportunity.[44]

43. '... céder il y a quatre mois sur ce mot constituait une capitulation et un aveu d'impuissance. Actuellement nous avons réaffirmé la souveraineté et la puissance françaises, rétabli l'ordre en Cochinchine, au Cambodge et dans une partie du Laos et de l'Annam, et nous allons arriver en force aux portes du Tonkin. Nous pouvons en toute souveraineté et au meilleur prix parler avec les Annamites et concéder.' Tel. Cororient to Chiefs of Staff (EMGDN), no. 501/4, 14 Feb. 1946, AOM, Tels/933; Devillers, *Paris-Saigon-Hanoi*, 137.

44. '1° Gouvernement français reconnaît à Viet-nam le principe d'un self-government, mais pose à cette reconnaissance les conditions ci-après énumérées: Vietnam restera dans l'Union française, acceptera conseillers et techniciens français, garantira à la France le maintien et même le développement de ses avantages économiques, adoptera la même position sur le plan culturel, invitera l'armée française à relever sans délai les troupes chinoises au Tonkin.' Tel. Cororient à Cominindo et à EMGDN, no. 515/Cab, Saigon, 17 Feb. 1946. MAE, AO/IC/179.

Ho asked for the GPRF's terms to be sent via Sainteny, and promised his acceptance. Further, Sainteny indicated Lu Han's willingness to back France's initiative. The extent of Ho's concessions was spelled out by Leclerc:

a) Ho Chi Minh has definitively abandoned his claim to the term 'independence'.

b) The term 'self government' was chosen by Ho Chi Minh himself, at Sainteny's suggestion, in preference to 'government freedom' and 'freedom within French Union'.

c) Ho Chi Minh accepts the inclusion of Vietnam in the Indochinese Federation.

d) Ho Chi Minh seems to have given up the idea of United Nations representation.

e) Sainteny established the principle that Cochinchina should decide its own future.[45]

On this understanding, Comindo met on 20 February to discuss the terms of d'Argenlieu's reply. As Laurentie argued in his brief for the meeting, things had come a long way in the few months since the first French landings:

It is quite clear, from a consideration of the difference between our position in September and Mr. Ho Chi Minh's proposals, that we have succeeded to such an extent that it would be a great mistake to risk compromising that success in the slightest by seeking further gains. In the circumstances, the only way we can be clever is by accepting these proposals as rapidly and openly as possible.[46]

Apart from responding point-for-point to the terms of Leclerc's telegramme of 17 February, d'Argenlieu's reply, agreed at the meeting of Comindo, also included two important qualifications. First, the inclusion of Vietnam in the French Union and the

45. 'a) Ho Chi Minh renonce définitivement au mot indépendance.
  'b) Le terme self-government a été choisi par Ho Chi Minh lui-même, sur proposition de Sainteny, de préférence à terme de liberté de gouvernement et liberté dans Union française.
  'c) Ho Chi Minh admet intégration du Viêt-nam dans Fédération indochinoise.
  'd) Ho Chi Minh semble abandonner désir de représentation dans l'ONU.
  'e) Sainteny a posé le principe que Cochinchine déciderait elle-même de sa position future.' Ibid.
46. 'Il est tout à fait clair que si l'on mesure la différence entre notre situation en septembre et les propositions de M. Ho Chi Minh, le succès est si éclatant que ce serait une grande faute de risquer le moins du monde de le compromettre en cherchant à obtenir un avantage supplémentaire. La seule habileté en l'espèce, c'est la rapidité et la franchise de l'acceptation.' 'Note pour le Conseil des Ministres', 18 Feb. 1946, AN, 72AJ539.

Indochinese Federation implied that France alone was responsible for Vietnam's overseas representation, though Indochinese officials in some French missions might act for Indochinese interests. And second, d'Argenlieu argued that the question of the three *ky* was still wide open, and in particular the mention of Cochinchina in no sense implied that the question of fusing Annam and Tonkin had been settled.[47]

It seemed briefly as if France had achieved all of its principal objectives in one stroke. French optimism proved premature, however, as over the following three weeks an extraordinary bout of three-way arm-wrestling ensued. First, Ho's concessions turned out to have been the result of temporary weakness in his own personal position. In his talks with Sainteny on 16 February, Ho had called for a rapid declaration by the GPRF in order to shore up his position against the Chinese and the opposition, and had spoken of perhaps having to step down, if only temporarily.[48] As rumours of Ho's talks filtered out, the VNQDD started to agitate against the 'Government of Traitors', and in favour of a new cabinet headed by Vinh Thuy. On 23 February, Ho even offered to change places with Vinh Thuy and to accept demotion as Supreme Counsellor, but that same evening he apologized to Vinh Thuy for a moment of weakness. The following day an agreement was signed between the three main parties and the smaller Democrat Party (*Parti Démocrate*) establishing the Governement of Union presented to the National Assembly on 3 March, with Ho still at its head, but with Dong Minh Hoi and VNQDD members in key positions including the Vice-Presidency. By seeking to ensure Chinese cooperation, and to share responsibility for negotiations with the Opposition, Ho could now also apply pressure in his daily negotiations with Sainteny, refusing to accept the imminent arrival of French troops in Hanoi, and holding out on Cochinchina, which he insisted formed an integral part of Vietnam.[49]

It was now the turn of the Chinese to threaten French plans. Following the Chungking government's concession to French insistence that the French relief of Chinese occupying forces be agreed before Chinese demands were met, a Franco-Chinese Treaty was initialled on 28 February, providing for the arrival of French forces between 1 and 15 March. The French fleet, having sailed from Saigon, was due to arrive in the Bay of Haiphong on 5 March,

47. In d'Argenlieu, *Chronique*, 160–61.
48. Tel. no. 515/Cab, 17 Feb. 1946, loc.cit.
49. Devillers, *Paris-Saigon-Hanoi*, 143–45.

ready to land the Expeditionary Corps on the 6th. But on 4 March, aboard the cruiser *Richelieu* riding off Haiphong, Leclerc discovered that the Chinese military authorities at Haiphong had no orders concerning the French landings. Since aborting the mission was inconceivable (and was not discussed), the alternative to Franco-Chinese hostilities was an immediate Franco-Vietnamese agreement, to ensure law and order in the wake of the Chinese departure. While Salan, French Commander North of the 16th Parallel, parleyed with the Chinese, Leclerc urged Sainteny, in a letter written by one of his staff-officers, Colonel Lecomte, to reach agreement at any cost:

> Given the gravity of the situation and the extent of eventual conflict, I beg of you on behalf of General Leclerc, who has given me authorisation to do so, to do everything within your power to reach agreement as soon as possible, *even if this means taking initiatives which could later be disavowed.*[50]

Sainteny was thus given carte blanche to finalise the Accords, which were signed on the 6th and witnessed by Chinese, British, and American observers. When shots were fired by the Chinese in Haiphong, the French riposted, inflicting heavy damage, but a ceasefire was quickly arranged and the landings proceeded smoothly thereafter. After a further nine days, Lu Han and Leclerc reached agreement concerning the stationing of French forces in Hanoi. On 18 March, a column of a thousand French troops marched into Hanoi to be greeted by the ecstatic French population. As was already clear, however, Leclerc's breezy greeting to President Ho, 'So, Mr. President, do we now see eye to eye?', was a courteous oversimplification.[51]

The major Accord signed on 6 March 1946 was the Preliminary Convention (*Convention Préliminaire*) which, in three short paragraphs, developed the terms of Sainteny's agreement with Ho three weeks earlier and which, by the same token, reflected the earlier policy debate. The political terms of the agreement, in the first paragraph, were more precise than previously. The indeterminate

---

50. 'Etant donné la gravité de la situation et l'ampleur du conflit possible, je vous demande instamment au nom du général Leclerc qui m'a donné pouvoir de vous le dire, de faire tout ce qui est en votre pouvoir pour arriver au plus tôt à un accord, *fût-ce au prix d'initiatives qui pourraient être désavouées.*' Lettre du Lieutenant-Colonel Lecomte àM.Sainteny, Commissaire de la République à Hanoi, 5 Mar. 1946, in d'Argenlieu, *Chronique*, 439, emphasis added. See also Devillers, *Paris-Saigon-Hanoi*, 146–47.

51. 'Alors, monsieur le Président, on est d'accord maintenant?' Devillers, *Paris-Saigon-Hanoi*, 154–55.

notion of 'self-government' was dropped, and the question of the three *ky* was now at the heart of the agreement:

> 1. The French Government recognises the Republic of Vietnam as a Free State with its own government, parliament, army, and finances, forming a part of the Indochinese Federation and of the French Union. Concerning the union of the three ky, the French Government undertakes to respect the decisions taken by the people and expressed in a referendum.[52]

As d'Argenlieu noted, there was nothing here that contradicted his own instructions of 20 February, although on the three *ky* he regretted the passing of France's earlier 'clear position based on the Declaration of 24 March 1945'.[53] The second paragraph was also unproblematic, concerning the Hanoi government's willingness to welcome French troops. And the third paragraph called for a ceasefire in order to create a suitable atmosphere for further negotiations. The seat of an eventual conference was to be Paris, Saigon, or Hanoi, and the proposed topics for negotiation included Vietnam's diplomatic relations with third countries, its future status, and French economic and cultural interests in Vietnam. Although these, along with the core issues of independence and national unity, were to fuel controversy over the coming months, no qualms on this score are recorded by d'Argenlieu in his *Chronique d'Indochine*.

More immediately controversial was the Annex Accord (*Accord Annexe*) signed at the same time, which was intended to fix the modalities of the French military takeover. In fact, it went considerably further than a mere relief of troops ('relève'). The first paragraph was concerned with troop numbers: the relief troops were to be composed of ten thousand Vietnamese troops and a total of fifteen thousand French, including those French forces already based in the North. Only metropolitan French troops were to be used, except for the guarding of Japanese prisoners, who were to be evacuated, and their guards repatriated, within ten months. Overall responsibility was given to the French High Command,

---

52. '1° Le Gouvernement français reconnaît la République du Viet-nam comme un Etat libre ayant son gouvernement, son parlement, son armée et ses finances, faisant partie de la Fédération indochinoise et de l'Union française. En ce qui concerne la réunion des trois ky, le Gouvernement français s'engage à entériner les décisions prises par la population consultée par référendum.' Convention Préliminaire and Accord Annexe, full text in d'Argenlieu, *Chronique*, 188–90.

53. '... [la] position claire, issue de la déclaration du 24 mars'. Ibid., 190.

assisted by Vietnamese delegates. The controversy came in the second paragraph which provided for the progressive Vietnamese relief over five years of all French troops. If the Admiral had been unable to pin down his lingering discomfiture in reading the Convention, it was easily identifiable in the case of the Annex: 'The future of French land, sea and air forces has hereby been signed away without a second thought'.[54] D'Argenlieu cabled to Sainteny demanding an explanation of this apparent *fait accompli*, and delayed transmitting the Annex to Paris, fearing the document's likely repercussions. Leclerc reassured him that the Accord might serve as the 'basis for useful discussions', since it provided for the continued French defence of unspecified naval and airbases. Sainteny explained that the Annex was his work and Pignon's, with Salan's agreement, but that the question of the 'relève' had been mentioned by Ho on the last day; refusal to accept any part of the Accords at that late stage would have meant the failure of the Accords as a whole. On 11 March, d'Argenlieu finally transmitted the text of the Annex to Paris, with a covering note employing both Leclerc's and Sainteny's arguments.[55]

An astute bargaining ploy on Ho's part to exploit French discomfiture, the proposal for French troop withdrawals over five years also helped Ho consolidate his domestic position. When news of the Accords leaked, the VNQDD prepared to mobilise. But at a rally on 7 March, Ho, Vo Nguyen Giap, and Vu Hong Khanh, VNQDD leader and co-signatory of the Convention, sought to justify the agreement with the French. Giap stressed Vietnam's isolation and her need for economic aid and for food supplies from Cochinchina. (Famine in Tonkin had been averted by a mixture of hardship policies and mass mobilisation to grow vegetables.) Arguing that complete independence could not be realised immediately, he evoked the 1918 Brest-Litovsk Treaty to show how a revolutionary government made temporary concessions in adversity. On the three *ky*, he argued that the result of any referendum on the issue was easily predictable. Khanh too stressed the final goal of complete independence. But it fell to Ho, on whose authority and prestige the Accords rested (and to a certain extent vice versa), to press home the purpose of his own diplomacy: what was the point of fighting to prevent the arrival of French

54. 'Voilà le devenir de l'ensemble des forces françaises de terre, de mer, de l'air prématurément engagé'. Ibid., 191.
55. Ibid., 193, 201–203.

troops, when there would only be fifteen thousand of them, and when they would be gone in five years?[56] By the end of the rally, Ho Chi Minh had won his case, but the equilibrium established was as fragile for Ho as for the French.

—— ∞∞ ——

Although quickly hailed as a triumph for French liberalism, the Accords of 6 March were fatally compromised by the fact that they emerged from crisis, with the result that, at bottom, they suited no-one. On the face of it, the Preliminary Convention corresponded to the kind of solution advocated by Laurentie and his allies at the Rue Oudinot: Vietnam was to be a part of both the Indochinese Federation and the French Union; the issue of internal unity stood a chance of being resolved peacefully and equitably; and for the moment nationalist interlocutors and a set of suitably liberal polices had been given the benefit of the doubt. At the very least, France had scored a 'first' in an international context, as Laurentie argued in a circular to the colonial Governors and Governors-General:

> We must consider that opinion in Asia is generally hostile to the colonial powers. Britain's difficulties in India, and those of the Dutch in Indonesia, are ample proof of this. It is therefore remarkable that our country should by amicable means have arrived at a definition of common ground with Annamite nationalism.

As he stressed, much depended on the sensitivity ('délicatesse') with which French negotiators set about constructing the autonomy of the new Vietnam. But Laurentie was careful to qualify the extent to which the Vietnamese case should be seen as setting an example elsewhere in the French empire:

> The autonomy thus publicly granted the Republic of Vietnam may appear to draw France towards a policy of self-government. You must not make overhasty generalisations along these lines on the basis of a purely local solution.[57]

---

56. Devillers, *Histoire*, 228–30. In private Ho preferred a graphic metaphor: 'Better to sniff the French dungheap for five years than to have to eat Chinese dung forever!' ('*Mieux vaut renifler la crotte française pendant cinq ans, que manger la crotte chinoise pour toujours!*')

57. 'Il faut considérer en effet que l'état d'esprit en Asie est d'une façon générale hostile aux puissances coloniales. Les difficultés de la Grande-Bretagne dans l'Inde et de la Hollande en Indonésie en sont le témoignage. Il est donc remarquable que

As he pointed out, at the same time as France was recognizing the Republic of Vietnam, she was also about to transform the Antilles, Guyane, and Réunion into French *départements*. Different solutions applied to different cases: French policy was at one and the same time liberal and 'empirical'.

The lessons which could be drawn from this episode by the High Commissioner in Saigon were rather different. The first was that, even in the absence of de Gaulle at the head of the Government, and notwithstanding the professed liberalism of the administration in Paris, the 'bottom line' for the GPRF remained the maintenance of French sovereignty. This was especially the case for conservatives such as Bidault. As d'Argenlieu had feared, after they had belatedly been informed of the Annex Accord, the GPRF's delight at the Accords turned instantly to displeasure. On 9 March, officials met to draw up the agenda for Cominindo on 13 March, which was largely devoted to arrangements for the negotiations prescribed by the Accords.[58] Over the intervening weekend, however, d'Argenlieu cabled the contents of the Annex. Moutet's congratulations of the 9th were now followed by a reprimand:

> Your telegramme transmitting the Annex Accord of 6 March only reached us on 12 March. The Government has now been presented with a fait accompli concerning points on which it has never been consulted. I instruct you in future never to conclude an accord of whatever nature without first submitting the text in advance for the Government's agreement. Express reservations concerning the relief of troops.[59]

The Cominindo meeting on the 13th was dominated by the new development, with Bidault taking the lead in denouncing the deal on troop withdrawals. In his brief for the meeting Philippe Baudet,

---

notre pays ait pu trouver à l'amiable un terrain d'entente avec le nationalisme annamite. ... l'autonomie donnée publiquement à la République du Viet-Nam peut paraître entraîner notre pays vers une politique de self government. Il ne faut pas que vous tiriez de cette solution locale des généralisations trop hâtives dans ce sens.' Tel. no. 262 Circ/AP, ref.HL/bp, Secret, 8 Mar. 1946. AN, 72AJ535.

58. Comité Interministériel de l'Indochine, Ordre du jour de la séance du mardi 13 mars 1946, 9 Apr. 1946, MAE, AO/IC/179.

59. 'Votre télégramme donnant les accords annexes du 6 mars nous parvient seulement le 12 mars. Le Gouvernement est maintenant mis en présence d'un fait accompli concernant des points sur lesquels il n'a jamais été consulté. Je vous prie à l'avenir de ne conclure aucun accord de quelque nature que ce soit sans que le texte ait été au préalable soumis à l'accord du Gouvernement. Faites des réserves pour la relève des troupes.' Tel. Moutet to d'Argenlieu, no. 237/CI, 13 Apr. 1946, in d'Argenlieu, *Chronique*, 207.

Director of the Asia-Oceania Division at the Quai d'Orsay, gloomily predicted that France would lose her foothold in all three *ky,* and that Cambodian and Laotian security within the Indochinese Federation would crumble under pressure from Vietnam in the East and in the West from Thailand (which at this date still occupied the provinces of Battambang and Siam-Reap annexed in 1940). As Baudet commented: 'At first sight it looks like another Syrio-Lebanese affair'.[60]

However, a second lesson which could be concluded from the affair concerned the potential for autonomous decision making by the administration in Indochina: Paris was apparently quite prepared to let its agents in the Far East act independently in the rather alarming way which had led to the Accords, and to accept the results of their independent initiatives. To be sure, in this instance the March Accords represented the temporary seal on the controversy which had marked the internal policy debate, but in fact the planning and strategy of the Paris administration had counted for little. In particular, what 'liberal' input there had been into the negotiating process had come from officials in Indochina and especially from Leclerc. Moreover, notwithstanding the furore, the Accords were not disavowed, although this was an option mentioned in Baudet's briefing, and was therefore presumably raised by Bidault at Cominindo. On 18 March, as French troops marched into Hanoi, Moutet sent a further telegramme of congratulations to d'Argenlieu, promising his full support in the Assembly for the Accords, 'which I fully support', and pointing out that it was Bidault who had protested against them.[61] Alongside some of the initiatives which d'Argenlieu was contemplating, the agreement reached on 6 March would soon be remembered as a peak of liberalism in France's Indochina policy.

60. 'A première vue, c'est une nouvelle affaire syro-libanaise' Note pour le Ministre, ref.PB/-, 13 Mar. 1946, in Devillers, *Paris-Saigon-Hanoi,* 166.

61. Tels. Moutet to d'Argenlieu, 263/CI 1005, 13 Mar. 1946; 264/CI 1006, 14 Apr. 1946; 289/CI 1042, 18 Mar. 1946: in d'Argenlieu, *Chronique,* 210–11, 215.

7

WHO RULES: PARIS OR SAIGON?

The Dalat Conference and the Cochinchina Policy,
March–June 1946

With the signing of the Accords of 6 March 1946, a second phase of
the Accords policy began, in which the GPRF and the Republic of
Vietnam sought to engage in the 'frank and friendly negotiations'
prescribed by the Preliminary Convention. The aim of this process
was to settle the issues left unresolved in the Accords, including
still the two principal questions which divided the French and the
Vietnamese: Vietnam's status within the French Union and internationally, and the question of the three *ky*. The Accords also
brought to an end the improvisation and hectic parleying which
had marked the policy-making process in the first months following the 'return', and which had temporarily resolved the
controversy over the terms of the nascent Accords policy. This
controversy would now be re-opened, and indeed deepened and
broadened, for the issues which had separated 'liberal' and 'conservative' opinion were now increasingly reflected in the attitudes
and actions of two rival French centres of decision making: Paris
and Saigon.

This chapter is thus concerned with the emergence of rivalry
between central government and local administration, which had
remained latent in the period up to the signing of the Accords, but
which was now to become an established characteristic of French
policy making, contributing to the breakdown of policy and leading ultimately to the outbreak of war. Although chiefly manifested
in differences of approach to policy, it may be argued that this
rivalry stemmed from the divergent interests and perspectives of
the two centres. Thus, for the GPRF, Indochina took its place in the

background of the intensifying political crisis accompanying the Constitution-making process; nonetheless, it was an issue which Paris was now concerned to dominate, especially given the potentially disastrous consequences of the local initiative taken in the run-up to 6 March. On the other hand, the High Commission's much closer focus on Indochina threw into relief the problems created by the Accords rather than the positive achievements of French policy. Saigon's increasing antagonism towards the Hanoi government was thus directed against the Accords, which were therefore to be compromised or diverted. Both positions may be distinguished from that of officials at the Ministry of Overseas France, seeking to regain their influence following the Ministry's eclipse in the preceding few months.

In particular, the chapter shows how the rival interests and perceptions of the two centres came to be reflected, within weeks of the signing of the Accords, in their differing approaches to two issues, corresponding to the two outstanding questions identified above. The first was the issue of negotiations between the French and the Vietnamese. Were these to take the shape of an inter-governmental conference, as the text of the Accords implied, thus contributing to the idea that Vietnam was acquiring the attributes of sovereignty? Alternatively, should agreement be reached between Ho Chi Minh, understood as leader of one of the constituent 'lands' of the Indochinese Federation, and the appointed head of that Federation, the High Commissioner? This question was temporarily resolved with a compromise, in the form of a Preparatory Conference held in April–May 1946 at Dalat, the proposed Federal capital of Indochina, preceding a full Franco-Vietnamese Conference to be held in France. The second issue was the increasingly vigorous Cochinchina policy ('politique cochinchinoise'), with which the Saigon administration supported and encouraged a separatist movement in Cochinchina, the Southern *ky*. Was this a legitimate attempt to promote a Nationalist alternative to the Viet Minh in Hanoi, or merely a retrograde attempt by Saigon to apply the outdated terms of the March 1945 Declaration and to block Vietnamese ambitions to unify their country? The controversy surrounding this issue reached a climax on 1 June 1946 when, as a Vietnamese delegation headed by Ho Chi Minh left Hanoi for the Fontainebleau Conference, the High Commissioner declared the Autonomous Republic of Cochinchina, in a first recourse to the unilateral action which was increasingly to characterise Saigon's policy.

'To make nothing of Dalat so that Paris is everything'.[1]

As suggested in an earlier chapter, the two critical developments in French domestic politics in 1946, de Gaulle's resignation and the Constitution-making process, both had a profound impact on colonial policy making.[2] In the aftermath of the signing of the Accords of 6 March, the full implications of this impact for Indochina policy had yet to be realised, but its effects may nonetheless be detected in the GPRF's decreasing confidence and sense of certainty, and in Saigon's tendency to set the terms and the pace of policy, a tendency which had prevailed before 6 March and which Paris now sought to reverse. The first hints of an emerging rivalry came in preparations for the Preparatory Conference held at Dalat in April–May. In the run-up to this conference, both sides sought to impose their own control on the negotiating process, while showing an apparent unwillingness to trust the other's capacity for decision making. The Dalat Conference, however, was to prove a minor setback for Saigon, which had failed to allow for the strategy of the third player, in the shape of the Hanoi government.

Controversy erupted quickly concerning the siting of an eventual Franco-Vietnamese Conference. Dalat, a hill station in the South Annamese highlands which was to become the capital of the Indochinese Federation, was proposed by d'Argenlieu in reaction to Ho Chi Minh's insistence on going to Paris to negotiate, but his proposal also stemmed from a highly restrictive interpretation of the March Accords. Of the three possible host cities named in the Accords, Saigon seems not to have been seriously considered, and Hanoi was quickly ruled out by Sainteny and Pignon as being too close to the sources of Vietnamese pressure and Chinese influence.[3] D'Argenlieu explained his reasons for refusing Ho in a telegramme to Paris:

> Ho's aim is to see the planned conference open in Paris as soon as possible. This would be a grave mistake in all respects. Since his government has resolved with him to remain within the Indochinese federation, it is indispensable that we keep it within this

1. 'Faire que Dalat ne soit rien pour que Paris soit tout': see below.
2. See above, Ch. 4.
3. Tel., Sainteny to d'Argenlieu, 7 Mar. 1946, in P. Devillers, *Paris-Saigon-Hanoi, Les archives de la guerre, 1944–1947*, Paris, 1988, 169.

framework for the whole of this preliminary period. Not to do so would constitute a flagrant injustice towards the Cambodian and Laotian sovereigns.

At Dalat, however, a conference could proceed 'in a calm, serene atmosphere away from the pressure of mass demonstrations, whether spontaneous or organised'.[4] Cominindo's response, which crossed with d'Argenlieu's delayed despatch of the controversial Annex to the March Accords, agreed to rule out Paris, but pointed out that the choice of Dalat contravened the Accords. Suggesting two 'tiers' of negotiations, at Hanoi and then at Dalat, it also made two proposals potentially more worrying to the High Commissioner: that he should be supported at the various stages of negotiation by ministerial delegates sent from Paris for this purpose; and that a committee should be established in Paris reporting to Cominindo on the 'federal and diplomatic problem'.[5]

The rationale for these provisions by Cominindo officials was not stated, but in a note issued for a subsequent meeting of Cominindo, Philippe Baudet, Director of the Asia-Oceania Division at the Quai d'Orsay, commented that ministerial representatives would ensure that no more 'hasty and irresponsible commitments' were made in Saigon without reference to the GPRF.[6] In other words, d'Argenlieu was somewhat unfairly being blamed for the signing of the Annex to the Accords. This line of reasoning was apparently already on d'Argenlieu's mind at a special meeting of his Federal Council on 11 March, when he criticised what he called the 'extreme distortion' of the Indochinese problem, which tended to 'put metropolitan institutions in charge, which bore no direct responsibility for the Indochinese populations'.[7] The ostensible reason for d'Argenlieu's 'surprise' was that

4. 'Il [i.e., Ho] ambitionne de voir à très bref délai s'ouvrir à Paris la conférence prévue. Ce serait une erreur grave à tous égards. Puisque son gouvernement a résolu avec lui de faire partie de la Fédération indochinoise, il est indispensable de le maintenir dans ce cadre durant toute cette période préliminaire. Ce serait injustice flagrante vis-à-vis des souverains du Cambodge et du Laos. ... dans une atmosphère calme et sereine à l'abri de toute manifestation spontanée ou organisée de foule'. Hau[t Commi]ssaire to Cominindo, 8 Mar. 1946, in G. Thierry d'Argenlieu, *Chronique d'Indochine, 1945–1947*, Paris, 1985, 198–99.

5. Tel. no. 958–960 CI, 9 Mar. 1946, in d'Argenlieu, *Chronique*, 204.

6. '... des engagements hâtifs et irresponsables'. Note pour le Ministre, a.s. Comité de l'Indochine du 28 mars, ref.PB/LD, 28 Mar. 1946, MAE, AO/IC/179.

7. 'le gauchissement extrême.. [qui tend à] coiffer ce problème par des organismes métropolitains, irresponsables vis-à-vis des populations indochinoises'. D'Argenlieu, *Chronique*, 204.

Paris's suggestion would make it easier for Ho to step free of the framework of the Indochinese Federation, 'without which there will be no Indochina'. To impress this point upon Paris, the High Commissioner despatched a telegramme presenting an extremely limited idea of the agreement signed on 6 March:

> It has a local character. Signed by the Commissioner for the Republic in Tonkin, with the de facto Hanoi government, it explicitly defers to an eventual decision by the populations of Cochinchina and Annam concerning the eventual union of the three ky. It does not therefore differ in substance from the Agreement signed with Cambodia.[8]

In other words, the March Accords were to be seen as the equivalent of the Franco-Cambodian *modus vivendi* of 7 January 1946, signed within the framework of the March 1945 Declaration.

Insistence on Paris as the site of an eventual conference was part of a concerted campaign by the Hanoi government to press home the advantages which it perceived as flowing from the March Accords. This campaign was adroitly whipped up by the Viet Minh's propaganda machine in Hanoi, in the press and in a series of public demonstrations which threatened to jeopardize the triumphal arrival of Leclerc and his troops into Hanoi, planned for 18 March. The campaign included also the efforts by Ho, firmly rebuffed by Saigon, to have Viet Minh representatives administer the ceasefire agreement south of the 16th Parallel, and complaints to Félix Gouin about alleged French violations of the ceasefire (which Gouin referred to Cominindo); it also took the form of appeals for recognition to the British, American, Soviet, and Chinese Military Missions in Hanoi and to the Secretary-General of the United Nations, which were forwarded to the Quai d'Orsay but otherwise ignored.[9] On 17 March, d'Argenlieu responded to the insistence of Sainteny and Leclerc in Hanoi, and asked permission of Cominindo to announce publicly (while keeping his and its options open) that Ho would shortly be invited

---

8. 'Il a un caractère local. Signé par le Commissaire de la République pour le Tonkin, avec le gouvernement annamite de fait siégeant à Hanoi, il réserve expressément la décision des populations de la Cochinchine et de l'Annam touchant la fusion éventuelle des trois ky. Par sa nature, il ne diffère donc pas de celui qui est intervenu avec le Cambodge.' D'Argenlieu à Cominindo, Saigon, 442F, 12 Mar. 1946: d'Argenlieu, *Chronique*, 205–06.

9. Tel. Cominindo to Saigon, no. CI 1072, 21 Mar. 1946; Br. Embassy, Paris, to Bidault, no. 328, ref. 19/54/46, 2 Apr. 1946; MAE to Chungking, Washington, Moscow, no. 158, 1018, 750, 8 Apr. 1946: MAE, AO/IC/68.

to Paris, though he argued that such a plan was still ill-advised, and that Sainteny had committed himself too far on this subject. Moutet agreed immediately, but without apparently understanding the limited nature of the permission being asked, since he added that more could be achieved in Paris, 'since the principal character would be removed from the influences which usually surrounded him'.[10]

Even without waiting for Paris's approval, d'Argenlieu set about striking a compromise with Ho according to his own counsel. In a memorandum to Sainteny, dated 17 March, he proposed a meeting aboard the cruiser *Emile Bertin* in the Bay of Along, at which President Ho would receive all the 'honours due to his rank, a gun salute, crew lining the decks and cheering, and so forth'.[11] This meeting took place on Sunday 24 March. After their glacial formal exchanges, the aristocratic Admiral and the former Comintern agent got down to business. To counter Ho's 'obsession' with the idea of a conference in Paris, since 'you don't go to Paris just like that', d'Argenlieu proposed a preparatory conference at Dalat, and suggested that Hanoi should also send a parliamentary good will mission to Paris. These would then lead the way to a conference in the metropole at which agreement would be finalised; this, it was hoped, could take place by the second half of May. President Ho, who reportedly found the Admiral 'very polite and affable', accepted this proposition, and the meeting ended with toasts and speeches.[12]

D'Argenlieu's cable to Paris on his return to Saigon, coupled with his own commentary in his diary, reveal in almost equal measure his suspicion of Ho's motivation and his doubts as to the GPRF's capacity to handle the negotiations. As he explained to Cominindo, Ho's position was wholly tactical:

> The President has all the techniques of a revolutionary leader, which are those of the party by which he was trained.
>
> His policy will now be to evade all the provisions of the 6 March Accords which make the difference between the agreed

10. '… le principal personnage étant soustrait aux influences de son milieu'. D'Argenlieu to Cominindo, 472F, 17 Mar. 1946; Moutet to d'Argenlieu, 289/CI 1042, 18 Mar. 1946: d'Argenlieu, *Chronique*, 213, 215.

11. '… les honneurs dus à son rang, salves d'artillerie, équipage à la bande, hurrahs, etc.' Devillers, *Paris-Saigon-Hanoi*, 172.

12. '… on ne va pas à Paris comme cela', d'Argenlieu, *Chronique*, 229–34; 'très poli et très affable', Devillers, *Paris-Saigon-Hanoi*, 173.

formula of a 'Free State forming a part of the Indochinese Federation and of the French Union' and full independence.[13]

Ho's aim in wanting to negotiate in Paris, it was suggested, was to gain media and public attention, awaken party interest, and to put pressure on the Government. In private, d'Argenlieu's commented that Ho was hoping to 'exert a powerful influence on left-wing political circles and thus put pressure on the Provisional Government'. Cominindo sent its approval on 3 April.[14]

Having accepted d'Argenlieu's proposal and, to a large extent, his reasoning, Cominindo was now concerned to retain the initiative in the run-up to Dalat. The agenda for the Conference, following the Accords, covered three main points: Vietnam's diplomatic relations with third countries, the future status of Indochina, and French economic and cultural interests in Vietnam. Given the nature of these issues, the Quai d'Orsay now largely took charge. Baudet thus provided the clinching diplomatic argument for not holding the initial conference in Paris:

> Welcoming Ho Chi Minh in Paris would in itself pose problems of protocol which it would be impossible to resolve given the fact that there is no certainty whatsover as to the extent of his authority, whether in territorial or moral terms.[15]

On the other hand, he supported the signature of a final accord in Paris, once initial agreement had been reached. To counter possible independent initiatives by the High Commission's representatives at the Conference, a prestigious political figure was chosen to head the delegation, Max André, backed personally by both Bidault and Edmond Michelet (MRP), Minister of Armies. (Baudet was concerned that Clarac, d'Argenlieu's Diplomatic Counsellor, was already a senior diplomat whom it would be difficult for an official

---

13. 'Le Président possède la technique d'un chef révolutionnaire, la même que celle du parti à l'école duquel il a été formé.

'Sa politique va consister maintenant à éluder les dispositions qui distinguent le statut fixé par la Convention du 6 mars: 'Etat libre faisant partie de la Fédération indochinoise et de l'Union française' de l'indépendance tout court.' Tel. no. 532F, Haussaire to Cominindo, 29 Mar. 1946, MAE, EA/36/15.

14. '... agir puissament sur les milieux politiques de gauche et faire ainsi pression sur le Gouvernement provisoire', d'Argenlieu, *Chronique*, 247; Cominindo to Haussaire, No. 370/CI 1146, 3 Apr. 1946, in d'Argenlieu, *Chronique*, loc.cit.

15. 'Le seul accueil de Ho Chi Minh à Paris poserait des problèmes de protocole impossibles à résoudre étant donné l'incertitude complète qui règne encore sur l'étendue territoriale et morale de son autorité.' Note pour le Ministre, a.s. Comité de l'Indochine du 28 mars, 28 Mar. 1946, MAE, AO/IC/179.

appointee to outrank.) A member of the General Council (*Conseil Général*) for Paris, and reputedly the only atheist in the leadership of the predominantly Catholic MRP, André was also known as 'a pure reactionary'.[16] His delegation of politicians and officials complemented the team from Saigon, consisting of Pignon (appointed Political Counsellor at the Palais Norodom in April), Clarac, Torel, Legal Counsellor (and d'Argenlieu's *éminence grise*, according to Devillers), the Economic, Financial, and Educational Counsellors, and Salan, Commander of French Forces in the North.[17]

Paris's efforts to control the agenda, however, were impaired by uncertainty in the face of the provisional nature of France's domestic political arrangements: a referendum on the Constitutional draft was set for 2 May. Baudet's memorandum for Bidault and his department's instructions for the Conference reveal the state of opinion at the Quai d'Orsay at this time. It was in seeking to define the Indochinese Federation's relations with France that Baudet was most constrained, advocating:

> an extremely flexible Federal plan which would not challenge Vietnam's nationalism head-on, but which would maintain the principle of continuity in Indochina's foreign policy, economy and finances and its defence, for all the countries of the Federation. It is a matter of deliberate policy that only careful mention is made of the ties between the Federation and the Metropole within the framework of the French Union, given that the Constitution has not yet been approved.[18]

Baudet offered only limited room for manoeuvre on three issues of direct relevance to his Ministry. First, concerning Vietnam's overseas representation, Baudet argued that Ho's efforts to see this resolved by stealth went against the principle of the Indochinese Federation. However, he accepted that Vietnamese representatives,

---

16. '... un réactionnaire à l'état pur'. G. Elgey, La république des illusions, 1945–1951, ou la vie secrète de la IVe République, Paris, 1965, 148–49.

17. P. Devillers, *Histoire du Viet-Nam de 1940 à 1952*, Paris, 1952, 256–57.

18. '... un projet de Fédération très souple qui vise à ne pas heurter de front le nationalisme du Viêt-Nam, mais qui sauvegarde le principe d'une conduite continue, pour les pays de la Fédération, de la politique extérieure de l'Indochine, de son économie et finances, enfin de sa défense. C'est à dessein qu'il n'y est fait qu'une très prudente mention des liens de la Fédération avec la Métropole dans le cadre de l'Union Française, la Constitution n'étant pas encore votée.' Note, 28 Mar. 1946, loc.cit; see also the 'Instructions du MAE pour la négociation d'un accord avec le Gouvernement Provisoire du Viêt-Nam', 29 Mar. 1946, MAE, AO/IC/54.

along with Laotians and Cambodians (and possibly Cochinchinese), might serve in French delegations to neighbouring countries and major powers (United States, Great Britain, USSR). These proposed Agencies of the Indochinese Federation ('Agences de la Fédération Indochinoise') were seen as analagous to proposals for India Agencies to be located in some British embassies. Moreover, as Baudet commented, though not in the Ministry's official instructions: 'If, at a later stage, the Federation were to be granted Dominion status, these Agencies could become distinct diplomatic missions'.[19] Second, how should agreements be reached with third countries concerning Indochina? Here too Vietnam would be prevented from stepping out of the federal framework. Close coordination would be needed, both between the federal and local Indochinese administrations on the one hand, and between the Indochinese administration and the metropole and/or the future French Union on the other. Third, Ho's demand for participation in the United Nations was to be discouraged as being incompatible with the Indochinese Federation. However, given India's separate UN membership and the Netherlands' proposed sponsorship of Indonesia, Indochina might join in its own right, since these precedents would otherwise undermine prolonged French opposition; the selection of Indochinese representatives remained problematic, given the competing wealth and size of the member countries of the Federation.[20]

In the event, Cominindo's discussion of detail was rendered otiose by the provisional, prefatory nature of the Dalat Conference itself, which lasted three weeks from 19 April to 11 May without really getting to grips with the issues.[21] A spirit of bonhomie was scrupulously maintained, and some French delegates, to the discomfiture of their colleagues, even went so far as to address their Vietnamese counterparts by the familiar and comradely *tu*-form, as if between revolutionaries.[22] But nothing could disguise the fundamental disagreements which persisted between the two sides. Of the four Commissions which divided up the Conference agenda, for Political Affairs, Economy and Finances, Military Affairs, and Culture, none advanced much beyond the basic agreements set down in the March Accords. Thus the Political

19. Si, plus tard, un statut de 'Dominion' était accordé à la Fédération, ces Agences prendraient le statut de représentations diplomatiques distinctes.' Loc.cit.
20. Note, Instructions, loc.cit.
21. Devillers, *Histoire*, 266.
22. Referred to as 'le tutoiement révolutionnaire' in ibid., 263.

Commission agreed Vietnam's status as an Associated State within the French Union, but deferred to a later discussion the terms of Vietnam's participation in the proposed High Council of the French Union (*Conseil supérieur de l'Union française*). But the Vietnamese delegation made no concessions on the three points at issue in Bidault's instructions: full sovereignty and true independence remained the declared Vietnamese aims.[23] The Economic and Financial Commission agreed that France should play a preeminent part in providing aid, especially in the form of French technicians, and called for a customs union and the free circulation of goods and persons; but it expressed Vietnamese reservations concerning monetary union, and there was no agreement concerning the role or protection of French businesses in Indochina.[24] In the Military Commission, Vo Nguyen Giap, the senior Viet Minh delegate present, repeatedly stressed that the effective defence of Indochina rested on close Franco-Vietnamese cooperation. The existing basis for this cooperation, however, was still far from Vietnamese conceptions, while fundamental disagreements remained on Vietnamese troop-training, the unity of command, the nature of French Union forces based in Indochina, and on the strategic bases mentioned in the Annex to the 6 March Accords.[25] The pattern was repeated even in the Cultural Commission: France was free to establish schools in Vietnam, and there were no objections to Franco-Vietnamese cultural exchanges; but the Vietnamese delegation refused to accept French as the sole medium of education above the primary level, or to return to French control educational establishments including the French School in the Far East (*Ecole française d'Extrême-Orient*), the Pasteur Institute, and Hanoi University.[26]

The French delegation remained unflustered, although they had in effect been duped by the Vietnamese aim at the Conference, successfully realised, to 'make nothing of Dalat so that Paris is everything'. In effect, d'Argenlieu had failed in his stratagem to

23. Minutes for 8 May 1946 and 10 May 1946 sessions, in d'Argenlieu, *Chronique*, 257–59.

24. Minutes of 29 Apr., 4 May and 13 May 1946 sessions, in d'Argenlieu, *Chronique*, 259; Devillers, *Histoire*, 261.

25. Minutes, 11 May 1946, in d'Argenlieu, *Chronique*, 259; Devillers, *Histoire*, 262. Giap, Ho's Minister of Defence, was second-in-command of the Vietnamese delegation, which was headed by Nguyen Tuong Tam, leader of the VNQDD and Foreign Minister.

26. D'Argenlieu, *Chronique*, 260.

force agreement on his terms in Dalat, rather than at the politically more highly-charged Paris Conference still to come. As Torel argued to d'Argenlieu:

> The Hanoi Government's principal concern would seem to have been to maintain its freedom of manoeuvre with a view to the forthcoming negotiations in Paris. This is why they did not see fit to go beyond their initial position on most of the important issues, but maintained that the discussion could be resumed in Paris. We should not therefore be surprised at the relatively limited number of agreements reached.[27]

By the same token, Hanoi and Paris had achieved a curious tactical community of interest in the face of the High Commissioner's ambitions. It remained to be seen whether agreement could be extended in France beyond the irregular verb shared by both sides at Dalat: I stand firm, you (even 'tu') refuse to budge, he has 'an essentially negative attitude', we keep smiling and agree to disagree.[28]

More worrying for the French was the looming presence of the Cochinchina question, which at times quite overshadowed the proceedings at Dalat. Indeed, the issue had almost caused the Conference to fail on the first day as the two sides clashed over continued hostilities south of the 16th Parallel. Were these the result of police action ('opérations de police') against undisciplined irregulars, as the French maintained, refusing to discuss an issue beyond the Conference's powers; or were the French attacking troops of the Vietnamese Army, in violation of the 6 March ceasefire? As Giap argued, these troops were no more irregulars or gangsters than the Resistance had been in occupied France.[29] Notwithstanding the French concession of a Joint Commission (*commission mixte*) to treat with Nguyen Binh, the Vietnamese commander in the south, the core issue remained. On the last day of the Conference, the Vietnamese again stated their position: that

27. 'Le gouvernement de Hanoi semble avoir eu pour principal souci de réserver sa liberté d'action en vue des négociations qui s'ouvriront prochainement à Paris. C'est la raison pour laquelle ils ne se sont pas cru autorisés à s'abandonner leur position initiale sur la plupart des points importants tout en déclarant que la discussion pourrait être reprise en France. Il ne faut donc pas s'étonner du nombre relativement restreint des accords réalisés.' Rapport de M. Torel, 21 May 1946, in d'Argenlieu, *Chronique*, 260.

28. '... une attitude essentiellement négative', Minutes, Cultural Commission, 29 Apr. 1946, ibid.

29. Devillers, *Histoire*, 257.

Cochinchina – *Nam Bô* – was part of Vietnam and that the purpose of a referendum, as provided for in the Accords, was to resolve a purely administrative question concerning Cochinchinese autonomy within the Vietnamese polity. To the French delegation's insistence on the terms of the March 6 Accords, Hoang Xuan Han responded with a stirring closing speech, expressing his hope 'that this land will soon be returned to the bosom of our common Fatherland: Vietnam', and the Vietnamese delegation left the conference chamber in tears.[30] On this theatrical note the Conference came to an inconclusive end. All attention was now free to centre on this essential bone of contention.

Cochinchina Policy

Apart from the independence issue, the other essential question left unresolved by the March Accords concerned the three *ky*. Indeed, the promise of a referendum to settle the issue had arguably exacerbated the problem from the French perspective by making it a hostage to precarious political fortune south of the 16th Parallel. Thus, it allowed the Viet Minh to play to its strengths as an efficient disseminator of propaganda, with an easy case to be made in favour of national unity in terms of both nationalism and anti-colonialism. By the same token, it also strengthened Saigon's hand in dealing with Paris. The lesson of the Dalat Conference was that Franco-Vietnamese negotiations would sooner or later have to take place in Paris, beyond d'Argenlieu's reach. But the Cochinchina question lay much more clearly within the High Commissioner's domain. Pursued with increasing vigour after 6 March, the cause of Cochinchinese separatism thus proved to be a potent instrument, not only in Saigon's campaign to recast the Viet Minh as the enemies of French policy, but also in its contest with Paris for policy-making primacy. The first fruit of this campaign was the Autonomous Republic of Cochinchina, declared by d'Argenlieu without prior consultation with Paris on 1 June 1946.

Cochinchina provided the natural focus for a conservative approach to Indochina policy, not simply as the French stronghold after October 1945, but also as the nub of French economic and strategic interests in Indochina, and historically as the heart of the

---

30. '... que ... cette terre revienne bientôt au sein de notre patrie commune: le Viet-Nam', ibid., 264–66.

French colonial regime in Indochina; Cochinchina was France's only *de jure* colony in the Far East, and had formerly sent a *député* to Paris along with France's other Old Colonies. By contrast, Cochinchinese separatism had its origins in the attempts of the Commissioner for the Republic in Cochinchina, Governor Jean Cédile, to establish a Representative Assembly in Saigon in the spirit of Brazzaville. Cédile had served before the war in Cameroun, where he rallied to de Gaulle in 1940; as Director of Pleven's private office (*directeur du cabinet*) in Algiers, he had collaborated with Laurentie in organising the Brazzaville Conference.[31] Parachuted into Saigon in August 1945, he liaised successfully if controversially both with the southern Viet Minh and with the British Commander in Saigon, General Gracey, before concentrating on his primary political task in Saigon.[32]

By October 1945, Cédile had prepared plans for a Consultative Assembly on the Parisian model, numbering perhaps eighty members. However, he had not allowed for the influence and 'advice' of local colonial interests, backed by the old administration, who, fearing a return to the near-anarchy of August-September, proposed a small Consultative Council to draft a constitution. The problem then was to find suitable political figures untainted by hostile nationalism. One such figure was Dr Nguyen Van Thinh, leader since before the war of the moderate Democrat Party, and briefly a prisoner of the Viet Minh. But Thinh was 'too upright', as Devillers puts it ('trop droit'), and as a counterweight to Thinh's party a Cochinchinese Party was formed in November 1945 with the support of the French settlers, and with the stated aim of achieving Cochinchinese autonomy by every legal means. Moreover, Thinh had difficulty in recruiting from amongst the Saigon intelligentsia without explicit official support for his aim of forming a democratic government. The Consultative Council invested on 4 February 1946 thus bore a close resemblance to the pre-war puppet councils, with four French and eight Cochinchinese members: Thinh and three party colleagues, the leader of the Cochinchinese Party, and three others. Of these eight, seven were naturalised French. The Council's role was threefold: to mediate with the Commissioner, to advise him on matters of Cochinchinese concern, and

31. 'Notice biographique' in Commandant G. Bodinier, ed., *Le retour de la France en Indochine, 1945–1946*, Vincennes, 1987, 111.

32. See P. Isoart, 'Aux origines d'une guerre: l'Indochine française (1940–1945)', in P. Isoart, ed., *L'Indochine française, 1940–1945*, Paris, 1983, 66–67.

to draw up a constitution.[33] Coming a month before the signing of the Accords in Hanoi, the Council was a compromised and, even in its own terms, heavily outdated last bid to apply the terms of the March 1945 Declaration.

Confronted with Hanoi's claims to speak for a unified Vietnam, however, the Administration turned to the Consultative Council as the germ of a new initiative, which appealed both to Paris and to Saigon. Ironically, one of the earliest to mention the idea was Moutet, cabling Cominindo's criticisms of the March Accords:

> It has been indicated to me that it might be possible, with the help of those who know Cochinchina well, to organise a propaganda campaign to prevent its union with Tonkin, under the slogan 'Cochinchina for the Cochinchinese'. This might bring us considerable political success.[34]

The idea as conceived by Saigon, however, lacked this democratic gloss. Returning from his meeting with Ho in the Bay of Along, d'Argenlieu found the Consultative Council preparing for the next move. On 26 March, the Council voted for the creation of a 'Provisional Government of the Republic of Cochinchina', with Dr Thinh as its President. On 30 March, d'Argenlieu informed the Federal Council (composed of senior officials) of this plan, which was lent urgency by revived terrorist activity in the south: the day before, one of the Cochinchinese Councillors had been assassinated. As d'Argenlieu reported to Paris on 3 April, this and another failed attack had strengthened Cochinchinese opinion in favour of autonomy. The main problem foreseen by the Admiral was the likely violent reaction from Hanoi when the new Cochinchina Government was announced. The announcement would therefore be timed to minimise this reaction: he suggested the moment of the Vietnamese parliamentary delegation's departure for Paris. He also proposed sending a Cochinchinese parliamentary delegation simultaneously.[35]

By now Moutet and his men were beginning to have reservations about the implications of Saigon's Cochinchina policy, which

33. Devillers, *Histoire*, 172–76. On Thinh, see also Bodinier, *Le retour*, 126.

34. 'On me signale qu'il serait possible d'organiser, avec des personnes connaissant bien la Cochinchine, tout une propagande pour empêcher sa réunion avec le Tonkin, sous le slogan: "La Cochinchine aux Cochinchinois". Nous pourrions remporter à cet égard un grand succès politique.' Tel. Moutet to d'Argenlieu, no. 237/CI, 13 Apr. 1946, in d'Argenlieu, *Chronique*, 207.

35. D'Argenlieu to Cominindo, no. 556F, 3 Apr. 1946, in d'Argenlieu, *Chronique*, 268–69.

threatened to wreck the good relations so painstakingly established with Hanoi. As Laurentie warned Moutet:

> I detect signs here and in Saigon of a growing temptation to divide and rule. Cédile, with his usual heavy-footed enthusiasm, is throwing himself into a Cochinchina policy. The Admiral is saying nothing against it. If you do not straighten things out, we will lose all the benefits of our agreement with Vietnam in the twinkling of an eye.[36]

D'Argenlieu's diary records his mounting frustration at the apparent change of heart stealing over the Rue Oudinot during April, culminating in a telegramme from Labrouquère (SFIO), the new Secretary-General at Comonindo, dated 21 April, two days after the opening of the Conference at Dalat. As Labrouquère argued, nothing should be done to jeopardise the agreement reached six weeks before, including anything that might be interpreted as propaganda in favour of Cochinchinese autonomy. France should 'dominate the debate and act as arbiter', though it was not explained how it was possible to dominate debate while avoiding political initiatives.[37] Labrouquère advised against the formation of a Cochinchinese government and the despatch of a Cochinchinese delegation to Paris. He did not think that the Cochinchinese could harbour any bitterness for such a position: soon, after all, the referendum would allow them to register their own opinion.

D'Argenlieu responded to the increasingly hesitant line issuing from Paris with a robust restatement of his own view of Indochina policy, in a memorandum entitled 'Political Turning Point in Indochina' ('Tournant Politique en Indochine') which undertook to place the Cochinchina question in a wider Indochinese context.[38] As he saw it, French sovereignty, which he glossed as 'authority', was well on its way to full restoration across the Indochinese Federation. The first obligation remaining was to maintain and consolidate eight months' work in restoring French authority; and d'Argenlieu's principal preoccupation was with Cochinchina, over which hung the 'threat' of a referendum:

---

36. 'Je crois deviner qu'ici m,me et à Saigon s'insinue la tentation de diviser pour régner. Cédile s'élance, avec sa fougue un peu fruste, dans une politique cochinchinoise. L'Amiral n'y contredit pas. Si vous n'y mettez pas bon ordre, nous perdrons en un tournemain tout le bénéfice de notre accord avec le Viêt-Nam.' NOTE pour Monsieur le Ministre, ref.HL/bp, 20 Mar. 1946. AN, 72AJ535.

37. Comonindo (Labrouquère) to d'Argenlieu, no. 502/CI 1343, 21 Apr. 1946, d'Argenlieu, *Chronique*, 271–72.

38. 26 Apr. 1946, in d'Argenlieu, *Chronique*, 274–77.

The chances of a strong majority in favour of autonomy depends chiefly on the clarity of our policy. Until 6 March our policy was clear enough.... A provisional government was about to be formed, and Cochinchina was to become an autonomous state within the Indochinese Federation and the French Union. All clarity has vanished since 6 March.

France had a choice: it could back Cochinchinese autonomy, and risk the Hanoi government's displeasure, or it could support the union of the three *ky*, 'at the expense of French authority'. Having thus indicated his own preference, d'Argenlieu reiterated the arguments against Vietnamese unity, on historic and economic grounds. Moreover, he argued, Cochinchina was bound by the Mekong to Cambodia and Laos, and cut off from Tonkin by the Annamese highlands; and the linguistic argument in favour of national unity was either puerile or tinged with racism:

Was not the argument of linguistic unity used by the Führer to force German minorities to join the Reich? In Indochina it has always been, and remains, France's mission to protect the ethnic minorities against the Annamite tendency to imperialism.[39]

As d'Argenlieu argued, granting Vietnamese unity would constitute an injustice against the loyal populations of Laos, Cambodia, and, above all, Cochinchina. If Cochinchina slipped from France's grasp following a poorly prepared referendum, the Federation would collapse and Laos and Cambodia would be absorbed, sooner or later, into 'Greater Annam'. For the moment, however, Cochinchina was solidly held, and constituted one of France's best cards in the forthcoming negotiations in Paris: d'Argenlieu drew from Dalat the lesson that Hanoi had no desire to break off talks. But, as he further argued, it would not necessarily be a disaster if the talks failed: after a period in which Vietnam was allowed to drift as a 'Free State within the French Union', while the Indochinese Federation developed without it, d'Argenlieu predicted that Vietnam would seek re-admittance. As d'Argenlieu concluded,

39. 'La part de chances d'une forte majorité en faveur de l'autonomie dépend principalement en ce pays de la clarté de notre politique. Elle existait jusqu'au 6 mars.... Un gouvernement provisoire allait se constituer librement et la Cochinchine devenir un Etat autonome au sein de la Fédération indochinoise et de l'Union française. Depuis le 6 mars, cette clarté n'existe plus.... L'argument de l'unité linguistique ne fut-il pas celui du Führer pour contraindre les minorités germaniques à se dissoudre dans le grand Reich.... Or, en Indochine, la mission de la France fut et reste de protéger les minorités ethniques contre la tendance impérialiste annamite.' Ibid., 276.

the important thing was for the Government to decide on a policy one way or the other.[40]

Moutet and the Government were unable to share Saigon's certainties. Nor may the inconsistencies detected by the Admiral in the instructions issuing from Paris be attributed to changes in personnel.[41] Rather, officials at the Rue Oudinot faced a dilemma. On the one hand, negotiating with the Hanoi government had increased, rather than lessened, official distaste for the task in hand, as expressed in a despatch to the High Commissioner drafted by Laurentie:

> I understand your concern not to want to give way unconditionally to the Hanoi Government's demands. It is clear that the people we are dealing with are both brutal and childish and that, though they may clamour for independence, they would never be able to make the most of it. In the specific case of Cochinchina they are showing signs of appetite way in excess of their likely digestive capacities.[42]

On the other hand, it was essential not to allow the Cochinchina question to become a bone of contention between Hanoi and the French. As Laurentie explained to Pignon, this was more than a matter of shameful appeasement. First there was the risk of losing the international moral credit earned as a result of the March Accords. If the Tonkinese were left to 'stew in their own juice, while we acted purely according to our own lights in Cochinchina', their disillusionment and isolation might reopen the door, even assuming it was fully closed, to a renewed Chinese offensive which this time might succeed more fully. Moreover, it would become increasingly difficult to avoid international control of the forthcoming referendum: 'We will have involved the Americans, the Chinese and the Russians in questions which up until now

40. Ibid., 277. As he noted six months later: 'On 20 October 1946 the Government has not yet responded'. ('Aucune réponse n'est encore faite par le Gouvernement à la date du 20 octobre 1946'.)

41. D'Argenlieu, *Chronique*, 271–72. Commenting on Labrouquère, d'Argenlieu concludes: 'Is he not in the end a faithful Socialist party man?' ('N'est-il pas au reste un fidèle SFIO?') De Langlade announced his resignation shortly after de Gaulle's, but stayed on during negotiations with Hanoi.

42. 'Je conçois très bien votre préoccupation … de ne pas vouloir faire droit sans réserves aux demandes du Gouvernement de Hanoi. Il est évident en effet que nous avons affaire à une équipe à la fois brutale et puérile qui [n]e saura jamais tirer parti de l'indépendance qu'elle exige et qui dans le cas particulier de la Cochinchine manifeste un appétit très supérieur à ses facultés de digestion.' Tel. FOM to Haussaire Saigon, ref.HL/ocg, in reply to d'Argenlieu's no. 702F and to Pignon's letter of 27 Apr. 1946, AN, 72AJ539.

have been treated as a family matter'. As he noted, this was despite the fact that American policy was becoming both increasingly conservative and anti-Russian, and therefore tended to favour the French position in Indochina. Worse would follow if France resorted to force, a possibility which Laurentie suspected had not been ruled out by Pignon.[43]

Apart from its international ramifications, Laurentie also doubted that a Cochinchina policy was effective against Hanoi's undoubted nationalist appeal. Applying the lessons of the previous summer, Laurentie argued that nationalism should be fought with the same weapons, not with the subterfuge of separatism, nor with the authoritarian reflexes of traditional colonial rule:

> The acute crisis of nationalism we are witnessing cannot be tackled head-on, nor should we act according to our traditional understanding that we can always resort to force when things go wrong. We are up against a movement which, however childish, will only strengthen if we start to use apparently authoritarian methods.[44]

Laurentie was impressed by the mettle of the Cochinchinese delegation whose potential he praised to Cédile, recognizing their political appeal in the south to a more Francophile audience in the face of the intransigent nationalism of the 'Hanoi intellectuals'. Cédile's policy was nonetheless unsuitable because it did not match like with like:

> We are not dealing with nationalism in Cochinchina, but rather with a tangle of different political sympathies and interests which are both rational and useful to us, but which are not backed by the sort of nerve shown by Hanoi, whose sole appeal is to the national idea.[45]

43. '... mariner ... dans leur jus, cependant que nous agirions selon notre conception purement personnelle en Cochinchine. ... nous aurons introduit les Américains, les Chinois et les Russes dans une affaire qui restait jusqu'à présent une affaire de famille.' Laurentie to Pignon, 18 May 1946; Laurentie to Cédile, 20 May 1946: AN, 72AJ539.

44. '... la crise du nationalisme aigu à laquelle nous assistons ne peut pas à mon avis être traitée par des moyens directs ni avec l'arrière-pensée bien établie du recours à la force en cas d'échec. C'est en effet une poussée qui quelle que soit sa puérilité ne peut que croître devant le déploiement de procédés apparemment autoritaires.' Tel. FOM to Haussaire, 13 May 1946, loc.cit.

45. '... ce n'est pas à un nationalisme que nous avons affaire en Cochinchine mais peut-être à un faisceau de tendances et d'intérêts à la fois raisonnables et utiles à quoi pourtant manquera le nerf que nous constatons chez les gens de Hanoi parce que ceux-ci s'appuient uniquement sur l'idée nationale.' Tel. FOM to Haussaire, 13 May 1946, loc.cit.

The unrepresentative nature of the Cochinchinese separatists was exemplified in the leader of the Cochinchinese delegation, *Doc Phu* (Prefect) Chan, but especially in his deputy, and future Prime Minister at the time of the Bao Dai solution, Colonel Nguyen Van Xuan. When Xuan returned to Paris in December 1946, Laurentie's letter of introduction to General de Gaulle depicted the Colonel as the model assimilated colonial, but by the same token an imperfectly 'national' figure:

> ... a colonial artillery colonel to the core. Not only is he a Polytechnique graduate, but he also served for a long time in Paris, and in his manner, background and methods he is as much one of us as is possible (to the extent that he can hardly make a speech in Vietnamese).[46]

Although politely received by Gouin and others, including the Socialist former Governor-General Alexandre Varenne, the delegation had been largely neglected, and its enthusiastic reports back to Saigon dismissed by Labrouquère, who transmitted them, as a 'purely personal point of view'.[47]

As an alternative to the dangers of the Cochinchina policy, as he perceived them in May 1946, Laurentie proposed harnessing the force of Vietnamese nationalism to French advantage. Dismissing Cédile's contention that 'ninety percent of Cochinchina is naturally separatist', he argued that separatism was probably a conditional response to the Hanoi government's unreasonable nature, which might well be softened by the responsibilities of power. If this happened, it would be difficult to resist the appeal to uncontrollable gut feeling inherent in 'this pan-Annamite fever' ('cette fièvre pan-annamite'), which would undermine any autonomy achieved by Cochinchina in the meantime.[48] The key to Laurentie's proposed strategy was the referendum, discussion of which had foundered at Dalat: as Laurentie noted, each side seemed prepared to accept only the result it wanted, while Hanoi was unwilling to discuss even the terms on which the referendum would be

---

46. '... un 'vrai' colonel de l'artillerie coloniale. Elève de Polytechnique, il a longtemps servi à Paris et il est, de manières, d'[éducation], et de méthode, aussi proche de nous qu'il est possible (au point qu'il a peine à faire un discours en annamite).' Note pour M. le Général de Gaulle, 23 Dec. 1946, AN, 72AJ539. The *Ecole Polytechnique* is the most prestigious of the military and administrative academies (*grandes écoles*) founded in the Revolutionary period (1789–1815).

47. '... un point de vue ... strictement personnel', in d'Argenlieu, *Chronique*, 273.

48. Cédile to Laurentie, 22 Apr. 1946, note introducing Cochinchinese delegation; FOM to Haussaire, 13 May 1946; Laurentie to Cédile, 20 May 1946: AN, 72AJ539.

conducted. To break the logjam, Laurentie proposed vigorous advocacy of the referendum on Hanoi's terms, but on two conditions: a special statute for Cochinchina within a united Vietnam; and guaranteed Cochinchinese cabinet posts within the Vietnamese government. In this way France would be seen to respect the Vietnamese national idea while preserving a separate identity for Cochinchina and ensuring that the new government would include 'men we can trust and who might be far more skilled than the Tonkinese when it comes to administration and government.[49] Laurentie's plan was thus to 'put a stop to the Hanoi government's naïve but dangerous brutality', but to do so from within, in the tried and trusted manner of the Trojan Horse.

Laurentie's proposals are best understood as a fascinating exercise in sounding, and perhaps guiding, official opinion, but with little chance of being realised in practice. In the final analysis, the High Commissioner was unlikely to perform such a complete U-turn; nor by the same token was it likely that Moutet or his colleagues would have contemplated the political dangers of such a move. Laurentie's draft telegramme of 13 May went unsigned by Moutet, though Laurentie sent a copy to Pignon. As he commented, apparently without malice, Moutet was hesitating over Cochinchina, and 'does not wish to commit himself too explicitly'.[50] Moutet's hesitations reflected the pressures of France's second governmental crisis of 1946. In the referendum of 5 May, the French electorate rejected the draft Constitution submitted to it, which had been drawn up under the influence of Communists and Socialists in the Constituent Assembly. Elections to a new Assembly were set for 2 June, and with the political mood in France shifting to the right, the MRP was widely expected to make significant gains. The time was unripe for fresh initiatives from the GPRF, and especially from its SFIO members.

Conversely, it was an auspicious moment for Saigon to take matters into its own hands. On 1 June, following a request from the (French) President of the Consultative Council, d'Argenlieu proclaimed the Autonomous Republic of Cochinchina; Dr Thinh

49. '... des hommes à nous et qui aurons au surplus des qualités administratives et peut-être gouvernementales très supérieures à celles des Tonkinois ... faire échec à la naïve mais dangereuse brutalité du Gouvernement de Hanoi'. FOM to Haussaire, 13 May 1946, loc.cit.

50. '... le Ministre hésite longuement sur cette question de Cochinchine et ne veut pas prendre des responsabilités trop précises.' Laurentie to Pignon, 18 May 1946, loc.cit.

was appointed President and Colonel Xuan Vice-President of a provisional government.[51] One other event determined d'Argenlieu's timing: the day before, on 31 May, Ho Chi Minh left Hanoi on his way for Paris at the head of the Vietnamese delegation for the forthcoming Fontainebleau Conference. His cable to Ho, via the French embassy in Cairo, was withheld on the orders of the Quai d'Orsay, and Ho learned the news from his escort, General Salan.[52] The High Commission had calculated correctly: on 5 June, Moutet cabled Cominindo's assent to the initiative, although he stressed that the new Government should not 'be seen to be a creation of, or a screen for, the French administration'. Unless he believed it himself, however, Moutet was presumably suggesting an approved 'official version' when he urged Saigon to argue to Hanoi that the situation created by the proclamation 'does not in any way preempt a definitive solution'.[53] Saigon's intention, in creating the Cochinchinese Republic, to force the Paris government's hand may be detected in Cédile's belated reply to Laurentie's letter of 16 May:

> The provision for a referendum in the 6 March Accords presented Cochinchina with a fait accompli, and we had to find a way out of a blind alley. The fact is, after 6 March I felt obliged to do something; my firm conviction is that the solution dictated by French national interests is a split between Cochinchina and Vietnam. I might add that this is what is wanted by the majority of the Cochinchinese.[54]

The Administration in Saigon was thus calculatedly upping the stakes in the forthcoming negotiations, in a determined effort not to lose the initiative. In effect, with the edifice of the Accords policy supposedly about to be completed, its foundations had just been decisively undermined by its more unwilling architects.

51. Devillers, *Paris-Saigon-Hanoi*, 188–89.

52. D'Argenlieu, *Chronique*, 285; Devillers, *Paris-Saigon-Hanoi*, 189.

53. '… apparaître comme une création des autorités françaises et comme un paravent de celles-ci … la situation de fait … ne préjuge en rien de la solution définitive'. Tel., Présidence Paris to Haussaire, no. 926/CI 1789, 5 Jun. 1946, in d'Argenlieu, *Chronique*, 285–86.

54. 'Les accords du 6 mars, en prévoyant le référendum, ont mis la Cochinchine devant le fait accompli … et il a fallu trouver un moyen de sortir de l'impasse....
Le fait est qu'après le 6 mars je me suis trouvé dans l'obligation de faire quelque chose[;] mon avis, définitif, est que la solution d'intérêt national français est la scission Cochinchine-Vietnam [*sic*]. J'ajoute qu'elle est voulue par la majorité des Cochinchinois.' Cédile to Laurentie, Saigon, 16 Jun. 1946, AN, 72AJ539.

—

On the eve of the Fontainebleau Conference, the rivalry between the two decision-making centres of Paris and Saigon was already well established. In contrast with its rather secondary and reactive role during the negotiations leading to the March Accords, and helped indirectly by the inconclusive outcome of the Dalat Conference, the GPRF was now poised to retake the initiative with the Vietnamese delegation's arrival on French soil. Moreover, following the setback of de Gaulle's resignation in January, and the consequent ministerial reshuffle, a new Minister of Overseas France was making his mark on policy making. The veteran Minister's dynamism and his control of Indochina policy were registered by d'Argenlieu, in ironic vein, during the controversy over the Annex to the March Accords:

> While his friend President Gouin willingly slips into the background, Moutet relishes the personal control he can now exercise over Cominindo. Perhaps this means a return to the happy days when he was Léon Blum's handpicked Minister of Colonies in 1936!

As d'Argenlieu also noted, Moutet's influence was further enhanced by François de Langlade's replacement as Secretary-General of Cominindo, an SFIO *député* in the Constituent Assembly and a member of Moutet's private office at the Rue Oudinot.[55] Laurentie's satisfaction at the new rhythm of work following the inertia of Giacobbi's ministry has already been recorded.[56] This was marked by his increased participation in the dialogue between Paris and Saigon concerning the terms of the Cochinchina policy. However, this rediscovered sense of purpose at the Rue Oudinot was more than offset by the hesitations and reversals of domestic politics and Constitution-making. Not only was the GPRF unable to offer a clear idea of what Vietnam had to gain from membership of the French Union (since the French Union did not exist), it also had to watch its back during the elections which followed the rejection of the first Constitutional draft in the referendum of 5 May. As if to make just this point, the Vietnamese delegation arrived in

55. 'Celui-ci [Moutet], vu l'effacement volontaire du président Gouin, son ami, savoure d'avoir à diriger désormais en personne le Comité [interministériel]. Les beaux jours du ministre des Colonies qu'il fut en 1936, lors choisi par Léon Blum, vont peut-être revivre!' As a sign of Moutet's confidence in him, Labrouquère retained his post as *chef-adjoint du cabinet*: d'Argenlieu, *Chronique*, 208, 273–74; Devillers, *Histoire*, 268.

56. See above, Ch. 4.

France in the midst of the ministerial crisis which followed the elections of 2 June.

It is difficult not to conclude that the initiative remained in the hands of the High Commissioner and his administration in Saigon. This was after all the true message of d'Argenlieu's telegraphic lectures and sermons on the rationale for a Cochinchina policy. As the pages of the *Chronique* reveal, moreover, d'Argenlieu had taken into account the possible consequences of the line of action he was taking over Cochinchina. Instructing General Valluy on his duties covering for Sainteny, while the latter accompanied the Vietnamese parliamentary delegation in April, d'Argenlieu was apparently ready to contemplate the 'worst case' which might result from the creation of a separate Cochinchina. As he argued:

> By ruling out any recourse to the ultima ratio, we would be risking the loss of French Indochina and gravely compromising the first aim of our mission, which is to restore France's authority not only in law but in fact.[57]

What he meant by 'the *ultima ratio*' was made clear by Valluy, whose Directive no. 2, dated 10 April 1946, instructed French garrison commanders to prepare for what he termed 'a coup d'état scenario'.[58] Seen in this light, d'Argenlieu's initiative in proclaiming the Autonomous Republic of Cochinchina at the moment of greatest potential embarrassment to the GPRF was only a foretaste of things to come.

---

57. 'Nous interdire, comme une règle, le recours à l'*ultima ratio* serait risquer la perte de l'Indochine française, et compromettre gravement le but premier de notre mission qui est d'y rétablir l'autorité de la France, non seulement en droit mais en fait.' D'Argenlieu, *Chronique*, 283. 'Ultima ratio' (Latin) = 'the ultimate reason' or 'the last resort'.

58. '… un scénario de coup d'Etat'. Devillers, *Paris-Saigon-Hanoi*, 179. The document was quoted in a memorandum issued by the Hanoi Government on 31 Dec. 1946.

8

'A ROUND OF THE BATTLE WE ARE FIGHTING'

The Fontainebleau Conference, June–September 1946

The Franco-Vietnamese Conference, which met at Fontainebleau between 6 July and 10 September 1946 with the aim of
drawing up a definitive agreement between France and Vietnam,
should by rights have marked the culmination of the Accords policy pursued since the beginning of the year. Instead, it served not
only to emphasise the differences which still separated the two
sides, but also to accentuate the conflict and rivalry which now
dominated relations between the GPRF and the High Commissioner in Indochina. It was clear by the opening of the Conference
that Paris and Saigon had diverged further in their respective
approaches since their quarrels in the spring: while officials and
ministers sought to maintain the momentum of negotiations,
Admiral d'Argenlieu and his lieutenants were now openly hostile
towards Hanoi, and portrayed the Conference as merely a surro-
gate battle in a struggle, with fewer and fewer holds barred, to
maintain a French presence in Indochina: 'a round of the battle
we are fighting'.[1] Translated into action, this attitude took the
form of a series of dramatic coups effected in Indochina without
consultation with Paris, culminating in August in the convening
of a second Dalat Conference, apparently designed to undermine
or compromise the negotiations in France. If this was the aim, its
success was marked by Moutet's and Ho Chi Minh's wearied
signing of a *modus vivendi* on 14 September, which brought the
period of direct negotiations to an inconclusive end.

1. '… une phase du combat que nous livrons', Pignon to Laurentie, 5 Jul. 1946,
AN, 72AJ539.

This chapter is concerned with the developing rivalry between the two decision-making centres of Paris and Saigon, against the background of the negotiations at Fontainebleau. In particular, it illustrates the effects of an ostensible shift to Paris in the focus of policy making. Colonial policy making tends to be focused on the colonial periphery, away from the metropolitan centre. But what happens when this focus is reversed, and when the shift occurs at a moment of intense political flux? Far from succeeding in their bid to regain the initiative from Saigon, policy makers in Paris were frustrated by the prolongation of domestic political crisis. Indeed, the Conference could hardly have been worse timed: arriving in France on 12 June, the Vietnamese delegation had to be entertained at Biarritz for two weeks while the parties manoeuvred to form a government. The elections of 2 June, following the no-vote in the referendum of 5 May, had marked the temporary retrenchment of the Communist vote and a moderate gain in support for the MRP, which emerged as the largest party in the Second Constituent Assembly. The arithmetic of the 'tripartite' coalition pointed to no obvious candidate as the new leader of the GPRF; despite SFIO hopes that Gouin might keep the job, Bidault was nominated by the Assembly on 19 June, and formed a government on 24 June.[2]

The scale of the ensuing problem may be gauged from a brief consideration of the domestic parameters of policy making enunciated in an earlier chapter.[3] In terms of **institutional solidarity** the situation was hardly encouraging, even aside from the core problem of weakening links in the chain of command. With the GPRF's authority more doubtful than at any time since the Liberation, Moutet's control of the levers of Indochina policy was now compromised by Bidault's *ex officio* chairmanship of Cominindo. A Government split on policy now became more likely, since the MRP leader, although untried in colonial policy, was not noted as a liberal. Moreover, de Gaulle chose this moment to stage his re-entry into the political fray with his speech at Bayeux on 16 June, thus throwing open the question of Gaullist loyalties within the administration. This was of particular significance with regard to d'Argenlieu, who arrived from Saigon just in time to be present at de Gaulle's side.[4] By the same token, the General's Bayeux speech

2. B.D. Graham, *The French Socialists and Tripartisme, 1944–1947*, London and Canberra, 1964, 181–83.

3. See above, Ch. 4.

4. G. Thierry d'Argenlieu, *Chronique d'Indochine, 1945–1947*, Paris, 1985, 293.

found resonance with a growing mood of conservatism in France, thus throwing into doubt the question of the **ideological acceptability** of a liberal policy for Indochina. Alongside his proposals for a bicameral, presidential régime, de Gaulle called for a tighter imperial structure. Controversy on the imperial issue was thus assured in the new Assembly, especially given the increased Nationalist showing, particularly amongst Algerian and Malagasy *députés*. As observed earlier, a second factor of growing significance for the ideological basis of policy was the increasingly overt anti-Communist tendency of non-Communist politicians and officials.

Most dramatically altered by the shift in focus to Paris was the **political salience** of Indochina policy. Ho Chi Minh's presence in France could not fail to create a political stir. Even in Biarritz, Ho and his men received pilgrimages from representatives of the Left. This was precisely the propaganda effect which Saigon had feared. Indeed, it was at d'Argenlieu's suggestion that the site of the conference itself was moved away from the glare of publicity, from Paris to Fontainebleau.[5] Even then, it was clear that the aims behind Ho's ambition to come to Paris had been realised; notwithstanding the problems of protocol raised earlier by the Quai d'Orsay, the ceremonial aspects of his 'state visit' went ahead in early July, thus effecting a large measure of diplomatic recognition for the fledgeling Republic of Vietnam.[6] Moreover, while Pham Van Dong headed the Vietnamese delegation to Fontainebleau, Ho continued to receive a stream of visitors, such as Maurice Thorez, Secretary-General of the PCF, and Jacques Rabemananjara, the newly elected Malagasy nationalist *député*, who gave Ho a copy of a blueprint for the French Union drawn up by Rabemanajara's party, the Democratic Movement for Malagasy Renovation (*Mouvement Démocratique pour la Rénovation Malgache*, or MDRM).[7] Meanwhile, the press made the most of Ho's exotic presence, especially following his press conference on 12 July. As one reporter had it:

> Mr. Ho Chi Minh holds forth arrogantly in gilded salons while every day Frenchmen are ambushed and killed in Indochina. He is too clever by half, and his cruel eyes allow glimpses of the fine

5. D'Argenlieu to Bidault, 19 Jun. 1946, d'Argenlieu, *Chronique*, 297.

6. P. Devillers, *Paris-Saigon-Hanoi, Les archives de la guerre, 1944–1947*, Paris, 1988, 192–93.

7. J. Tronchon, *L'insurrection malgache*, Paris and Fianarantsoa, 1974/1986, 335–37.

intelligence that one might expect of a cat that had suddenly acquired the gift of speech.[8]

The colonial lobby now had an immediate target for its hostility, and the effect on opinion, not least in the Constituent Assembly, of this highly visible and eloquent spokesman for colonial independence cannot be underestimated. Although colonial policy was now assured the political salience which policy makers had craved since the Liberation, the political climate was such as to reduce still further the likelihood of a liberal outcome to the negotiations, especially given the coincidence of Fontainebleau with the acrimonious constitutional debate on the French Union. Ironically, even now Indochina policy took second place on the political agenda in Paris behind preparations for the projected Peace Conference with Germany.[9]

The Drawing of Battle Lines

It was against this inauspicious background that the administration prepared its negotiating position for Fontainebleau. It was apparent well before the Conference opened on 6 July that the policy dispute between Paris and Saigon was intensifying. In public, little discord was visible between the GPRF and the High Commission in Indochina. This harmony was even maintained when French forces in Indochina, on orders from d'Argenlieu in Paris, staged a military takeover of the Moi plateaux of Southern Annam on 21 June and, four days later, re-occupied the Government General in Hanoi. Like the creation of the Cochinchinese Republic three weeks before, this unilateral action by the High Commissioner was swiftly backed up by the GPRF in Paris.[10] In private, however, ministry officials and their Saigon colleagues clashed over the purpose of the Conference and indeed of the Accords policy as a whole.

8. 'M. Ho Chi Minh pérore avec arrogance dans des salons dorés tandis que des Français tombent chaque jour dans des embuscades en Indochine. [Il est,] dans son genre, un petit rigolo ... supérieurement adroit et ses yeux cruels laissent filtrer une belle intelligence, une sorte d'intelligence de chat qui aurait brusquement le don de la parole.' J. Imbert, *Dépêche de Paris*, 13 Jul. 1946; in a 'dossier de presse', MAE, AO/IC/54.

9. J. Valette, 'La Conférence de Fontainebleau (1946)', in IHTP, *Les chemins de la décolonisation de l'empire français, 1936–1956*, Paris, 1986, 241.

10. Devillers, *Paris-Saigon-Hanoi*, 193.

The ministerial crisis in June precluded a repetition of the detailed discussions which preceded the Dalat Conference, even if they had been necessary. Since Dalat had decided nothing, the agenda was broadly speaking the same, and although it was clear that the stakes were this time significantly raised, Paris did its best to maintain the impression of continuity. By the time of Ho's arrival in Paris, on 24 June, a final decision had still to be reached on the composition of the French delegation. Acting as liaison with the Vietnamese delegations, Laurentie reported to Cominindo that Ho was keen to see a fresh delegation appointed and, in particular, the inclusion of parliamentary representatives. Resisting this attempt by Ho to politicise the Conference, the Secretary-General of Cominindo argued that the Dalat team were clearly qualified to conduct the conversations which they had initiated, and that the inclusion of parliamentarians would work against the idea that the Conference was at governmental level. The French delegation at Fontainebleau, still headed by Max André, was thus essentially the same as before, with the addition of token representatives from the Tripartite coalition parties who, in the event, played little part in the proceedings.[11]

Notwithstanding the fact that the main agenda at Fontainebleau was to be carried over from Dalat, the proclamation of the Cochinchinese Republic made it likely that the Conference would be dominated by the question of the three *ky* and the referendum laid down in the March Accords. The case for a liberal approach to this question was wearing thin by now, but it was reiterated by Laurentie, for whom the global perspective was as important as ever. As he argued, what happened to Cochinchina would determine France's Indochina policy as a whole. He envisaged two possible solutions. The first was the imposition of a federal structure for Indochina, in pursuance of the terms of the March 1945 Declaration. This would necessitate tight control by France if the encroachment of 'Annam' into the affairs of Cambodia and Laos was to be avoided, and the maintenance of complete Cochinchinese independence from Annam. The second, preferred, solution was a more flexible Indochinese Union, based essentially on economic and financial arrangements, and in which France's role would be one of overseer or arbitrator. This, he suggested, would

11. Note, Secrétariat-Général du CI, 27 Jun. 1946, MAE, AO/IC/54. The party delegates were: J.-J. Juglas (MRP); H. Lozeray (PCF); P. Rivet (SFIO). The delegation included three new 'experts', including the staff officer Admiral Barjot: d'Argenlieu, *Chronique*, 300.

lessen the danger of Vietnamese encroachment into Cambodia and Laos, while France might hope to maintain some control over Cochinchina, within the general framework of Vietnamese sovereignty in the South guaranteed by France. This last would depend on the outcome of the referendum. Whilst the Vietnamese apparently believed that the referendum would go the way the dominant political authority wanted, many French officials were opposed to the holding of a referendum. For Laurentie, however, even if a result was doubtful in favour of Cochinchinese independence, the same was not true for the idea of broad Cochinchinese autonomy under Vietnamese sovereignty.[12] For Laurentie, therefore, much turned on the organisation of a referendum, although, as he also argued to Cédile even this would not bring matters to their conclusion, since the fundamental debate hinged rather on the intangible and unpredictable character of modern nationalism.[13]

The principal problem with Laurentie's thinking was that few if any Saigon officials now shared his Olympian vision.[14] Nor on the eve of the Conference was there much sign on the French side of the goodwill which Laurentie's solution presupposed. Rather, the attitude of Saigon officials seemed increasingly likely to jeopardize Franco-Vietnamese agreement on any subject. Léon Pignon, a key player at Fontainebleau as he had been at Dalat, now displayed overt hostility towards the Vietnamese, responding angrily to Laurentie's criticisms of policy emanating from Saigon:

> You think that we are starting to live a lie, that our position is unworthy of France and untenable. If there is a lie, it is the one that has led us to sign accords with people who know, as we know ourselves, that we are enemies. The lie is lived only by those who do not recognise this fact.[15]

---

12. Note, Sec.-Gen. du CI, 27 Jun. 1946, loc.cit.

13. Laurentie to Cédile, 13 Jul. 1946, AN, 72AJ539.

14. As he wrote to Cédile, a touch naïvely, 'When one is in the thick of things, one does not have the same perspective, and one can reflect more clearly with the benefit of time and distance'. (*'Quand on est "sur le tas" la perspective n'est plus la même, la réflexion gagne avec le temps et l'éloignement.'*): ibid.

15. 'Vous estimez que nous débutons dans le mensonge et que notre position est indigne de la France et insoutenable.... Si mensonge il y a, il réside dans le fait de vouloir signer des accords avec des gens qui savent, comme nous le savons nous-mêmes, que nous sommes adversaires. Le mensonge n'existe que pour ceux qui ignorent cet aspect.' Pignon to Laurentie, 5 Jul. 1946. AN, 72AJ539. Laurentie's letter is not extant.

In defence of Saigon's Cochinchina policy, in which he was instrumental, Pignon admitted only to 'some clumsiness'. Cochinchina
was 'the essential stronghold for any reconquest of Indochina', and
he painted a grim picture of the consequences of Vietnamese involvement of any kind in Cochinchina:

> We will lose the confidence of Cambodia and Laos and of all those
> in the Annamite lands who had believed in us. Far worse than
> that, we will be delivering them up along with their families to be
> tortured and killed. I would personally feel guiltier and less wor-
> thy of being French by sacrificing our allies than by playing tricks
> on our enemies.[16]

Pignon refuted Laurentie's charges of duplicity, pointing to the
transparency and consistency of d'Argenlieu's policies since the
spring. As Pignon argued disarmingly, 'We may be "colonialists"
but we are not playing an ambiguous game'. Saigon's aim was
neither to return to the past, nor to allow Indochina to fall beneath
the yoke of a 'hated, incompetent minority'.[17]

Writing on the day before the conference was due to start,
Pignon was alarmingly pessimistic as to the purpose and likely
outcome of the negotiations. Echoing Laurentie's own views, he
observed that, skilled propagandists though they might be, the
Vietnamese delegation in Paris were unrepresentative of either
Indochina or of the whole of 'Annam'. But for Pignon, the dramatic effect of the Vietnamese delegation on French public opinion was the pursuit, by other means and on other terrain, of the
policy which had so far been fruitless on the battlefield. The same
was even more true of the Fontainebleau Conference:

> Tomorrow's negotiations are a round in the battle we are fighting,
> in which we are trying to reinstate ourselves in Indochina and they
> are trying to see us off. It is as simple as that. The question we

---

16. '… la place d'armes indispensable pour la *reconquête* de l'Indochine…. Nous
perdons la confiance du Cambodge et du Laos et dans tous les pays annamites de
ceux qui ont cru en nous. Nous faisons pire, nous les livrons, eux et leurs familles
à la torture et à la mort. Personnellement,… je m'estimerais plus coupable et plus
indigne du nom français en sacrifiant nos partisans qu'en rusant avec *des ennemis*.'
Laurentie's underlining and marginal note: 'Playing tricks on our enemies? Reconquest? This would suggest winning by force of arms. Will this be allowed by
France and the world?' ('Ruser avec des ennemis? Reconquérir? finalement cela
veut dire: vaincre par les armes. La France et le monde le permettront-ils?')

17. 'Nous sommes peut-être des "colonialistes" mais notre jeu n'est pas équiv-
oque … une minorité détestée et incapable'. Ibid.

should be asking ourselves at this moment is the following: do we or do we not wish to keep Indochina?[18]

Pignon was now inclined to disown the entire Accords policy, which he had in part masterminded. As he claimed, he realised his mistake too late to reverse the process, and had left Hanoi unable to stomach further a policy of weakness. He concluded that it would be better to abandon France's exposed and vulnerable economic interests in Indochina than to pursue policies which did not maintain the minimum authority necessary. Even discounting the fact that Pignon was responding to criticisms of his judgement, the views of France's most competent and best-informed negotiator can only have dismayed Laurentie, who responded with head-shaking resignation.[19]

Pignon's hostile attitude was consistent with the approach of his superior, Admiral d'Argenlieu, who, keen to belittle the importance of the Conference, wrote to Bidault on the day he was named President of the GPRF, placing Fontainebleau in the context of a long line of 'conversations' with Ho Chi Minh which had taken place since 6 March in Hanoi, the Bay of Along, Dalat, and Hanoi again. Although his arguments were respected concerning the retention of the Dalat negotiating team, his attitude may be contrasted with that of Cominindo which sought to ascribe a 'definitive character' to the conference, for example in its 29 May session.[20] More potentially damaging was the effect of his two new *coups de théâtre* which, with impeccable timing, coincided with the formation of the new government. In a long letter to Bidault, d'Argenlieu set out his reasoning for these two further acts of indiscipline. Thus, the reoccupation of the Government General in Hanoi had been carried out in accordance with Franco-Chinese agreements. Moreover, given the building's symbolic value to both the Indochinese and the French, it was important

18. 'Les négociations qui s'ouvrent demain sont une phase du combat que nous livrons nous pour nous réinstaller en Indochine, eux pour nous en chasser, un point c'est tout. A l'heure actuelle, la question doit être envisagée sous l'angle suivant: voulons-nous, oui ou non, conserver l'Indochine?' Ibid.

19. As he wrote in the margin, 'Essentially, Pignon blames France for being what she is. The world is also what it is. In politics you always have to start by accepting things the way they are'. ('En somme, Pignon reproche à la France d'être ce qu'elle est. Le monde aussi est ce qu'il est. En politique il faut d'abord accepter les données du problème.') Ibid.

20. D'Argenlieu to Bidault, 19 Jun. 1946, in d'Argenlieu, *Chronique*, 295; Commission Consultative du CI, 29 May 1946, MAE, AO/IC/179.

that France should enjoy the same authority and prerogatives as the Chinese, who had vacated it a few days before.[21] The occupation of the Moi plateaux lay closer to the heart of traditional 'colonial' concerns in Indochina: the 'protection' of Indochina's largest ethnic minority; and the rubber plantations, which had constituted the most dynamic element of Indochina's pre-war economy, as d'Argenlieu remembered. In May, the High Commissioner had been welcomed at Ban Me Thuot, in the Annamese highlands. In a ceremony which, for d'Argenlieu, had the value of a plebiscite, 2,400 headmen had given a Grand Oath ('Grand Serment') of loyalty to France. This and other moral, social, historical, and juridical factors served to justify the action, if not its timing. Although he argued that France was in a strong position at the Comonindo session of 29 June, he said nothing to dispel the impression that his major concern was to wrest the initiative from the media-friendly Vietnamese and, for that matter, from the Parisian authorities.[22]

Fontainebleau … and Dalat

D'Argenlieu's initiatives ensured a rocky start to the Fontainebleau Conference on 6 July. Pham Van Dong replied to André's speech of welcome by denouncing Saigon's recent faits accomplis. While affirming that he wished to reach agreement with France, he condemned France's actions in occupying the 'rich plateaux of Pleiku and Kontum' and the Government General, but above all, as he went on, the Vietnamese delegation wished to protest, 'with all the force which a nation of twenty millions can muster when it is united in a supreme effort of legitimate defence, against the mutilation of our Fatherland, against the creation of a Free State of Cochinchina'.[23] André's response was to suspend this first public session of the Conference; it resumed the following day, and by the 9th an agenda had been drawn up. Instructed by d'Argenlieu, Sainteny registered a verbal protest to Ho. Further, in a letter to Bidault, the Admiral insisted that, if the Government did not

21. Haussaire au Président du Comonindo, no. 22 Cab/P, 4 Jul. 1946, MAE, AO/IC/69.

22. Séance du CI du 29 Jun. 1946, MAE, AO/IC/179.

23. '… nous tenons à protester, avec toute la force dont est capable un peuple de vingt millions d'hommes dressé dans un suprême élan de légitime défense, contre la mutilation de notre patrie, contre la création d'un Etat libre de Cochinchine.' *Le Monde*, 7 Jul. 1946; Devillers, *Paris-Saigon-Hanoi*, 194.

make clear that it would tolerate no affront to its authority on the part of its guests, 'our partners (enemies at heart) will immediately take advantage by upping their demands and reiterating their grievances'.[24] As he stressed, the French were now strong enough to impose a 'liberal and enlightened policy' ('une politique libérale et éclairée') in Indochina. After a further meeting with Bidault on 9 July, d'Argenlieu left for Saigon. With the rapid onset of stalemate at Fontainebleau, it did not take long for the High Commissioner to make plain his idea of liberalism and enlightenment, with his announcement of a second Dalat Conference.

Meanwhile, and until the end of the month, the two delegations engaged in negotiating the substance of their ambitious agenda, covering five issues: Vietnam's position in the French Union and its diplomatic relations with third countries; the elaboration of the Indochinese Federation; the union of the three *ky* and the Cochinchina referendum; economic problems; the drafting of a treaty.[25] However, it soon became clear from the work of the conference committees, which met from 13 to 30 July, that neither side's position had changed in substance since Dalat, even if both sides made resolutely conciliatory noises in public.[26] The Vietnamese case was eloquently explained for a wider French public by Ho Chi Minh himself, in a press conference on 12 July. Ho claimed the right of self-determination for Vietnam; accepted the notion of the Indochinese Federation, which (like Laurentie) he saw as having an essentially economic function, rather than being a Government-General in disguise; and offered aid to Laos and Cambodia, since Vietnam was 'in a more favourable position than its two neighbours'.[27] On the French side, Baudet made a public speech at the Conference on 20 July, on the core issue of Vietnam's diplomatic status: allowing for possible consular representation for a 'Free State' ('Etat libre'), he also stressed that France would probably accept Indochinese membership of the United Nations. But he avoided prejudging the issue of separate Vietnamese status, as opposed to participation within the context of the Indochinese Federation. Accepting the talks' diplomatic dimension, he

24. '… nos partenaires (au fond des adversaires) s'en prévaudront aussitôt pour augmenter leurs exigences et réitérer leurs inconvenances.' Haussaire au Prés. du GPRF, no. 24 Cab/F, 7 Jul. 1946, d'Argenlieu, *Chronique*, 301.

25. Devillers, *Paris-Saigon-Hanoi*, 195.

26. The Vietnamese and French texts are compared in 'Conférence de Fontainebleau – Principaux points de désaccord', n.d. (July 1946), MAE, AO/IC/69.

27. *Le Monde*, 13–14 Jul. 1946.

stressed another aspect, 'that of discussions between members of the same community, or even almost the same family'.[28] The French position was restricted for as long as the French Union remained, as Laurentie put it, 'a soul without a body, a purely juridical conception'. Thus the highly concrete Vietnamese demands were met only with vague talk of 'the great and powerful community which *will be called* the French Union'.[29]

On Cochinchina, Pignon's robust presentation of the French case was more than matched by the Vietnamese, who now increasingly presented Cochinchina as the determining issue on which agreement depended.[30] Thus, Ho presented in highly emotive terms the case for integrating Cochinchina into Vietnam: 'It is Vietnamese land. It is the flesh of our flesh, the blood of our blood.... Even before Corsica became French, Cochinchina was Vietnamese'.[31] He expressed his own preference for reaching agreement without the expense of a referendum; but promised that if necessary this would be held in good faith, and the result would still favour the Vietnamese cause. Increasingly the fate of the conference depended on settlement of this one issue. As one delegate argued:

> For as long as Cochinchina remains detached from Vietnam, there can be no understanding between France and Vietnam. Everything depends on the Cochinchina question: Franco-Vietnamese friendship, peace and order in Vietnam, the future of our relations. We must settle this affair as quickly as possible.[32]

As Pignon observed, such rhetoric appealed to the French public's bad conscience with regard to Cochinchina; it was all the more

28. '… celui de conversations entre membres d'une même communauté, je dirais presque d'une même famille': 'Relations diplomatiques du Viêt-Nam avec l'étranger', Exposé de M. Baudet du 20 Juillet à Fontainebleau, MAE, AO/IC/54.

29. '… une âme sans corps, une simple virtualité juridique … la grande et puissante communauté qui *s'appellera* l'Union française'. 'Note sur la nécessité d'une constitution de l'Union française', n.d. (July 1946), AN, 72AJ535, also reproduced as EMGDN, *Bulletin d'études* no. 32. Emphasis in text.

30. Note (Pignon), n.d. (July 1946). And see his 'exposé oral to the Commission Consultative meeting of Comindo, 29 Jun. 1946, MAE, AO/IC/54.

31. 'C'est une terre vietnamienne. C'est la chair de notre chair, c'est le sang de notre sang.... Avant que la Corse fût française, la Cochinchine était déjà vietnamienne.' Loc.cit.

32. 'Tant que la Cochinchine, d'une manière ou d'une autre, sera détachée du Viêt-Nam, il n'y aura pas d'entente possible entre la France et le Viêt-Nam. Tout dépend de la question de Cochinchine, l'amitié franco-vietnamienne, la paix comme l'ordre dans le Viêt-Nam, l'avenir de nos relations. Il faut régler cette affaire le plus tôt possible.' Duong Bach Mai, in Devillers, *Paris-Saigon-Hanoi*, 199.

necessary therefore for the French delegation to present a united front in the continuing debate.[33]

The next decisive move came almost inevitably from Saigon. On 22 July, d'Argenlieu announced that a 'Preparatory Conference to study the status of the Federation' ('Conférence préparatoire d'étude du statut de la Fédération') would open at Dalat on 1 August. To make matters worse, the news broke, and Ho protested to Moutet, before d'Argenlieu had officially informed Paris.[34] D'Argenlieu had been planning this conference for more than a month. His ostensible concern was wholly legitimate: since 6 March, Vietnam had stolen the limelight from the other parts of the future Indochinese Federation, which was especially worrying given Vietnam's potential for dominating the Federation even without Cochinchinese union. As d'Argenlieu argued in a telegramme to Saigon: 'Just as the question of new relations between Vietnam and France must be settled by those two countries, so also must the organisation of the Indochinese Federation be settled by all member states working together on the basis of equality'.[35] On this basis, replying to Moutet on 30 July, d'Argenlieu claimed even that the new conference had effectively been approved by the Government in April, when the first Dalat Conference was in preparation.[36] However, beyond the equitable organisation of the Federation, his intention was to set up a rival bloc to counter the influence of Hanoi, as he had already hinted in a policy paper in April. In a diary entry for 21 June, d'Argenlieu reasoned that a new Dalat Conference would allow Hanoi's views to be resisted by a 'barrage' of other states: 'If, as is possible, we arrived at a satisfactory solution with the other states at Dalat, we could turn this to good account in favour of the masterplan of a Mekong bloc, while at the same time maintaining the Hanoi's government's ties with the French Union'.[37]

33. Note (Pignon), loc.cit.

34. Tel. 1324/CI, Moutet to d'Argenlieu, 24 Jul. 1946, Devillers, *Paris-Saigon-Hanoi*, 201.

35. 'Si la question des rapports nouveaux entre le Viêt-Nam et la France est à régler entre ces deux pays ... tous les Etats membres doivent être appelés à collaborer sur un pied d'égalité [à] l'organisation de la Fédération indochinoise.' Tel. no. 2482/CHA no. 29/CAB, Defnat Paris to Haussaire Indo Saigon, signé d'Argenlieu, 4 Jul. 1946, in d'Argenlieu, *Chronique*, 299.

36. Tel. no. 1149 F, Haussaire to Comindo, 30 Jul. 1946, d'Argenlieu, *Chronique*, 247.

37. 'Si comme il est possible nous arrivions à une solution satisfaisante avec les autres Etats à Dalat nous pourrions en tirer parti pour *l'idée maîtresse du bloc du Mékong* ... tout en ayant maintenu le lien du gouvernement de Hanoi avec l'Union

Apart from the conference's overt rationale and the inklings of d'Argenlieu's grand plan, however, there was also the question of timing. Protesting to Saigon, Moutet noted that the High Commissioner's latest action might serve a purpose, but it gave the impression that the French government was not holding to the terms of the 6 March Accords.[38] Moutet's fears were quickly realised. On the day the rival conference opened at Dalat, 1 August, Pham Van Dong presented what amounted to an ultimatum:

> Either it is the French authorities in Cochinchina which are responsible for the fate of Cochinchina, South Annam, the High Plateaux and the status of the Indochinese Federation. In this case, the 6 March Convention loses its purpose and our conference at Fontainebleau has no further reason to meet. Or the 6 March Convention must be put into effect, in which case the Fontainebleau Conference is the sole appropriate forum for the discussion of these problems.[39]

While waiting for this ambiguity to be resolved, the Vietnamese delegation had no option but to suspend their participation in the Conference. Bidault's quandary is reflected in his 3 August cable to Saigon which, while not directly criticising d'Argenlieu, underlined the consequences of his action, and suggested that Dong wished to provoke the GPRF into disavowing the High Commissioner. Bidault denied that he would do this, but in order to bring the Vietnamese back to the conference table he asked d'Argenlieu not to inflate the importance of the Dalat Conference, and to keep it short and consultative in scope. D'Argenlieu replied that the proceedings were due to last until 10 or 11 August, but that it would an injustice and an affront to the kings of Laos and Cambodia to cut short the conference just to please Vietnam.[40]

---

française.' D'Argenlieu, *Chronique*, 299, emphasis added; cf. 'Tournant Politique en Indochine', 26 Apr. 1946, d'Argenlieu, *Chronique*, 274–77 and see above, Ch. 7.

33. Note (Pignon), loc.cit.

34. Tel 38. Tel. no. 1324/CI, loc.cit.

39. '… ou bien ce sont les autorités françaises en Cochinchine qui décident du sort de la Cochinchine, du Sud-Annam, des Hauts Plateaux et du statut de la Fédération indochinoise. Dans ce cas, la Convention du 6 mars devient sans objet, et notre conférence de Fontainebleau n'a plus raison d'être. Ou bien la Convention du 6 mars doit recevoir application, auquel cas seule la conférence de Fontainebleau a qualité pour discuter de ces problèmes.' Quoted in Tel. no. 49/c.d., Présiparis to Haussaire, 3 Aug. 1946, MAE, EA/36/15.

40. Ibid., and Tel. no. 111, Haussaire to Cominindo, 5 Aug. 1946, d'Argenlieu, *Chronique*, 309.

D'Argenlieu's preference for the complete abandonment of the Fontainebleau Conference was made clear in a memorandum dated 2 August, a tendentious account of the consistency of his policy since the previous autumn, which he contrasted with the GPRF's indecision and inconstancy. Thus he stressed his adherence to the principles enshrined in the March 1945 Declaration, upon which the GPRF had not formally reneged, he noted French and Indochinese perceptions that Paris's sense of purpose was faltering; and he praised the Expeditionary Corps' part in the restoration of French authority. As he argued, the Government should suspend the conference if it could not reverse the current momentum of events, for if colonial confidence was lost, all that would be left for France would be to 'prepare to leave or to envisage an armed reconquest'. Noting the coincidence of the conference with the work of the Second Constituent Assembly he predicted that the former would either differ in its findings from the latter, or influence it adversely. The likely outcome either way was a French Union which was merely 'a formula to paper over the probably terminal decline of France and her overseas territories'. In conclusion, d'Argenlieu asked that no decisions concerning the Federation be made before he could address Comenindo in late August.[41] The High Commissioner now largely dismissed the authority and sense of purpose of his political masters. Writing to de Gaulle on 27 July, he expressed dismay at the 'crisis of authority' ('crise d'autorité') which he had witnessed during his three weeks in Paris, and its likely effect on Indochina policy. In particular he criticised the French decision to allow Siam's case concerning the two provinces annexed in 1940 to come before the International Court of Justice at the Hague. If any historical parallels were needed, his diary provided them in the form of references to Munich and Chamberlain.[42] In the well-tried manner of the colonial proconsul, he laid down two conditions for achieving France's 'political, liberal and democratic goals in Indochina': that Comenindo should drop its suspicions of his actions; and that the Government should remain firm.[43]

41. '... préparer un départ ou à envisager une reconquête par la force ... une formule couvrant le déclin probablement irréversible de la France et de ses territoires d'outre-mer'. Note, 'Incidences des Conférences de Fontainebleau et Dalat sur le devenir de l'Indochine française', Dalat, 2 Aug. 1946, MAE, AO/IC/54.
42. D'Argenlieu, *Chronique*, 308, 312.
43. Note, 2 Aug. 1946, loc.cit.

In effect, d'Argenlieu was challenging the whole thrust of the Accords policy. Moreover, he was backed by his lieutenants, including Pignon, who drafted a note for Cominindo, on 'the Viet Minh's takeover of power in Indochina'. The implication was clear: Ho and his men, by their violent methods and lack of respect for democratic principles, were unworthy negotiating partners for France.[44] As if to prove Saigon's point, on 3 August, a French convoy was reported ambushed on the road from Hanoi to Langson, at Bac Ninh. The incident brought accusations that France was breaking the military agreement of 6 March, which did not provide for a garrison at Langson. The incident was quickly resolved by staff on both sides, but if nothing else it served to demonstrate the futility of ascribing too much importance to the talks in Paris.[45]

Maintaining the Accords Policy

This evidence of the fragility of the peace in Indochina did not deter Moutet from reacting to the broadside from Saigon with a stout defence of the Accords policy. As Baudet wrote to Clarac in Saigon, the Vietnamese had come close to splitting both the French Delegation and the Government, when the 'rather too heavy hint of blackmail' in Dong's statement concerning the Dalat Conference and the Bac Ninh incident had brought a change of heart.[46] In the end, Moutet carried the day with a touch of the required firmness, combined with a determined effort to bring about conciliation. Although it could not save the conference, this approach was to lead to the compromise solution of a *modus vivendi* between the two sides.

In a note dated 8 August, Moutet set about striking the balance: deploring the Vietnamese ultimatum concerning Cochinchina, he also criticised the 'lack of national discipline during sensitive negotiations', though he tactfully referred only to partisan disputes in the Parisian press. Calling for clear Government unity, he reiterated the need for a Accords policy:

44. 'La prise du pouvoir en Indochine par le parti Viêt Minh', Compte-rendu, 5 Aug. 1946, no. 103 CD, signé Labrouquère, MAE, AO/IC/54.
45. As later emerged from intercepted signals, the Vietnamese army had reacted to reports of the convoy firing on civilians: Devillers, *Paris-Saigon-Hanoi*, 206; d'Argenlieu, *Chronique*, 310–11.
46. '… note de chantage un peu trop accentuée', Baudet to Clarac, Conseiller Diplomatique du Hau-Commissaire, 21 Aug. 1946, MAE, AO/IC/54.

The 6 March Accords must be our charter and the terms of the Accords must be carried out in good faith. For me, the Accords will not be purely and simply a point of departure for the restoration of French sovereignty by force.[47]

The use of force would put relations with Hanoi on a war footing, risk Ho's overthrow by even more radical nationalists probably backed by China, and embroil France in what Leclerc had called 'our Spanish Civil War' ('notre guerre d'Espagne'). He disputed that agreement amounted to abandonment. Admitting the inadequacy of the historical case for Vietnamese national unity, which had lasted a mere fifty years, he also argued that North and South would almost inevitably be drawn together, given that the Tonkinese workforce was economically complemented by the ricefields of Cochinchina. Like Laurentie, Moutet placed his faith in a fair referendum, conducted without pressure from either the French military or Viet Minh terrorism, leading to autonomy for Cochinchina within a loose Vietnamese union.[48]

The immediate priority, however, was to effect a return to the negotiating table at Fontainebleau. On 11 August, d'Argenlieu brought the Dalat Conference to a triumphant close, after ten days of 'excellent work', which he contrasted with the 'recantations at Fontainebleau'.[49] In meetings on 10 and 12 August, Cominindo rejected the Admiral's advice on Fontainebleau and drew up an *aide-mémoire* stating the French position and expressing the desire to resume negotiations in a draft joint declaration. Approved by the GPRF on 19 August, this was conveyed to Ho by his preferred French emissary, Sainteny. Ho's initial response was to suggest improvement to the French *aide-mémoire*. But on the 20th, the Vietnamese produced their own declaration and *aide-mémoire*, purporting to be conciliatory, and based on the French plan. In fact, these new texts suggested that the Vietnamese position had hardened: citing the British Dominions as proof of France's interest in

47. '... l'accord du 6 mars doit être notre charte et cet accord doit être exécuté de bonne foi. Il ne saurait être pour moi considéré comme un point de départ pour rétablir purement et simplement par la force la souveraineté française sur l'Indochine.' Note de Mr Marius Moutet a/s de la Conférence de Fontainebleau, 8 Aug. 1946, MAE, EA/36/15.

48. Ibid.

49. '... les palinodies de Fontainebleau', d'Argenlieu, *Chronique*, 306, 310. See also a 'Rapport sur la Situation Politique Intérieure de l'Indochine au 10 août 1946', 30 Aug. 1946, noting the 'comforting atmosphere of fruitful work' ('l'atmosphère réconfortante de travail fécond') at Dalat, MAE, AO/IC/139.

accepting Vietnamese independence, the *aide-mémoire* called for independence within three years.[50] Pignon reacted with a stern set of 'Observations on the Vietnamese Aide-Mémoire', ruling out independence and stressing the 'permanence of the French mission in Indochina'. For Pignon, the new texts were a Vietnamese attempt to make up ground lost at Dalat and even in the March Accords: 'Once again President Ho Chi Minh has built a stage set for our benefit; it would seem that we must inform him clearly of our decision not be be taken in by his make-believe'.[51] Baudet's view was that the Vietnamese were playing for time and that, while avoiding a complete breakdown, they were unwilling to come to terms. After apparently angling in early August to force a stalemate at the Conference and return home, Ho now talked of leaving in October; Baudet speculated that, having failed his coup, Ho was seeking to exploit the potential of the forthcoming elections.[52]

Notwithstanding continuing pressure to allow the conference to fail, Moutet was now seeking a compromise with a face-saving accord falling short of definitive agreement but building on the March Accords. Replying to d'Argenlieu's memorandum of 2 August, he restated the purpose of an Accords policy. As he argued, though there had been frequent Vietnamese violations of the March Accords, the French had to decide whether they were looking for a reason to break off relations or whether they wanted a policy based on amicable agreement. Ruling out reconquest, even given the change in France's military fortunes since March, and discounting thoughts of substituting a Quisling government ('gouvernement fantoche') of the kind which had been so recently discredited by the Germans and Japanese, Moutet endorsed Ho's status as an acceptable negotiating partner:

> We have chosen Ho Chi Minh as a negotiating partner, and I believe that he is the only figure to represent any kind of authority, however

50. Réunion de la délégation française en séance privée, 19 Aug. 1946, MAE, AO/IC/54; Devillers, *Paris-Saigon-Hanoi*, 210–12.

51. '... la pérennité de l'oeuvre française en Extrême-Orient.... C'est encore une fois un décor de théâtre que le Président HO CHI MINH a bâti à notre usage. Il paraît nécessaire de lui faire connaître avec netteté que nous ne sommes pas décidés à accepter un pareil marché de dupes.' 'Observations sur l'Aide-Mémoire Viêtnamien', N.d. (22 Aug. 1946?), MAE, AO/IC/54.

52. Baudet to Clarac, 21 Aug. 1946, loc.cit; Réunion de la Délégation Française, 19 Aug. 1946, loc.cit.

limited. As soon as he realises fully that he derives his essential power from us, he will have to act loyally and properly.[53]

Agreement was not to be equated with appeasement, however, even if complete agreement was still impossible, as Moutet suspected. As it was, the French would have to be content with achieving a small measure of progress. To this end, a more peaceable atmosphere was needed, including the cessation of anti-French propaganda and acts of violence. Two stumbling blocks remained: the question of independence, and the date and conditions of the referendum on Cochinchina. Moutet considered that this last trump card should be played only if all other conditions were met.[54]

Moutet was effectively setting the agenda which led to the *modus vivendi* almost four weeks later, although the initiative for this has also been attributed to Bidault's advisers at the Quai d'Orsay.[55] However, it took a further two weeks of hesitation and unofficial meetings with Ho before Moutet felt able to spell out the alternatives to Saigon: either a limited agreement, or 'breaking off the Conference with the all the ensuing consequences' ('la rupture de la Conférence avec toutes les conséquences qui s'ensuivent'). As he argued, the consequences might be serious for France, given the present strength of guerilla forces in the South and the forthcoming relief of experienced French troops by new recruits (though he played down the significance of the latter).[56] In the meantime, Pignon and Laurentie (presumably armed with stick and carrot respectively) were charged by Moutet to negotiate a new Memorandum (*note verbale*) with Ho. This re-admitted to the agenda the issue of the referendum, omitted from the *aide-mémoire* of 14 August. A further note dated 6 September set out the French position on the key issue: it would organise a referendum on Cochinchina just as soon as peace and order had been restored through a series of measures to be carried out both by France's agents in Indochina and by the Government of the Democratic

---

53. 'Nous avons choisi Ho Chi Minh pour traiter et je crois bien qu'il est le seul représentant une autorité qui, pour limitée qu'elle soit, n'en existe moins. Le jour où il sera bien convaincu qu'il tire de nous sa force essentielle, il sera bien obligé d'agir avec loyauté et correction.' Moutet to Haussaire, 19 Aug. 1946, d'Argenlieu, *Chronique*, 312–14.

54. Ibid.

55. Valette, 'La Conférence', 246–47.

56. Moutet to Haussaire, 3 Sep. 1946, d'Argenlieu, *Chronique*, 317–18, Devillers, *Paris-Saigon-Hanoi*, 213.

Republic of Vietnam. This last note was approved by Ho on 7 September.[57] But it took a further three days of talks before the two delegations, in plenary session on the morning of 10 September, reached the point of agreement. Then, in the afternoon session, to French astonishment, Pham Van Dong proposed re-opening discussion of the whole text, or at least omitting from the final protocol certain arrangements having a bearing on Vietnamese sovereignty. Further he demanded a definite French commitment as to the date and modalities of the referendum. Max André, presiding, had no option but to adjourn what proved to be the last meeting of the two delegations. Four days, later the Vietnamese delegation embarked at Marseille aboard the *Pasteur*, bound for Haiphong.[58]

Although by now it was clear that the Fontainebleau Conference had failed in its central purpose of reaching a definitive agreement between the two sides, neither the French nor the Vietnamese were happy to allow a complete breakdown in relations. Indeed, the Vietnamese delegation parted quite amicably and with the declared intention of reaching partial agreements with the French administration in Indochina and thus proving its desire for peace and cooperation with France. Ho meanwhile explained to the press in Paris that Franco-Vietnamese disagreements were of a kind found in any family. However, he also criticised French proposals for the disarming and repatriation of Vietnamese troops in the South, and he called for the liberation of all political prisoners.[59] On 13 September, in a cable intercepted by the French, the Hanoi government laid down three conditions for an eventual accord: that it should be global in scope, covering political, economic, financial and cultural matters; that any ceasefire in Cochinchina should be accompanied by the accordance of democratic liberties, and should avoid stationing Vietnamese troops in fixed locations more liable to French attack; and that the accord should be free of the ambiguities which had attached to the 6 March Convention.[60] These three conditions were largely met, on a provisional basis, in the *modus vivendi* signed by Moutet and Ho in the small hours of 15 September. This reaffirmed the Accords policy inaugurated on 6 March and elaborated at the (first) Dalat and

57. Note verbale, 2 Sep. 1946, Devillers, *Paris-Saigon-Hanoi*, 215; Note, 6 Sep. 1946, and covering letter, MAE, EA/36/15.
58. Devillers, *Paris-Saigon-Hanoi*, 217–19.
59. *Le Monde*, 13–14 Sep. 1946; *Libération*, 12 Sep. 1946.
60. D'Argenlieu, *Chronique*, 319.

Fontainebleau Conferences; and expressed the conviction that it would establish a 'climate of calm and confidence' ('un climat de calme et de confiance') permitting the resumption of the Fontainebleau Conference, which was set for January 1947. There followed articles on the agreed political, economic, financial, and cultural provisions. Article IX provided for the ceasefire, release of prisoners, guarantee of democratic liberties, etc., thus reflecting the bulk of Vietnamese concerns. Not coincidentally, it was also to be the focus of Saigon's criticisms. The *modus vivendi* was to come into effect on 30 October.[61]

The two sides now had six weeks to prepare for the *modus vivendi*'s entry into force, which d'Argenlieu deemed to be 'impossible'.[62] In the meantime, on 19 October, Ho left for home on board the French cruiser *Dumont d'Urville*, arriving home a month later, on 20 October. Although to Sainteny he cited health reasons for not flying home, it is tempting to speculate why he thus placed himself effectively incommunicado: he certainly needed time to recuperate and reflect; but was he setting himself up as a moderate to counter the zeal of Vo Nguyen Giap or Nguyen Binh (guerilla leader in the South)? Or was he anxious to delay the increasingly inevitable showdown?[63] Certainly the famous image which he provided for the journalist David Schoenbrun of an eventual Franco-Vietnamese conflict gave little ground for optimism — France was depicted as the all-powerful but ponderous elephant slowly bleeding to death from the attacks of the weaker but more cunning and more implacable Vietnamese tiger.[64]

———— ✦ ————

The *modus vivendi* marked the far from satisfactory end to the period of high-level Franco-Vietnamese negotiations. The Fontainebleau Conference never resumed, and it was not until 1954 that the Hanoi government would find themselves again across a

61. 'Déclaration conjointe des Gouvernements de la République Française et de la République Démocratique du Viêt-Nam', 14 Sep. 1946, in Commandant G. Bodinier, ed., *Le retour de la France en Indochine, 1945–1946*, Vincennes, 1987, 287–91; although dated the 14th, it was signed at 1 a.m. on the 15th: see a 'Note sur la Déclaration Conjointe et du Modus Vivendi', à l'attention du Chef de l'EMGDN, 16 Sep. 1946, ibid., 291–93.

62. 'L'impossible application du *modus vivendi*', chapter title in d'Argenlieu, *Chronique*, 325.

63. J. Sainteny, *Histoire d'une paix manquée*, Paris, 1967, 210; S. Tønnesson, *1946: Déclenchement de la guerre d'Indochine*, Paris, 1987, 41.

64. D. Schoenbrun, *As France Goes*, London, 1957, 233.

conference table from French government representatives. Even Moutet was little inclined to make the best of a bad job. In a set of instructions issued to d'Argenlieu on 21 September, he wearily foresaw a long road ahead to further agreement:

> The Franco-Vietnamese *modus vivendi* of 14 September no doubt constitutes a marked advance on the Preliminary Convention of 6 March. However, this new provisional accord may not be regarded as the basis for a new departure and does not allow us so much as a glimpse of a final settlement of the Indochinese problem.
>
> This agreement must be carried out loyally by us, but this is above all so that we can bring about a relaxation of tension. This will allow us to carry out the vital overhaul of our whole policy.[65]

Also at an end was the temporary, and misleading, focus of Indochina policy making on Paris. Indeed, it is doubtful whether this conjunction of events had achieved more than to obscure the proper object of policy, namely the situation in Indochina. If ministers and officials had hoped to regain the initiative by bringing Ho and his men to Paris, this hope quickly vanished. With its options limited by the increased publicity accorded colonial policy and by the mood of increasing conservatism in France, its confidence further sapped by domestic political uncertainties, the GPRF was outmatched both by the rhetoric and theatricality of the Vietnamese delegation and by the Saigon administration's increasing inclination to control the pace and direction of policy.

By contrast, though d'Argenlieu saw the *modus vivendi* variously as appeasement of the hateful *de facto* Government in Hanoi, as the result of cynical electioneering by the politically less clubbable members of the GPRF (chiefly the Socialist Moutet),[66] and as the unacceptable and unworkable product of the failed Accords policy, he could at least draw a kind of satisfaction from his success in imposing his own view of events over the preceding two months. Moreover, the ball was now back where he wanted it, in his court. Debriefing the federal members of the French delegation, Pignon, Torel, and Gonon, he smugly divided the talks at

---

65. 'Le *modus vivendi* franco-vietnamien du 14 septembre ... constitue sans doute un progrès sensible sur la Convention préliminaire du 6 mars. Toutefois, il ne nous est pas possible de considérer cet accord provisoire comme la base de départ susceptible de nous laisser entrevoir le règlement 'au fond' du problème indochinois.

S'il doit être appliqué avec loyauté de notre part, c'est avant tout en vue de susciter une détente, à la faveur de laquelle il est indispensable de reconsidérer l'ensemble de notre politique.' Devillers, *Paris-Saigon-Hanoi*, 225–26.

66. D'Argenlieu, *Chronique*, 321.

Fontainebleau into three phases: the first consisted of the 'sterile labours' ('travaux stériles') up to 2 August; the second was the 'vague phase' ('phase floue') when the Government had presented a tougher line, while Ho had 'pretended not to understand' ('feint de ne pas comprendre'); the third, 'healthy period' ('période saine') was distinguished by the Vietnamese decision to work with d'Argenlieu's men on the French side. As he put it: 'Our partners understood that with the others, matters never progressed further than mere words'.[67] This, then, was the Admiral's blithe and unrepentant verdict on the negotiations in France which he and his men had been in large part responsible for wrecking.

67. 'Nos partenaires ont compris qu'avec les autres l'on en restait toujours aux paroles', 28 Sep. 1946, ibid.

9

THE NARROWING OF FRENCH POLICY OPTIONS, AUTUMN 1946

The Accords Policy Abandoned?

The *modus vivendi* signed by Marius Moutet and Ho Chi Minh on 14 September 1946 was equally unsatisfactory whether considered from the perspective of Paris, Saigon or Hanoi: it was after all a compromise settlement resolving nothing, signed *in extremis* by two principal actors, and despised by a third (d'Argenlieu). However, it possessed at least the virtue of providing a six-week breathing space, since it was to come into effect, at Ho's insistence, only on 30 October. This allowed the Vietnamese to strengthen their political and military positions both north and south of the 16th Parallel, but it also gave the French the chance to steady their nerves and to review their options. As this chapter shows, these options were extremely limited at best. While Moutet remained committed to the Accords policy, on which his political credibility depended, Henri Laurentie and his colleague in Saigon, Léon Pignon, now favoured a more effective, less equivocal, but nonetheless broadly continuous Indochina policy. Meanwhile, also in Saigon, officials were drawn increasingly to the idea of a third, more 'hawkish', option: a military strike against Hanoi. As the deadline passed for the application of the *modus vivendi*, however, it was clear that France's room for manoeuvre was dwindling alarmingly in the face of Vietnamese political successes, the disarray of Saigon's Cochinchinese collaborators, continuing French domestic chaos, and, most disastrous of all, the growing autonomy of action exercised by the military and administration in Indochina, resulting in the bombardment of Haiphong in late November.

The preceding chapters have traced the evolution of Indochina policy from an internal debate between 'liberals' and 'conservatives' to a growing split on policy between the rival decision-making centres of Paris and Saigon. It has been shown how this split was not only based on differences of approach (liberal/conservative, concessionary/intransigent) and emphasis (the March 1946 Accords versus the March 1945 Declaration), but also resulted from a divergence of interests and perspective. Thus, whilst the Parisian perspective necessarily took in domestic and international factors, and indeed was often dominated by them, that of the High Commission in Saigon was more fully occupied by events in Indochina. Furthermore, it has been shown that this split was exacerbated by ambiguities in the chain of command, resulting in independent policy initiatives undertaken by the administration in Indochina. Nonetheless, it might be argued that decision-making rivalry and policy disputes did not preclude a common strategic view of aims and objectives. Stated at its simplest, this strategy was directed towards reaching a durable settlement to maintain a French presence in Indochina, avoiding the extremes of a return by force to the colonial status quo ante, on the one hand, and the granting of total independence on the other.

In the period following the signing of the *modus vivendi* this strategic view was still maintained, and most clearly informed the policy proposals of two officials: Henri Laurentie, Director of Political Affairs at the Ministry for Overseas France in Paris, and Léon Pignon, Federal Counsellor for Political Affairs in Saigon. However, this chapter shows how the effect on policy making of deepening crisis on all fronts was to overwhelm the rational terms of policy debate, as it had been conducted hitherto; the common strategic view identified above was thus increasingly obscured or rejected. This process is discernible already in the lull preceding the 30 October deadline, as the GPRF insisted on the provisions of the *modus vivendi*, in increasingly unrealistic pursuit of the Accords policy, while 'hawks' in Saigon considered a full-scale resort to force. By the time of the Haiphong and Langson incidents at the end of November, the polarisation of policy between the two centres of decision making was threatening to pull that policy apart. It remained to be seen whether this collapse of policy could be halted in time to head off full-scale Franco-Vietnamese hostilities. Before turning to the growing crisis in Indochina, this chapter considers the debate conducted in the calm before the storm, as officials weighed up the alternatives to the by now heavily compromised Accords policy.

The *Modus Vivendi* and French Policy Options

As the preceding chapter suggested, the *modus vivendi* was intended in the first instance more as a face-saving tactic to wind up the proceedings at Fontainebleau than as a binding agreement to determine the nature of Franco-Vietnamese relations. Moreover, the impression is palpable thereafter that Moutet and his colleagues in the GPRF were relieved to unburden themselves, at least temporarily, of the Vietnamese question during the forthcoming referendum and election campaigns. The lack of realism displayed in the GPRF's instructions concerning the application of the *modus vivendi* may be contrasted with the debate conducted by the administration in Paris and Saigon at this time, as they contemplated revision or even – in the case of the military option – reversal of existing Indochina policy. Indeed, far from remaining constant in the face of the worsening crisis, even Laurentie's perspective reveals something of the limitations of his distinctively liberal approach to colonial policy.

The GPRF's decreasing interest in Indochina emerges obliquely from Moutet's instructions of 21 September.[1] Moutet was above all concerned to maintain the Accords policy following the Fontainebleau fiasco. Nonetheless, his instructions gave some indication as to the future direction of French policy, particularly with regard to Cochinchina, depicted as the 'pivot' of France's Indochina on which France's whole future in the Far East now depended. Between the two alternatives for action in Cochinchina, it was clear which he favoured:

> We can either step up our military effort, with all the reprecussions that such an attitude might have in Indochina, in France and in terms of internaional opinion, or, on the contrary, we can come to terms with any government having a broad enough representative base to allow it to work effectively towards restoring order with our support.

Moutet thus argued for a new, truly democratic Cochinchina policy. Defending the controversial Article IX of the *modus vivendi*,

---

1. P. Devillers, *Paris-Saigon-Hanoi, Les archives de la guerre, 1944–1947*, Paris, 1988, 225–27; see above, Ch. 8.

he suggested that the French make the first steps towards establishing democratic liberties in advance of the 30 October deadline, in order to steal a march over Hanoi, which was likely to maintain its 'totalitarian' approach to policy. Furthermore, he advocated broadening the Thinh government's political base, with the inclusion of unionists:

> We should not rule out the eventual participation of figures who are open about their sympathy for the union of the three *ky*. The French Government does not fear the development in Cochinchina of a sincere democracy, even if such a free regime leads sooner or later to the union of the three *ky*, in one form or another.[2]

Moutet denied that his proposals constituted a policy of scuttle ('une politique d'abandon'); rather, they were intended to allow the calming of the political situation, and thus facilitate economic recovery. Indeed, he argued that the *modus vivendi* marked an improvement in the north, especially concerning French property and cultural rights.

Although Moutet may be excused for trying to put a brave face on things, in effect he was demanding the impossible: that peace should be achieved by peaceful means. Moreover, his suggestion that the French, rather than the Hanoi government, stood to gain from the propaganda value of democratic freedoms ('les libertés démocratiques') must surely have raised some eyebrows in the Norodom Palace, since the phrase had been adopted by Ho largely as a stick with which to beat the 'colonial' regime in the south. This impression of the GPRF's lack of realism was reinforced in the instructions issued by the Chiefs of Staff (*Etat-Major Général de la Défense Nationale*, or EMGDN), signed by Barjot, which explained that the *modus vivendi* was intended to 'create a climate in which the pacification of Cochinchina may proceed, with Ho Chi Minh's cooperation in the disarming of unbeaten extremist elements, but with the aim of total peace achieved in such a way as to preempt

---

2. '... ou accentuer notre effort militaire, avec toutes les répercussions qu'une telle attitude peut entrainer en Indochine, en France et devant l'opinion internationale, ou, au contraire, composer avec des gouvernements ayant une base représentative assez large pour travailler efficacement au rétablissement de l'ordre en profitant de notre soutien.... Le concours éventuel de personnalités qui ne cachent pas leurs sympathies pour l'union des trois ky n'est nullement à exclure. Le Gouvernement français ne redoute pas le développement en Cochinchine d'une démocratie sincère, même si un tel régime de liberté doit aboutir tôt ou tard à l'union des trois ky, sous une forme ou sous une autre.' Ibid.

as far as possible any pretext for reaction.[3] Barjot thus expected Vietnamese troops in the south to be disarmed without the use of force, despite the categorical refusal of Ho and Pham Van Dong at Fontainebleau to allow this.[4] It was small comfort that these instructions played down Article IX's significance, arguing that it should be taken in its entirety, and depended on military agreements which still had to be reached. In this light, d'Argenlieu's criticism of the *modus vivendi*, that articles I-VIII were unexceptionable but that IX cast into doubt the whole future of French Indochina, appears partially justified.[5]

While Moutet and others in Paris sought to pull together the strands of an increasingly threadbare Accords policy, Pignon and Laurentie turned their efforts to a revised policy consistent with the reality of the situation in Indochina. Inevitably, Pignon's analysis in September contained an element of recrimination, especially concerning Cochinchina. Responding to the suggestion implicit in Moutet's instructions that Paris had now abandoned its intermittent support for the Cochinchina policy pursued in Saigon since the spring, Pignon blamed Paris for the failure of Cochinchinese separatism in the first place, through its policy of friendship towards Vietnam. This had been most damaging at the time of Fontainebleau. Aware of French uncertainties, the Cochinchinese sought to avoid taking sides except where it was necessary to make pledges ('des gages') to the Vietnamese to cover themselves. However, they still hoped for some kind of autonomy for Cochinchina, which might include some kind of sentimental attachment to Greater Vietnam. Pignon also cited in this regard Thinh's failure to capture popular support.[6]

More worrying still, and at the root of Saigon's anxieties concerning Article IX, the military situation in the south was poor and deteriorating all the time, as Pignon explained in a letter to Laurentie. For, while the negotiating teams had been at work over the summer, French control in the south had slipped badly. As

3. '... créer un climat favorable à une politique de pacification en Cochinchine avec le concours de l'autorité d'Hô Chi Minh en permettant de désarmer les éléments extrémistes et irréductibles mais avec le souci d'apaisement total et de manière à prévenir dans la mesure du possible tout prétexte de réaction.' Barjot to Haussaire, 1 Oct. 1946, Devillers, *Paris-Saigon-Hanoi*, 227–28.

4. S. Tønnesson, *1946: Le déclenchement de la guerre d'Indochine*, Paris, 1987, 39.

5. G. Thierry d'Argenlieu, *Chronique d'Indochine, 1945–1947*, Paris, 1985, 321.

6. NOTE SOMMAIRE sur la situation politique nouvelle en Indochine, n.d. (Sep. 1946), AN, 72AJ539.

Pignon noted, matters were not likely to improve with the imminent departure of the 9th Division of Colonial Infantry (9e DIC) and of Massu's armoured group who, since arriving in Indochina the year before, had acquired valuable experience of the terrain and of the 'particular conditions imposed by their semi-political, semi-military mission'.[7] Moreover, troop deployment on the Indochinese-Thai frontier was draining French resources. Meanwhile, French military blunders and occasional crimes were weighed in local eyes against the Viet Minh's perceived virtue of being 'less blind'. Secondly, the resurgence of Vietnamese terrorism and military action since March could be blamed directly on the Accords. As Pignon saw it, Hanoi was trying to exploit French weariness to bring about Cochinchinese union with Vietnam. By early October, terrorism in the south was decreasing, but this could be ascribed more to Vietnamese successes than to French: as Pignon contended, the Hanoi government was developing its administrative capacities, and preparing for the legal status which the *modus vivendi* would allow it south of the 16th Parallel. This gloomy picture could be contrasted with that in Cambodia and Laos, which presented few immediate problems, with Thailand about to hand back the annexed provinces of Battambang and Siam-Reap. In the High Plateaux of South Annam, the Mois had welcomed French troops as liberators. Even north of the 16th Parallel, Pignon noted that French forces were well protected and in control of the strategically crucial Delta region. But the price of relative stability in Tonkin had been paid in collaboration with Hanoi, including acquiescence in the crushing of anti-Viet Minh opposition. This had resulted in the consolidation of Ho's power, since the alternative groups to Ho had all collaborated with the Japanese or the Chinese. Moreover, it was precisely this dichotomy in French policy between north and south which was most worrying to Pignon:

> At the moment we are confronting the paradox of a policy which is contradictory and apparently irreconcilable between north and south in Indochina: in Tonkin we pursue a policy of friendship and, to an extent, weakness, while in Cochinchina and South Annam our policy is one of combat and open hostility.[8]

7. '... l'expérience du milieu et des conditions très particulières de leur action mi-politique, mi-guerrière', Pignon to Laurentie, 5 Oct. 1946, AN, 72AJ539.

8. 'Nous vivons actuellement dans le paradoxe d'une politique contradictoire et apparemment inconciliable selon qu'elle s'applique au nord ou au sud de l'Indochine: politique d'amitié et, dans une certaine mesure, de faiblesse, au Tonkin,

Like Moutet, Pignon saw Cochinchina as the principal focus for French policy. Indeed, as he argued, the problems stemming from the division of Indochina at Potsdam, which the March Accords were intended to solve, had in fact become so acute that the question of Cochinchina's relations with the North now threatened France's future in Indochina. Any policy revision would have to address this issue as a matter of urgency.

One further factor was brought to bear in favour of fresh initiatives in Indochina by Henri Laurentie in instructions for General Valluy, appointed to stand in for d'Argenlieu while the High Commissioner returned for talks in Paris from early November. As Laurentie argued, France stood to gain from a temporary respite in the international situation, brought about by 'a balance of forces in the Far East and the desire on the part of the Americans and the Russians not to compromise this balance by taking position prematurely in South East Asia'.[9] France's hold in Indochina thus precluded the need for either side to commit itself. China was also tied up by its own internal problems; Thailand had ceased to be a threat by deciding, with some American persuasion, to return the Cambodian provinces annexed in 1941; and India, notwithstanding its emblematic status as champion of Asian nationalism, was unable or unwilling to act in Vietnam's favour. Only the new United Nations Organisation might embarrass France, but even then without affecting the main lines of international politics.[10] This equilibrium would be threatened if Ho took over completely, thus committing the US and the USSR, tempting the Chinese, and encouraging other regional nationalists, while destroying Cambodian and Laotian confidence and leaving France only an 'honorific title' in Indochina. The US would have several options for taking over in Indochina, but would probably choose the capitalist path, with the Chinese in their train, thus cheating both the French and the Viet Minh of a role in Indochina.[11] France should therefore act swiftly to secure its position.

---

politique de combat et d'hostilité ouverte en Cochinchine et dans le Sud-Annam.' Note Sommaire, loc.cit.

9. '... l'équilibre actuel des forces en Extrême-Orient et par la volonté, tant du côté russe que du côté américain, de ne pas compromettre cet équilibre par une prise de position prématurée dans le sud-est asiatique.' Projet d'Instructions pour le Haut Commissaire par intérim, Très Secret, ref HL/BP, 28 Oct. 1946, MAE, EA/36/15. See also a 'NOTE PERSONNELLE à Monsieur le MINISTRE sur la politique en INDOCHINE', ref HL/BP, 21 Oct. 1946, MAE, EA/36/15.

10. Projets d'instructions, loc.cit.

11. Note, loc.cit.

The proposals for a revised Indochina policy were based on this analysis of a highly uncertain situation which was nonetheless fast approaching the moment of decision. The guiding principles of this policy were set out by Pignon in his September report, and by Laurentie in his instructions for General Valluy.[12] As was already clear from Pignon's enunciation of these principles, the new policy stemmed from a far greater willingness to 'think the unthinkable' than had been the case with Moutet's instructions, which it resembled only superficially. First, and most importantly, Pignon argued that French confidence should no longer be placed in the Hanoi government. This had been the High Commission's position since March, but had become confused with Saigon's disruptive Cochinchina policy, the ostensible purpose of which had been to spike the Accords policy. With Fontainebleau aborted, and the Hanoi delegation back in Indochina where they could wreak less damage on French public opinion, it was tempting to dispense altogether with Ho. Second, given the eradication of the opposition in the north, anti-Viet Minh opinion would have to spread from Cochinchina, although the French could also expect support from traditionalist and Catholic elements in North- and South-Annam. Third, the Cochinchinese government would have to be restructured, with the removal of Thinh and the introduction of more liberal elements. The government would be enlarged, not merely for reasons of democracy, but in order to establish the government-in-waiting of a united Vietnam. This would then pave the way for Vietnamese unification (or, as the French chose to see it, Cochinchinese union with Vietnam), with guarantees for French economic and strategic interests and for Cochinchinese autonomy within 'Greater Vietnam'. In other words, as Laurentie put it to de Gaulle in a note accompanying a copy of the report, the aim of French policy should be 'to use Cochinchina to retake Tonkin'.[13]

Laurentie's instructions to Valluy reprised Pignon's proposals, leaving the choice of personnel and the timing of the operation to Valluy as Acting High Commissioner, but emphasising the importance of a revamped Cochinchinese government:

> It is important that an eventual Government should be *representative*, that is, drawing on groups with a reputation and a strong popular following, *social*, that is, committed to finding its support

---

12. Loc.cit.
13. '… la reprise du Tonkin par la Cochinchine'. NOTE pour Monsieur le Général de GAULLE, 3 Oct. 1946. AN, 72AJ539.

amongst groups other than the big landowners and wedded to a policy of land reform and equitable wages, *national*, that is, not resistant to the nationalist movement.[14]

He commented that, given the political progress of unionism, it would be impolitic to be seen to oppose it. Unionists would be admitted to the government, but on the understanding that union was not purely and simply subordination to the Viet Minh. Thus Laurentie agreed with both Moutet and Pignon concerning the failure of separatism. He even implied the GPRF's partial responsibility, arguing that Thinh's successor should be granted the external marks of French deference to ensure his government's prestige:

> Cochinchinese government members must be given the best administrative buildings, fine houses, cars, credit, etc. They should not appear in the least beholden to the High Commission, to the Commissioner for the Republic or to their agents.

He contrasted this policy of 'personal honour' ('politique d'honneur personnel') with the preceding 'rather artificial policy complete with Cochinchinese flag, national anthem and "Free Republic"'.[15]

It is idle to speculate as to whether such a government might have worked, or whether it would have been seen merely as a more skilfully installed puppet. Certainly neither Pignon nor Laurentie underestimated the Hanoi government's continuing appeal to nationalist sentiments. By contrast, as Pignon noted in a further letter to Laurentie, the Cochinchinese elite, although terrified by what they saw as the imminent prospect of a Communist takeover, were disunited and barely organised, with little hope of countering either the Viet Minh or a re-emergent Communist Party.[16] As a solution to this problem, Pignon had one other wild card to play, amounting to a prototype of the Bao Dai solution. As he suggested:

---

14. 'Il importe que le gouvernement qui sera finalement mis en place soit … *représentatif*, c'est-à-dire composés d'éléments réputés et populaires, *social*, c'est-à-dire décidé àchercher ses appuis ailleurs que chez les grands propriétaires et résolu à entreprendre une politique de réforme agraire et de justes salaires, *national*, c'est-à-dire non réfractaire au mouvement nationaliste.' Projet d'Instructions, loc.cit. Emphasis in text.

15. 'Il faut donner aux gouvernants cochinchinois les meilleurs bâtiments administratifs, de belles habitations, des voitures, des crédits, etc. Il ne faut pas qu'ils paraissent le moins du monde subordonnés aux services du Haut-Commissariat, au Commissaire de la République et à ses services … la politique assez factice de drapeau cochinchinois, d'hymne national et de "république libre"' Ibid.

16. Pignon to Laurentie, Saigon, 25 Oct. 1946, MAE, EA/36/15.

Many of the great and good are convinced that our only chance of staying in this country is through the French restoration by force of the Annamite monarchy, accompanied by the proclamation of Greater Vietnam and inspired by liberal, bourgeois socialist principles; either that, or we must envisage immediate recourse to the ultimate fallback position, which is the proclamation of independence.

Bao Dai, however, was still under a cloud following his collaboration with the Japanese (and with Ho), and the idea was stillborn, for the moment at least.[17]

The problem was always going to be one of persuading the Government in Paris to act, for its capacity for swift action was severely hampered by France's domestic situation. Laurentie in particular was aghast at the continuing disorder and political chaos in Paris, further fuelled by the intrusion of colonial affairs:

The Indochina question is just one of the many trials and tribulations which weigh down national life and complicate action by any government. Indochina in these conditions has simply become an excuse for polemics and a battleground on which the hot-headed fight it out with the merely ignorant.[18]

The constitutional saga by now left the electorate bored or indifferent. On 13 October, the referendum on the second constitutional draft was passed by 36.1 percent; 31.3 percent voted against, on the advice of the Radicals, Independents, and de Gaulle, and 31.2 percent apparently preferred to spend the day fishing (the traditional occupation of French abstainers).[19] But apart from signalling the growing apathy of French voters, the passing of the referendum meant fresh elections, and further disillusionment. As Laurentie wrote to Pignon at the end of October:

The French are being called out to another election, but think that 'it won't change anything'. This belief, unwarranted in a democracy,

17. 'Beaucoup de bons esprits sont convaincus qu'une restauration par la force française de la monarchie annamite avec proclamation d'un grand Viêt-Nam Fédéral et inspiré d'un socialisme libéral et bourgeois contribue notre seule chance de maintien dans ce pays, si l'on ne veut pas envisager tout de suite l'ultime position de repli, c'est-à-dire, la proclamation de l'indépendance.' Ibid.; Laurentie to Pignon, 9 Nov. 1946, AN, 72AJ539.

18. '… l'affaire d'Indochine s'ajoute à toutes les rivalités, épreuves et équivoques qui rendent la vie nationale si lourde et l'action de tout gouvernement si complexe. Elle est devenue, dans ces conditions, un pur motif de polémique où la passion et l'ignorance se disputent l'avantage.' Projet d'instructions, loc.cit.

19. J.-P. Rioux, *La France de la Quatrième République*, 2 vols, vol. 1, *L'ardeur et la nécessité, 1944–1952*, Paris, 1980, 153.

leads rightly or wrongly to a sort of despair which finds expression in hatred, furious egotism and scepticism. The so-called government is both sinned against and sinning in this muddle. It is one of the most remarkable examples of anarchy on record.[20]

Thus, France entered the crucial period for its policy in Indochina with an indecisive caretaker government, a divided and acrimonious outgoing Assembly, and an electorate bored already of the rebirth of French political life and legitimacy.

Pignon has been identified as the 'Machiavelli of the federal government' and as the 'brains' behind Saigon's subsequent warmongering.[21] However justified this reputation, it needs qualification concerning his relationship with the 'liberal' Henri Laurentie. For, as late as October, Pignon and Laurentie saw largely eye to eye in favouring what amounted to a renunciation of the Accords policy, albeit for differing reasons: Pignon's distaste for the prospect of renewed dealings with Hanoi was mirrored by Laurentie's disdain for the cowardly muddle of metropolitan politics. The corollary of this stance was a willingness to contemplate military action. Thus, on 25 October, on the eve of his departure for Hanoi to oversee the Vietnamese application of the *modus vivendi*, Pignon wrote to Laurentie:

> I don't wish to sound like a Cassandra; but I feel obliged to say that the metropole may one day find itself confronted with a formidable dilemma: either the more or less complete abandonment of our position in Indochina, or a considerable reinforcement of our military effort. It is clear that by signing the modus vivendi, which was something I was very much in favour of, we have been brought very rapidly to the moment of truth which we have been avoiding until now.[22]

20. 'Les Français sont convoqués aux élections, mais ils pensent que "ça ne changera rien". Cette conviction, inhabituelle en démocratie, les conduit, qu'elle soit justifiée ou non, àune sorte de désespoir qui s'exprime par la haine, l'égoisme furieux et le scepticisme. Le 'gouvernement', dans cette confusion, est à la fois cible et acteur. C'est l'un des plus remarquables exemples d'anarchie qu'on ait enregistrés.' Laurentie to Pignon, 29 Oct. 1946, loc.cit.

21. '... le «Machiavel» du gouvernement fédéral', Tønnesson, *1946*, 29; 'le cerveau de toute l'affaire', Devillers, *Paris-Saigon-Hanoi*, 331.

22. 'Je ne veux donc pas jouer les Cassandre; mais j'ai le devoir de dire que la Métropole se trouvera peut-être placée un jour devant un redoutable dilemme: ou un abandon à peu près complet de notre position en Indochine, ou un renforcement considérable de son effort militaire.... Il est évident que la signature du modus vivendi, que j'ai moi-même cependant vivement désirée, nous a amenés très rapidement devant les décisions, que nous avions jusqu'à ce jour éludées.' Pignon to Laurentie, 25 Oct. 1946, loc.cit.

Even accepting that Ho could be relied upon to delay the inevitable, he foresaw that this would allow a respite of only a few weeks or months, following which France would still be confronted with the fateful choice.

Laurentie, for his part, was apparently prepared to make the same choice as Pignon in this regard. Reflecting on the GPRF's 'almost physical inability to have a policy on any subject', he underlined the important role that might be played by middle-ranking administrators:

> As far as we are concerned, the danger is clear: France's action in Indochina risks losing any sense of leadership, unless a close understanding can be reached between certain relatively junior officials in Indochina and their counterparts in Paris to the effect that they will, at whatever cost, take on certain responsibilities which belong by rights elsewhere.[23]

As Laurentie pointed out, such autonomous action was not without precedent in France's colonial history. The danger came from what Laurentie termed 'betrayal from on high, by which I mean giving into to the soft option, which is the temptation of peace at any price. So we must put the fear of God in them.'[24] What action was Laurentie prepared to contemplate? To Pignon he suggested only that Saigon should remain pessimistic in its despatches, in order to 'send a shiver down their spines' ('provoquer le petit frisson'). On 9 November, on the eve of the elections, he even preached improbably to the converted, advising Pignon of Saigon's decisive role in the weeks to come, suggesting that they should rely only on themselves, not on Paris. Here traces may be discerned of the Gaullist instinct to act in the name of a higher national interest, even in defiance of government authority; perhaps this explains why, by his own admission, he was 'not in people's best books at the moment' ('plutôt mal vu en ce moment'). Even before the onset of crisis, then, Laurentie's outlook suggests

---

23. '... l'impossibilité, on pouvait dire physique, d'avoir, en aucune matière, une politique.... Pour ce qui nous touche, vous mesurez le péril: l'action de la France en Indochine risque de n'être plus conduite, à moins qu'une entente étroite, à l'échelon dit subalterne, ne se fasse entre certains agents d'exéc[utif] d'Indochine et certains autres de Paris pour assumer coûte que coûte les responsabilités qui devraient en théorie appartenir à d'autres'. Laurentie to Pignon, 9 Nov. 1946, loc.cit.

24. '... la trahison des 'hautes sphères', j'entends par là le fait de céder à la tentation molle, la tentation de la paix à tout prix. Aussi faut-il leur faire peur.' Ibid.

that the subsequent 'defeat of the Rue Oudinot' identified by Tønnesson resembles more closely its fall from grace.[25]

Laurentie's concept of 'betrayal from on high' was reflected
also in his reservations concerning the High Commissioner. Significantly, these were expressed in his continuing communications
with de Gaulle. Thus, he criticised as troublesome d'Argenlieu's
attempts to achieve administrative autonomy from Paris. As he
argued, Pignon's report 'concluded, no doubt regretfully, that a
broader policy was needed than that pursued to date by the High
Commissioner'. Laurentie saw d'Argenlieu's primary aim as
being to restore the French administration as the 'keystone of the
federal system'.[26] Acting upon this idea, in his instructions for
Valluy, Laurentie announced that a new administrative Secretary-
General, Governor Digo, would maintain 'order and efficiency'
('l'ordre et l'efficacité') at the Norodom Palace. Pignon was also
worried by d'Argenlieu's tougher stance, as revealed by Cédile's
replacement as Commissioner for the Republic: Torel, formerly
Federal Commissioner for Legal Affairs (*Commissaire aux Affaires
Légales*) and, unlike Cédile, an old Indochina hand. As Pignon
noted, Torel might have imposed a separatist solution in Cochinchina, but the timing of his appointment seemed intended to provoke Paris.[27]

Although Pignon and Laurentie thus effectively dismissed the
Accords policy, they also distanced themselves from any suggestion of a *coup de force*. Thus, Laurentie's fundamental point in his
note to de Gaulle was that 'we must rule out resorting to the use
of force by purely French forces'.[28] Even taking into account the
teasing implications of Laurentie's phrasing (what did he mean by
'purely French forces', for instance?), it is clear that he was ruling
out a purely military option. Again, this was a subtle and nuanced
position: Laurentie was returning to his argument, first enunciated in his response to the Sétif and Damascus crises of May 1945,
that the wholesale use of force, as opposed to a carefully managed
show of limited force, was unsustainable, and would be interpreted as a sign of French weakness. Pignon argued a similar

25. 'La défaite de la rue Oudinot', chapter heading in Tønnesson, *1946*, 132–37.

26. '… conclut – à regret sans doute – à une politique moins étroite que celle qui
fut jusqu'à présent tentée par le Haut-Commissaire. Il s'agissait pour l'Amiral de
réhabiliter l'administration française comme clef de voûte d'un système fédéral.'
NOTE pour Monsieur le Général de GAULLE, 3 Oct. 1946, loc.cit.

27. Projet d'instructions, loc.cit.; Pignon to Laurentie, 5 Oct. 1946, loc.cit.

28. '… un recours à la force par des forces purement françaises doit être écartée'. Ibid.

point in his report, when he noted his fears that General Valluy, who had succeeded Leclerc in July in command of the Expeditionary Corps, was seeking to eliminate the civil element in favour of a purely military command structure. This was to Pignon's mind a grave mistake, for, as he saw it, 'we are distancing ourselves increasingly from the populace and we give the impression of making our arrangements to pull out'.[29] Thus, however critical of the Accords policy, Laurentie's and Pignon's proposals were broadly continuous with that policy.

This continuity obtained in one crucial respect, namely in the emphasis placed on the Cochinchinese 'pivot', as Moutet had termed it. It was this refusal to contemplate a more radical reversal of policy which chiefly distinguished the line taken by Laurentie and Pignon, however critical, from that of a further approach in preparation in the Palais Norodom. To the hawkish instincts of the new military Commander, Valluy, as well as to a High Commissioner increasingly intolerant both of the equivocations of Paris, and of the resilience of the Hanoi regime, it seemed obvious and potentially glorious to 'strike at the head' ('frapper à la tête') in a swift attack on Hanoi. Valluy has already been noted as a 'hawk', with his preparations for a 'coup d'état' in April 1946.[30] His thinking had now proceeded a full step further. Reporting to d'Argenlieu on 14 October 1946, Valluy aimed higher than merely shoring up the existing military status quo. Rather, as he argued:

> One aspect of our policy which I would imagine to be feasible might be that, instead of contenting ourselves with controlling rebel attacks in the south, we should put serious pressure on the rebels by taking large-scale initiatives in Hanoi and Annam. This seems to me to be to be an inevitable recourse to the ultima ratio.[31]

29. '... l'élimination pure et simple de l'élément civil au profit du commandement unique militaire ... nous nous éloignons de plus en plus de la population et nous avons l'air de mettre en place un dispositif d'abandon.' Ibid. On Sétif and Damascus, see above, Ch. 3. Civil and military powers were combined only in December 1950, when General de Lattre de Tassigny took over as High Commissioner from none other than Léon Pignon: J. Dalloz, *La guerre d'Indochine, 1945–1954*, Paris, 1987, 188–89.

30. See above, Ch. 7.

31. '... l'un des aspects que j'imagine possible de notre politique peut être, non de se contenter de maîtriser les attaques des rebelles, mais au contraire de faire une pression radicale sur ces derniers en prenant des initiatives d'envergure à Hanoi et en Annam. Cet appel à l'«ultima ratio» me semble présenter un caractère de fatalité.' Rapport du Général Valluy à l'Amiral d'Argenlieu, Saigon, 14 Oct. 1946, in

The timing for this operation was flexible: if the new government were to commit itself after the forthcoming elections, Valluy's plan would go into operation in February-March 1947 at the latest. He thus argued the case for the retention of remaining units of the 9e DIC, but also for some 'white' (that is, metropolitan French) reinforcements, perhaps numbering ten thousand men. These should be constituted in cohesive, seasoned units ('des unités homogènes et aguerries'), in contrast to the 'magma' currently trickling through. As he argued, he would otherwise be unable to 'take over Hanoi and Hué as cleanly as possible and overpower armed Vietnamese contingents in one blow'.[32] Valluy was thus the first general in post-war South-East Asia to employ the rhetoric of the 'surgical strike'.

This rhetoric was not without effect on the High Commissioner who, on 18 October, welcomed the returning Ho Chi Minh aboard the *Dumont d'Urville* in Cam Ranh Bay. In a memorandum to Moutet, d'Argenlieu reported that Ho seemed anxious about the situation in Hanoi, and therefore likely to cooperate with the *modus vivendi*. This guarded optimism was tempered with a warning that Ho's friendliness would probably turn out to mask attempts to blackmail and intimidate the French over Cochinchina.[33] A secret telegramme to Bidault and General Juin (Chief of the Defence Staff) was more substantial, setting out in five points the essentials of Valluy's analysis, encoded for governmental consumption.[34] First, he noted that Ho would probably use the *modus vivendi* to obtain political and military advantages in the south. Second, he pointed out that while the Hanoi government's military potential was steadily increasing, no assurance had been given that the Expeditionary Corps' strength in 1947 would even be maintained at seventy-five thousand. Moreover, third, the reoccupation of the two Western provinces would further drain French manpower. Fourth, he argued that the hypothesis that Hanoi would resort to force could not be ruled out, and that, while such a threat could be met in the short term, in the longer

Commandant G. Bodinier, ed., *Le retour de la France en Indochine, 1945–1946*, Vincennes, 1987, 296.

32. '… m'emparer le plus proprement possible d'Hanoi et d'Hué et maîtriser d'emblée les contingents vietnamiens armés', ibid.

33. No. 1659 F, H.C. à l'attention du ministre FOM, 18 Oct. 1946, in d'Argenlieu, *Chronique*, 336.

34. Tel., Amiral d'Argenlieu to Défense Nationale, 19 Oct. 1946, in Bodinier, *Le retour*, 300–302.

term French military morale and public opinion were likely to be affected. Fifth, therefore, he put his case for the reinforcement of the Corps with a lightly armoured division of ten thousand men, in order to provide 'an instant response in Hanoi and Annam' ('une riposte immédiate ... à Hanoi et en Annam'). Such reinforcements would also be needed in Cambodia, and in order to neutralise subversives and terrorists in the south. The question of reinforcements was discussed at an interministerial meeting of officials on 23 October, and accepted in principle a few days later by General Juin.[35]

By the end of October 1946, three options presented themselves for French policy in Indochina. First, the Accords policy could be maintained. This option, to which Moutet and a 'lame-duck' government remained politically committed, possessed the virtue of appeasing international opinion and maintaining a working relationship with the strongest political forces on the ground; but its internal contradictions were increasing as France's collaborators in the south became demoralised by Viet Minh political and paramilitary successes. Second, addressing these contradictions, Laurentie and Pignon argued for a partial abandonment of the Accords policy. Pragmatic and intellectually rigorous, their case was also hopelessly over-subtle in the volatile political climate of both Paris and Saigon. Third came the lure of a quick military fix and, in Saigon, Valluy's sense of an 'inevitable' resort to force was winning over staff at the High Commission. When crisis broke, the chances of a rational choice between policy options were to diminish so completely as to appear to vanish altogether.

The Onset of Crisis in Indochina

Indochina had been in a state of permanent crisis since long before the French 'return' in October 1945, and it could be said that since that date the French had succeeded only in managing their relations with the Vietnamese in ways which had just barely warded off overt hostilities. Nonetheless, the final breakdown in those relations which led to war came swiftly and, with hindsight, unmistakeably. Four stages may be identified along the way to war, each of which discredited the arguments for peace and eroded French capacities for rational policy making. For French aims now

35. Bodinier, *Le retour*, 78; Devillers, *Paris-Saigon-Hanoi*, 233.

depended, however implicitly, on four factors: the *modus vivendi* as an albeit makeshift product of Franco-Vietnamese accord; the chances of maintaining a cohesive and potentially effective Cochinchinese government; the revival of firm government in Paris; and the maintenance of a fragile military status quo north of the 16th Parallel. One by one, each of these was demonstrated to be a chimera.

Ironically, the first event to precipitate crisis was one from which the French expected to benefit: the passing of the deadline for the *modus vivendi* at midnight on 30 October 1946, which was to be marked by a ceasefire. The ceasefire was the first death-blow of Moutet's policy, not because it failed but because of its success. In his draft instructions for Valluy, Laurentie had betrayed a natural enough French assumption that the *modus vivendi* depended primarily on French initiative, suggesting that 'the terms of the *modus vivendi* must be carried out without restrictions, but we should not count on Hanoi's instructions being sufficient to bring order in Cochinchina'.[36] In the week preceding the 30 October, the Vietnamese press in Hanoi reported the orders of Nguyen Binh, Viet Minh military leader in Cochinchina, for the ceasefire. These orders were carried out to the letter, so that, on 3 November, Saigon was able to report almost complete calm and a halt to all terrorist activities in Cochinchina.[37] It did not last long, and by 9 November, the Cochinchinese Council was protesting about ceasefire violations; on 23 November, d'Argenlieu reported to Cominindo that terrorist activity had returned to pre-ceasefire levels in the south by the 20th. In political terms, however, the point had been made: Southern 'terrorists', 'insurgents', and 'bandits' were firmly under Hanoi's orders. Moreover, the Viet Minh's Provisional Administrative Committee, which had governed Cochinchina briefly before the British landings in September 1945, emerged from hiding in September 1946 and was issuing orders concerning the *modus vivendi* even before the deadline. France thus risked losing the propaganda war whichever way it turned: even applying the terms of the agreement, the French would be seen to recognize Vietnamese authority in the south. Protests against the establishment of a Resistance Committee, and the

---

36. 'L'exécution du modus vivendi doit se faire sans restrictions de notre part mais il ne faut pas non plus escompter que les instructions de Hanoi suffiront à ramener l'ordre en Cochinchine.' Projet d'instructions, 28 Oct. 1946, loc.cit.

37. Tønnesson, *1946*, 57; Haussaire to Cominindo, 3 Nov. 1946, AOM, Tels/938.

refusal to accept its President, Pham Van Bach, as Ho's representative in Saigon under the terms of the *modus vivendi*, counted for
little in the climate thus created.[38]

The second event to step up the crisis was the dramatic demise
of the policy of Cochinchinese separatism, symbolically marked
by the suicide of Dr Nguyen Van Thinh. Hanoi's increasing confidence and authority in South-Annam and Cochinchina, and the
emergence of a body claiming sole legal authority in Cochinchina
(as did the Viet Minh's Administrative Council on 22 September)
dealt a further blow to the Thinh government, which was already
shaken by Paris's waning interest in separatism. On 31 October,
the Cochinchinese Council demanded a reshuffle of Thinh's cabinet. When, a week later, Thinh had still not formed a new government, he was attacked for his government's disunity. He asked for
more time, and lamented the hybrid nature of the polity he was
called upon to govern: was it a colony or a republic? As a symp-
tom of this uncertainty, the Commissioner for the Republic, who
would have to approve Thinh's choice of ministers, attended the
Council session. On 10 November, Thinh was found hanged at his
home. Before leaving for Paris on 13 November, d'Argenlieu
approved the nomination of Le Van Hoach, Thinh's main critic, as
the new leader. But the French had driven themselves into an
impasse, and their hapless protégés with them. D'Argenlieu's
public response was to blame those opinion makers under the
sway of Hanoi, and to warn that the *modus vivendi* would facilitate
further attacks on the integrity of the Cochinchinese government.[39] In a later note to de Gaulle, Laurentie provided a more balanced view, describing Thinh's suicide as:

> the Confucian climax to a series of errors: too much rigidity in
> social matters, too much autonomy for Cochinchina and, above all,
> a lack of due deference and confidence; while Ho Chi Minh was the
> centre of attention in Paris, we were giving the impression of not
> playing along with Thinh, to whom we refused credits, a police
> force, proper administrative quarters, etc.[40]

---

38. Tønnesson, *1946*, 60–61.
39. Ibid., 50–51.
40. '… [la] conclusion confucianiste de plusieurs erreurs: trop d'étroitesse dans le
domaine social, excès d'autonomisme cochinchinois et surtout, de notre part,
manque d'égards et de confiance; tandis que Hô Chi Minh faisait l'intéressant à
Paris, nous donnions l'impression de ne pas jouer le jeu avec THINH, à qui nous
refusions crédits, police, locaux, etc.' Note pour Monsieur le Général de Gaulle, 22
Dec. 1946. AN, 72AJ539.

While this analysis was consistent with Laurentie's proposals for Cochinchina, in his draft instructions for Valluy, it may be noted that these had also written off the unfortunate Thinh. In the short term, however, the sound of pigeons coming home to roost in the Norodom Palace went undetected by the hawks already in residence; the immediate effect of this abrupt end to Saigon's Cochinchina policy was to introduce an element of pugnacious unpredictability into its future actions.

More predictable but equally dispiriting, third, was the outcome of the first general election to be held under the new Constitution, on the same day as Thinh's suicide. For the next pillar of Indochina policy to crumble further was that of metropolitan political will. For the Administration in Paris, the election was depressing for two reasons. First, the Communists were now the largest party in the Assembly with 28.6 percent of the vote, overtaking the MRP which slipped to 26.3 percent and gaining further ground over the SFIO which received only 17.9 percent of the vote (while 21.9 percent abstained). But second, a long war of attrition was likely before a government could be decided upon. Parliamentary practice dictated that Maurice Thorez and Georges Bidault should be granted the opportunity to form a government in turn, but the open divisions within the Tripartite coalition made it unlikely that the MRP and the PCF would emerge as mutually acceptable partners. Only when the alternatives of 'Thorez without Bidault' and 'Bidault without Thorez' had been tried could the option of a Socialist-led government be attempted. In the event, Léon Blum was nominated as the first Prime Minister of the Fourth Republic on 12 December, and it was not until the 16th, a full five weeks after the elections, that his all-Socialist Council of Ministers was approved.[41] Meanwhile, France was rudderless, thus increasing the scope for officials' autonomy of action.

The fourth event leading to crisis, and probably the Rubicon for France on the way to war with the Vietnamese, was the battle of Haiphong which erupted in mid-November. While this ground has been well covered elsewhere, it is essential to recall briefly the sequence of events at Haiphong, and also at Langson, where a lesser confrontation between the French and Vietnamese occurred at the same time.[42] An awful logic may be detected in the events

---

41. B.D. Graham, *French Socialists and Tripartisme 1944–1947*, London and Canberra, 1965, 230–43. Figures are for metropolitan France only.
42. See Tønnesson, *1946*, 81–120.

which culminated in the bombardment of the Chinese and Vietnamese quarters at Haiphong, resulting in the deaths of thousands of the local population. Haiphong was the principal Tonkinese port, serving Hanoi, 'the lungs of Tonkin',[43] and thus of crucial strategic, political, and commercial importance to both the French and Vietnamese, as it had been to the occupying Chinese, the last elements of whose army pulled out on 18 September. Not least, Hanoi depended on arms and fuel supplies, which were exchanged for rice. By November, Haiphong was the centre of a Franco-Vietnamese dispute over customs. On 10 September, four days before the signing of the *modus vivendi*, which enshrined proposals for a federal customs union, General Morlière, commander of French forces in the North and acting Commissioner for the Republic in Sainteny's absence, ordered the creation of an agency to supervise Saigon's ban on Tonkinese rice exports and the fuel import monopoly granted to Western oil companies. The Navy was to enforce the measures with seaborne inspections. The Chinese and Vietnamese resented what one French official described as 'not a blockade, but at least a tightening of imports to Tonkin' ('sinon ... un blocus, au moins un reserrement des importations au Tonkin'), but which was explained officially as a bid to combat trafficking in rice and foodstuffs. In fact, the French were concerned to stop a run on the *piastre* caused by a negative trade balance in the north, to integrate Tonkin into the French economic system, and to stem the flow of arms to the Vietnamese army. In early November, the Hanoi government further raised tensions by introducing measures directed towards economic self-sufficiency, in an apparent reversal of its economic modernisation programme; the French police (*Sûreté*) also reported that the Vietnamese Economic Commission was considering an economic and monetary offensive against the French, including renewed printing of its own rival currency. As Pignon speculated, the Vietnamese aimed to exclude the French from the economy, to persuade them to leave of their own accord. Meanwhile, rumours were rife in Haiphong of a French attack on Vietnamese positions; and at the end of October, the local French commander, Colonel Dèbes, issued secret orders detailing the use of tanks and artillery in case of French intervention.[44]

43. '... le poumon du Tonkin', P. Mus, *Viêt Nam – Sociologie d'une Guerre*, Paris, 1952, 73.
44. Tønnesson, *1946*, 84–85, 89–91.

In this highly charged atmosphere, the 'inevitable' happened on 20 November, when a French attempt to seize an illegal cargo of fuel oil led to shooting between French and Vietnamese, which in turn escalated into a pitched battle. By the evening of the 20th, French troops had secured vital strategic points in the city at the cost of 240 Vietnamese and seven French lives. Blame for the original incident attaches perhaps to both sides: the Vietnamese were nervous and inexperienced in combat, while the French seemingly became daily more trigger-happy. On 23 October, after a ceasefire had been agreed by the Franco-Vietnamese Joint Commission (*Commission Mixte*, another product of the *modus vivendi*) and broken, and after the Vietnamese failed to meet an ultimatum delivered in Haiphong against the orders of Morlière in Hanoi, Colonel Dèbes ordered a prolonged military and naval bombardment which, over two days, reduced the Vietnamese quarter to rubble; fleeing refugees were strafed by Spitfires, and the town of Kien An, the regional Vietnamese military headquarters to which refugees had been directed, was shelled by the cruiser *Savorgnan de Brazza*. Vietnamese casualties numbered somewhere between Valluy's figure of three hundred, the long accepted figure of six thousand and Vietnamese propaganda claims of sixty thousand.[45] Over the same period, at the frontier garrison town of Langson, a further incident escalated in similar fashion, when Vietnamese troops ambushed (or were attacked by) French troops exhuming the bodies of servicemen killed by the Japanese after 9 March 1945. After parleying failed, and after an ultimatum had not been met, the French commander stormed and captured the town. The two incidents were unrelated, but aggression on both sides at Langson was probably fuelled by news of the events in Haiphong.[46]

The Haiphong and Langson 'incidents' probably turned the tide of events in favour of war, and overwhelmed what little chance remained of pursuing the Accords policy. Two aspects of the conflicts warrant discussion in the present context. The first of these was the readiness of senior figures within the administration and, in this instance particularly, the military hierarchy, to exploit relatively minor incidents in order to press home major strategic advantages and to do so without fully informing, or being explicitly covered by, Paris. Indeed, Haiphong may be seen as a dress

45. Tønnesson, *1946*, 91–106; cf Dèbes's report, 10 Dec. 1946, covering the period 20 Nov.-2 Dec. 1946, in Bodinier, *Le retour*, 343–63.
46. Tønnesson, *1946*, 106–12.

rehearsal for Valluy's proposed strategy of a strike in Tonkin. Colonel Dèbes at Haiphong certainly bears a large part of the blame for fanning the original flames, and for the tactically immaculate bombardment, which Sainteny described as 'extremely brilliant but extremely brutal'.[47] The chief culprit, however, was General Valluy who, on 22 November, ordered Dèbes to 'take maximum advantage of this incident in order to improve our position in Haiphong' ('exploiter au maximum ce grave incident pour améliorer notre position Haiphong'), thus countermanding Morlière's orders in his attempts to impose a peaceful solution. Also on 22 November, Morlière warned Valluy that taking the town would involve flattening a large part of it in order to avoid heavy French casualties, would lead to a breach of the 6 March Accords and the *modus vivendi*, and that the conflict would almost certainly spread to embrace all French garrisons in Tonkin. Morlière's message crossed with Valluy's cable which effectively sealed Haiphong's fate:

> It seems clear that we are facing premeditated aggression, carefully planned by the regular Vietnamese army which seems no longer to be following its Government's orders.... The moment has arrived to teach a hard lesson to those who have so treacherously attacked us. By every possible means you must take complete control of Haiphong and force the Vietnamese government and army into submission.[48]

The only senior French figure to emerge with honour was thus General Morlière, who sought in vain to rein in his subordinate Dèbes. Morlière was unable to cable Paris directly, which received copies of Valluy's orders, but was unaware of Valluy's and Morlière's differences, or of the real situation at Haiphong.

When Moutet visited Indochina six weeks later on a carefully managed tour which otherwise recalled the Empress Catherine's excursions with Potemkin, Morlière gave him a truer picture, which he followed up with a full report. At the end of January 1947, he was dismissed and replaced by Dèbes, who was promoted

47. '... très brillante, mais très brutale', Tønnesson, *1946*, 103.
48. 'Il apparaît nettement que nous sommes en face agression préméditée, soigneusement préparée par l'armée régulière vietnamienne qui semble ne plus obéir aux ordres de son Gouvernement.... Le moment est venu de donner une dure leçon à ceux qui nous ont traîtreusement attaqués. Par tous les moyens à votre disposition vous devez vous rendre maître complètement de Haiphong et amener le gouvernement et l'armée vietnamienne àresipiscence.' Valluy to Morlière and Dèbes, 22 Nov. 1946, quoted in Tønnesson, *1946*, 98.

and later raised to the Legion of Honour.[49] At this time, d'Argenlieu praised Morlière for his efforts to maintain good relations with Hanoi, in line with the Accords policy, but also gave a curiously frank appraisal of the General's untimely peacemaking:

> As I was in Paris when disorder erupted in Haiphong on 20 November, I was unable to make my own assessment of events. General Valluy criticised Morlière for not acting quickly enough to derive all possible political benefit from the situation. Especially given the complexity of the events, it would be consistent with Morlière's extremely conciliatory methods that he should be overzealous in this way.[50]

Morlière's undoing, therefore, was his fidelity to the spirit of existing policy, and his disloyalty to the military ethic: as Tønnesson points out, without Morlière's intervention, his superior Valluy would not have been obliged to show his hand, and history would have laid the blame conveniently on the local commander.[51]

The second significant aspect of the battles of November 1946 concerns their interpretation by ministers and officials in Paris. This, like the unrolling of the events themselves, was largely dictated or supervised by Saigon. In part this was a question of the imperfect state of communications (here understood in the literal sense) between Saigon and Paris, which inevitably delayed the drafting, transmission, and decoding of signals. Tønnesson offers one striking example of this: when Comindo met on the afternoon of 23 November, the bombardment of Haiphong, unleashed at 1005 hours local time, had been in progress since the small hours of the Parisian morning. However, even Valluy's orders of 22 November, quoted above, were only decoded in Paris after the meeting had convened.[52] As a consequence, the matter was not raised – there had after all been other confrontations both at Haiphong and at Langson – and d'Argenlieu was able to escape with

49. G. Chaffard, *Les carnets secrets de la décolonisation*, 2 vols, vol. 1, Paris, 1965, 90–94; Morlière's report, 12 Dec. 1946, in Bodinier, *Le retour*, 365–72.

50. 'Etant à Paris lors des désordres survenus à Haiphong le 20 novembre, je n'ai pu apprécier sur place leur déroulement. Le général Valluy a alors reproché à Morlière de n'avoir pas su tirer assez vite de ces incidents tout le *bénéfice politique désirable*. Il est normal que, fidèle à sa méthode conciliatrice à l'extrême et engagé dans une affaire complexe, Morlière ait peut-être excédé dans ce sens.' Tel no. 41CIP, Haussaire to Paris, 30 Jan. 1947, d'Argenlieu, *Chronique*, 360.

51. Tønnesson, *1946*, 114–15.

52. Tønnesson suggests another possible reason for the reticence of Moutet et al.: the presence of the Communist Air Minister, Charles Tillon; in *1946*, 125.

only an oblique reference to 'recent incidents'. Ironically, this was in support of his main purpose at the meeting, which was to urge the abandonment of the *modus vivendi*.[53] Moreover, in a telegramme to Valluy the following day, in which he approved Valluy's actions, d'Argenlieu quoted Bidault's instruction to 'use all means to ensure that law and order are respected'; but Bidault was apparently referring to Cochinchina.[54] How different might the response have been had Paris been better apprised of the situation, or had Morlière's role been known? One possible answer to this question is that it might not have differed substantially, given the extent to which the deepening crisis on all fronts was affecting the policy makers' responses. Although this theme provides the core of the following chapter's concerns, the case of Laurentie may be cited here, for whom the crisis served to confirm the change of direction in his recent policy proposals. Briefing Moutet for the Cominindo meeting on 29 November, Laurentie restated the aims of his policy since the signing of the *modus vivendi*:

1. The organisation of a French administration capable of providing for Indochina's general needs.
2. The creation from within Cochinchina of a socially and if necessary nationally viable anti-Viet Minh movement, on the understanding that such a movement can only be established and developed if we protect it by standing firm.[55]

As he argued, the case for this policy was reinforced both by Thinh's suicide and by what Laurentie saw as the Viet Minh going to war ('l'entrée en guerre du Viet Minh'). As seen above, Laurentie took a robust view of Thinh's failure, arguing even before his suicide for his removal. Laurentie's other contention was more problematic: that the Haiphong incident signalled Hanoi's abandonment of the Accords policy in favour of war. Again, his logic was clear: Hanoi's actions (as seen from Paris) proved their untrustworthiness, and argued further in favour of a restructured

53. Mémorandum présenté le 23 novembre au Cominindo, d'Argenlieu, *Chronique*, 345.

54. '... faire respecter l'ordre et la loi par tous les moyens contre qui que ce soit' Tel no. 20/DC, 24 Nov. 1946, d'Argenlieu, *Chronique*, 345, 358.

55. '1°/ organisation d'une administration française, capable de pourvoir aux besoins généraux de l'Indochine,

'2°/ création, à partir de la Cochinchine, d'un mouvement social et au besoin national anti Viet-Minh, étant entendu qu'un tel mouvement ne peut naître et se développer qu'à l'abri de notre fermeté.' Note pour Monsieur le Ministre, 27 Nov. 1946, MAE, EA/36/15.

Cochinchina government capable of ruling a Vietnam united from the south. Ho was now accused, albeit obliquely, of abandoning the nationalist cause in favour of international Communism:

> The fact that the Viet Minh have now gone to war proves, if it needed proving, that Ho Chi Minh receives his instructions and derives his power from something other than nationalism pure and simple. That is where we must look if we are to find the origins of the insuperable obstacles on which the Accords policy has come to grief.

Moreover, Laurentie showed a new, or at least newly unequivocal, willingness to accept the challenge supposedly thrown down by the Viet Minh. As he continued:

> The Viet Minh will from now on be actively seeking to resort to force, although they know it will bring about their downfall. If we now back down in the slightest, after a year of poor administration and political failure, we will lose our last chance.[56]

It is unclear how representative Laurentie's views were at this stage; and his analysis was rather eccentric in places, for instance his judgement that 'French opinion will be behind us' ('l'opinion française ... sera avec nous'), which contradicted his earlier estimation of public indifference to colonial affairs. Moreover, as will be seen, Laurentie soon recovered his poise as a qualified opponent of a policy of force. But if Laurentie relished the roles of maverick and devil's advocate, his arguments reflected also the growing sense of uncertainty and powerlessness governing the actions of a caretaker government and its hamstrung administration as they confronted the facts, insofar as they were in possession of them, in the face of deepening crisis.

By late November 1946, the basis for rational policy making was fast disappearing. The French saw their options in Indochina eroded to almost nothing in the space of a few weeks by Vietnamese successes in exploiting the *modus vivendi*, the collapse of Cochinchi-

---

56. 'L'entrée en guerre du Viet Minh prouve, s'il était besoin de le prouver, que Hô Chi Minh reçoit ses enseignements et tire sa vertu d'autre chose que le nationalisme pur et simple. C'est là qu'il faut chercher la cause des impossibilités où la politique des accords s'est brisée. L'emploi de la force est désormais voulu par le Viet-Minh, qui sait pourtant que c'est sa perte. N'hésitons pas à entrer dans le jeu. Toute reculade, après un an de mauvaise administration et d'insuccès politique, nous ferait perdre nos dernières chances.' Ibid.

nese separatism (marked with 'Confucian' finality by Thinh's suicide), the dangerous bathos of the referendum and elections in
France, and the disasters of Haiphong and Langson. Indeed, the
likelihood of a collapse of policy was increased not only by ministerial indecision, as the political leaders of the brand-new Fourth
Republic struggled to form a new Government, but also by the
pugnacious and insubordinate approach adopted by the administration in Saigon, the logical conclusion of which was outright
Franco-Vietnamese hostilities. Was war now inevitable? The next
chapter considers the attempts made in Paris, however half-hearted
and against the odds, to answer this question in the negative.

The likelihood of war was not diminished by the fact that,
amongst the middle-ranking officials to whom Laurentie attached
so much importance, the recent sequence of events had been
largely accepted as ineluctable. As his attitude at the time of Fontainebleau suggests, this was perhaps not so surprising in the case
of Pignon, though he was still uncommitted to the role of 'brains'
in a Saigon-led conspiracy. In Laurentie's case, this fatalism may be
attributed not only to deficiencies in the Parisian perspective, but
also to an interpretation coloured by newly dominant ideological
factors. Thus, he unwittingly based his analysis of Haiphong on an
only partial version of events, which failed to implicate French
actors, but he also showed an apparent willingness to suspend
belief in the principles underpinning his earlier policy. For these
principles, which had formed the basis for the liberal Brazzaville
policy, and hence also for the Accords policy in Indochina, were
now undermined by anti-Communist considerations, which identified Ho Chi Minh as an enemy, and by a wholly Gaullist yearn-
ing for a return to strong government.

10

'THE TONKIN VESPERS', DECEMBER 1946

Burying the Accords Policy

The start of France's eight-year war with Vietnam was marked by the 'Tonkin Vespers' ('les vêpres tonkinoises') on 19 December 1946.[1] It took a few days short of a hundred after the signing of the *modus vivendi* for Franco-Vietnamese relations to break down completely in this way. As suggested in the previous chapter, this breakdown was probably inevitable after the Haiphong incident, whether it was seen as a 'flashpoint' resulting from an inherently unstable and volatile situation in Indochina, as an act of war by the Viet Minh, or as a sign of willingness on the part of the French military and administration in Indochina to pursue policy wholly according to their own lights. Nonetheless, in the four weeks which elapsed between Haiphong and the outbreak of open hostilities marked by the Vietnamese attack on French positions in Hanoi, policy makers in Paris made a final effort to regain control of events in Indochina, and to make policy on their terms. That this attempt was unsuccessful was in part because the situation in Indochina had by now developed an unstoppable dynamic, in part because Saigon was pursuing an agenda of its own, in defiance of the impotent prohibitions and hasty *ex post facto* rationalisations emanating from the metropole. Indeed, the evidence increasingly suggests, though it does not yet prove, that the administration in Saigon cynically provoked the Hanoi government into action, in a bid to sweep it aside once and for all. Although the French failed to topple Ho Chi Minh in

---

1. The name recalls the Sicilian Vespers, the massacre of the French in Sicily on Easter Day, 1282.

favour of a more pliant nationalist interlocutor, the Accords policy had nevertheless been dealt its *coup de grâce*.

The theme of this concluding chapter is thus the final breakdown of the policy pursued with only intermittent and qualified success since France's 'return' to Indochina in October 1945. The focus in this, as in previous chapters, is largely fixed on Paris, on the efforts of the government and senior officials to maintain and impose a rational policy in the teeth of crisis both in Indochina and in the metropole. Indeed, as if to underline the intimate link between policy making and French domestic politics, the chapter shows how Saigon achieved its immediate goal (if not its purpose) only two days after the formation of an all-Socialist government in Paris, led by the man who might otherwise have stood the best chance of making peace, Léon Blum. And yet, as will be shown, notwithstanding the temporisation, improvisation, and sheer panic which marked these critical weeks, the administration in Paris displayed a considerable degree of equanimity, the implications of which need to be teased out. No doubt the *sangfroid* shown by officials in Paris reflected in part their ignorance of the true picture, as Saigon continued to exploit, and to widen, the information gap identified in the previous chapter; this process was to be vividly illustrated by Saigon's careful management of Moutet's tour of Indochina in late December-early January. No doubt also, even as the army was digging in for the first of France's long wars of decolonisation, French optimism flowed from a simple lack of predictive powers. However, a third possibility is that, given a shift in the parameters of policy identified in earlier chapters, the train of events in Indochina was no longer entirely inimical to erstwhile colonial liberals. Thus, having argued a convincing case in their efforts to brake Saigon's slide towards hostilities, centring on the impracticability of full-scale colonial war in military, economic, and diplomatic terms, officials largely abandoned this case thereafter as France geared up to fight its own front of the fast-approaching Cold War. In a changing domestic and international environment, the policy debate which restarted soon after the New Year 1947 pointed already to a resurrected Accords policy in the bastard form of the Bao Dai Solution.

Even given Paris's imperfect understanding of events, the Haiphong incident heightened a sense of urgency and prompted a new round in the policy debate. Against the background of the continuing ministerial crisis, it fell to officials to restate the rationale for avoiding fullscale hostilities with Hanoi, as they prepared a fresh set of instructions for the High Commissioner. Meanwhile in Saigon, in the absence of d'Argenlieu, the administration wavered between keeping the peace, as far as the febrile state of Franco-Vietnamese relations permitted, and putting into effect the hawks' evolving strategy for a strike against the hated 'de facto government' in Hanoi. Ironically, the apparent catalyst for this latter course of action was the nomination as Prime Minister of the veteran SFIO leader, Léon Blum, whose first major act in office was thus his resigned acceptance of Saigon's *fait accompli*.

The preliminary, inconclusive, round of the renewed policy debate in Paris took place even before the Haiphong crisis had been resolved, prompted by the decision to draw up instructions for the High Commissioner, since, remarkably, none had been issued since October 1945.[2] A set of instructions was drafted by senior officials for consideration at a Cominindo meeting scheduled for 29 November; Pierre Messmer, now Secretary-General of Cominindo, thus summoned Baudet, Laurentie, Admiral Barjot, acting Chief of the Defence Staff in General Juin's absence, and d'Arcy, a member of Michelet's private office (*chef-adjoint du cabinet*) at the Ministry of Armies.[3]

No record survives of the meeting but Laurentie's rather bellicose stance may be deduced from his memorandum discussed in the previous chapter.[4] By contrast, Admiral Barjot was emerging as the foremost opponent of a military solution to the Indochina problem. In a series of reports and bulletins on the Haiphong and Langson incidents, Barjot showed some inkling of d'Argenlieu's secret agenda, and warned against Saigon's tendency to fix its attention increasingly on Tonkin. As he put it in a major report dated 29 November:

> The key element for our security in Indochina is Cochinchina and not Tonkin. We cannot maintain a general presence and occupy every point in strength. We must exercise choice, and the choice is obvious: the keystone of of our presence in Indochina is Cochinchina. That is where our forces should be concentrated.[5]

2. See above, Ch. 6.

3. Secrétaire-Général, Cominindo, Invitation à une réunion, 27 Nov. 1946, MAE, AO/IC/179. Messmer (future Prime Minister under Pompidou) replaced Labrouquère early in Bidault's premiership.

4. Note pour Monsieur le Ministre, 27 Nov. 1946, MAE, EA/36/15; see above, Ch. 9.

5. 'La pièce maîtresse de notre sécurité en Indochine est la Cochinchine et non le Tonkin. Nous ne pouvons pas être présents partout à la fois et occuper en force

Further, Barjot indicated the dangers of troop transfers to the north – which were already taking place. And he argued that the conquest by force of all three *ky* would require reinforcements far in excess of the ten to fifteen thousand requested by Valluy; he mentioned the figure of 250,000 which, as he pointed out, would deprive France of its reserves in case of troubles in Africa, 'the most compact part of the French Union' ('la partie la plus compacte de l'Union Française'). A similar case was made also by General Humbert, the head of Bidault's military office (*chef du cabinet militaire*), who argued that war in Indochina would be a repeat of the Rif War of 1925, a bottomless pit into which France would pour its inadequate manpower resources.[6] At the Cominindo meeting of 29 November, ministers approved Valluy's request for reinforcements but, as Humbert pointed out, this was intended only as a gesture in the wake of Haiphong, not as a prelude to a policy decision to use force.[7] Thus, while Laurentie's liberalism underwent a momentary lapse, it fell to the army to draw out the disparity between France's limited military means and the increasingly aggressive intentions of some its policy makers.

In the event, little was decided at the Cominindo meeting of 29 November, preceded the day before by the Bidault government's resignation. However, Barjot's advice was apparently heeded by Bidault, who remained head of the caretaker government, and whose overriding anxiety was to avoid presenting his successor with a dangerous *fait accompli*. As it was argued at the meeting, 'nothing must be done which might serve as a precedent, particularly in respect of Morocco or Tunisia, by way of either concessions or new initiatives'. In addition to the military case, the meeting also recalled the diplomatic arguments against purely military action in Indochina, although this was qualified with a restatement of France's strength of purpose:

> The problem as a whole cannot be settled by the use of force alone.
> International political opinion would not allow to take such a step,
> nor would we have the support of the French nation. But we must

---

tous les points. Il faut savoir choisir. Le choix est évident: la clef de voûte de notre présence en Indochine, c'est la Cochinchine. C'est là qu'il faut concentrer nos forces.' 'Rapport sur les incidents de Haiphong et de Langson du 20 au 28 novembre 1946', 29 Nov. 1946, quoted in S. Tønnesson, *1946: Le déclenchement de la guerre d'Indochine*, Paris, 1987, 139.

6. Fiche 6645/Cab.mil., 30 Nov. 1946, in P. Devillers, *Paris-Saigon-Hanoi, Les archives de la guerre, 1944–1947*, Paris, 1988, 257–58.

7. Ibid.

make it clear that France does not intend to quit Indochina, and she will defend her presence by every possible means.[8]

Overall, the impression left was of a powerless ex-government hedging its bets in the face of considerable uncertainties. The instructions largely reiterated Laurentie's proposals of the preceding weeks: a new Cochinchinese government composed of moderate unionists and nationalists renouncing violence; the unification of Vietnam within which there would exist distinct administrative units corresponding to its three constituent parts; and continued respect for the *modus vivendi*. No allusion was made to recent events, other than to the occupation of Langson, which made it easier for France to protect the minority ethnic groups in the Sino-Vietnamese frontier region. The draft concluded with a restatement of the increasingly implausible conviction that the proper application of the *modus vivendi* would enable Indochina to leave behind its present troubles and disorganisation. As if to underline the weakness of Paris's position, it was decided on 29 November merely to await the appointment of a new government before despatching any instructions.[9]

Indecision in Paris was matched by General Valluy's hesitations as Acting High Commissioner, particularly concerning the overtly military bias of his emerging strategy. Thus, even while giving the Vietnamese a 'hard lesson' at Haiphong, Valluy was following Pignon's advice to avoid a political break with Hanoi. At the end of November, Sainteny was due to return as Commissioner for the Republic in Hanoi. Remembering his expulsion from the Government General in Hanoi a year before, Sainteny planned to reoccupy the palace. Replying to d'Argenlieu in Paris, Valluy and Pignon thought this an unnecessary provocation:

> This question has always been a particularly sensitive one for the Vietnamese Government. In the present circumstances, and in the wake of the very serious incidents at Haiphong and Langson,

---

8. '... il ne faut rien faire en Indochine qui puisse servir de précédent, notamment au regard du Maroc ou de la Tunisie, ni sur le plan des concessions, ni sur le plan des initiatives.... L'ensemble de ce problème ne peut être réglé par le recours à la force seule.... Nous ne recevrions pas de l'opinion publique mondiale la liberté de le faire et nous n'aurions pas non plus le support de la nation française. Mais il faut faire connaître fermement que la France ne quittera pas l'Indochine et qu'elle défendra sa présence par tous les moyens.' Notes Ségalat, 29 Nov. 1946, Devillers, *Paris-Saigon-Hanoi*, 257.

9. Devillers, *Paris-Saigon-Hanoi*, 255–56.

occupying the palace will be interpreted as a provocation indicating our desire to break off relations.[10]

Valluy's initial reaction to Sainteny's return was that it would compromise the latter's credit for him to deal with an affair that was best kept at a purely military level. However, by the end of the month, Valluy had changed his mind and sent Sainteny north to Hanoi as the man who alone was 'in a position fully to exploit the situation's political implications' ('en mesure de poursuivre l'exploitation politique de la situation'). In a further re-interpretation, Haiphong and Langson were now presented as an test of strength deliberately staged by the Hanoi government in order to take its own people 'in hand' and reawaken flagging nationalist loyalties. As Valluy explained:

It was not an option, if we did not wish to jeopardize the whole future of France in Indochina, to accept the provocation without an appropriate military reaction. Clearly, our interest was and remains to use the opportunity to gain an ascendancy over the Hanoi Government in order to bring it to the negotiating table in good faith according to the letter and spirit of the *modus vivendi*.[11]

Sainteny's mission was thus to exploit France's supposed success in the wake of Haiphong and Langson and to work towards creating an atmosphere in which the *modus vivendi* could be applied and negotiations eventually resumed in Paris.

Sainteny's prestige was still high in Hanoi as the 'Man of 6 March', but the feasibility of his mission to Hanoi in December 1946 was uncertain. Sainteny was instructed to bring his influence to bear on the Hanoi government, backing Ho and his supposed moderate allies against the hardliners, allowing them to 'save face' and to resist extremist pressures from within the government.[12] From the start, it was clear which side was playing with a stronger

10. 'Cette question a toujours tenu particulièrement à coeur au Gouvernement Viet Namien. Dans les circonstances présentes, et après les très graves incidents de Haiphong et de Langson, cette occupation sera interprétée comme une provocation signifiant notre volonté de rupture.' Tél. no. 1888, Valluy and Pignon to d'Argenlieu, 23 Nov. 1946, MAE, EA/36/15.

11. 'Il ne nous était pas permis, sans mettre en cause l'avenir même de la France en Indochine, d'accepter cette provocation sans réagir d'une manière appropriée sur le terrain militaire.... Il est évident que notre intérêt était et reste de prendre à cette occasion un ascendant sur le Gouvernement d'Hanoi pour l'amener à négocier de bonne foi suivant la lettre et l'esprit du *modus vivendi*.' Tel., Haussaire Saigon to Paris, no. 1924 F, 30 Nov. 1946, AOM, Tels/938.

12. Valluy to Sainteny, no. 3147, 2 Dec. 1946, Devillers, *Paris-Saigon-Hanoi*, 263–64.

hand. Sainteny reported, after his only meeting with Ho on this mission, that Ho and his allies wished to avoid a complete break with the French. However, as he continued, he had no way of knowing who these allies were, and what influence they still possessed, not only on Ho, but also, more importantly, on public opinion.[13] Sainteny's principal interlocutor thereafter was Hoang Minh Giam, recently returned from his post as Hanoi's emissary to Paris. Giam listened politely to Sainteny's demand for a reshuffle to avoid open Franco-Vietnamese conflict; but as Sainteny admitted, it was unclear what influence Giam still possessed. Meanwhile, Ho Chi Minh's aim seems to have been to stall for time, awaiting the formation in Paris of a government more favourable to the Vietnamese cause.[14]

In fact, Valluy was pursuing a two-pronged strategy, and while encouraging Sainteny's vain efforts to bring about a change of heart in Hanoi, he prepared for a confrontation, although he veered between plans for an immediate offensive and a more restrained policy dependent on reinforcements. On 6 December, he sent his most outspoken telegramme to date in an attempt, as Devillers surmises, to prepare Paris in the event of further military action.[15] Reiterating the thesis of Vietnamese provocation at Haiphong and Langson, he painted a sombre picture of Hanoi's alleged preparations for an offensive, including threats to the crucial supply-line from Haiphong to Hanoi, and the proliferation of barricades, mines, and pill-boxes in Hanoi itself. Morlière, who with the return of Sainteny had gratefully resumed his purely military duties, was now identified as an over-cautious appeaser:

> It will not be possible to approve for much longer General Morlière's apparent scrupulous concern not to heighten local tension by implementing legitimate and indeed indispensable counter-measures. I am advising French authorities in Hanoi to indicate once again to the Vietnamese that their present military dispositions are provocative in nature and that we will be obliged in our turn to take the steps strictly dictated by prudence.[16]

13. Sainteny to Valluy, 3 Dec. 1946, Devillers, *Paris-Saigon-Hanoi*, 267.

14. Comrep Hanoi to Haussaire (Saigon), no. 709/H, 5 Dec. 1946, Devillers, *Paris-Saigon-Hanoi*, 258, 262, 268.

15. Tel., no. 1001/EMHC, Valluy to Cominindo, 6 Dec. 1946, Devillers, *Paris-Saigon-Hanoi*, 273–75.

16. 'Le souci scrupuleux dont témoigne le général Morlière de ne pas aggraver la tension locale par des légitimes et mêmes indispensables contre-mesures ne peut être désormais plus longtemps approuvé. Je prescris aux autorités françaises de

Valluy envisaged reopening the Hanoi-Haiphong road by force. Troops would move out from Haiphong in an attempt to contain the conflict. However, he warned that containment would be difficult, and that a break ('la rupture') with Hanoi was increasingly inevitable as a result of the Hanoi Government's 'hatred and bad faith' ('la haine et la mauvaise foi').

As he argued, France's military position would rapidly worsen after February 1947, as a result of troop replacements, seasonal changes (the same which had dictated the timing of the March 1946 landings), and the Vietnamese army's recovery from the setback which it had suffered at Haiphong. As he concluded, the only way to avoid conflict was to step up France's military presence, in order to convince the Vietnamese of French determination to stay.

Was Valluy preparing for action on 6 December, or merely galvanising Paris into firm action over reinforcements? In the former case, he soon reconsidered his position. In a note dated 8 December, which argued that France could not immediately confront the military problems it would face in Tonkin in case of widespread conflict, he estimated that it would be better to await the arrival of reinforcements expected by 15 January 1947. However, if he aimed to scare Paris into action, then this was partly achieved, though not in the manner intended. At the climax of the ministerial crisis, Bidault and Moutet steered Valluy away from a showdown. On 10 December, the Government's instructions were approved at a special meeting of Comindindo, signed by Bidault, Moutet and Michelet and despatched.[17] On the 12th, Bidault replied directly to Valluy's alarmism:

> In your telegramme no. 1001 of 6 December, you reported growing tension in Tonkin. I wish to underline that I was surprised by the terms of this telegramme, which described an alarming situation which could not have been foreseen from any of your earlier communications.[18]

Hanoi de remontrer aux Vietnamiens le caractère provocateur de ces dispositions militaires et la nécessité dans laquelle nous sommes de prendre à notre tour de strictes mesures de prudence.' Ibid.

17. Tønnesson, *1946*, 129.

18. 'Par votre télégramme n° 1001 du 6 décembre, vous m'avez rendu compte de la tension croissante au Tonkin.... Je désire ... souligner que j'ai été surpris des termes de votre télégramme précité, qui font subitement état d'une situation alarmante que rien ne laissait prévoir dans vos communications précédentes.' Tel., Présidence to Haussaire Saigon, CI/3466, 12 Dec. 1946, AOM, Tels/915. In an earlier draft Bidault had added that he hoped Valluy was not merely trying to cover himself and to shed responsibility in any eventuality: see Tønnesson, *1946*, 137.

Cominindo had now had ample opportunity to reflect on the lessons of Haiphong. On 8 December, Admiral Barjot again criticised Saigon's new Tonkin-based strategy, which, as he pointed out, contravened the titular High Commissioner's own instructions issued after the signing of the *modus vivendi*. But his arguments centred on the military impracticability of the strategy, when Vietnamese forces were increasing in strength, and when there was still fighting in the south:

> Was the French Command aware of the size of the Vietnamese Army before it embarked on a trial of strength? Also, given the decision to centre this trial of strength on Tonkin, was it prudent to do so when there was still sporadic guerilla fighting in Cochinchina?[19]

Far from strengthening France's position in the north, he argued, by 'striking at the head' ('frapper à la tête'), as in the operations at Haiphong, Saigon would merely succeed in concentrating Vietnamese military efforts in the Tonkin delta.

Barjot's case was bolstered by Valluy's predecessor as Commander-in-Chief in Indochina, General Leclerc, who weighed in with a memorandum adding political acumen to Barjot's primarily military perspective. Leclerc recalled his own part in the negotiations leading up to the March Accords:

> The problem was to reconcile as far as possible French interests and those of Vietnam. This was feasible, thanks to the existence of the Ho Chi Minh government. Much could be achieved in dealings with this government as long as great care was taken with regard to questions of 'face'.
>
> To sum up, since we did not have the means at our disposal to break the back of Vietnamese nationalism by force of arms, France was obliged to seek every means to bring about the coincidence of French and Vietnamese interests.[20]

19. 'Le Commandement français avait-il conscience de l'importance de l'armée vietnamienne avant d'engager l'épreuve de force? D'autre part, avant d'accepter de centrer cette épreuve de force sur le Tonkin, convenait-il de laisser en Cochinchine des réminiscences de guérilla?' EMGDN, Bulletin d'études no. 48, 8 Dec. 1946, Devillers, *Paris-Saigon-Hanoi*, 277–79.

20. 'Le problème consistait à concilier au maximum les intérêts de la France et ceux du Viêt-Nam. La chose était possible, grâce à l'existence du gouvernement Hô Chi Minh ... beaucoup pouvait être obtenu de ce gouvernement en ménageant avec grands soins toutes les questions de «face».

'En résumé, n'ayant pas les moyens de briser par les armes le nationalisme vietnamien, la France devait par tous les moyens chercher à faire coïncider ses intérêts avec ceux du Viêt-Nam.' Note du Général Leclerc, 5 Dec. 1946. Commandant G. Bodinier, ed., *Le retour de la France en Indochine, 1945–1946*, Vincennes, 1987, 339–41.

Emphasising the need for timely concessions to preserve what was essential, he drew an unfavourable comparison with British policy in Egypt where, as he put it, 'The British have negotiated and flattered and so will not be releasing their grip on the Suez Canal'.[21] This diplomatic approach, where everything was possible given time and a degree of tact, had formed the basis for French successes from March to August, but had since been lost to view. In the midst of the chaos reigning in Paris, however, Leclerc's arguments fell on deaf ears, although they served as a reminder of the qualities which were to recommend him to Blum, who sent Leclerc on a mission of inspection in Indochina at the end of December, and even offered him his Command in Indochina back.[22] Barjot fared worse, as d'Argenlieu objected strenuously to one Admiral warning ministers against the policies of another, and protested to General Juin on his return about Barjot breaking the rules of military discipline. Juin concurred, but it transpired that Barjot's reports had not been circulated, on Messmer's initiative, on the grounds that they dealt with matters which were outside the EMGDN's sphere of competence.[23] Thus, the information gap was being maintained even by those Parisian actors best placed to bridge it.

Although his call to reason was ignored, Leclerc's recognition of France's limited means found an echo in two texts bearing Laurentie's imprimatur. The first of these was the preamble to the Instructions signed on 10 December, drafted by Laurentie and Messmer. In unprecedentedly narrow terms, this defined three sets of French interests in Indochina: the maintenance and development of France's cultural influence and economic interests; the protection of the ethnic minorities; and the security of its strategic bases.[24] The authors thus steered a course made circuitous by the need to please an Interministerial Committee including PCF representation while partially accommodating some of Saigon's less maximalist designs. For instance, the question of colonial 'protection' had been raised by the occupation of the Moi Plateaux in June, which had jeopardized France's negotiating position at Fontainebleau, and by the recent occupation of Langson. The position argued was an essentially minimalist one, as was made clear in a comparison with France's rival Powers. Whereas the United States

---

21. 'Les Anglais ont négocié, flatté, ... et ne lâcheront pas le canal de Suez'. Ibid.
22. See below and Devillers, *Paris-Saigon-Hanoi*, 326.
23. Tønnesson, *1946*, 139–40.
24. Projet d'Instructions, 29 Nov. 1946, quoted in Tønnesson, *1946*, 129–30.

could achieve its economic ends overseas by means of its economic and financial aid programme, France herself was in need of economic reconstruction, while the Soviet Union's policy with regard to the peripheral Soviet Republics was only practical because of their geographical contiguity. And while a symbolic Commonwealth might have been ideal in other circumstances, in the case of the French Union it would lead to 'France's complete abdication and sacrifice of all her interests'.[25] In other words, France must walk a political tightrope to defend her interests in Indochina, since she had neither the military nor the economic means, nor the confidence, to do otherwise. No mention was made of a more purely ideological justification for France's presence overseas (nor for British, American, or Soviet imperialism).

France's more immediate aims in Indochina were outlined by Laurentie in an auxiliary set of instructions drawn up on 10 December, also replying to Valluy's telegramme no. 1001.[26] These gave a more prosaic argument than either Barjot's or Leclerc's against Saigon's adventurism: the Government was unable to send substantial reinforcements, since this could be an obstacle to French economic recovery. Laurentie, apparently recanting his earlier belligerent stance, opposed the undertaking of any military operation requiring reinforcements, arguing that France 'should not be confronted with a choice between providing an excessive military effort and leaving Indochina'.[27] Secondly, while noting the dangerous way in which the Viet Minh had enflamed nationalist passions in Hanoi and Tonkin, he ruled out any attempt to drive Ho Chi Minh from power. Here too, Laurentie's position had become more cautious since his initial reaction to the news from Haiphong. Thus, Ho was still to be seen as a relative moderate who could be trusted to respect French interests, while his removal would lead to 'a period of tawdry rivalry which would work to the advantage of those who do not see their future lying with France alone'.[28] This trust, however, did not devolve on to Ho's government as a whole; Laurentie therefore backed Sainteny's mission to influence the Hanoi government's attitude. As

---

25. '… une démission totale de la France et le sacrifice de tous ses intérêts'. Ibid.

26. Moutet to Valluy, HL/HP, réf. votre 1001/EMHC, 11 Dec. 1946, Devillers, *Paris-Saigon-Hanoi*, 280–81.

27. 'La France ne doit pas être placée devant l'alternative ou de fournir un effort excessif pour ses moyens, ou de se retirer d'Indochine.' Ibid.

28. '… une période de médiocres compétitions qui favoriserait finalement ceux qui n'attendent pas leur avenir que de la France.' Ibid.

he proposed, if Ho was no longer in a position of strength within the Hanoi government, then France should come to his aid. No judgement was offered as to how this might be possible. Nonetheless, the High Commission was instructed to report on Sainteny's achievements before contemplating any further military action. Finally, the importance of Cochinchina was reiterated.

If Valluy's telegramme had been intended to elicit a guarantee that Paris would cover for his future actions, the main purpose of these instructions was to mark the Minister of Overseas France's refusal to shoulder such a responsibility, either as a member of the outgoing government or on behalf of the new government which at last was about to materialise. In doing so, however, Moutet and Laurentie implicitly recognized the extent to which Saigon held the initiative; even the stress laid on Sainteny's futile mission seemed very much like clutching at straws. In any event, in the heat of the approaching crisis, the instructions were never sent.[29]

Léon Blum's nomination as Prime Minister on 12 December brought onto the scene a prestigious new actor (or rather, old stager). On the 10th, the SFIO newspaper *Le Populaire* published Ho's appeal to the French National Assembly broadcast a few days before, accompanied by an article by Blum which urged a new resolve for French policy: 'There is one way, and one way only, to maintain in Indochina the prestige of our civilisation, of our political and spiritual influence, and of our legitimate interests: we must reach agreement on the basis of independence, we must keep confidence and preserve friendship'. Objecting to the firmness ('fermeté') exercised so far in the name of the Accords policy, he argued that firmness consisted in keeping one's promises. And he criticised both the present system of decision making, and Saigon's predominance within it:

> Decision making should be a matter not for the military authorities or civilian settlers in Indochina, but for the Government in Paris. And when I say Government, I do not mean one of these interministerial committees which have been just as ineffective over Indochina as they have over Germany, I mean the Cabinet and the Minister responsible.[30]

29. Tønnesson, *1946*, 136.

30. 'Il n'existe qu'un moyen, et un seul, de préserver le prestige en Indochine de notre civilisation, notre influence politique et spirituelle, et aussi ceux de nos intérêts légitimes: c'est l'accord sincère sur la base de l'indépendance, c'est la confiance, c'est l'amitié.... La décision doit appartenir non pas aux autorités militaires

Thus Blum heralded the imminent abolition of Cominindo, an institution which he and Moutet blamed for Paris's ill-coordinated policy initiatives. It took Blum four days after his nomination to form a government. His first attempt, a government of National Union composing members of all major parties, failed when the PCF insisted on one of the three big ministries (Defence, Foreign Affairs, Interior) which de Gaulle had denied the party the year before.[31] Only on the 17th, two days before the showdown in Hanoi, was Blum's homogeneous, all-Socialist government given a vote of confidence in the Assembly by 544 votes to two. Of the key ministers in the outgoing government, Moutet was one of only four to keep his job.[32]

The resolution of the political crisis in Paris brought to an end the indecision which had blunted Saigon's purpose in the three weeks since Haiphong. For, of all the possible choices as Prime Minister, Blum was perhaps the most likely to achieve a reconciliation with Ho. Postponing military action pending the arrival of reinforcements was thus futile. On 14 December, Cominindo heard Valluy's aide de camp, Colonel Le Puloch, present the case for direct and immediate military action:

> We have the military means to prevail in Hanoi and Haiphong, to restore communications between the two cities, and to expel the Vietnam Government from Hanoi. This government has itself stated that it could not survive outside Hanoi, since this would deprive it, amongst other things, of the means to finance its guerilla war.

In the ensuing discussion, it fell to Messmer to make the government's opposing case, but neither side had anything new to add to its previously stated position.[33]

---

ou aux colons civils d'Indochine, mais au gouvernement siégeant à Paris. Et quand je dis gouvernement, je n'entends pas l'un de ces comités inter-ministériels qui n'ont pas mieux réussi dans l'affaire indochinoise que dans l'affaire allemande, mais le Cabinet et le ministre responsable.' *Le Populaire*, 10 Dec. 1946; Devillers, *Paris-Saigon-Hanoi*, 285–86.

31. See above, Ch. 4. Cominindo was abolished in January 1947.

32. B.D. Graham, *French Socialists and Tripartisme, 1944–1947*, London and Canberra, 1965, 241–43. The others were Naegelen (Education), Moch (Public Works, Transport and Reconstruction) and Mayer (Labour and Social Security).

33. 'Nous avons les moyens militaires de nous imposer à Hanoi et Haiphong, de rétablir les communications entre les deux villes et de chasser de Hanoi le gouvernement du Viêt-Nam. Or ce gouvernement ne survivrait pas, selon lui, à une expulsion d'Hanoi qui, entre autres choses, le priverait des moyens de financer la guérilla.' 'Note sur la situation militaire en Indochine', 14 Dec. 1946, Devillers, *Paris-Saigon-Hanoi*, 286–87.

The extent to which Saigon had dropped all pretence of defending official policy emerges from a report by Pignon, for whom the waiting game was over, and who now identified himself with the hawks in Saigon. Effectively, Pignon was refuting the points made, for example, in Laurentie's auxiliary instructions. Thus, his starting point was to write off the Hanoi government once and for all, including Ho Chi Minh, whom Pignon depicted as a duplicitous schemer:

> More cunning than some of his younger colleagues, more moderate in his statements and in some of his public gestures, largely because of his age, he nonetheless shares the aims of the Viet Minh's central committee, of which he is the most eminent if no longer the most influential member. Any reshuffle of his government can only amount to a trap.

In this way, the thesis of a split in the Hanoi government, which had underpinned Sainteny's mission in Hanoi, was dropped almost casually. Secondly, perhaps for the first time in clear terms, Pignon challenged the notion of the Cochinchina 'pivot':

> Contrary to what may be thought, the solution to the Indochina problem does not lie in Cochinchina; it lies exclusively in Tonkin and centres on the fact that the Viet Minh remains on the political scene. Many Annamites are aware that this totalitarian party stands in the way of the prompt and peaceful realisation of their national aspirations: independence and the union of the three *ky*.[34]

Thus, both Morlière's provisions for the defence of Hanoi and French commitment to Vietnamese independence and national unity were now tied to the cause of a Saigon administration thirsty for action. On 16 December, Valluy summoned Sainteny, Morlière and Dèbes to a secret meeting in Haiphong. No minutes have survived for this meeting, but it bore all the signs of a war council.[35]

---

34. 'Plus habile que certains de ses jeunes coéquipiers, plus mesuré dans ses propos et ses manifestations extérieures en raison surtout de son âge, ses objectifs ne sont pas autres que ceux du Tong Bô central du Viêt Minh dont il est le membre le plus éminent, sinon aujourd'hui le plus influent. Tout remaniement de son ministère ne peut être qu'un piège.... Contrairement à ce que certains peuvent penser, la solution du problème indochinois n'est pas en Cochinchine; elle réside uniquement et seulement au Tonkin et dans la présence sur la scène politique du parti Viêt Minh.... Bon nombre d'Annamites ... savent que ce parti totalitaire ... est l'obstacle à la prompte et pacifique réalisation de leurs aspirations nationales: l'indépendance et l'union des trois ky.' 'Rapport sur la situation politique intérieure de l'Indochine', L.Pignon, 17 Dec. 1946, Devillers, *Paris-Saigon-Hanoi*, 293–94.

35. Devillers, *Paris-Saigon-Hanoi*, 293; Tønnesson, *1946*, 187–88.

Three days later, the break was made complete. No hypothesis concerning the events of 19 December combines simplicity and plausibility. The official version on both sides, positing Vietnamese aggression, has now been discredited: as Tønnesson suggests, while the French were eager to appear innocent and aggrieved, the Vietnamese were unwilling to be portrayed as dupes.[36] But research has so far only muddied the waters. Perhaps there is no single explanation of what happened next. On the 17th, Valluy ordered the removal of the barricades which had sprung up in Hanoi since the beginning of the month. The violence and counter-violence which followed brought the situation in Hanoi to breaking-point by the morning of the 19th. A Vietnamese attack on French positions was scheduled for 1900 hours on the 19th, but when the Central Committee (*Tong Bô*) met in the early afternoon, more peaceful counsel prevailed in response to two French initiatives: first, in an effort to reduce tension, Morlière stood down French troops in Hanoi; secondly, news arrived of Moutet's forthcoming mission of inspection. Ho immediately drafted a cable for Blum welcoming the Moutet mission. In the late afternoon, however, Morlière recalled his men to barracks on Sainteny's advice. Shortly after that, a report was received from Fernand Petit, a Eurasian spy who had infiltrated the Vietnamese militia (*Tu Ve*), and who had caught wind of the original plan of attack.[37] But nothing happened at 1900 hours, and it was thus assumed that the attack had been cancelled. An hour later, a power-cut at the main power station signalled to *Tu Ve* detachments in the city that the moment had arrived to strike. The French were thus taken by surprise by the *Tu Ve*'s concerted attack; one of the first casualties was Sainteny, who was seriously injured when his armoured vehicle hit a mine. Before leaving for home, he had again recommended reoccupying the Government General, in a further effort to raise the stakes so as to force Hanoi's hand. Meanwhile, on the Vietnamese side, it remains unclear whether the attack was unleashed by *agents provocateurs* working for the beleaguered VNQDD and/ or the French *Sûreté*; by hardliners acting independently of Vo Nguyen Giap, Ho's Minister of Defence, who reacted furiously by holding back the regular army (which only joined the attack some

36. Tønnesson, *1946*, 195–96.
37. The fullest account of the events of 19 December, in Tønnesson, *1946*, 195–244, discounts the traditional version according to which the troops were recalled to barracks as a result of Petit's warning. See also Devillers, *Paris-Saigon-Hanoi*, 294–99.

hours later); by Giap working without Ho's prior consent; or by Giap in collaboration with Ho.[38] The ensuing battle was a fiasco for both sides. Perhaps the best evidence of a lack of Vietnamese premeditation lies in the uncoordinated and improvised way in which the attack spread: the regular army joined the fray from its positions around Hanoi only after considerable delay, and the advantage of surprise was completely lost in the attacks on French garrisons in the rest of Tonkin, which failed almost without exception. On the evening of the 20th, Ho finally issued the agreed signal for the general offensive, calling on the Vietnamese people to attack with firearms, picks, shovels, and sticks.[39] But the French coup d'état, envisaged by Valluy as long ago as April, had also failed. At one point, Ho was nearly captured, but he escaped with the rest of the government to set up his headquarters in the mountains near the Chinese border. On the 25th, the convalescent Sainteny occupied the Government General at last, but, as he reported to d'Argenlieu, newly arrived in Saigon, the battle was not going well for the French:

a) VM – I repeat VM – Resistance is much more stubborn than foreseen. Fanatical would not be too strong a word to describe the combattants at all levels.

b) French Command making the most of the means at its disposal and is controlling local situation well but the time needed to clear Hanoi and environs was considerably underestimated.

c) After 5th day of battle certain objectives have only just been met which should have required only a few hours.[40]

Hanoi was not secured until February 1947, in part because the tactics employed at Haiphong were unfeasible in full view of foreign diplomats; and by this time the full logic of an inexorable guerilla war was beginning to be felt.

However, it was surely Léon Blum whose expectations were most cruelly deceived. A pacifist and Socialist, Blum was obliged to

---

38. Tønnesson, *1946*, 232–33.

39. Ibid, 196–97.

40. 'a) Résistance VM – je dis VM – beaucoup plus opiniâtre que prévu. Il n'est pas exagéré parler d'un véritable fanatisme chez combattants toutes catégories.

'b) Commandement français tire maximum des moyens dont il dispose et a bien situation locale en main mais délais envisagés pour dégagement Hanoi et périphérie avaient été très sous-estimés.

'c) Après 5e jour bataille sont à peine atteints certains objectifs qui devaient être dégagés en quelques heures.' Sainteny to d'Argenlieu, 25 Dec. 1946, Devillers, *Paris-Saigon-Hanoi*, 303.

accept a state of war, colonial war at that, against a government led by a former Socialist comrade. D'Argenlieu, who respected Blum only because 'one can sense that he is on a higher plane than all those of the same party whom I have met', recorded an exchange with the Prime Minister on the 19th, a day before he left to resume his duties in Saigon. When d'Argenlieu resorted to a 'dogmatic' position by evoking France's good works in Indochina, Blum responded by gently belittling them: 'Oh! si peu'.[41] But at a distance of several thousand miles, Blum could do little to prevent the defence of the despised colonial edifice. Blum kept up his efforts to stop the war, but was eventually obliged to accept a *fait accompli*. On the 15th, Ho sent his congratulations to Blum via Sainteny, who added his own dismissive commentary, but his message was delayed in Saigon, and was only deciphered in Paris on the 20th. On the afternoon of the 20th, having learnt of the attack in the morning, Blum cabled Ho, calling for a ceasefire, and Juin ordered Valluy to stop fighting 'if you can see a way which does not compromise the position of French troops and civilians'.[42] Valluy's reply took up Juin's heavy hint, advising against a ceasefire on the grounds of both local difficulty, since Ho had broken contact with the French authorities, and French prestige, since the Hanoi government was 'clearly the aggressor in both French and foreign eyes' and the initiative for a ceasefire should therefore come from them. He even offered to broadcast Blum's message on Radio-Saigon if Morlière was unable to pass it on, but there was a catch:

> However, I feel obliged to draw the government's attention to the deleterious effect that such a broadcast would have on the morale of troops engaged in bitter combat and on that of civilians grieving their compatriots savagely and treacherously murdered in circumstances of which you will be informed separately. I should add that native public opinion would not understand either.[43]

41. '… on le sent au-dessus de tous ceux du même parti que j'ai rencontrés …' G. Thierry d'Argenlieu, *Chronique d'Indochine, 1945–1947*, Paris, 1985, 368–69.
42. '… si vous en voyez la possibilité sans compromettre la situation des troupes et des ressortissants français.' Blum to Ho Chi Minh, tel. DN/Cab. 265, 20 Dec. 1946; Juin to Valluy, tel. DN/Cab. 264; AOM, Tels/933.
43. 'Je crois devoir cependant attirer attention du gouvernement sur les inconvénients très graves qu'aurait cette diffusion sur moral des troupes engagées dans un dur combat et sur celui des civils très émus par les assassinats perpétrés sur leurs concitoyens avec une sauvagerie et une perfidie qui vous seront relatées ailleurs. J'ajoute que l'opinion publique autochtone elle-même ne comprendrait pas.' '… indubitablement pour tous observateurs français et étrangers l'agresseur' Haussaire to FOM and to EMGDN, 21 Dec. 1946, AOM, Tels/933.

Blum's message was delivered by a Vietnamese officer released from captivity by Morlière, and Ho replied in kind.[44] But Saigon's screening prevented any dialogue between the two heads of government. On 23 December, Blum announced in the National Assembly that Moutet and Leclerc were both to be sent on missions of inspection. Affirming that his government was obliged to confront violence, he also stated that nothing could alter the guiding principles of his government's policy. As he explained, to protests from the Right, he aimed to create 'a free Vietnam within an Indochinese Union freely associated with the French Union'. Unfortunately, this aim could only be revived once peace had been restored.[45]

With Blum's acceptance of hostilities, all that remained was for Saigon to stage-manage Moutet's and Leclerc's tours of inspection. The latter was particularly threatening to d'Argenlieu, who protested to Blum at the implied questioning of his competence; as Blum later related, if d'Argenlieu had offered his resignation it would have been immediately accepted.[46] The main question for both men, however, was: would they succeed in making contact with Ho Chi Minh? The importance of meeting Ho was recognized by Leclerc, who made Hanoi his first port of call after arriving in Saigon on the 28th. But he could not act without Moutet's authority, and the Minister had apparently placed Hanoi last on his list of Indochinese capitals: arriving in Saigon on the 25th, he had first met representatives of the Cochinchinese government before leaving for Phnom Penh and Vientiane. On 1 January, Ho broadcast a polite New Year message to the French government, expressing his willingness for a meeting with Moutet. D'Argenlieu condemned Ho's ruse, which seemed to pretend that nothing had happened in the north, and advised strongly against a meeting, which should not be considered to have been accomplished simply by Ho's mention of it.[47]

By the time Moutet arrived in Hanoi on 2 January, Leclerc had left to inspect Langson and Haiphong. Already hesitant about meeting Ho, Moutet's mind was made up by his conducted tour

44. Devillers, *Paris-Saigon-Hanoi*, 302–03.

45. '... un Viêt-Nam libre ... dans une Union indochinoise librement associé à l'Union française'. *Journal Officiel, Assemblée Nationale, Débats parlementaires*, 24 Dec. 1946, 320. His restatement of his anti-colonial principles on this occasion is quoted above, Ch. 4.

46. 'Hommage à Leclerc', *Le Populaire*, 18 Jun. 1949; Devillers, *Paris-Saigon-Hanoi*, 317.

47. D'Argenlieu to Moutet, no. 3220, 1 Jan. 1947, in d'Argenlieu, *Chronique*, 375.

of the battlefield of central Hanoi, past the remains of barricades and other evidence of Vietnamese 'premeditation', where fighting continued day and night around the Sino-Vietnamese quarter. After thirty hours in Hanoi, he had seen enough. As he declared at a press conference before leaving:

> Those responsible for this tragedy have systematically destroyed many people's hopes and have compromised the efforts in which we had invested our good will. Before any negotiation, it is now necessary that there should be a military outcome. I regret this, but no-one shoud be allowed to get away with such acts of madness as those committed by the Viet Minh. I could not be convinced any differently by staying longer. The premeditation involved is just too obvious.[48]

Explaining why he had had no contact with the Viet Minh, he pointed out that the necessary invitation had not been issued. As he later discovered, a letter from Ho had been received on 3 January and kept back from him. This letter proposed a four-point peace plan: the immediate cessation of hostilities, including a return to the positions of 3 April and the liberation of prisoners; an immediate stop to the despatch of reinforcements; a meeting between Moutet and Ho, on the basis of the 6 March Accord, to agree upon the terms of a treaty; and a conference in Paris to draw up the treaty.[49] And so Moutet returned to Paris overwhelmed by his close-range but nonetheless selective and indeed deceptive view of the situation in Hanoi. For d'Argenlieu, the ministerial visit was a success: to de Gaulle, he wrote that keeping Moutet away from Ho represented 'a point to chalk up in our favour'. As the British Consul-General in Saigon concluded: 'Moutet venit, vidit, d'Argenlieu vicit'.[50]

---

48. 'Les responsables de cette tragédie ont systématiquement détruit beaucoup d'espoirs et ont compromis la tentative dans laquelle nous avions mis notre bonne volonté. Avant toute négociation, il est aujourd'hui nécessaire d'avoir une décision militaire. Je le regrette, mais on ne commet pas impunément de folies pareilles à celles que les Viêt Minh ont commises.... Rester plus longtemps ne m'aurait pas appris davantage. La préméditation est trop évidente.' P. Devillers, Histoire du Viet-Nam de 1940 à 1952, Paris, 1952, 363.

49. Devillers, Paris-Saigon-Hanoi, 321.

50. '... un premier point de marqué', d'Argenlieu to de Gaulle, 14 Jan. 1947, Chronique, 386; Meiklereid to FO, no. 10, 17 Jan. 1947, FO/371/63432.

Although the case is not yet proven, it would seem that Saigon thus succeeded in its bid to provoke the Hanoi government into full-scale hostilities, but failed to bring off a swift coup d'état overthrowing Ho Chi Minh's hated Government. But at the same time, even with the best will in the world on all sides, Paris's rather half-hearted efforts to cling to the vestiges of rational policy making were probably a lost cause anyway, given the increasingly precarious situation in Indochina, and especially in Hanoi, in December 1946. Neither the attempts by Barjot and Laurentie to restate the purpose and rationale of the Accords policy, nor Blum's and Leclerc's appeals to reason, were so much as heeded, let alone followed, in the crisis which gripped the French both in Indochina and in Paris. Indeed, it is difficult to imagine how this could have been otherwise, given the primacy which Saigon had by now firmly established for itself within the decision-making process. Léon Blum's investiture as the first Prime Minister of the Fourth Republic thus not only galvanised Saigon into action, but also, by its tardiness and by its singularly unrepresentative all-Socialist composition, epitomised the crisis which had impeded policy makers in Paris since the Liberation, and especially since de Gaulle's departure eleven months before.

In conclusion, although the outbreak of war marked the end of the policy whose formulation, attempted implementation, and failure have been examined here, the attitudes of some of the key policy makers in the immediate aftermath of the 'Tonkin Vespers' of 19 December 1946 may shed further light on the reasons for the breakdown of policy making. For, in contrast with Léon Blum's sense of tragedy, the view of officials in this opening stage of France's war in Indochina was remarkably sanguine. This was particularly the case for Henri Laurentie, whose first reaction to the news from Hanoi was to see it as a great political opportunity: in a letter to de Gaulle, introducing the Cochinchinese Vice-President Colonel Xuan, he argued that France should exploit 'our show of force' ('la manifestation de notre force') and Ho Chi Minh's flight beyond the pale of Hanoi, in order to implement the policy he had been advocating for some months.[51] In early January, after the full import of the events in Hanoi had sunk in, Laurentie recognised that the opportunity for a short war had already

---

51. Note pour Monsieur le Général de Gaulle, 22 Dec. 1946, AOM, 72AJ539.

passed, and welcomed Moutet's firm stance in Hanoi. As he argued, in a note to Gaston Defferre, junior minister (*Sous-Secrétaire d'Etat*) at the Ministry for Overseas France:

> Calling a halt today to military action would amount to capitulation, the effects of which in Indochina would work decisively against us. In Cochinchina and Annam we would lose all the chances which have come back within our grasp; we would lose forever the confidence of Laos and Cambodia; we would lose Indochina. It is difficult to imagine how the rest of the Empire would resist the process. So our duty has been mapped out for us. M. Moutet has understood this and said as much. The case rests.[52]

Thus, having championed a 'liberal' interpretation of the Brazzaville policy based on negotiations with the authentic representatives of colonial nationalism, and having loyally played his part in the attempts made in Paris to head off conflict with Ho, Laurentie now returned to the stance he had adopted in the wake of the Haiphong crisis, according to which Ho was to be written off as an enemy of France.

Arguing from a quite separate direction, in his report on his mission of inspection, General Leclerc reached rather similar conclusions concerning the purpose of military action in Indochina, against which he had provided perhaps the most convincing arguments. On the premise that the 'Indochina problem is above all a *political problem*', he argued that France's military aim was to permit a return to discussion of the key political issues:

> The present military situation is certainly one of *crisis*, but the problem for the French Command is much a more question of the longer term than one of crisis as one might be tempted to think....
>
> A first political phase, starting ten months ago, has finished in failure. We must now *hold out* militarily, in order to allow the development of a second constructive phase which might allow us to achieve our politico-military objectives.[53]

52. '... la cessation aujourd'hui de l'action militaire équivaudrait à une capitulation dont les effets, en Indochine même, seraient décisifs contre nous. Nous perdrions en Cochinchine et en Annam toutes les chances que nous venons de rattraper; nous perdrions à tout jamais la confiance du Cambodge et du Laos; nous perdrions l'Indochine. Et l'on ne sait pas comment le reste de l'Empire résisterait à l'opération. Ainsi notre devoir est-il tracé. M. MOUTET l'a compris et proclamé. La cause est donc entendue.' NOTE pour Monsieur le MINISTRE, 7 Jan. 1947, AOM, 72AJ539.

53. 'Le problème indochinois est avant tout un *problème politique*.... La situation militaire actuelle, si elle est un problème de *crise*, pose davantage au commandement un problème de *durée* qu'un problème de crise comme on serait tenté de croire....

Unlike Laurentie, he also argued that the resumption of policy making in the wake of military action might include negotiation with the Viet Minh, whom he condemned only for having acted 'like fanatics or even like nervy, unstable children'.[54] It was this balanced and forgiving approach, perhaps, which commended Leclerc to Blum, who, following his return to Paris, offered him his old Command in Indochina, on the understanding that he might soon take over the High Commission as well, in place of the unreliable d'Argenlieu. Having consulted de Gaulle, however, who vehemently blamed 'the System' rather than the Admiral, Leclerc refused.[55] Ten months later, Leclerc was killed in a plane crash in Algeria.

The third perspective which may be noted in the aftermath of the events of December is that of Saigon, and, in particular, of Léon Pignon, whom Devillers identifies as 'the brains of the affair', and who was still unrepentant and optimistic when he wrote to Laurentie two months into the war: 'The situation in Indochina is far from being as bad as is sometimes imagined. We have made considerable progress since September 1945, and the only real danger if the troubles drag on comes from failure on the part of the metropole or from foreign intervention'.[56] Characteristically, Pignon had already set down the basis for future policy in a long position paper ('Note d'Orientation') the month before, which argued two essential points. First, in contrast with Leclerc, he argued for ruling out further negotiations should with Ho's government, whose sole objective had always been total independence and the expulsion of the French. Secondly, however, he stressed that the Viet Minh should in no sense be identified with 'the national cause'; and that, conversely, the French should harness the national idea to French

---

'Une première phase politique commencée il y a dix mois se termine par un échec. Il faut à présent *durer assez* militairement, pour permettre le développement d'une 2e phase constructive et susceptible de mener au terme de l'entreprise politico-militaire.' Projet de Rapport du Général Leclerc, 7 Jan. 1947, Bodinier, *Le retour*, 382–91; see also V. Auriol, *Journal du Septennat*, Paris, 1970–1980, 7 vols, vol. 1, 661–64. Emphases in text.

54. '... comme des fanatiques ou encore comme des enfants nerveux et instables'. Ibid.

55. Devillers, *Paris-Saigon-Hanoi*, 236.

56. '... la situation en Indochine est loin d'être aussi mauvaise qu'on imagine parfois. Les progrès depuis septembre 1945 sont considérables et il n'existe de réel danger à la prolongation des troubles qu'en fonction soit d'une défaillance de la Métropole, soit d'une intervention étrangère.' Pignon to Laurentie, Saigon, 18 Feb. 1947, AN, 72AJ539; '... le cerveau de toute l'affaire', Devillers, *Paris-Saigon-Hanoi*, 331.

ends, even if this meant tackling the issues which had prevented progress on the Accords policy: independence and national unity.

As he argued: 'We cannot now hope to drive a wedge between the masses and the Viet Minh unless we can show by what we say and do that we do not represent a threat to the national idea'. Thus, it was important to break none of the promises made in the 6 March Accords, although the *modus vivendi* was dismissed as merely an expedient intended to prepare the way for a definitive agreement.[57] But there were to be no superficial concessions, and in particular the name 'Vietnam' was dismissed as a tendentious and misleading term which had only ever been used by the French 'out of courtesy' ('dans un souci de courtoisie'). In a circular drafted in Pignon's office and issued by d'Argenlieu on 15 January, the term was proscribed from all official correspondence.[58]

If these proposals apparently promised in some respects a reprise of the Accords policy, their corollary was in fact the Bao Dai Solution, according to which the ex-Emperor was to be reinstated as head of the united 'Annamite lands'. Although not mentioned in Pignon's position paper, its purpose was nonetheless suggested, as a shield to deflect Franco-Vietnamese antagonism:

> Our aim is clear: we must transfer to a domestic Annamite level the quarrel we have with the Viet Minh party and be involved as little as possible in the campaigns and reprisals which must be seen to be the work of the local opponents of this party.[59]

Thus, Bao Dai was to assist the 'Vietnamisation' (the French term was 'jaunissement') of the war, or, in other words, to transform it into civil war. This idea was not new in early 1947. It had its origins in the plans entertained by de Gaulle more than a year earlier for the reinvestiture of Bao Dai's exiled cousin Vinh San; and had recently been discussed in theory by Laurentie and Pignon. D'Argenlieu very quickly made the idea his own, in a major policy

---

57. 'Nous ne pouvons, actuellement, espérer désolidariser la masse du Viêt Minh qu'en montrant, par nos propos et par nos actes, que l'idée nationale n'est pas mise par nous en péril.' Note d'Orientation no. 9, 4 Jan. 1947, Devillers, *Paris-Saigon-Hanoi*, 331–34.

58. Note circulaire, no. 215/CP.Cab, 15 Jan. 1947, Devillers, *Paris-Saigon-Hanoi*, 334–37.

59. 'Notre objectif est clairement déterminé: transporter sur le plan intérieur annamite la querelle que nous avons avec le parti Viêt Minh et nous engager nous-mêmes le moins possible dans des campagnes et des représailles qui doivent être le fait des adversaires autochtones de ce parti.' Loc.cit.

document.[60] But before Bao Dai could be accepted as a plausible Head of State – he had after all been the puppet of, successively, the French, the Japanese, and the Viet Minh – he had to be seen to meet one other essential criterion, as an anti-Communist. As Laurentie argued to Defferre in January 1947, only weeks before Truman's capital speech to Congress of 12 March 1947 setting out the Truman Doctrine, the White House was torn between the 'need to check communism in South East Asia', and the desire to be seen by American public opinion to disapprove of a colonial war.[61] Thus Bao Dai came to be seen as the best way to flatter President Truman's sensibilities both as a democrat and as a Cold Warrior.[62]

In the New Year 1947, however, this 'solution' to France's problems in Indochina was still some way off, since neither Léon Blum nor his SFIO successor as Prime Minister, Paul Ramadier, was prepared to abandon all hope of resuming talks with Ho Chi Minh. Moreover, the political crisis in Paris was well on the way to an albeit temporary resolution when, on 16 January, Léon Blum resigned to mark the election of Vincent Auriol as first President of the Fourth Republic. One of the first decisive actions of the new President and Prime Minister, over the following month, was to engineer the removal of d'Argenlieu, whose threat to resign over the question of breaking with Ho was finally accepted on 1 March. Léon Pignon was appointed Commissioner for the Republic in Phnom Penh by d'Argenlieu's successor, Emile Bollaert, only to replace Bollaert in his turn as France's third High Commissioner in Indochina, in October 1948. There was to be one further sacrifice to the 'winds of change' in Paris: as an outspoken and rather unpredictable critic of official policy, and no doubt also as a Gaullist, Henri Laurentie was no longer acceptable to Moutet in the Political Affairs Division at the Rue Oudinot, and in March 1947 he was replaced by the older and more tactful Robert Delavignette, who had also served in Moutet's private office during the

---

60. See above, Chs 6, 9; see also NOTE pour Monsieur le MINISTRE, 7 Jan. 1947, loc.cit; 'Tournant politique en Indochine', 14 Jan. 1947, Devillers, *Paris-Saigon-Hanoi*, 337–43.

61. '… la nécessité de faire pièce au communisme dans le sud-est asiatique'. Loc.cit.

62. See M.J. Shipway, 'British perceptions of French policy in Indochina from the March 1946 accords to the inception of the Bao Dai régime, 1946–1949: a meeting of "Official Minds"?', in C.-R. Ageron and M. Michel, eds, *L'ère des décolonisations*, Paris, 1995, 83–96.

Popular Front.[63] Henri Laurentie, still only forty-five years old, was 'kicked upstairs' to the United Nations, where he served on the Trusteeship Council.[64] As if to confirm the demise of the Brazzaville policy, almost the first dossier to hit Delavignette's desk concerned the outbreak of the Malagasy insurrection at the end of March 1947.

63. Fichier des Anciens Elèves de l'ENFOM, AOM, 39APOM2.

64. For a caustic account of his functions in New York, cf. his January 1948 letter to Pignon: 'There's always the United Nations. I sit there behind M. Garreau and listen to him with dread that I have so far failed to control, as he launches into bizarre speeches which turn out in ways that even he had not expected. And yet I'm the one who is still considered dangerous.' ('Il y a bien les Nations Unies. Je m'y assieds derrière M. Garreau et l'écoute, avec une appréhension que je n'ai pas su calmer, se livrer à des interventions pittoresques et inattendues, même de lui. C'est moi, cependant, que l'on continue de trouver dangereux.': AN, 72AJ539.

In 1951, he returned briefly to administrative office in Paris, as Technical Adviser (*conseiller technique*) in the prime-ministerial *cabinet* of his former boss, René Pleven.

CONCLUSION

*It was one of those difficult periods in which anyone is
likely to get it wrong, and to an extent everyone does get
it wrong, because of the weight of circumstance.
De Gaulle, d'Argenlieu, Moutet, Mérat, Chevance-
Bertin, the MRP, the PRL and co. can all say what they
like: France's principle fault in colonial matters has been
her weakness. French weakness is obvious and long-last-
ing, much like Britain's or Holland's, and why not call
yourself a Communist or a Nationalist, and be as intransigent as possible whatever the label you choose, when the
Empire you belong to is so feebly kept in hand.*[1]

In these words, Governor Henri Laurentie summed up the failure of the French colonial administration's attempts, following
the Liberation, to find a new formula for French colonial rule
which would balance the terms of an imperial equation, contributing to the restoration of French greatness in the wake of
humiliating defeat and occupation while at the same time seeking
an accommodation with newly powerful and confident colonial
nationalist movements. Writing only a year after the breakdown
of policy in its first and most important test-case, Indochina, Laurentie was perhaps too closely involved, not to say implicated, in

---

1. 'C'était l'une de ses périodes difficiles où chacun risque de se tromper, et dans
une certaine mesure se trompe, tant est lourd le poids des circonstances admises....
    '... De Gaulle, d'Argenlieu, Moutet, Mérat, Chevance-Bertin, le MRP, le PRL,
etc., auront beau dire, la France n'a commis, ou éprouvé, qu'une faute principale en
matière coloniale, celle d'être faible. La faiblesse de la France est évidente et
durable, tout comme celle de l'Angleterre et de la Hollande, et comment ne pas être
ou communiste, ou nationaliste, et se montrer aussi intransigeant sous une étiquette que sous l'autre, quand on est le sujet d'un empire si pauvrement possédé.'
Laurentie to Pignon, New York, 8 Jan. 1948, AN, 72AJ539.

the events which led to war to be reliable as a balanced or objective interpreter of those events. (His correspondent, Léon Pignon, was even more deeply implicated.) Nonetheless, his views plausibly convey the sense of an ineluctable process with a momentum of its own: France was too weak, her policy makers too fallible, to bring off the 'massive operation to capture hearts and minds' which Laurentie, with characteristic grandiloquence, had been advocating.[2] Now that we know more or less the 'whole story' of European decolonisation which, along with the Cold War, so dominated the international system following the Second World War, we can add to Laurentie's analysis the perception that it was probably an illusion for post-war policy makers to suppose that France's colonial empire would remain intact for long, even if allowed to drift with the tide of colonial nationalism, rather than being anchored against it.

However, far from advocating a Whiggish view of the decolonisation process, or suggesting a kind of tragic inevitability to the collapse of relations between the French and Ho Chi Minh's regime in Hanoi, the purpose of this study has been to study a complex instance of breakdown in policy making. The policy which has been observed breaking down is the so-called Brazzaville policy, and its Indochinese offshoot, the Accords policy. But the peculiar difficulty which has been identified for policy makers lay not simply in the magnitude of the task envisaged, but in the extent to which policy straddled two very different, and quite separate, sets of concerns, corresponding to the two sides of the imperial equation. Thus, on the one hand, policy makers drawn from the ranks of the colonial administration sought to wrestle with the new and changing colonial and international parameters of policy; on the other hand, they were constrained also to operate within the framework of French domestic political concerns and interests. Moreover, confronted with acute crisis both in colonial affairs and in domestic politics, policy makers found themselves adapting policy to keep pace with the former, while unwillingly or unwittingly responding to changes wrought by domestic crisis to the political, ideological, and institutional basis for policy. Thus, confronted with a moving target, French policy makers found themselves constrained also to take aim and fire from a moving train.

---

2. '… une grande opération du coeur et de la raison', NOTE, 20–21 juin 1945, AN, 72AJ535. See above, Ch. 3.

What happens to policy making in these circumstances? An answer to this question in general terms is suggested in Part One of this study. It has been shown how officials, having offered a guardedly generous interpretation of France's imperial mission at the Brazzaville Conference in early 1944 and thereafter (Chapters 1 and 2), responded to their perception of colonial crisis by advocating extensive concessions to local nationalists which would nonetheless preserve essential French interests (Chapter 3). Indochina's role has also been recognised as a paradigm for the Brazzaville policy, as set out in the March 1945 Declaration on Indochina (Chapter 2). However, it has been demonstrated that this highly 'excentric' policy, to borrow Ronald Robinson's coinage, was subordinated from the start to domestic ideological concerns and political interests; and overlaid by misleading associations with domestic myths, ranging from those surrounding de Gaulle to the supposedly discredited myth of an assimilated 'France of a hundred million people' (Chapters 1 and 2). Further, it has been argued that colonial policy makers implicitly assumed a model for the functioning of domestic politics which would allow them to concentrate on their own 'external' concerns. Three sets of parameters for this model were identified, relating to the salience of colonial affairs on the political agenda; the acceptability of policy within perceived ideological norms, mainly Gaullist or Republican in origin; and the loyalty and cohesion of the institutions on which policy depended. These domestic parameters of policy were probably imperfectly understood by policy makers, and were anyway highly ambiguous, but they briefly offered a reasonably stable context in which colonial policy could be conducted. However, far from remaining stable, these domestic parameters of policy were increasingly volatile as a result of the prolonged political crisis which marked the Constitution-making process in Paris, especially as a result of de Gaulle's resignation in January 1946. Thus, colonial policy's place on the domestic political agenda was uncertain, and its intermittent political salience was in itself problematic. The ideological acceptability of the Brazzaville policy was subject to varying ideological interpretations of that policy, as its Gaullist and Republican foundations shifted, and as new ideological factors came to prominence, notably anti-Communism. And, in terms of institutional solidarity, its fate was too obviously tied to the Gaullist institutional model, and to the loyalty which de Gaulle alone inspired in some quarters of the colonial hierarchy (Chapter 4).

Extending the general thesis, advanced in Part One, of distortions in the colonial policy-making process brought about by domestic instability and crisis, Part Two has examined the evidence of more direct interference in, and manipulation of, policy in the specific case of Indochina. Thus it has been shown how, even before the French 'return' in September 1945, Indochina policy was subject to widely diverging interpretations, as liberal colonial officials clashed with de Gaulle over the conflicting priorities suggested by the proposals of Laurentie and his colleagues, on the one hand, and the narrow application of French interests on the other (Chapter 5). It has been suggested that the Accords policy which followed the French 'return' resolved this controversy only partially and superficially in favour of the liberal camp. Thus the March 1946 Accords, supposedly a triumph for liberal policy, were in fact seen by conservatives as a hard-driven bargain, which thus served indirectly to fuel resistance to the liberal prescriptions for policy emanating from Paris (Chapter 6). It has been shown how this resistance took the form of a bid by the colonial administration in Saigon to set itself up as a decision-making centre rivalling Paris. This rivalry, which was manifested soon after the signing of the March Accords, took the form of *faits accomplis* undertaken without consultation with Paris, apparently designed to undermine Paris's authority to determine and conduct policy (Chapter 7). Indeed, it is argued that Saigon was thus partly responsible for the failure of the Fontainebleau Conference, which was intended to mark the culmination of the Accords policy, but which ended ignominiously with the signing of a compromise *modus vivendi* in September 1946 (Chapter 8). Saigon's insubordination became more brazen thereafter, as it became plain that, not only was the Accords policy crumbling, but so also was the basis for Saigon's own rival policy. It has been suggested that Saigon's fanning of the flames at Haiphong in late November 1946 may be seen as a trial run for the 'last ditch' option of a military strike against Hanoi (Chapter 9). Saigon's partial success (or rather, only partial failure) in working out this strategy, and Paris's last attempts to retake the reins of effective policy making, have been traced to their conclusion in the 'Tonkin Vespers' of 19 December 1946, which marked the outbreak of the war in Indochina, and thus the complete breakdown of the Accords policy which Paris had sought to implement (Chapter 10).

Was it an illusion to suppose that a deal could be struck with colonial nationalists such as the Viet Minh, enabling France to reconcile her imperial interests with Vietnamese aspirations to national unity and self-determination? If so, the illusion was shared by policy makers both in the Hague and in London. Thus, a year after the signing of the Accords in Hanoi, in March 1947, a similar agreement was signed at Linggadjati in the Dutch East Indies by the Dutch Lieutenant Governor-General, the British High Commissioner, and the Prime Minister of the Indonesian Republic; it took little more than two months for the agreement to break down.[3] British self-deception in South Asia was more persistent, however, and Laurentie's arguments have their echo, for instance, in Patrick Gordon-Walker's summary, as Commonwealth Secretary in 1948, of British policy towards Ceylon: 'It is hardly too much to say that if we treat them strictly as a dominion they will behave very like a loyal colony; whereas if we treat then as a Colony we may end in driving them out of the Commonwealth'.[4] With hindsight, we can perhaps identify the fallacy of liberals in the French colonial administration: even while recognizing the importance of nationalism, Laurentie et al. were unwilling or unable to see that the strength of the national idea lay precisely in its espousal of the cause of independence, which meant exactly what that term implied, notwithstanding French attempts to place their own limiting interpretations upon it. This failure of perception may be attributed to the fact that French liberals and conservatives alike came to colonial policy making in the post-war period with nationalist designs of their own: imperial restoration and, in the case under consideration, the project of a 'return' to Indochina were both tied into grander plans, Gaullist in origin but embraced across the French political spectrum (however refracted that spectrum became), for the political, economic, and moral renewal of French society and the French state following the depredations of the war-years. It was unfortunate but inevitable that French nationalism should thus meet its match in the equal but opposite force of the Vietnamese national idea. However, as this study has argued, the breakdown in policy which led to war was hastened or facilitated, if not directly caused, by political or ideological ambiguities and institutional weaknesses in the policy-making process, many of which had their source in that same

3. See J.J.P. de Jong, *Diplomatie of stryd, het Nederlandse beleid tegenover de Indonesische revolutie, 1945–1947*, Amsterdam, 1988.
4. Quoted by J. Darwin, *Britain and Decolonisation, The Retreat from Empire in the Post-War World*, Basingstoke, 1988, 106.

need for national renewal. Thus, France's liberal policy in Indochina failed, not only because it mistook its aim but also because it fell victim to systemic flaws which it had been in part designed to mend.

The Accords policy in Indochina was not the last attempt by French colonial liberals to manage or check the decolonisation process. Traces of Laurentie's 'thesis' may be found in the 1956 Framework Law for the devolution of power in Black Africa (the *Loi Defferre*), which granted effective self-government to France's African dependencies within the French Union, and in de Gaulle's African policy after 1958; it would be instructive also to compare the Rocard government's New Caledonia policy from 1988. However, the debacle in Indochina prepared the way both for later policy, and for further recourse by France's colonial 'proconsuls' to conspiracy, or at least to what might be termed 'crisis management with extreme prejudice'. As Georgette Elgey comments, 'From this moment on, France's future policy was established with regard to emerging nationalisms within the French Union: no negotiations without military victory'.[5] It was a brave politician indeed in the Fourth Republic who would court responsibility for scuttling the Empire. Three months after cutting the Gordian knot of the French war in Indochina, at the 1954 Geneva Conference, Pierre Mendès-France and his Interior Minister, François Mitterrand, were confronted with the insurrection of the National Liberation Front (*Front de Libération Nationale*, FLN) in Algeria which broke out on 1 November 1954. Without the humiliating experience of defeat and withdrawal in Indochina, it is difficult to imagine the strength of the Army's support for the cause of French Algeria, sustained as it was by the myth of a political stab in the back after Dien Bien Phu. After his return to power in 1958, not even the rule of de Gaulle, the rebellious generals' rebellious general, was immune to further military insubordination. By the same token, although Algeria was a far more intractable case even than Indochina, it is a measure of the sheer scale of France's colonial dilemma after 1945, that, even after de Gaulle returned to power at the head of the kind of regime he had been advocating for eighteen years, it took a further four years before the conflict was

---

5. 'Dès ce moment, toute la politique future de la France à l'égard des nationalismes qui se manifesteront dans l'Union Française est définie: pas de négociations sans une victoire militaire.' G. Elgey, *La république des illusions, 1945–1951, ou la vie secrète de la IVe République* Paris, 1965, 171.

finally resolved in favour of Algerian independence. Perhaps, therefore, we should not judge too harshly the record of policy makers in the immediate aftermath of the Second World War. In conclusion, it is tempting to speculate on an alternative outcome for a French policy of liberal reformism circa 1945. Surely not a transformed Empire, in the guise of a new multi-continental francophone community, in which Ho Chi Minh might have rubbed shoulders with Senghor, Bourguiba or, for that matter, de Gaulle. Conceivably, however, a policy of concessions conducted with sincerity, and perhaps a measure of face-saving 'Anglo-Saxon' self-delusion, might have led France peacefully and with honour out of Vietnam, and thus set a valuable precedent for the decolonisation of the rest of the French Union. As it was, a quite different precedent was set, and it was to take a decade and a half of colonial and domestic conflict, for which the events described in this study provide only a foretaste, before de Gaulle arrived at his breath-taking redefinition of French interests, enabling him to state that 'decolonisation is in our interest and is therefore our policy'.[6]

---

6. '... la décolonisation est notre intérêt et, par conséquent, notre politique'. 12 Apr. 1961, *Discours et messages*, 3 vols, vol. 3, *Avec le renouveau, 1958–1962*, Paris, 1970, 292.

APPENDIX I

The Administrative Structure of the French Empire, 1945

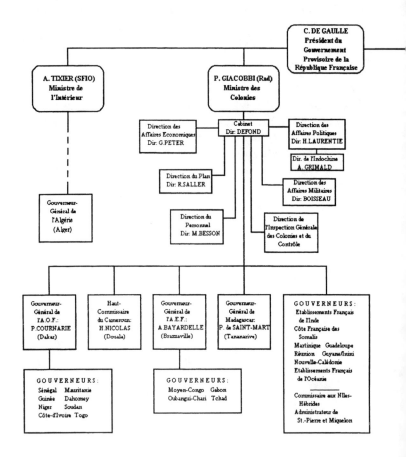

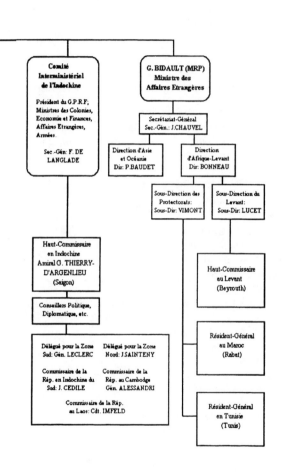

Comité Interministériel de l'Indochine

Président du G.P.R.F;
Ministres des Colonies,
Economie et Finances,
Affaires Etrangères,
Armées.

Sec.-Gén: F. DE LANGLADE

**G. BIDAULT (MRP)
Ministre des Affaires Etrangères**

Secrétariat-Général
Sec.-Gén.: J.CHAUVEL

Direction d'Asie et Océanie
Dir: P.BAUDET

Direction d'Afrique-Levant
Dir: BONNEAU

Sous-Direction des Protectorats:
Sous-Dir: VIMONT

Sous-Direction du Levant:
Sous-Dir: LUCET

Haut-Commissaire en Indochine
Amiral G. THIERRY-D'ARGENLIEU
(Saigon)

Haut-Commissaire au Levant
(Beyrouth)

Conseillers Politique, Diplomatique, etc.

Délégué pour la Zone Sud: Gén. LECLERC

Délégué pour la Zone Nord: J.SAINTENY

Résident-Général au Maroc
(Rabat)

Commissaire de la Rép. en Indochine du Sud: J. CEDILE

Commissaire de la Rép. au Cambodge
Gén. ALESSANDRI

Commissaire de la Rép. au Laos: Cdt. IMFELD

Résident-Général en Tunisie
(Tunis)

APPENDIX II

Chronology of Events in France and Indochina, 1944–1947[1]

		France: Politics and Diplomacy	Indochina and the Far East
1943		Establishment of the CFLN at Algiers (July), Pleven is Commissioner for the Colonies; Empire united under Gaullist authority, except for Indochina; Levant Crisis (Nov.)	CFLN establishes diplomatic relations with Nationalist China (July); Declaration on Indochina (8 Dec.)
1944	January	Brazzaville Conference (30 Jan.–8 Feb.)	
	June	CFLN becomes GPRF (2); Normandy landings (6)	
	July	De Gaulle in US (6–10); endorses idea of a French Federation (10)	
	August	Liberation of Paris (19–25)	Decoux declares full powers in Indochina
	September	First GPRF Council of Ministers (2); FFI incorporated into French Army (23)	
	October	Allied recognition of GPRF (23); de Gaulle lends support for 'a French system where everyone would have a role to play' (25); FTP disbanded (28)	American landings in Philippines; de Langlade's intelligence mission to Indochina
	November	SFIO extraordinary congress (9–12); MRP founding Congress (26); Thorez returns to Paris (27); Pleven replaced by Giacobbi as Minister of Colonies	

1. Sources include: J.-P. Rioux, *La France de la Quatrième République*, vol. 1, Paris, 1980, 267–73; Commander G. Bodinier, *Le retour de la France en Indochine, 1945–46*, Vincennes, 1987, 11–18.

1944	December	Franco-Soviet pact signed, Moscow (10); first edition of *Le Monde* (18)	
1945	January	Nationalisation of Renault (16); Yalta Conference goes ahead without France	
	February	Yalta Accords (12); creation of Cominindo (15), de Langlade is Secretary-General	
	March	Allies reach the Rhine (4)	Japanese overthrow of Decoux administration and takeover (9); Bao Dai declares Vietnamese independence and national unity (11); Sihanouk declares Cambodian independence (13); Giacobbi makes Declaration on Indochina (24)
	April	Death of Roosevelt; accession of Truman to US Presidency (12); opening of San Francisco Conference (26); first round of municipal elections (29)	Independence of Laos declared (8); Tran Trong Kim forms Government in Hanoi (17)
	May	VE-Day (8); insurrection and repression of same in Eastern Algeria (8–12); 'Thanks to her Empire France counts amongst the victors!' (Monnerville, 15); France becomes permanent member of UN Security Council (16); Syrian crisis culminating in British-imposed ceasefire (30)	
	June	France acquires an occupation zone in Germany (5); 'We are in the midst of colonial crisis' (Laurentie, 20/21); end of San Francisco Conference and UN Charter (26); end of French Mandate in Syria and Lebanon	Leclerc charged with formation of French Far East Expeditionary Corps (CEFEO) (7)
	July	Pétain's trial begins (23)	Potsdam Conference decides to divide Indochina along 16th Parallel for receiving Japanese surrender (23)
	August	D'Argenlieu named High Commissioner in Indochina (16); Laurentie passes over as his Political Counsellor	End of Potsdam Conference (2); atomic bombs dropped on Hiroshima (6) and Nagasaki (9); USSR declares war on Japan (8); Ho Chi Minh calls

1945	August (cont.)		for general insurrection (10); Japanese capitulation (15); Viet Minh takes over power (19); Sainteny arrives in Hanoi (22); Cédile parachutes into Saigon (24); Ho forms cabinet, Bao Dai abdicates (25); arrival of first Chinese troops, commanded by General Lu Han (28); 'a situation as vague as it is confusing' (Laurentie, 29)
	September	D'Argenlieu leaves Paris for Chandernagor (5); Laurentie's press conferences (13–14)	Ho Chi Minh declares independence (2); Leclerc represents France at signing of Japanese surrender (2); arrival of British troops, commanded by General Gracey, in Saigon (12); rearmed French troops take over public buildings in Saigon (23); massacre of about 100 French in *cité Héraud*, Saigon (24)
	October	Trial and execution of Laval (4–15); referendum and legislative elections (21)	General Leclerc arrives in Saigon (5); arrival of first detachments of CEFEO; Admiral d'Argenlieu arrives in Saigon (30); start of pacification campaign
	November	Gouin made President of Constituent Assembly (8); formation of de Gaulle's government (21), Soustelle is Minister of Colonies	Leclerc's pacification campaign continues
	December	Vinh San meets de Gaulle (14) and dies in air crash (26); prompting de Gaulle's comment that 'France certainly is unlucky.'	
1946	January	De Gaulle resigns as President of the GPRF (20); agreement signed between MRP, SFIO and PCF (24); Gouin government formed (26–29), with Moutet as Minister of Overseas France; Auriol President of the Constituent Assembly (31)	Elections to Vietnamese Constituent Assembly (6); Franco-Khmer *modus vivendi* signed (7); General Gracey leaves Saigon (28)
	February	D'Argenlieu in Paris (13–27); vote on French Union in Constituent Assembly	Conchinchinese Consultative Council meets (12); breakthrough in Sainteny's negotiations with Ho Chi Minh (16);

1946 February (cont.)

March   Churchill's speech at Fulton, Missouri (5)

April   Constitutional draft adopted by Assembly (19); creation of FIDES, Overseas Departments (*départements d'Outre-mer*), abolition of forced labour

May   Constitutional draft rejected in referendum (5)

June   Legislative elections (2); de Gaulle's speech at Bayeux (16); Ho arrives in France (12), entertained at Biarritz, pending formation of Bidault government (23–26)

July   Ho shown sights of Paris; opening of Fontainebleau Conference (6)

August   Breakdown of talks at Fontainbleau (1); debate in Constituent Assembly on revision of French Union articles in Constitution; 'France would become the colony of her former colonies' (Herriot, 27)

September   Fontainebleau Conference adjourned (10); Ho Chi Minh and Moutet sign *modus vivendi* (14); Constitutional draft adopted by Assembly (29)

agreement reached in Chungking concerning French relief relief of Chinese troops north of 16th Parallel (28)

Accords signed in Hanoi by Sainteny and Ho, French troop landing at Haiphong (6); 'Better to sniff the French dungheap for five years ...' (Ho, 7); arrival of Leclerc and French troops in Hanoi (18); d'Argenlieu meets Ho aboard *Emile Bertin* in Bay of Along (24); formation of a Provisional Government of the Republic Cochinchina, headed by Dr Nguyen Van Trinh (26)

Opening of Dalat Conference (19)

D'Argenlieu receives Moi oath of loyalty at Ban Me Thuot (14); Lu Han leaves Tonkin (30); Ho Chi Minh leaves for France at head of Vietnamese delegation (31)

Proclamation of Autonomous Republic of Cochinchina (1); French occupation of Moi Plateaux (21–27) and Government-General in Hanoi (25)

Leclerc replaced as Military Commander in Indochina by General Valluy (18)

Second Dalat Conference (1–13); Bac Ninh incident (3); Franco-Lao *modus vivendi* (27)

1946	October	Yes vote in referendum on Constitution (13)	Siam returns annexed Laotian and Cambodian provinces to France (15); d'Argenlieu welcomes Ho on his return, aboard the *Dumont d'Urville* in Cam Ranh Bay (18); *modus vivendi* comes into force (30)
	November	Legislative elections (10); d'Argenlieu arrives in Paris (18); first round of elections to Council of the Republic (24); Bidault government resigns (28)	Nguyen Van Thinh commits suicide (10); start of Haiphong 'incident' (20), leading to French bombardment of the town, 'to teach a hard lesson' (Valluy, 23); Langson occupied, following a further' incident' (25)
	December	Auriol President of National Assembly (3); formation of of Blum government (16)	Sainteny returns to Hanoi (2); growing tensions in Hanoi lead to insurrection by Vietnamese militia, flight of Ho government from city and breakdown of Franco-Vietnamese relations (19); arrival of Moutet (25) and Leclerc (28) in Indochina on missions of inspection
1947	January	Auriol elected President of the Republic, Blum government resigns, to be replaced by Ramadier (16); abolition of Cominindo	Moutet and Leclerc leave Indochina (8–9); 'I regret this, but no-one should be allowed to get away with such acts of madness as those committed by the Viet Minh ...' (Moutet, 8)
	February		'The situation in Indochina is far from being as bad as is sometimes imagined ...' (Pignon, 18)
	March	D'Argenlieu's resignation accepted by Ramadier (1); he is replaced by Emile Bollaert (6); Truman enunciates his Doctrine in Congress (12); military credits voted for Indochina (22); Delavignette replaces Laurentie as Director of Political Affairs at the Ministry for Overseas France; start of insurrection in Madagascar (29–30)	
	May	Communist ministers expelled from Ramadier government (5)	

BIBLIOGRAPHY

I. Archival Sources

Archives Nationales, Paris (AN):
72 AJ 535–541   Archives du Comité d'Histoire de la Seconde Guerre Mondiale, Papiers du Gouverneur Henri Laurentie

Dépôt des Archives d'Outre-Mer, Aix-en-Provence (AOM):
AP   Direction des Affaires Politiques du Ministère des Colonies / de la France d'Outre-mer
INF   Indochine Nouveau Fonds
CP   Conseiller Politique, Saigon
Tels   Télégrammes, départ et arrivée, du Ministère des Colonies / de la France d'Outre-mer
Cab   Cabinet du Ministre des Colonies, 1945
39 APOM   Fichier des Anciens Elèves de l'Ecole Nationale de la France d'Outre-Mer
2G   Gouvernement-Général de l'Afrique Occidentale Française, Dakar (microfilmed copy from Senegalese National Archives)

Archives diplomatiques, Ministère des Affaires Etrangères, Paris (MAE):
AO   Direction Asie-Océanie
EA   Archives de l'ancien Ministère des Etats Associés*
Y   Conférences internationales, 1944–1949
Guerre   Guerre 1939–1945, Londres/Alger

Journal Officiel de la République Française. Débats.
JOACP   Assemblée Consultative Provisoire, Alger/Paris, 1943–1945
JOANC   Assemblée Nationale Constituante, Paris, 1945–1946
JOAN   Assemblée Nationale, Paris, 1946–

Public Record Office, Kew (PRO):
FO 371   Foreign Office general files

---

* Includes *Comité Interministériel de l'Indochine* (Cominindo) papers from January 1945. Mr Stein Tønnesson kindly provided me with copies of documents from this file, access to which was restricted shortly before I was able to consult it.

II. Press

Le Monde
Combat
Renaissances
Marchés coloniaux
Dépêche de Paris

Observer
Times
Manchester Guardian
Daily Herald

III. Published Documents and Memoirs

Argenlieu, Amiral Georges Thierry d'. *Chronique d'Indochine, 1945–1947*. Paris: Albin Michel, 1985.

Auriol, Vincent. *Journal du septennat*. Paris: Armand Colin, 1970–1980.

Bodinier, Commandant Gilbert, ed. *Retour de la France en Indochine, 1945–1946*. Vincennes: Service Historique de l'Armée de Terre, 1987.

Chauvel, Jean. *Commentaire*. vols II and III, *1944–1962*. Paris: Fayard, 1972–1973.

Decoux, Amiral Jean. *A la barre de l'Indochine*. Paris: Plon, 1949.

Deschamps, Hubert. *Roi de la brousse. Mémoires d'autres Mondes*. Paris: Berger-Levrault, 1975.

Devillers, Philippe. *Paris-Saigon-Hanoi. Les archives de la guerre, 1944–1947*. Paris: Gallimard/Julliard, 1988.

Dumaine, Jacques. *Quai d'Orsay (1945–1951)*. Paris: Julliard, 1955.

Foreign Relations of the United States. Conference at Berlin. vols I and II. Washington, 1960.

Gaulle, Charles de. *Mémoires de guerre*. Paris: coll.ed. Plon, 1970..

    t. 1: *L'appel. 1940–1942*.

    t. 2: *L'unité. 1942–1944*.

    t. 3: *Le salut. 1944–1946*.

———. *Discours et messages*. Paris: coll.ed. Plon, 1970.

    t. 1: *Pendant la guerre, juin 1940–janvier 1946*.

    t. 2: *Dans l'attente, février 1946–avril 1958*.

    t. 3: *Avec le renouveau, mai 1958–juillet 1962*.

Patti, Archimedes. *Why Vietnam? Prelude to America's Albatross*. Berkeley: University of California Press, 1980.

Sainteny, Jean. *Histoire d'une paix manquée*. Paris: rev.ed, Fayard, 1967.

Salan, Raoul. *Mémoires*. t. 1, *Fin d'un Empire*. Paris: Presses de la Cité, 1970.

Sanmarco, Louis. *Le colonial colonisé*. Paris: Favre, 1983.

IV. Works Quoted or Consulted

Ageron, Charles-Robert. *France coloniale ou parti colonial*. Paris: PUF, 1978.

———. 'L'opinion publique et l'Union Française (étude de sondages)'. In *Les chemins de la décolonisation de l'empire français*, I.H.T.P., q.v., 33–48.

———. 'La préparation de la Conférence de Brazzaville et ses enseignements'. In *Brazzaville, aux sources de la décolonisation*, Institut Charles-de-Gaulle, q.v., 29–41.

———. *La décolonisation française*. Paris: Armand Colin, 1991.

———, and Marc Michel, eds. *L'ère des décolonisations. Actes du Colloque d'Aix-en-Provence*. Paris: Karthala, 1995.

Albertini, Rudolf Von, with Albert Wirz. *Decolonization*. New York: Doubleday, 1970.

———. *European Colonial Rule, 1880–1940. The Impact of the West on India, Southeast Asia, and Africa*. Trans. J.G. Williamson. Oxford: Clio Press, 1982.

Anderson, Benedict. *Imagined Communities. Reflections on the Origins and Spread of Nationalism.* London: Verso, 1983.

Andrew, Christopher M., and A.S. Kanya-Forstner. *The Great War and the Climax of French Colonial Expansion.* London: Longman, 1981.

———. 'France: Adjustment to Change'. In *The Expansion of International Society.* Ed. Hedley Bull and Adam Watson, q.v., 335–44.

Aujoulat, Louis. *La vie et l'avenir de l'Union Française.* Paris: Société d'Editions Républicaines Populaires, 1948.

Benoist, Joseph-Roger de. *La balkanisation de l'Afrique Occidentale Française.* Dakar/Abidjan: Nouvelles Editions Africaines, 1979.

———. *L'Afrique Occidentale Française.* Dakar/Abidjan: Nouvelles Editions Africaines, 1980.

Bernard, Stéphane. *Le conflit franco-marocain, 1943–1956.* T. 1, *Historique.* Bruxelles: Editions de l'Institut de Sociologie de l'Université libre de Bruxelles, 1963. Trans: *The Franco-Moroccan Crisis, 1943–1956.* New Haven, CT, and London: Yale University Press, 1968.

Bodinier, Comandant Gilbert, and Général Philippe Duplay. 'Montrer sa force et négocier: le général Leclerc et la négociation annamite'. In *Leclerc et l'Indochine, 1945–1947,* Guy Pedroncini and Général Philippe Duplay, eds, q.v., 181–97.

Borella, François. *Evolution juridique et politique de l'Union Française après 1946.* Paris: Librairie générale de droit et de jurisprudence, 1958.

Bottin Administratif. Paris: Bottin, 1945, 1946, 1947.

Bouche, Denise. 'Autrefois notre pays s'appelait la Gaule. Remarques sur l'adaptation de l'enseignement au Sénégal'. *Cahiers d'Etudes Africaines,* 8 (1968).

———. 'Problèmes de sécurité en A.O.F. à l'heure de la réorganisation de l'armée française'. In *De Gaulle et la Nation face aux problèmes de la défense,* Institut Charles-de-Gaulle, q.v., 240–46.

———. 'L'administration de l'Afrique occidentale française et les libertés démocratiques (1944–1946)'. In *Les chemins de la décolonisation de l'empire français,* IHTP, q.v., 467–79.

———. 'La réception des principes de Brazzaville par l'administration en A.O.F'. In *Brazzaville, aux sources de la décolonisation,* Institut Charles-de-Gaulle, q.v., 207–21.

Branca, Eric. 'De Gaulle et la lutte avec l'Empire. 1940–1944'. In *De Gaulle et le tiers monde,* Institut Charles de Gaulle, q.v., 40–61.

Brunschwig, Henri. 'De l'assimilation à la décolonisation'. In *Les chemins de la décolonisation de l'empire français, 1936–1956,* I.H.T.P., q.v. 49–53.

Bull, Hedley, and Adam Watson, eds. *The Expansion of International Society.* Oxford: Oxford University Press, 1984.

Chaffard, Georges. *Les carnets secrets de la décolonisation,* 2 vols. Paris: Calmann-Lévy, 1965, 1967.

———. *Les deux guerres du Vietnam.* Paris: La Table Ronde, 1969.

Chagnollaud, Dominique. 'De Gaulle, chef du gouvernement provisoire: recouvrer et rénover l'Empire (Juin 1944–Janvier 1946)'. In *De Gaulle et le tiers monde,* Institut Charles de Gaulle, q.v., 61–72.

Chevance-Bertin, Maurice. *La communauté française, principe d'une nouvelle politique.* Paris: La Communauté Française, 1946.

Cobban, Alfred. *The Nation State and National Self-Determination*. First publ., Oxford: Oxford University Press/Royal Institute for International Affairs, 1945; revised edn., London: Collins, 1969.

Cohen, William B. *Rulers of Empire: The French Colonial Service in Africa*. Stanford, CA: Hoover Institute Press, 1971.

——. 'The Colonial Policy of the Popular Front'. *FHS*, vol.VII, no. 3, Spring 1972, 368–93.

Cointet, Jean-Paul. 'Le général de Gaulle et l'Empire (1940–1946)'. In *De Gaulle et le tiers monde*, Institut Charles de Gaulle, q.v., 73–94.

Conférence Africaine Française, La. Brazzaville: Editions du Baobab, 1944.

Conférence Africaine Française, La. Paris: Ministère des Colonies, 1945.

Cornford, F.M. *Microcosmographia Academica*. Cambridge, 1908.

Dalloz, Jacques. *La France de la Libération, 1944–46*. Paris: Le Seuil, 1983.

——. *La guerre d'Indochine, 1945–1954*. Paris: Le Seuil, 1987.

Darwin, John. *Britain and Decolonisation. The Retreat from Empire in the Post-War World*. Basingstoke: Macmillan, 1988.

Descamps, Henri. *La Démocratie chrétienne et le MRP de 1946 à 1959*. Paris: Fayard, 1981.

Devèze, Michel. *La France d'Outre-mer: de l'Empire colonial à l'Union française, 1938–1947*. Paris: Hachette, 1948.

Devillers, Philippe. *L'Histoire du Viêt-Nam de 1940 à 1952*. Paris: Le Seuil, 1952.

——. 'Le choix de la voie négociée'. In *Leclerc et l'Indochine, 1945–1947*, Guy Pedroncini and Général P. Duplay, eds. q.v., p. 139–66.

Duff Cooper, Arthur. *Old Men Forget*. London: Hart-Davis, 1953.

Duncanson, Dennis J. 'General Gracey and the Viet Minh'. In *Royal Central Asian Journal*, vol. LV, 1967, 288–97.

——. *Government and Revolution in Vietnam*. Oxford: Oxford University Press/Royal Institute for International Affairs, 1968.

Dunn, Peter M. *The First Indochina War*. London: Hurst, 1985.

Duroselle, Jean-Baptiste. *Politique étrangère de la France. La décadence. 1932–1939*. Paris: Imprimerie nationale de la France, 1979.

——. *Politique étrangère de la France. L'abîme. 1939–1945*. Paris: Imprimerie nationale de la France, 1982.

Éboué, Félix. 'La nouvelle politique indigène. Circulaire du 8 novembre 1941'. In *La fédération française*, Jean de la Roche and Jean Gottmann, eds., q.v., 586–627.

Elgey, Georgette. *La république des illusions, 1945–1951, ou la vie secrète de la IVe République*. Paris: Fayard, 1965.

Faligot, Roger, and Pascal Krop. *La piscine. Les services secrets français, 1944–1984*. Paris: Le Seuil, 1985.

Folin, Jacques de. *Indochine, 1940–1955. La fin d'un rêve*. Paris: Perrin, 1993.

Gallagher, John. *The Decline, Revival and Fall of the British Empire. The Ford Lectures and other essays*. Ed. Anil Seal. Cambridge: Cambridge University Press, 1982.

Gardinier, D.E. 'Les recommandations de la Conférence de Brazzaville sur les problèmes d'éducation'. In *Brazzaville, aux sources de la décolonisation*, Institut Charles-de-Gaulle, q.v., 170–80.

Gifford, Prosser, and Wm. Roger Louis, eds. *France and Britain in Africa. Imperial Rivalry and Colonial Rule*. New Haven, CT, and London: Yale University Press, 1971.

——. *The Transfer of Power in Africa. Decolonization 1940–1960*. New Haven, CT, and London: Yale University Press, 1982.

——. *Decolonisation and African Independence: the transfers of power 1960–1980*. New Haven, CT, and London: Yale University Press, 1988.

Girardet, Raoul. *L'idée coloniale en France de 1871 à 1962*. Paris: Table ronde, 1972.

Graham, B.D. *The French Socialists and Tripartisme, 1944–1947*. London and Canberra: Weidenfeld and Nicolson and Australian National University, 1965.

Grimal, Henri. *La décolonisation de 1919 à nos jours*. Bruxelles: nlle ed., Complexe, 1985.

Grosser, Alfred. *La IVe République et sa politique extérieure*. Paris: Armand Colin, 1961.

——. *Affaires Extérieures*. Paris: Flammarion, 1984.

Hammer, Ellen J. *The Struggle for Indochina*. Stanford, CA: Stanford University Press, 1954.

Hargreaves, John. *Decolonization in Africa*. London: Longman, 1988.

Hémery, Daniel. *Révolutionnaires et pouvoir colonial en Indochine*. Paris: Maspéro, 1975.

Hémery, Daniel. 'Aux origines des guerres d'indépendence vietnamiennes: pouvoir colonial et phénomène communiste en Indochine avant la Seconde Guerre mondiale'. *Le mouvement social*, no. 101, octobre–décembre 1977, 4–35.

Hesse d'Alzon, Claude. *La présence française en Indochine (1940–1945)*. Vincennes: Service Historique de l'Armée de Terre, 1985.

Holland, R.F., and G. Rizvi, eds. *Perspectives on Imperialism and Decolonization. Essays in Honour of A.F.Madden*. London: Cass, 1984.

——. *European Decolonization 1918–1981: An Introductory Survey*. London and Basingstoke: Macmillan, 1985.

Institut Charles-De-Gaulle. *Le général de Gaulle et l'Indochine, 1940–1946. Colloque tenu par l'Institut Charles de Gaulle les 20 et 21 février 1981*. Gilbert Pilleul, ed. Paris: Plon, 1982.

——. *De Gaulle et la Nation face aux problèmes de défense (1945–1946.) Colloque organisé par l'Institut d'Histoire du Temps Présent et l'Institut Charles-de-Gaulle, les 21 et 22 octobre 1982*. Paris: Plon, 1983.

——. *De Gaulle et le tiers monde. Actes du colloque organisé par la Faculté de Droit et des Sciences Economiques, l'Institut de Droit de la Paix et du Développement de l'Université de Nice, et l'Institut Charles de Gaulle. Nice, 25–26 février 1983*. Paris: Pedone, 1984.

—— and Institut d'Histoire du Temps Présent. *Brazzaville, Janvier–Février 1944. Aux sources de la décolonisation. Colloque organisé par l'Institut Charles-de-Gaulle et l'I.H.T.P. les 22 et 23 mai 1987*. Paris: Plon, 1988.

Institut d'Histoire du Temps Présent. *Les chemins de la décolonisation de l'empire français, 1936–1956. Colloque organisé par l'I.H.T.P. les 4 et 5 octobre 1984*. Paris: Editions du C.N.R.S., 1986.

Institut d'Histoire Comparée des Civilisations and Institut d'Histoire du Temps Présent. *Décolonisations européennes. Actes du Colloque international "Décolonisations comparées"*. Aix-en-Provence: Publications de l'Université de Provence, 1995.

Irving, R.E.M. *Christian Democracy in France*. London: Allen and Unwin, 1973.

——. *The First Indochina War. French and American Policy, 1945–1954*. London: Croom Helm, 1975.

Isoart, Paul, ed. *L'Indochine Française, 1940–1945*. Paris: P.U.F, 1984.

——. 'Aux origines de la guerre d'Indochine'. In *L'Indochine française, 1940–1945*, in Paul Isoart, ed., q.v., 1–71.

———. 'Les aspects politiques, constitutionnels et administratifs des Recommandations'. In *Brazzaville, aux sources de la décolonisation*, Institut Charles-de-Gaulle, q.v., 90–96.

Jeffrey, Robin. *Asia – the winning of independence*. London: Macmillan, 1981.

Johnson, Harry M. 'Ideology and the Social System'. In *International Encyclopedia of the Social Sciences*, ed. D.L. Sills, vol. VII, 76–85. New York, NY: Macmillan and The Free Press, 1979.

Julien, Charles-André. *L'Afrique du nord en marche. Nationalismes musulmans et souveraineté française*. 1st edn, Paris: Julliard, 1952; 3rd edn, Paris: Julliard, 1972.

———. 'Léon Blum et les pays d'outre-mer'. In *Léon Blum. Chef de Gouvernement*, Pierre Renouvin and René Rémond, eds., q.v., 377–90.

Kahler, Miles. *Decolonization in Britain and France. The Domestic Consequences of International Relations*. Princeton, NJ: Princeton University Press, 1984.

Lacouture, Jean. *Hô Chi Minh*. Paris: Le Seuil, 1967.

———. *Léon Blum*. Paris: Le Seuil, 1977.

———. *De Gaulle*. Tôme 2, *Le politique, 1944–1959*. Paris: Le Seuil, 1985.

Lancaster, David. *The Emancipation of French Indochina*. Oxford: Oxford University Press/Royal Institute for International Affairs, 1961.

Lanne, Bernard. 'Le Tchad pendant la guerre'. In *Les chemins de la décolonisation de l'empire français*, I.H.T.P., q.v., 439–54.

Lapie, Pierre-Olivier. 'Pour une politique coloniale nouvelle'. In *Renaissances*, numéro spécial, q.v., 1620.

La Roche, Jean de, and Jean Gottmann. *La fédération française. Contacts et civilisations d'outre-mer*. Montréal: Editions de l'arbre, 1945.

Laurentie, Henri. 'Notes sur une philosophie de la politique coloniale française'. In *Renaissances*, numéro spécial, q.v., 9–15.

———. 'Témoignage du gouverneur-général Henri Laurentie'. In *Le général de Gaulle et l'Indochine*, 230–42

Le Couriard, Daniel. 'Les Socialistes et les débuts de la guerre d'Indochine (1946–1947)', *Revue d'histoire moderne et contemporaine*, 31 (1984), 334–53.

Le Tourneau, Roger. *Evolution politique de l'Afrique du Nord musulmane: 1920–1961*. Paris: Armand Colin, 1962.

Lewis, Martin Deming. 'One Hundred Million Frenchmen: The "Assimilation" Theory in French Colonial Policy'. In *Comparative Studies in Society and History*, 4, 1961–1962, 129–53.

Longrigg, Stephen Hemsley. *Syria and Lebanon under French Mandate*. Oxford: Oxford University Press/Royal Institute for International Affairs, 1958.

Louis, Wm. Roger. *Imperialism at Bay, 1941–1945. The United States and The Decolonization of the British Empire*. Oxford: Oxford University Press, 1977.

———. *The British Empire in the Middle East, 1945–51*. Oxford: Oxford University Press, 1984.

M'bokolo, Elikia. 'French Colonial Policy in Equatorial Africa in the 1940s and 1950s'. In *The Transfer of Power, Decolonization 1940–1960*, P. Gifford and W.R. Louis, eds., q.v., 172–92.

Madjarian, Grégoire. *La question coloniale et la politique du Parti communiste français, 1944–1947*. Paris: Maspero, 1977.

Marr, David G. *Vietnamese Tradition on Trial, 1920–1945*. Berkeley, CA: University of California Press, 1981.

Marseille, Jacques. *Empire colonial et capitalisme français. Histoire d'un divorce*. Paris: Albin Michel, 1984.

———. 'La Conférence de Brazzaville et l'économie impériale: «des innovations éclatantes» ou des recommandations «prudentes»?'. In *Brazzaville, aux sources de la décolonisation*, Institut Charles-de-Gaulle, q.v., 107–15.

Marshall, D. Bruce. *The French Colonial Myth and Constitution-Making in the Fourth Republic.* New Haven, Ct.: Yale University Press, 1973.

Marsot, Alain-Gérard. 'The Crucial Year: Indochina 1946'. In *Journal of Contemporary History*, vol. 19, 1984, 337–54.

Mérat, Louis. *Fictions ... et réalités coloniales.* Paris: Sirey, 1946.

Michel, Marc. 'Decolonisation, French Attitudes and Policies, 1944–46'. In *France in the World*, Peter Morris and S.Williams, eds, 81–86. London: Pinter, 1985.

Miège, Jean-Louis. *Expansion européenne et décolonisation. De 1870 à nos jours.* Paris: PUF, 1973.

Moneta, Jakob. *La politique du Parti communiste français dans la question coloniale, 1920–1963.* Paris: Maspéro, 1971.

Morgenthau, Ruth Schachter. *Political Parties in French-speaking West Africa.* London: Oxford University Press, 1964.

Morlat, Patrice. *La répression coloniale au Vietnam (1908–1940).* Paris: L'Harmattan, 1990.

Mortimer, Edward. *France and the Africans, 1944–1960. A Political History.* London: Faber, 1969.

Mus, Paul. *Viêt Nam – Sociologie d'une Guerre.* Paris: Le Seuil, 1952.

Nguyen Quoc Dinh and Nguyen Dac Khê. *Le futur statut de l'Indochine. (Commentaire de la Déclaration Gouvernementale du 24 mars 1945).* Paris: Dalloz, 1945.

Novick, Peter. *The Resistance versus Vichy: The Purge of Collaborators in Liberated France.* London: Chatto and Windus, 1968.

Pedroncini, Guy, and Général Philippe Duplay, eds. *Leclerc et l'Indochine, 1945–1947, quand se noua le destin d'un empire.* Paris: Albin Michel, 1992.

Pervillé, Guy. 'La commission des réformes musulmanes de 1944 et l'élaboration d'une nouvelle politique algérienne de la France'. In *Les chemins de la décolonisation de l'empire français*, I.H.T.P., q.v., 357–65.

Quilliot, Roger. *La SFIO et l'exercice du pouvoir, 1944–1958.* Paris: Fayard, 1972.

Renaissances. Numéro spécial: 'Le problème colonial'. Algiers, 1944.

Renouvin, Pierre, and René Rémond, eds. *Léon Blum. Chef de Gouvernement.* Paris: Presses de la Fondation nationale des sciences politiques, 1967.

Rice-Maximin, Edward. *The French Left, Indochina and the Cold War.* New York, NY: Greenwood, 1986.

Richard-Molard, Jacques. *Afrique occidentale française.* Paris: Berger-Levrault, 1949.

Ridley, F., and J. Blondel. *Public Administration in France.* London: Routledge and Kegan Paul, 1964.

Rioux, Jean-Pierre. *La France de la Quatrième République.* T. 1: *L'ardeur et la nécessité, 1944–1952.* T. 2: *L'expansion et l'impuissance, 1952–1958.* Paris: Le Seuil, 1980, 1983.

———. 'A Changing of the Guard? Old and New Elites at the Liberation'. In *Elites in France: Origins, Reproduction and Power*, J. Howorth and P. Cerny, eds. London: Pinter, 1981.

Robinson, Ronald. 'Non-European foundations of European imperialism: a sketch for a theory of collaboration'. In *Studies in the Theory of Imperialism*. Ed. Roger Owen and Bob Sutcliffe. London: Longman, 1972, 117–40.

———. 'Imperial Theory and the Question of Imperialism after Empire'. In *Perspectives on Imperialism and Decolonization*. R.F. Holland and G. Rizvi, eds, q.v., 42–54.

Rous, Jean. *Chronique de la décolonisation*. Paris: Présence Africaine, 1965.

Ruscio, Alain. *Les communistes français et la guerre d'Indochine, 1944–1954*. Paris: L'Harmattan, 1985.

———. *Dien Bien Phu. La fin d'une illusion*. Paris: L'Harmattan, 1986.

———. *La décolonisation tragique: une histoire de la décolonisation française*. Paris: Messidor/Editions sociales, 1987.

Sarraut, Albert. *La mise en valeur des colonies françaises*. Paris: Payot, 1923.

Schoenbrun, David. *As France Goes*. London: Gollancz, 1957.

Shennan, Andrew. *Rethinking France. Plans for Renewal, 1940–1946*. Oxford: Oxford University Press, 1989.

Shipway, Martin James. 'The Brazzaville Conference, 1944: Colonial and Imperial Planning in a Wartime Setting'. Unpubl. M.Phil. thesis, University of Oxford, 1986.

———. 'The Brazzaville Conference, 1944: Origins of a Policy ... and a Myth'. In *Quinquereme*, 13 (1990–91), 53–70.

———. 'France's "Crise coloniale" and the Breakdown of Policy Making in Indochina, 1944–1947'. Unpubl. D. Phil. thesis, University of Oxford, 1992.

———. 'Creating an Emergency: Metropolitan Constraints on French Colonial Policy and its Breakdown in Indochina, 1945–1947', *Journal of Imperial and Commonwealth History*, vol. 21, no. 3, September 1993, 1–16. Also published in *Emergencies and Disorder in the European Empires after 1945*, ed. R.F. Holland, Frank Cass and Co, London, 1994, 1–16.

———. 'British perceptions of French policy in Indochina from the March 1946 Accords to the inception of the Bao Dai régime, 1946–1949: a meeting of "Official Minds"?' In Ageron and Michel, eds, 1995, q.v., 83–96.

———. '*Nous sommes en pleine crise coloniale*: French decolonisation, state violence and the limits of liberal reformism', in *Violence and Conflict in the Politics and Society of Modern France*, J. Windebank and R. Günther, eds. Lewiston, NY, Queenston, Ontario and Lampeter: Edwin Mellen Press, 1995, 73–87.

———. 'Madagascar on the eve of insurrection, 1944–1947: the impasse of a liberal colonial policy', *Journal of Commonwealth History*, vol. 24, no. 1, January 1996, 72–100.

Siriex, Paul-Henri. *Félix Houphouet-Boigny*. Paris and Dakar/Abidjan: Seghers and novelles Editions Africaines, 1975.

Smith, Ralph B. 'The Vietnamese Elite of French Cochinchina, 1943', *Modern Asian Studies*, vol. 6, 1972, no. 4, 459–82.

———. 'The Japanese Period in Indochina and the Coup of 9th March 1945'. In *Journal of Southeast Asian Studies*, vol. 9, 1978, 268–301.

———. 'The Work of the Provisional Government of Vietnam, August–December 1945', *Modern Asian Studies*, vol. 12, 1978, no. 4, 571–609.

Smith, Tony. *The Pattern of Imperialism. The United States, Great Britain and the late-industrializing World since 1815*. Cambridge: Cambridge University Press, 1981.

Sorum, Paul Clay. *Intellectuals and Decolonization in France*. Chapel Hill, NC: University of Nrth Carolina Press, 1977.

Suleiman, Ezra N. *Politics, Power and Bureaucracy in France*. Princeton, NJ: Princeton University Press, 1974.

Suret-Canale, Jean. *Afrique noire occidentale et centrale. L'ère coloniale (1900–1945)*. Paris: Editions Sociales, 1964.

———. *Afrique noire, de la colonisation aux indépendances, 1945–1960.* t. 1: *Crise du système colonial et capitalisme monopoliste d'état.* Paris: Editions Sociales, 1977.

Thorne, Christopher. 'Indochina and Anglo-American Relations, 1942–1945'. In *Pacific Historical Review*, vol. XLV, 1976, 73–96.

———. *Allies of a Kind. The United States, Britain and the War Against Japan, 1941–1945.* New York: Oxford University Press, 1979.

———. *The Issue of War. States, Societies and the Far Eastern Conflict of 1941–1945.* London: Hamish Hamilton, 1985.

Tønnesson, Stein. 'The Outbreak of the War in Indochina, 1946'. P.R.I.O.-Report 3/84 (unpubl.), Oslo, 1983.

———. 'The Longest Wars: Indochina 1945–75'. In *Journal of Peace Research*, vol. 22, no. 1, 1985, 1–25.

———. *1946: Déclenchement de la Guerre d'Indochine.* Paris: l'Harmattan, 1987.

Touchard, Jean. *Le gaullisme, 1940–1969.* Paris: Le Seuil, 1972.

Tronchon, Jacques. *L'insurrection malgache de 1947.* Paris and Fianarantsoa: Karthala and Ambozontany, 1974/1986.

Valette, Jacques. 'La Conférence de Fontainebleau (1946)'. In *Les chemins de la décolonisation de l'empire français*, I.H.T.P., q.v., 231–50.

Viard, Paul-Emile. 'Essai d'une organisation constitutionnelle de la "Communauté française"'. In *Renaissances*, numéro spécial, q.v., 21–41.

Viard, René. *La fin de l'Empire colonial français.* Paris: Maisonneuve and Larose, 1963.

Weinstein, Brian. *Eboué.* New York: Oxford University Press, 1972.

White, Dorothy Shipley. *Black Africa and de Gaulle. From the French Empire to Independence.* University Park, PA, and London: Pennsylvania State University Press, 1979.

Williams, Philip M. *Crisis and Compromise: Politics in the Fourth Republic.* London: 3rd edn. Longman, 1964.

Wright, Gordon. *The Reshaping of French Democracy.* London: Methuen, 1950.

Zieglé, Henri. *Afrique équatoriale française.* Collection 'L'Union française'. Paris: Berger-Levrault, 1952.

INDEX

DATE DUE

09 Apr 99		
APR 3 0 2000		
OCT 2 4 2001		
JAN 2 8 03		
MAR 1 0 03		
JUL 9 03		
NOV 1 3 03		
APR 1 5 2010		
NOV 2 1 2013		
GAYLORD		PRINTED IN U.S.A.